ANNUAL EDITIONS

Computers in Society *08/09*
Fourteenth Edition

EDITOR
Paul De Palma
Gonzaga University

Paul De Palma is Professor of Computer Science at Gonzaga University. When he discovered computers, he was working on a doctorate in English (at Berkeley). He retrained and spent a decade in the computer industry. After further training (at Temple), he joined the computer science faculty at Gonzaga. He is currently studying computational linguistics (at the University of New Mexico). His interests include artificial intelligence, and the social impact of computing.

Boston   Burr Ridge, IL   Dubuque, IA   New York   San Francisco   St. Louis
Bangkok   Bogotá   Caracas   Kuala Lumpur   Lisbon   London   Madrid   Mexico City
Milan   Montreal   New Delhi   Santiago   Seoul   Singapore   Sydney   Taipei   Toronto

Higher Education

ANNUAL EDITIONS: COMPUTERS IN SOCIETY, FOURTEENTH EDITION

Annual Editions® is a registered trademark of The McGraw-Hill Companies, Inc.

Annual Editions is published by the **Contemporary Learning Series** group within the McGraw-Hill Higher Education division.

This book is printed on recycled, acid-free paper containing 10% postconsumer waste.

1 2 3 4 5 6 7 8 9 0 QPD/QPD 0 9 8 7

ISBN 978–0–07–352848–9
MHID 0–07–352848–X
ISSN 1094-2629

Managing Editor: *Larry Loeppke*
Senior Managing Editor: *Faye Schilling*
Developmental Editor: *Dave Welsh*
Editorial Assistant: *Nancy Meissner*
Production Service Assistant: *Rita Hingtgen*
Permissions Coordinator: *Shirley Lanners*
Senior Marketing Manager: *Julie Keck*
Marketing Communications Specialist: *Mary Klein*
Marketing Coordinator: *Alice Link*
Project Manager: *Sandy Wille*
Design Specialist: *Tara McDermott*
Senior Administrative Assistant: *DeAnna Dausener*
Senior Operations Manager: *Pat Koch Krieger*
Cover Graphics: *Maggie Lytle*

Compositor: Laserwords Private Limited
Cover Image: Thinkstock/Jupiterimages and Digital Vision/Getty Images

Library in Congress Cataloging-in-Publication Data
Main entry under title: Annual Editions: Computers in Society. 2008/2009.
  1. Computers in Society—Periodicals. De Palma, Paul *comp*. II. Title: Computers in Society.
658'.05

www.mhhe.com

Editors/Advisory Board

Members of the Advisory Board are instrumental in the final selection of articles for each edition of ANNUAL EDITIONS. Their review of articles for content, level, currentness, and appropriateness provides critical direction to the editor and staff. We think that you will find their careful consideration well reflected in this volume.

Preface

In publishing ANNUAL EDITIONS we recognize the enormous role played by the magazines, newspapers, and journals of the public press in providing current, first-rate educational information in a broad spectrum of interest areas. Many of these articles are appropriate for students, researchers, and professionals seeking accurate, current material to help bridge the gap between principles and theories and the real world. These articles, however, become more useful for study when those of lasting value are carefully collected, organized, indexed, and reproduced in a low-cost format, which provides easy and permanent access when the material is needed. That is the role played by ANNUAL EDITIONS.

In a well-remembered scene from the 1968 movie, *The Graduate,* the hapless Ben is pulled aside at his graduation party by his father's business partner. He asks Ben about his plans, now that the young man has graduated. As Ben fumbles, the older man whispers the single word, "plastics," in his ear. Today, Ben is eligible for the senior discount at movie theatres. What advice would he offer to a new graduate? Surely not plastics, even though petrochemicals have transformed the way we live over the past four decades. Odds are that computers have replaced plastics in the imaginations of today's graduates, this despite the tech bubble that burst in 2000. To test this hypothesis, I did a Google search on the words "plastics," and "plastic." This produced about 240,000,000 hits, an indication that Ben was given good advice. I followed this with a search on "computers," and "computer," to which Google replied with an astonishing 1,340,000,000 hits. The point is that computers are a phenomenon to be reckoned with.

In netting articles for the 14th edition of *Annual Editions: Computers in Society* from the sea of contenders, I have tried to continue in the tradition of previous editors. The writers are journalists, computer scientists, lawyers, economists, and academics—the kinds of professions you would expect to find represented in a collection on the social implications of computing. They write for newspapers, business and general circulation magazines, academic journals, and professional publications. Their writing is free from both the unintelligible jargon and the breathless enthusiasm that prevents people from forming clear ideas about computing. This is by design, of course. I have long contended that it is possible to write clearly about any subject, even one as technically complex and clouded by marketing as information technology. I hope that after reading the selections, you will agree.

Annual Editions: Computers in Society 08/09 is organized around important dimensions of society rather than of computing. The Introduction begins the conversation with an article by the late Neil Postman who says "that every technology has a philosophy which is given expression in how the technology makes people use their minds." Sherry Turkle, one of the earliest and most eloquent commentators on the psychological changes wrought by computing, begins the final unit with a similar thought: "computational objects do not simply do things *for* us, they do things *to* us as people, to our ways of

being [in] the world, to our ways of seeing ourselves and others." In between, with the help of many other writers, a crucial question recurs like a leitmotif in a complex piece of music: to what extent is technology of any kind without a bias of its own and to what extent does it embody the world view, intentionally or not, of its creators? If the answer were simply that the good and the ill of computing depend upon how computers are used, those of us interested in the interaction of computers and society would be hard-pressed to claim your attention. We could simply exhort you to do no evil, as Google tells its employees (http://investor.google.com/conduct.html, retrieved 6/1/07). Good advice, certainly. But information technology demands a more nuanced stance. Sometimes computing systems have consequences not intended by their developers. The waste generated by cast-off computers is one example (Unit 7). The vulnerability of government documents is another (Unit 6). And at all times, "embedded in every technology there is a powerful idea" (Unit 1, "Five Things You Need to Know About Technological Change"). An essential task for students of technology is to learn to tease out these ideas, so that the consequences might be understood *before* the technology is adopted.

The book's major themes are the economy, community, politics considered broadly, and the balance of risk and reward. In a field as fluid as computing, the intersection of computers with each of these dimensions changes from year to year. Many articles in the 10th edition examined the growing importance of e-commerce. By the time of the 13th edition, e-commerce had nearly disappeared. This is not to imply that e-commerce became unimportant, only that in just a few years it had moved into the mainstream. The 14th edition replaces roughly half of the articles from the 13th. Computing is a rapidly changing field. We race to keep up.

More than any other technology, computers force us to think about limits. What does it mean to be human? Are there kinds of knowledge that should not be pursued? As Sherry Turkle asks, apropos of any complex technology, "Are you really you if you have a baboon's heart inside, had your face resculpted by Brazil's finest plastic surgeons, and are taking Zoloft to give you a competitive edge at work" (Turkle, 2003:6). Are we developing "increasingly intimate relationship with machines," as Turkle claims (Unit 8, "A Nascent Robotics Culture"), or, more prosaically, how do we keep e-commerce flowing when public-key cryptography becomes obsolete. These and other unresolved issues are explored in Unit 8, The Frontier of Computing.

A word of caution. Each article has been selected because it is topical and interesting. To say that an article is interesting, however, does not mean that it is right. This is as true of the facts presented in each article as it is of the point of view. When reading startling claims, whether in this volume or in the newspaper, it is wise to remember that writers gather facts from other sources who gathered them from still other sources, who may, ultimately, rely upon a selective method of fact-gathering. There may be no good solution to the problem of unsupported assertions, beyond rigorous peer review. But, then, most of us don't curl up each night with scientific journals, and even these can be flawed. The real antidote to poorly supported arguments is to become critical readers, no less of experts than of the daily newspaper. Having said that, I hope you will approach these articles as you might approach a good discussion among friends. You may not agree with all opinions, but you come away nudged in one direction or another by reasoned arguments, holding a richer, more informed, view of important issues.

This book includes several features that I hope will be helpful to students and professionals. Each article listed in the table of contents is preceded by a short abstract with key concepts in bold type. The social implications of computing, of course, are not limited to the eight broad areas represented by the unit titles. A topic guide lists each article by name and number along still other dimensions of computers in society.

We want *Annual Editions: Computers in Society* to help you participate more fully in some of the most important discussions of the time, those about the promises and risks of computing. Your suggestions and comments are very important to us. If you complete and return the postage-paid article rating form in the back of the book, we can consider them for inclusion in the next edition.

Paul De Palma
Editor

References

Turkle, S. (2003). Technology and Human Vulnerability. *Harvard Business Review*, 81(9): 43-50.

Contents

UNIT 1
Introduction

UNIT 2
The Economy

The concepts in bold italics are developed in the article. For further expansion, please refer to the Topic Guide.

UNIT 3
Work and the Workplace

The concepts in bold italics are developed in the article. For further expansion, please refer to the Topic Guide.

UNIT 4
Computers, People, and Social Participation

UNIT 5
Societal Institutions: Law, Politics, Education, and the Military

The concepts in bold italics are developed in the article. For further expansion, please refer to the Topic Guide.

UNIT 6
Risk and Avoiding Risk

The concepts in bold italics are developed in the article. For further expansion, please refer to the Topic Guide.

UNIT 7
International Perspectives and Issues

UNIT 8
The Frontier of Computing

The concepts in bold italics are developed in the article. For further expansion, please refer to the Topic Guide.

The concepts in bold italics are developed in the article. For further expansion, please refer to the Topic Guide.

Topic Guide

This topic guide suggests how the selections in this book relate to the subjects covered in your course. You may want to use the topics listed on these pages to search the Web more easily.

On the following pages a number of Web sites have been gathered specifically for this book. They are arranged to reflect the units of this *Annual Edition*. You can link to these sites by going to the student online support site at *http://www.mhcls.com/online/*.

ALL THE ARTICLES THAT RELATE TO EACH TOPIC ARE LISTED BELOW THE BOLD-FACED TERM.

Internet References

The following Internet sites have been carefully researched and selected to support the articles found in this reader. The easiest way to access these selected sites is to go to our student online support site at *http://www.mhcls.com/online/*.

AE: Computers in Society 08/09

The following sites were available at the time of publication. Visit our Web site—we update our student online support site regularly to reflect any changes.

General Sources

Livelink Intranet Guided Tour
http://www.opentext.com/

Livelink Intranet helps companies to manage and control documents, business processes, and projects more effectively. Take this tour to see how.

UNIT 1: Introduction

Beyond the Information Revolution
http://www.theatlantic.com/issues/99oct/9910drucker.htm

Peter Drucker has written a three-part article, available at this site, that uses history to gauge the significance of e-commerce—"a totally unexpected development"—to throw light on the future of, in his words, "the knowledge worker."

Short History of the Internet
http://w3.ag.uiuc.edu/AIM/scale/nethistory.html

Bruce Sterling begins with the development of the idea for the Internet by the cold war think tank, the Rand Corporation, and goes on to explain how computer networking works. There are links to other sites and to further reading.

UNIT 2: The Economy

CAUCE: Coalition Against Unsolicited Commercial Email
http://www.cauce.org

This all-volunteer organization was created to advocate for a legislative solution to the problem of UCE, better known as spam. Read about the fight and how you can help at this Web page.

E-Commerce Times
http://www.ecommercetimes.com/

E-Commerce Times is a gateway to a wealth of current information and resources concerning e-commerce.

The End of Cash (James Gleick)
http://www.around.com/money.html

This article, previously published in the *New York Times*, on June 16, 1996, discusses the obsolescence of cash.

Fight Spam on the Internet
http://spam.abuse.net

This is an anti-spam sight that has been in operation since 1996. Its purpose is to promote responsible net commerce, in part, by fighting spam. Up-to-date news about spam can be found on the home page.

The Linux Home Page
http://www.linux.org

This Web site explains that Linux is a free Unix-type operating system, originally created by Linus Torvalds, that is causing a revolution in the world of computers. The site features the latest news about Linux, and everything else you would need to know to switch to the service.

The Rise of the Informediary
http://www.ait.unl.edu/crane/misgrad/sglee/informediary.htm

The author of this site explains what an informediary is and what an informediary does. He also shows why the informediary is so important in today's business environment.

Smart Cards: A Primer
http://www.javaworld.com/javaworld/jw-12-1997/jw-12-javadev.html

This article by Rinaldo Di Giorgio brings the smart card to life with a real-world smart-card example. Five pages explain what a smart card is, how it is used, its limitations, and its strengths.

Smart Card Group
http://www.smartcard.co.uk

This Web site bills itself as "the definitive Web site for Smart Card Technology." At this site you can download Dr. David B. Everett's definitive "Introduction to Smart Cards."

UNIT 3: Work and the Workplace

American Telecommuting Association
http://www.knowledgetree.com/ata-adv.html

What is good about telecommuting is examined at this site that also offers information regarding concepts, experiences, and the future of telecommuting.

Computers in the Workplace

http://www.msci.memphis.edu/~ryburnp/cl/cis/workpl.html

In this lecture, some of the advantages of computers in the workplace are examined as well as some of the negative aspects, including issues of training, ethics, and privacy.

InfoWeb: Techno-rage

http://www.cciw.com/content/technorage.html

Techno-rage is becoming more and more common. This site provides information and resources regarding techno-rage and techno-stress.

STEP ON IT! Pedals: Repetitive Strain Injury

http://www.bilbo.com/rsi2.html

Data on carpal tunnel syndrome are presented here with links to alternative approaches to the computer keyboard, and links to related information.

What About Computers in the Workplace

http://law.freeadvice.com/intellectual_property/computer_law/computers_workplace.htm

This site, which is the leading legal site for consumers and small businesses, provides general legal information to help people understand their legal rights in 100 legal topics—including the answer to the question, "Can my boss watch what I'm doing?"

UNIT 4: Computers, People, and Social Participation

Adoption Agencies

http://www.amrex.org/

Here is an example of the much-talked-about new trend of online adoption agencies.

Alliance for Childhood: Computers and Children

http://www.allianceforchildhood.net/projects/computers/index.htm

How are computers affecting the intellectual growth of children? Here is one opinion provided by the Alliance for Childhood.

The Core Rules of Netiquette

http://www.albion.com/netiquette/corerules.html

Excerpted from Virginia Shea's book *Netiquette*, this is a classic work in the field of online communication.

How the Information Revolution Is Shaping Our Communities

http://www.plannersweb.com/articles/bla118.html

This article by Pamela Blais is from the Planning Commissioners Journal, Fall 1996 issue, and deals with our changing society. It points out and explains some of the far-reaching impacts of the information revolution, including the relocation of work from office to home.

SocioSite: Networks, Groups, and Social Interaction

http://www2.fmg.uva.nl/sociosite/topics/interaction.html

This site provides sociological and psychological resources and research regarding the effect of computers on social interaction.

UNIT 5: Societal Institutions: Law, Politics, Education, and the Military

ACLU: American Civil Liberties Union

http://www.aclu.org

Click on the Supreme Court's Internet decision, plus details of the case Reno v. ACLU, and the ACLU's campaign to restore information privacy; "Take Back Your Data"; and cyber-liberties and free speech for opinions on First Amendment rights as they apply to cyberspace.

Information Warfare and U.S. Critical Infrastructure

http://www.twurled-world.com/Infowar/Update3/cover.htm

The "twURLed World" contains a pie chart of URLs involved in IW (information warfare) as well as report main pages that list Internet domains, keywords in contexts and by individual terms, and listing of all URLs and links to details.

Living in the Electronic Village

http://www.rileyis.com/publications/phase1/usa.htm

This site addresses the impact of information in technology on government. Shown is the executive summary, but seven other sections are equally pertinent.

Patrolling the Empire

http://www.csrp.org/patrol.htm

Reprinted from CovertAction Quarterly, this article by Randy K. Schwartz details the plans of NIMA (National Imagery and Mapping Agency) for future wars by helping to fuse high-tech surveillance and weaponry.

United States Patent and Trademark Office

http://www.uspto.gov/

This is the official homepage of the U. S. Patent and Trademark Office. Use this site to search patents and trademarks, apply for patents, and more.

World Intellectual Property Organization

http://www.wipo.org/

Visit the World Intellectual Property Organization Web site to find information and issues pertaining to virtual and intellectual property.

UNIT 6: Risk and Avoiding Risk

AntiOnline: Hacking and Hackers

http://www.antionline.com/index.php

This site is designed to help the average person learn how to protect against hackers.

Copyright & Trademark Information for the IEEE Computer Society

http://computer.org/copyright.htm

Here is an example of how a publication on the Web is legally protected. The section on Intellectual Property Rights Information contains further information about reuse permission and copyright policies.

Electronic Privacy Information Center (EPIC)

http://epic.org

EPIC is a private research organization that was established to focus public attention on emerging civil liberties issues and to protect privacy, the First Amendment, and constitutional values. This site contains news, resources, policy archives, and a search mechanism.

Internet Privacy Coalition

http://www.epic.org/crypto/

The mission of the Internet Privacy Coalition is to promote privacy and security on the Internet through widespread public availability of strong encryption and the relaxation of export controls on cryptography.

Center for Democracy and Technology

http://www.cdt.org/crypto/

These pages are maintained for discussion and information about data privacy and security, encryption, and the need for policy reform. The site discusses pending legislation, Department of Commerce Export Regulations, and other initiatives.

Survive Spyware

http://www.cnet.com/internet/0-3761-8-3217791-1.html

Internet spying is a huge problem. Advertisers, Web designers, and even the government are using the Net to spy on you. CNET.com provides information about spyware and detecting spying eyes that will help you eliminate the threat.

An Electronic Pearl Harbor? Not Likely

http://www.nap.edu/issues/15.1/smith.htm

Is the threat of information warfare real? Yes. Do we need to be completely concerned? Probably not. This site tries to dispel some of the myths and hoaxes concerning information warfare.

UNIT 7: International Perspectives and Issues

Information Revolution and World Politics Project

http://www.ceip.org/files/projects/irwp/irwp_descrip.ASP

This project, launched by the Carnegie Foundation in 1999, has as its purpose to analyze the political, economic, and social dimensions of the world-wide information revolution and their implications for U.S. policy and global governance.

UNIT 8: The Frontier of Computing

Introduction to Artificial Intelligence (AI)

http://www-formal.stanford.edu/jmc/aiintro/aiintro.html

This statement describes A.I. Click on John McCarthy's home page for a list of additional papers.

Kasparov vs. Deep Blue: The Rematch

http://www.chess.ibm.com/home/html/b.html

Video clips and a discussion of the historic chess rematch between Garry Kasparov and Deep Blue are available on this site.

PHP-Nuke Powered Site: International Society for Artificial Life

http://alife.org/

Start here to find links to many alife (artificial life) Web sites, including demonstrations, research centers and groups, and other resources.

We highly recommend that you review our Web site for expanded information and our other product lines. We are continually updating and adding links to our Web site in order to offer you the most usable and useful information that will support and expand the value of your Annual Editions. You can reach us at: http://www.mhcls.com/annualeditions/.

UNIT 1

Introduction

Unit Selections

1. **Five Things We Need to Know About Technological Change,** Neil Postman
2. **Slouching Toward the Ordinary,** Susan C. Herring
3. **On the Nature of Computing,** Jon Crowcroft

Key Points to Consider

- All American school children learn that the first message Samuel F. B. Morse transmitted over his newly invented telegraph were the words, "What hath God wrought." What they probably do not learn is that Morse was quoting from the poem of Balaam in the Book of Numbers, chapter 23. Read the text of this poem. The overview to this unit presents two ways to understand technical and scientific discoveries. In which camp is Morse?

- Early on in *Walden,* Thoreau famously remarks that "Our inventions are wont to be pretty toys, which distract our attention from serious things. They are but an improved means to an unimproved end, an end that it was already but too easy to arrive at . . . . We are in great haste to construct a magnetic telegraph from Maine to Texas; but Maine and Texas, it may be, have nothing important to communicate." Substitute "Internet" for "magnetic telegraph." Do you agree or disagree with Thoreau? How do you think Jon Crowcroft ("On the Nature of Computing") might respond?

- Richard Lewontin, a Harvard geneticist ("The Politics of Science," *The New York Review of Books*, May 9, 2002), says that "The state of American science and its relation to the American state are the product of war." What does he mean? Is Lewontin over-stating his case? Use the Internet to find out more about Richard Lewontin.

- Susan Herring's "Slouching Toward the Ordinary," says that text-messaging is "perversely unergonomic." What does this mean? What accounts for its importance among teenagers?

Student Web Site
www.mhcls.com/online

Further information regarding these Web sites may be found in this book's preface or online.

Beyond the Information Revolution
http://www.theatlantic.com/issues/99oct/9910drucker.htm
Short History of the Internet
http://w3.ag.uiuc.edu/AIM/scale/nethistory.html

This book, Annual Editions: *Computers in Society 08/09,* is part of the Annual Editions series of books published by the McGraw-Hill/Contemporary Learning Series division. The series contains over seventy titles, among them American History, Sociology and World Politics. It is instructive to note that not one of them carries the final prepositional phrase "in Society." Why is that? Here is a first approximation. History, sociology, world politics, indeed, most of the other titles in the Annual Editions series are not in society, they are society. Suppose we produced an edited volume entitled "History in Society." If such a volume contained reflections on the social implications of the academic study of history, it would have a tiny and specialized readership. But you know that when we speak of "computers in society," we are not talking about the social implications of the academic study of computing. Here is one difference between this volume and the others in the series: it is possible to study computers without studying their social dimension.

But is it? Until not long ago, most people interested in the philosophy and sociology of science considered it value-neutral.

That is, a given technology carried no values of its own. The ethics of this or that technology depended on what was done with it. A vestige of this thinking is still with us. When people say, "Guns don't kill people. People kill people," they are asserting that technology somehow stands outside of society, waiting to be put to use for good or ill. The concern about intoxicated drivers is similar. All of us would live happier, safer lives if campaigns to remove drunken drivers from their cars were successful. But this still would not get to the heart of highway carnage that has to do with federal encouragement for far-flung suburbs, local patterns of land use, and a neglect of public transportation. Drunk-driving would not be the issue it is, if driving were not so vital to American life, and driving would not be so vital to American life if a cascade of social and political decisions had not come together in the middle of the twentieth century to favor the automobile.

The first article, "Five Things We Need to Know About Technological Change," makes this point eloquently: "Embedded in every technology there is a powerful idea. . . ." The observation is an important one that is shared by most of the more reflective

1

contemporary commentators on technology. The idea that technology can be studied apart from its social consequences owes some of its strength to the way many people imagine that scientific discoveries are made—since technology is just applied science. It is commonly imagined that scientists are disinterested observers of the natural world. In this view, science unfolds, and technology unfolds shortly after, according to the laws of nature and the passion of scientists. But, of course, scientists study those things that are socially valued. The particular expression of social value in the United States is National Science Foundation and National Institute of Health funding. We should not be surprised that the medical and computing sciences are funded generously, or, indeed, that our research physicians and computer scientists are paid better than English professors.

Perhaps a more accurate view of the relationship between technology and computing to society is that social values affect technical discovery which, in turn, affect social values. It is this intricate dance between computers and society—now one leading, now the other—that the writers in this volume struggle to understand, though most of them do it implicitly. But, before we try to understand the dance, it seems reasonable to understand what is meant by the word "computer." You will find in this volume a decided bias toward networked computers. A networked computer is one that can communicate with many millions of others through the global Internet. This is a new definition. As recently as 1996, less than 1 in 5 Americans had used the Internet (Blendon et al., 2001). Just as we mean networked computers when we use the word "computer" today, in the late eighties someone using the word would have meant a stand-alone PC, running, maybe a word processor, a spreadsheet, and some primitive games. A decade before to that, the word would have referred to a large, probably IBM, machine kept in an air-conditioned room and tended by an army of technicians. Prior to 1950, the word would have meant someone particularly adept in arithmetic calculations. The point here is that as the meaning of a single word has shifted, our understanding of the dance has to shift with it.

That this shift in meaning has occurred in just a few decades helps us understand why so many commentators use the word "revolution" to describe what computing has wrought. Just as technologies come with hidden meanings, so do words, themselves. The word "revolution," when it is applied to political upheaval, is used to describe something thought bad, or at least chaotic—the single contrary instance is the American Revolution. Not so when the word is applied to computing. Computing is thought to change quickly, but, more, it is thought to bring many benefits. A recent survey conducted by the Brookings Institution (Blendon et al., 2001) indicated that 90% of Americans believe that science and technology will make their lives easier and more comfortable. The real question to ask is more basic: whether or not Americans believe it, is it true? First, does the spread of computing constitute a revolution, or just, in Thoreau's words, "an improved means to an unimproved end." Second, revolutionary or not, have we grown smarter, healthier, happier with the coming of the computer? This is still an open question—as the Internet morphs from a novelty to an appliance—to a shrinking number of commentators.

Susan Herring's piece, "Slouching Toward the Ordinary," provides some much-needed historical perspective to the study of the social impact of computing. Who, ten years ago, would have predicted that an important form of electronic communication among teenagers and pre-teens would be the tightly constrained and "perversely unergonomic" medium of text-messaging? Or, for that matter, that most computer-mediated communication would be text-based, something the sunnier futurists not long ago might have predicted going the way of the typewriter: "the robust popularity of . . . email over the past 30 years," says the author, "suggests that it satisfies some important communication needs." We end this unit with a more traditional view of information technology. Jon Crowcroft's piece, "On the Nature of Computing," is a hymn to its limitless possibilities. As the subtitle asserts, "Computing is its own virtual world, bound only by its practitioners' imaginations and creativity." Read the article and see if you are persuaded.

References

Blendon, R., et al. (2001). Whom to Protect and How? *Brookings Review,* 9(1): 44–48.

Five Things We Need to Know About Technological Change

Neil Postman

Good morning your Eminences and Excellencies, ladies, and gentlemen.

The theme of this conference, "The New Technologies and the Human Person: Communicating the Faith in the New Millennium," suggests, of course, that you are concerned about what might happen to faith in the new millennium, as well you should be. In addition to our computers, which are close to having a nervous breakdown in anticipation of the year 2000, there is a great deal of frantic talk about the 21st century and how it will pose for us unique problems of which we know very little but for which, nonetheless, we are supposed to carefully prepare. Everyone seems to worry about this—business people, politicians, educators, as well as theologians.

> **The human dilemma is as it has always been, and it is a delusion to believe that the technological changes of our era have rendered irrelevant the wisdom of the ages and the sages.**

At the risk of sounding patronizing, may I try to put everyone's mind at ease? I doubt that the 21st century will pose for us problems that are more stunning, disorienting or complex than those we faced in this century, or the 19th, 18th, 17th, or for that matter, many of the centuries before that. But for those who are excessively nervous about the new millennium, I can provide, right at the start, some good advice about how to confront it. The advice comes from people whom we can trust, and whose thoughtfulness, it's safe to say, exceeds that of President Clinton, Newt Gingrich, or even Bill Gates. Here is what Henry David Thoreau told us: "All our inventions are but improved means to an unimproved end." Here is what Goethe told us: "One should, each day, try to hear a little song, read a good poem, see a fine picture, and, if possible, speak a few reasonable words." Socrates told us: "The unexamined life is not worth living." Rabbi Hillel told us: "What is hateful to thee, do not do to another." And here is the prophet Micah: "What does the Lord require of thee but to do justly, to love mercy and to walk hum-

bly with thy God." And I could say, if we had the time, (although you know it well enough) what Jesus, Isaiah, Mohammad, Spinoza, and Shakespeare told us. It is all the same: There is no escaping from ourselves. The human dilemma is as it has always been, and it is a delusion to believe that the technological changes of our era have rendered irrelevant the wisdom of the ages and the sages.

> **. . . all technological change is a trade-off . . . a Faustian bargain.**

Nonetheless, having said this, I know perfectly well that because we do live in a technological age, we have some special problems that Jesus, Hillel, Socrates, and Micah did not and could not speak of. I do not have the wisdom to say what we ought to do about such problems, and so my contribution must confine itself to some things we need to know in order to address the problems. I call my talk *Five Things We Need to Know About Technological Change.* I base these ideas on my thirty years of studying the history of technological change but I do not think these are academic or esoteric ideas. They are the sort of things everyone who is concerned with cultural stability and balance should know and I offer them to you in the hope that you will find them useful in thinking about the effects of technology on religious faith.

First Idea

The first idea is that all technological change is a trade-off. I like to call it a Faustian bargain. Technology giveth and technology taketh away. This means that for every advantage a new technology offers, there is always a corresponding disadvantage. The disadvantage may exceed in importance the advantage, or the advantage may well be worth the cost. Now, this may seem to be a rather obvious idea, but you would be surprised at how many people believe that new technologies are unmixed blessings. You need only think of the enthusiasms with which most people approach their understanding of computers. Ask anyone who knows something about computers to talk about them, and you will find that they will, unabashedly and relentlessly, extol the wonders of computers. You will also find that in most cases they will completely neglect to mention any of the liabilities of computers. This is a dangerous imbalance, since the greater the wonders of a technology, the greater will be its negative consequences.

Think of the automobile, which for all of its obvious advantages, has poisoned our air, choked our cities, and degraded the beauty of our natural landscape. Or you might reflect on the paradox of medical technology which brings wondrous cures but is, at the same time, a demonstrable cause of certain diseases and disabilities, and has played a significant role in reducing the diagnostic skills of physicians. It is also well to recall that for all of the intellectual and social benefits provided by the printing press, its costs were equally monumental. The printing press gave the Western world prose, but it made poetry into an exotic and elitist form of communication. It gave us inductive science, but it reduced religious sensibility to a form of fanciful superstition. Printing gave us the modern conception of nationwide, but in so doing turned patriotism into a sordid if not lethal emotion. We might even say that the printing of the Bible in vernacular languages introduced the impression that God was an Englishman or a German or a Frenchman—that is to say, printing reduced God to the dimensions of a local potentate.

Perhaps the best way I can express this idea is to say that the question, "What will a new technology do?" is no more important than the question, "What will a new technology undo?" Indeed, the latter question is more important, precisely because it is asked so infrequently. One might say, then, that a sophisticated perspective on technological change includes one's being skeptical of Utopian and Messianic visions drawn by those who have no sense of history or of the precarious balances on which culture depends. In fact, if it were up to me, I would forbid anyone from talking about the new information technologies unless the person can demonstrate that he or she knows something about the social and psychic effects of the alphabet, the mechanical clock, the printing press, and telegraphy. In other words, knows something about the costs of great technologies.

Idea Number One, then, is that culture always pays a price for technology.

Second Idea

This leads to the second idea, which is that the advantages and disadvantages of new technologies are never distributed evenly among the population. This means that every new technology benefits some and harms others. There are even some who are not affected at all. Consider again the case of the printing press in the 16th century, of which Martin Luther said it was "God's highest and extremest act of grace, whereby the business of the gospel is driven forward." By placing the word of God on every Christian's kitchen table, the mass-produced book undermined the authority of the church hierarchy, and hastened the breakup of the Holy Roman See. The Protestants of that time cheered this development. The Catholics were enraged and distraught. Since I am a Jew, had I lived at that time, I probably wouldn't have given a damn one way or another, since it would make no

difference whether a pogrom was inspired by Martin Luther or Pope Leo X. Some gain, some lose, a few remain as they were.

Let us take as another example, television, although here I should add at once that in the case of television there are very few indeed who are not affected in one way or another. In America, where television has taken hold more deeply than anywhere else, there are many people who find it a blessing, not least those who have achieved high-paying, gratifying careers in television as executives, technicians, directors, newscasters and entertainers. On the other hand, and in the long run, television may bring an end to the careers of school teachers since school was an invention of the printing press and must stand or fall on the issue of how much importance the printed word will have in the future. There is no chance, of course, that television will go away but school teachers who are enthusiastic about its presence always call to my mind an image of some turn-of-the-century blacksmith who not only is singing the praises of the automobile but who also believes that his business will be enhanced by it. We know now that his business was not enhanced by it; it was rendered obsolete by it, as perhaps an intelligent blacksmith would have known.

The questions, then, that are never far from the mind of a person who is knowledgeable about technological change are these: Who specifically benefits from the development of a new technology? Which groups, what type of person, what kind of industry will be favored? And, of course, which groups of people will thereby be harmed?

. . . there are always winners and losers in technological change.

These questions should certainly be on our minds when we think about computer technology. There is no doubt that the computer has been and will continue to be advantageous to large-scale organizations like the military or airline companies or banks or tax collecting institutions. And it is equally clear that the computer is now indispensable to high-level researchers in physics and other natural sciences. But to what extent has computer technology been an advantage to the masses of people? To steel workers, vegetable store owners, automobile mechanics, musicians, bakers, bricklayers, dentists, yes, theologians, and most of the rest into whose lives the computer now intrudes? These people have had their private matters made more accessible to powerful institutions. They are more easily tracked and controlled; they are subjected to more examinations, and are increasingly mystified by the decisions made about them. They are more than ever reduced to mere numerical objects. They are being buried by junk mail. They are easy targets for advertising agencies and political institutions.

In a word, these people are losers in the great computer revolution. The winners, which include among others computer companies, multi-national corporations and the nation state, will, of course, encourage the losers to be enthusiastic about computer technology. That is the way of winners, and so in the beginning they told the losers that with personal computers the average person can balance a checkbook more neatly, keep better track of recipes, and make more logical shopping lists. Then they told them that computers will make it possible to vote at home, shop at home, get all the entertainment they wish at home, and thus make community life unnecessary. And now, of course, the winners speak constantly of the Age of Information, always implying that the more information we have, the better we will be in solving significant problems—not only personal ones but large-scale social problems, as well. But how true is this? If there are children starving in the world—and there are—it is not because of insufficient information. We have known for a long time how to produce enough food to feed every child on the planet. How is it that we let so many of them starve? If there is violence on our streets, it is not because we have insufficient information. If women are abused, if divorce and pornography and mental illness are increasing, none of it has anything to do with insufficient information. I dare say it is because something else is missing, and I don't think I have to tell this audience what it is. Who knows? This age of information may turn out to be a curse if we are blinded by it so that we cannot see truly where our problems lie. That is why it is always necessary for us to ask of those who speak enthusiastically of computer technology, why do you do this? What interests do you represent? To whom are you hoping to give power? From whom will you be withholding power?

I do not mean to attribute unsavory, let alone sinister motives to anyone. I say only that since technology favors some people and harms others, these are questions that must always be asked. And so, that there are always winners and losers in technological change is the second idea.

Third Idea

Here is the third. Embedded in every technology there is a powerful idea, sometimes two or three powerful ideas. These ideas are often hidden from our view because they are of a somewhat abstract nature. But this should not be taken to mean that they do not have practical consequences.

The third idea is the sum and substance of what Marshall McLuhan meant when he coined the famous sentence, "The medium is the message."

Perhaps you are familiar with the old adage that says: To a man with a hammer, everything looks like a nail. We may extend that truism: To a person with a pencil, everything looks like a sentence. To a person with a TV camera, everything looks like an image. To a person with a computer, everything looks like data. I do not think we need to take these aphorisms literally. But what they call to our attention is that every technology has a prejudice. Like language itself, it predisposes us to favor and value certain perspectives and accomplishments. In a culture without writing, human memory is of the greatest importance, as are the proverbs, sayings and songs which contain the

accumulated oral wisdom of centuries. That is why Solomon was thought to be the wisest of men. In Kings I we are told he knew 3,000 proverbs. But in a culture with writing, such feats of memory are considered a waste of time, and proverbs are merely irrelevant fancies. The writing person favors logical organization and systematic analysis, not proverbs. The telegraphic person values speed, not introspection. The television person values immediacy, not history. And computer people, what shall we say of them? Perhaps we can say that the computer person values information, not knowledge, certainly not wisdom. Indeed, in the computer age, the concept of wisdom may vanish altogether.

The consequences of technological change are always vast, often unpredictable and largely irreversible.

The third idea, then, is that every technology has a philosophy which is given expression in how the technology makes people use their minds, in what it makes us do with our bodies, in how it codifies the world, in which of our senses it amplifies, in which of our emotional and intellectual tendencies it disregards. This idea is the sum and substance of what the great Catholic prophet, Marshall McLuhan meant when he coined the famous sentence, "The medium is the message."

Fourth Idea

Here is the fourth idea: Technological change is not additive; it is ecological. I can explain this best by an analogy. What happens if we place a drop of red dye into a beaker of clear water? Do we have clear water plus a spot of red dye? Obviously not. We have a new coloration to every molecule of water. That is what I mean by ecological change. A new medium does not add something; it changes everything. In the year 1500, after the printing press was invented, you did not have old Europe plus the printing press. You had a different Europe. After television, America was not America plus television. Television gave a new coloration to every political campaign, to every home, to every school, to every church, to every industry, and so on.

That is why we must be cautious about technological innovation. The consequences of technological change are always vast, often unpredictable and largely irreversible. That is also why we must be suspicious of capitalists. Capitalists are by definition not only personal risk takers but, more to the point, cultural risk takers. The most creative and daring of them hope to exploit new technologies to the fullest, and do not much care what traditions are overthrown in the process or whether or not a culture is prepared to function without such traditions. Capitalists are, in a word, radicals. In America, our most significant radicals have always been capitalists—men like Bell, Edison, Ford, Carnegie, Sarnoff, Goldwyn. These men obliterated the 19th century, and created the 20th, which is why it is a mystery to me that capitalists are thought to be conservative. Perhaps it is because they are inclined to wear dark suits and grey ties.

I trust you understand that in saying all this, I am making no argument for socialism. I say only that capitalists need to be carefully watched and disciplined. To be sure, they talk of family, marriage, piety, and honor but if allowed to exploit new technology to its fullest economic potential, they may undo the institutions that make such ideas possible. And here I might just give two examples of this point, taken from the American encounter with technology. The first concerns education. Who, we may ask, has had the greatest impact on American education in this century? If you are thinking of John Dewey or any other education philosopher, I must say you are quite wrong. The greatest impact has been made by quiet men in grey suits in a suburb of New York City called Princeton, New Jersey. There, they developed and promoted the technology known as the standardized test, such as IQ tests, the SATs and the GREs. Their tests redefined what we mean by learning, and have resulted in our reorganizing the curriculum to accommodate the tests.

A second example concerns our politics. It is clear by now that the people who have had the most radical effect on American politics in our time are not political ideologues or student protesters with long hair and copies of Karl Marx under their arms. The radicals who have changed the nature of politics in America are entrepreneurs in dark suits and grey ties who manage the large television industry in America. They did not mean to turn political discourse into a form of entertainment. They did not mean to make it impossible for an overweight person to run for high political office. They did not mean to reduce political campaigning to a 30-second TV commercial. All they were trying to do is to make television into a vast and unsleeping money machine. That they destroyed substantive political discourse in the process does not concern them.

Fifth Idea

I come now to the fifth and final idea, which is that media tend to become mythic. I use this word in the sense in which it was used by the French literary critic, Roland Barthes. He used the word "myth" to refer to a common tendency to think of our technological creations as if they were God-given, as if they were a part of the natural order of things. I have on occasion asked my students if they know when the alphabet was invented. The question astonishes them. It is as if I asked them when clouds and trees were invented. The alphabet, they believe, was not something that was invented. It just is. It is this way with many products of human culture but with none more consistently than technology. Cars, planes, TV, movies, newspapers—they have achieved mythic status because they are perceived as gifts of nature, not as artifacts produced in a specific political and historical context.

When a technology become mythic, it is always dangerous because it is then accepted as it is, and is therefore not easily susceptible to modification or control. If you should propose to the average American that television broadcasting should not begin until 5 P.M. and should cease at 11 P.M., or propose that there should be no television commercials, he will think the idea ridiculous. But not because he disagrees with your cultural agenda. He will think it ridiculous because he assumes you are proposing that something in nature be changed; as if you are suggesting that the sun should rise at 10 A.M. instead of at 6.

The best way to view technology is as a strange intruder.

Whenever I think about the capacity of technology to become mythic, I call to mind the remark made by Pope John Paul II. He said, "Science can purify religion from error and superstition. Religion can purify science from idolatry and false absolutes."

What I am saying is that our enthusiasm for technology can turn into a form of idolatry and our belief in its beneficence can be a false absolute. The best way to view technology is as a strange intruder, to remember that technology is not part of God's plan but a product of human creativity and hubris, and that its capacity for good or evil rests entirely on human awareness of what it does for us and to us.

Conclusion

And so, these are my five ideas about technological change. First, that we always pay a price for technology; the greater the technology, the greater the price. Second, that there are always winners and losers, and that the winners always try to persuade the losers that they are really winners. Third, that there is embedded in every great technology an epistemological, political or social prejudice. Sometimes that bias is greatly to our advantage. Sometimes it is not. The printing press annihilated the oral tradition; telegraphy annihilated space; television has humiliated the word; the computer, perhaps, will degrade community life. And so on. Fourth, technological change is not additive; it is ecological, which means, it changes everything and is, therefore too important to be left entirely in the hands of Bill Gates. And fifth, technology tends to become mythic; that is, perceived as part of the natural order of things, and therefore tends to control more of our lives than is good for us.

If we had more time, I could supply some additional important things about technological change but I will stand by these for the moment, and will close with this thought. In the past, we experienced technological change in the manner of sleepwalkers. Our unspoken slogan has been "technology über alles," and we have been willing to shape our lives to fit the requirements of technology, not the requirements of culture. This is a form of stupidity, especially in an age of vast technological change. We need to proceed with our eyes wide open so that we many use technology rather than be used by it.

Slouching Toward the Ordinary
Current Trends in Computer-Mediated Communication

Susan C. Herring

Introduction

It has become a truism that computer-mediated communication (CMC) systems, as compared with previous communication technologies, are cheap, fast, and democratic; as such, their popularity continues to grow. Every year, it seems, a new type of CMC enters the scene: ICQ ('I Seek You'), instant messaging (IM), short-messaging service (SMS, also known as text messaging or 'texting'), web logs (blogs). How has CMC technology changed, conceptually and feature-wise, from previous technologies? More importantly, is new CMC technology giving rise to new social practices, and if so, in what directions is it steering us?

These questions, which regularly frame inquiry into the design and use of CMC systems, reflect two underlying assumptions: first, that 'new' CMC technologies really are new; and second, that CMC technologies shape communication, and through it, social behavior. The first of these assumptions is rarely challenged, other than by historians who note parallels between the internet and previous teletechnologies such as the telegraph and telephone (Baron, 2000). After all, who could deny that the social hypertext of the world wide web (Erickson, 1996), for example, constituted a radical departure from what came before? The second assumption, technological determinism (Markus, 1994), was vigorously critiqued in the early to mid-1990s (Spears and Lea, 1992; Walther, 1996), but has been making a quiet comeback as a result of a growing body of empirical evidence that the medium can shape the message, or at least, how the message is packaged and processed (Condon and Čech, 2001). Now, the question is no longer: does technology shape human communication, but rather: under what circumstances, in what ways, and to what extent (Herring, 2001, 2003c)?

The above assumptions have given rise to a tendency for CMC scholarship to follow in the wake of the latest popular technologies, in an attempt to get a descriptive fix on their affordances and emergent cultures of use. Consider the rapid popularization of blogging, for example, and the scholarly attention that it is presently attracting. (Conversely, how many scholars are researching MOOs anymore?) Yet, although this technology-driven agenda may seem justified, it suffers from a systematic bias: it overestimates the novelty of much CMC, and

underestimates the effects of social forces such as mass popularization, according to which mundane uses of technologies tend to co-opt their destabilizing potentials over time. Brown (2000) flagged this process with respect to the commercialization of women's content on the world wide web several years ago. Could it be that the CMC of chatrooms, web boards, text messaging on mobile phones, blogs, and such like is also on its way to becoming mundane and ordinary? If so, how can this trajectory be reconciled with the perception of seemingly endless technological innovation?

Some answers to this apparent paradox suggest themselves when we reflect on the evolution of popular CMC systems and their social impacts over the past five years. A brief comparison between then and now reveals conflicting trends which nonetheless point toward a future convergence: CMC on the internet is slouching toward the ordinary. For the purposes of this survey, CMC is defined broadly to include both interactive, text-based modes and human to human communication via the world wide web.

Then
Technologies

CMC in the late 1990s was in some respects crude and fragmented. It was mostly text-based, and its various modes were accessed by disparate means: email required a mailer system, Usenet newsgroups a newsreader (already incorporated by that time into the Netscape browser, but requiring server set-up), Internet Relay Chat (IRC) required an IRC client, ICQ an ICQ client, and so forth. While both of these characteristics were beginning to change under the influence of the world wide web, many users still experienced CMC primarily as ASCII text, and one had to have a modicum of specialized knowledge in order to access its various forms (or be provided access to them through an internet service provider—ISP).

These circumstances in no way hindered the popularity of text-based technologies, however. Email was the acknowledged 'killer app', the default mode of CMC for most users. Discussion lists, a mainstay of academic discourse communities, were so active that many listservs had started to provide daily digests or 'header only' formats to reduce the email burden on overloaded subscribers. Usenet continued its mostly subterranean, exponential growth (Smith, 1999). When I conducted a six-month ethnographic study of it in 1998, EFNet (the largest IRC network) was bursting at the seams, a popular recreational hangout for young people in the US and abroad. Even MUDs (Multi-User Dungeons or Dimensions) and MOOs (MUDs, Object-Orientated) which previously had been known only in restricted circles, had attained a certain notoriety through published reports (e.g., Bruckman, 1993; Dibbell, 1993; Kendall, 1996; Kolko, 1995), and were beginning to develop a reputation as respectable teaching environments (Haynes and Holmevik, 1997). ICQ, which was newly introduced in 1996, was already attracting attention as an alternative to chat, especially for dyadic conversation.

The web, meanwhile, pursued a largely parallel course of development. By the late 1990s, with e-commerce as the dominant activity on the web, 'interactivity' was becoming a buzzword, although most webpages were in fact relatively static and allowed little human to human interaction (Ha and James, 1998). In the non-commercial realm, personal homepages were popular both among faculty at academic institutions (Arnold and Miller, 2000) and with young people, for whom the web offered an unprecedented opportunity for self-expression to a mass audience (Chandler, 1998). The 'jennicam', established in 1996 as one of the first personal webcam sites, received so many hits that Jennifer Ringley continued it after she graduated from college, adding a live-chat feature (O'Sullivan, 1999). Projections for the future of CMC at that time focused on increased use of multimedia, especially video and audio streaming. Graphical virtual worlds such as The Palace and ActiveWorlds, also introduced in 1996, were attracting communities of recreational users (Suler, 1996), and generating speculation about the potential of avatar-based communication in multi-dimensional, navigable environments.

Social Issues

In the late 1990s, the dominant discourses about CMC on the internet were a sometimes jarring juxtaposition of social concerns with commercial hype. Scholars, journalists, and other internet commentators expounded on the benefits (and challenges) of virtual community, anonymity and online romance, on the one hand, and e-commerce, 'stickiness', and trust (by which was meant users' willingness to provide their credit card numbers on commercial websites), on the other. Concerns that bridged the social/commercial gap included security, censorship, gender demographics, and online pornography. Views on the latter two were sharply divided: earlier utopian views of the internet as a gender equalizer enjoyed a renaissance as the number of female internet users climbed, and marketeers proclaimed them an important new market; others pointed to a by-then irrefutable body of evidence of online gender harassment (Herring, 1999, 2000). Web pornography was celebrated for being profitable (Rich, 2001); others critiqued it as socially harmful but, in keeping with libertarian fashion on the internet, advocated filtering it out rather than reducing its prevalence (Birsch, 1996). In a different domain, language purists warned

of linguistic decay as a result of the fragmented, abbreviated practices of chat users.

Throughout this period, Y2K loomed on the horizon, adding an overlay of anxiety to the generally positivist discourse about the internet. We surrendered to the internet, nervously accepted our dependence on it, as the extent of that dependency sunk in. It seemed the 'Net' would never stop growing and changing, leaving us forever scrambling to catch up. It was also exhilarating; we had the impression of living in important times. At the same time, for some, the novelty of CMC had already worn off: email had been around since 1972, listervs since at least 1975, chat since 1988, and some users who had been enthusiastic participants earlier had subsequently scaled back their use, disenchanted with the flame wars, repetitiousness, incoherence, and banality of online public discourse. By September 1999, according to Cyber Dialogue, 27.7 million adults in the US had tried the internet and discontinued its use (Pastore, 1999). Meanwhile, internet access was spreading globally and across class boundaries, bringing new and more diverse populations of communicators online.

Now
Technologies

Two internet-wide technological trends have affected broadly online communication practices over the past five years: increased bandwidth, and a growing tendency for different forms of CMC to be made available through a web browser interface. More bandwidth, which is available to home users through cable modem and DSL technologies, has meant faster connections and a greater ability to access multimedia applications. For CMC, this means that communication environments incorporating audio, video, and 3D graphics are increasingly available. Yet, despite the growing popularity of streaming audio and video for entertainment purposes, their use for communication outside of videocam sex chats (Kibby and Costello, 2001) is not yet widespread. Perhaps surprisingly, for those who had earlier predicted that multimedia would eclipse text, CMC has yet to embrace its full multimedia potential. Exceptions include peer-to-peer (P2P) music file transfer protocols such as Napster, and massively multi-player online role playing games (MMORPGs) such as EverQuest and Ultima Online which, crucially, involve rich sensory media. However, although these protocols allow some user-to-user communication, it is typically secondary to another purpose, such as downloading music or playing a 3D graphical game.

The second change, the integration of different CMC protocols within a web browser interface, provides greater convenience and ease of access to different online communication options. Synchronous chat, asynchronous discussion forums, and email are now accessible through the web. Usenet itself has been 'acquired' by Google; its archives are just a click away from the homepage of the popular search engine. This trend, in turn, has created de facto competition between web-based and older CMC protocols: web chat has attracted new chatters who would have gravitated to IRC in earlier days, and web boards have taken over partially the functions of listservs and newsgroups, such that both IRC and Usenet have declined in importance in recent years. MUDs and MOOs, which lack a web interface, have also receded into the shadows. Even participation in graphical virtual worlds, with the exception of game worlds, is down. The demographics of users have shifted as well, toward younger and less technically-skilled populations. The ease of access that makes public web CMC attractive to many users, including neophytes, tends also to lower the quality of discourse, making it more noisy, fragmented, and contentious than CMC in domains that are harder to access.

Meanwhile, new modes have emerged into mainstream consciousness. In the chat realm, ICQ, which featured a split-screen option with keystroke-by-keystroke message transmission, was bought by America Online and merged with its instant messenger protocol. Like IM, ICQ has a contact list that indicates when a friend is online and available to chat. Meanwhile, IM soared in popularity; Jupiter reported more than 67 million users by September 2001, including many in corporate contexts. Among young, recreational US users (according to informal surveys that I conduct whenever I give a lecture in a university other than my home institution), IM is edging out older modes of group chat. This is an interesting replacement, in that chatrooms allow large-scale, multi-participant conversations (many chatters in the same 'room' at the same time), whereas 'IMers' tend to engage in multiple simultaneous dyadic conversations. However, this appears to be mostly a US phenomenon as yet; in Germany, there is relatively little use of instant messaging, while group chat remains popular (Beißwenger, 2001), and Spain has high rates of both IM usage and chatroom participation (Greenspan, 2003).

There are geographical differences as well in the use of SMS on mobile phones. SMS is ubiquitous among teenage and preteenage users in industrialized nations outside North America. As of April 2001, 16 billion SMS messages had been sent, but SMS has only recently infiltrated the US communication ecology due to the complications caused by multiple network standards. Text messaging is perversely unergonomic: one 'types' words by repeatedly pressing miniature telephone buttons until the desired letter is reached; the tiny screen size limits message length to 160 characters, resulting in abbreviated patterns of language use. At the same time, a text message is cheaper, and because it is asynchronous, less intrusive than a phone call. SMS can be sent both to and from the internet (via a web interface), or between cellphones directly, making it the most mobile and ubiquitous of CMC modes in popular use at the present time.

The newest mode to attain widespread popularity is also text-based. Blogs are frequently updated websites in which messages are posted in reverse chronological sequence, typically by a single author. They are maintained both by tech-savvy insiders and including teenage girls to record personal observations and commentary; current estimates place the number of blogs at over four million (Perseus, 2003). In some milieux, they have replaced personal homepages as the preferred mode of self-presentation on the web. Additionally, some blogs permit readers to post comments directly to the web interface, making blogs a hybrid of webpages and interactive CMC (Herring et al., 2004). Group or 'community' blogs, such as Metafilter

(Krishnamurthy, 2002) and Slashdot, bear a strong resemblance to web-based asynchronous discussion forums.

IM, SMS and blogs are all 'new', but how different are they from what came before? Each contains a technical innovation: an awareness or 'social presence' indicator for IM, mobile access for SMS, and blog update capability that makes modifying a webpage as easy as posting a message to a discussion list. In other respects, all of them share more features with previous CMC technologies than they differ from them: IM is a form of synchronous chat, SMS is essentially email sent over mobile phones, and blogs are HTML documents, like other webpages. Even the keystroke-by-keystroke feature of ICQ was common to earlier forms of split-screen chat. Yet, more generally, all involve text messages that are composed and read via a digital interface, as do most currently popular forms of CMC. This is not for lack of ability to imagine different CMC systems: alternative text-based paradigms, voice-to-text and text-to-voice conversion systems, and multimedia protocols are being envisioned and designed continuously. Rather, the robust popularity of, for example, email over the past 30 years suggests that it satisfies some important communicative needs. It is an interesting question why the message-centered, text-interface paradigm still dominates the available options: is it due to historical precedence, lower cost, ease of production, viability across platforms, the comfort of familiarity, inertia, or all of the above? We revisit this question below.

Social Issues

Online discourse takes place today in a more subdued social, economic, and political climate. The past five years saw the dot com crash and a subsequent scaling-back of optimism about e-commerce. Although Y2K passed without major incident, the terrorist acts that followed continue to remind us of our vulnerability through technology. To be sure, the internet continues to grow; recent estimates place the number of global users around 700 million (CyberAtlas, 2003). However, although foreign adoption has increased such that US users now only make up only one-third of the online population, the percentage of English-language web pages remains disproportionately high (Lavoie et al., 2003), evidence of continuing global disparity.

Conversely, the gender gap appears to be closing. The number of female self-reported web users caught up with that of male users in the US in 2000 (Rickert and Sacharow, 2000) and continues to rise, although men still spend more time online per visit (Pastore, 2001) and dominate public discussion forums (Herring, 2003a). Indeed, the gender demographics, behaviors, and values of internet users now largely mirror those of mainstream society, as reflected also in the increasing 'mainstreamization' of web content (Brown, 2000). Gender issues have been replaced in popular awareness by other concerns. In a parody of the classic 1993 New Yorker cartoon ('On the internet, nobody knows you're a dog'), a recent cartoon shows the same dog reading on a computer screen: 'Welcome Canine User 39. Mutt, mostly black Lab. Enjoys pepperoni, fetching and sniffing other dog's heinies. Updating profile.' The underlying concern is no longer with liberation through anonymity from gender (and other forms of) discrimination, but with loss of personal privacy due to the ready availability of information about individuals online.

Even if Big Brother is not constantly watching, there is a growing awareness that our online communication leaves traces, in the form of archives, chat logs and navigational histories. Experienced users have become more cautious about what they say and do online. Relatedly, as abuses such as online harassment, cyberstalking, trolling, and spamming increase (Herring, 2003b), efforts are being made to filter and control abuser access to online environments through reputation systems and 'trust metrics', which require others to vouch for an individual, or for the individual to otherwise demonstrate trustworthiness, before he or she is allowed to participate fully. Legislation is also being promoted to restrict and punish anti-social behaviors, and to limit spamming. Whereas the libertarian ideology that characterized the internet in the 1990s required users to tolerate various forms of annoying behavior in the name of freedom of expression, users today are less tolerant of abuse and more willing to accept systems of control to restrict it. Maintaining a 'liveable' online environment is becoming increasingly important, as choosing to forego internet use becomes less of a practical option.

Other attitudes seem never to change. Language purists continue to fret about degradation of language through CMC, focusing currently on the IM and SMS messages exchanged by teenagers. However, the abbreviations and non-standard spellings typical of such messages are not really new (Thurlow, 2003). They carry on earlier practices from chat; going back further still, they function as a semi-private code to prevent teachers and parents from understanding what is written, much like teens of earlier generations passed notes 'encrypted' in special alphabets or writing permutations (Palfreyman and Al Khalil, 2003).

Whither CMC?

A colleague recently expressed consternation in a posting to a professional listserv that his undergraduate students no longer find the internet fascinating. They do not relate to the utopian and dystopian speculations of earlier decades, and find the debates of the 1990s about online democracy, identity, and virtuality hyped and vaguely silly. The explanation, it seems, is that they have grown up with the internet: using the web and communicating with others online are taken for granted. IM and SMS are no more exotic to this generation, it seems, than note-passing and talking on the telephone were to mine, and blogging is just the modern analog of keeping a personal journal.

Members of older generations as well have acquired extensive familiarity with CMC over the years, especially in the form of email, distribution lists, and webpages. While some embrace new paradigms, for others it is a relief that the pace of technological change seems to have slowed—or at least, that recent changes are less radical, building incrementally on established paradigms. Constant innovation and complexity in online communication tools exact a price; many users just want them to be stable, simple, and usable across computing platforms, an impetus that no doubt contributes to the enduring popularity of email.

In short, after barely more than 30 years of existence, CMC has become more of a practical necessity than an object of fascination and fetish. (Over)use, disenchantment, fatigue, ubiquity, indispensability, and the passage of time all contribute inexorably toward this end. The most popular technological trends that have emerged over the past five years lead in this direction as well. Despite the availability of increasingly sophisticated multimedia protocols, CMC remains predominantly grounded in 'old' textual practices. Idiosyncratic protocols are being united under a simpler browser-accessible format, and blogs integrate text-based CMC and HTML capabilities. The mobility of SMS (and wireless technologies more generally), and the presence indicators of IM and ICQ, blur the line between online and offline communication, a trend that is also evident in increased uses of traditional modes of CMC in order to establish face-to-face contact. These trends simplify CMC and appropriate it for ordinary interactional purposes.

Certainly, the sheen of novelty of computer-mediated communication has not yet worn off completely, save perhaps for the youngest generations of users. Designers still strive to innovate; superficially new technologies still exert an appeal. Yet I advance this prediction for the next five years: increasing technological integration, combined with assimilation of day-to-day uses and the corresponding need to ensure the trustworthiness of one's interlocutors, will continue to make the internet a simpler, safer, and—for better or for worse—less fascinating communication environment. If this prediction proves true, CMC researchers would do well to take a step back from the parade of passing technologies and consider more deeply the question of what determines people's use of mediated communication. In addition to technological determinism, the effects of time, familiarity, and mass popularization would need to be theorized and investigated.

References

Arnold, J. and H. Miller (2000) 'Same Old Gender Plot? Women Academics' Identities on the Web', URL (consulted July 2003): http://ess.ntu.ac.uk/miller/cyberpsych/gendplot.htm

Baron, N.S. (2000) *From Alphabet to Email: How Written English Evolved and Where It's Heading.* New York: Routledge.

Beißwenger, M. (ed.) (2001) *Chat-Kommunikation. Sprache, Interaktion, Sozialität & Identität in synchroner computervermittelter Kommunikation. Perspektiven auf ein interdisziplinäres Forschungsfeld.* Stuttgart: Ibidem Verlag.

Birsch, D. (1996, January 1) 'Sexually Explicit Materials and the Internet', *CMC Magazine,* URL (consulted July 2003): http://www.december.com/cmc/mag/1996/jan/birsch.html

Brown, J. (2000) 'What Happened to the Women's Web?', Salon.com, 25 August, URL (consulted July 2003): http://dir.salon.com/tech/feature/2000/08/25/womens_Web/index.html

Bruckman, A.S. (1993) 'Gender Swapping in Cyberspace', *Proceedings of INET 1993,* FTP (consulted June 2001): http://www.media.mit.edu in pub/MediaMOO/papers.gender-swapping

Chandler, D. (1998) 'Personal Homepages and the Construction of Identities on the Web', URL (consulted July 2003): http://www.aber.ac.uk/~dgc/Webident.html

Condon, S. and C. Čech (2001) 'Profiling Turns in Interaction: Discourse Structure and Function', *Proceedings of the 34th Hawaii International Conference on System Sciences,* (HICSS-34), 3–6 January, Maui, Hawaii (CD-ROM). Los Alamitos: IEEE Computer Society.

CyberAtlas (2003) 'Population Explosion!', 6 June, URL (consulted July 2003): http://cyberatlas.Internet.com/big_picture/geographics/article/0,,5911_151151,00.html

Dibbell, J. (1993) 'A Rape in Cyberspace, or How an Evil Clown, a Haitian Trickster Spirit, Two Wizards, and a Cast of Dozens Turned a Database into a Society', *Village Voice,* 21 December, pp. 36–42.

Erickson, T. (1996) 'The World Wide Web as Social Hypertext', in 'Viewpoints', *Communications of the ACM* 39(1): 15–7.

Greenspan, R. (2003) 'More than Half-billion Online Globally', *CyberAtlas,* 21 February, URL (consulted July 2003): http://cyberatlas.Internet.com/big_picture/geographics/article/0,,5911_1593591,00.html

Ha, L. and E.L. James (1998) 'Interactivity Re-examined: a Baseline Analysis of Early Business Web Sites', *Journal of Broadcasting and Electronic Media* 42(4): 457–74.

Haynes, C. and J.R. Holmevik (eds) (1997) *High Wired: on the Design, Use, and Theory of Educational MOOs.* Ann Arbor, MI: University of Michigan Press.

Herring, S.C. (1999) 'The Rhetorical Dynamics of Gender Harassment Online', *The Information Society* 15(3): 151–67.

Herring, S.C. (2000) 'Gender Differences in CMC: Findings and Implications', *Computer Professionals for Social Responsibility Journal,* Winter, URL (consulted July 2003): http://www.cpsr.org/publications/newsletters/issues/2000/Winter2000/index.html

Herring, S.C. (2001) 'Computer-mediated Discourse', in D. Schiffrin, D. Tannen and H. Hamilton (eds) *The Handbook of Discourse Analysis,* pp. 612–34. Oxford: Blackwell.

Herring, S.C. (2003a) 'Gender and Power in Online Communication', in J. Holmes and M. Meyerhoff (eds) *The Handbook of Language and Gender,* pp. 202–28. Oxford: Blackwell.

Herring, S.C. (2003b) 'Cyber Violence: Recognizing and Resisting Abuse in Online Environments', *Asian Women* 14(Summer): 187–212, available online: http://ella.slis.indiana.edu/~herring/violence.html

Herring, S.C. (2003c) 'Computer-mediated Discourse Analysis: an Approach to Researching Online Behavior', in S.A. Barab, R. Kling and J.H. Gray (eds) *Designing for Virtual Communities in the Service of Learning.* New York: Cambridge University Press.

Herring, S.C., L.A. Scheidt, S. Bonus and E. Wright (2004) 'Bridging the Gap: A Genre Analysis of Weblogs', Proceedings of the 37th Hawitt International Conference on System Sciences (HICSS-37), January 5–8, Big Island, Hawaii (CD-ROM).

Kendall, L. (1996) 'MUDder? I Hardly Know Er! Adventures of a Feminist MUDder', in L. Cherny and E.R. Weise (eds) *Wired Women: Gender and New Realities in Cyberspace,* pp. 207–23. Seattle, WA: Seal Press.

Kibby, M. and B. Costello (2001) 'Between the Image and the Act: Interactive Sex Entertainment on the Internet', *Sexualities: Studies in Culture and Society* 4(3): 353–69.

Kolko, B. (1995) 'Building a World with Words: the Narrative Reality of Virtual Communities', *Works and Days* 13(1–2): 105–26, available online: http://acorn.grove.iup.edu/en/workdays/toc.html

Krishnamurthy, S. (2002) 'The Multidimensionality of Blog Conversations: the Virtual Enactment of September 11', paper presented at the Association of Internet Researchers Conference 3.0, October, Maastricht, the Netherlands.

Lavoie, B.F., E.T. O'Neill and R. Bennett (2003, April) 'Trends in the Evolution of the Public Web 1998–2002', *D-Lib Magazine* 9(4), URL (consulted July 2003): http://www.dlib.org/dlib/april03/lavoie/04lavoie.html

Markus, M.L. (1994) 'Finding a Happy Medium: Explaining the Negative Effects of Electronic Communication on Social Life at Work', *ACM Transactions on Information Systems* 12(2): 119–49.

O'Sullivan, P. (1999) '"Personal Broadcasting": Theoretical Implications of the Web', URL (consulted July 2003): http://www.ilstu.edu/~posull/PersBroad.htm

Palfreyman, D. and M. Al Khalil (2003) 'Representing Gulf Arabic in Internet Messaging', *Journal of Computer-mediated Communication* 9(1). URL (consulted 12 November 2003): http://www.ascusc.org/jcmc/vol9/issue1/palfreyman.html

Pastore, M. (1999) 'US Internet Audience Growth Slowing', *CyberAtlas,* 29 November, URL (consulted July 2003): http://cyberatlas.Internet.com/big_picture/geographics/article/0,,5911_246241,00.html

Pastore, M. (2001) 'Internet Remains a Man's Domain', URL (consulted July 2003): http://cyberatlas.Internet.com/big_picture/demographics/

Perseus (2003) 'The Blogging Iceberg—4.2 Million Hosted Weblogs, Most Little Seen, Quickly Abandoned', URL (consulted 2 November 2003): http://www.perseus.com/blogsurvey

Rich, F. (2001) 'Naked Capitalists: There's No Business Like Porn Business', *New York Times,* 20 May, URL (consulted July 2003): http://www.bettydodson.com/nakedcapitalists.htm

Rickert, A. and A. Sacharow (2000) *It's a Woman's World Wide Web,* Media Metrix and Jupiter Communications, URL (consulted July 2003): http://www.mediametrix.com/data/MMXI-JUP-WWWW.pdf

Smith, M.A. (1999) 'Invisible Crowds in Cyberspace: Mapping the Social Structure of Usenet', in M. Smith and P. Kollock (eds) *Communities in Cyberspace,* pp. 195–219. London: Routledge.

Spears, R. and M. Lea (1992) 'Social Influence and the Influence of the "Social" in Computer-mediated Communication', in M. Lea (ed.) *Contexts of Computer-mediated Communication,* pp. 30–65. London: Harvester-Wheatsheaf.

Suler, J. (1996) *The Psychology of Cyberspace,* URL (consulted June 2001): http://www.rider.edu/users/suler/psycyber/psycyber.html

Thurlow, C. (2002) 'Generation Txt? Exposing the Sociolinguistics of Young People's Text Messaging', *Discourse Analysis Online.* URL (consulted 12 November 2003): http://www.shu.ac.uk/daol/articles/open/2002/003/thurlow2002003-01.html

Walther, J. (1996) 'Computer-mediated Communication: Personal, Interpersonal and Hyperpersonal Interaction', *Communication Research* 23(1): 3–43.

Susan Herring is Professor of Information Science and Adjunct Professor of Linguistics at Indiana University, Bloomington. One of the first researchers to apply linguistic analysis methods to interactive, text-based CMC in the early 1990s, in recent years she has extended her investigations to include multimedia Internet content, with a focus on the world wide web, *Address:* School of Library and Information Science, 10th Street and Jordan Avenue, Indiana University, Bloomington, IN 47405, USA. [email: herring@indiana.edu]

From *New Media & Society,* Vol. 6, no. 1, February 2004, pp. 26–36. Copyright © 2004 by Sage Publications, Ltd. Reprinted by permission.

On the Nature of Computing

Computing is its own virtual world, bound only by its practitioners' imaginations and creativity.

JON CROWCROFT

I would like to propose that computing's innate agenda is the virtual, rather than the natural or the artificial.

Each of us in the computing community experiences periodic bouts of navel gazing about the nature of our business. The related public debate typically polarizes us along a spectrum between engineering and science. At the engineering end are usually the engineers who design and manage systems, networks, and operating systems; at the science end are the ideas describing computability, complexity, and information theory. An extreme view of each end places practitioners within university electrical engineering departments, and theoreticians within university mathematics departments.

I studied the natural sciences at Cambridge University as an undergraduate. I was taught the value of studying the natural world, along with the use (and advance) of mathematics to describe and understand (and predict) its behavior. I have also spent more than a decade teaching courses in an electrical engineering department, where artificial systems are built according to models (often mathematical) with reliable and predictable behavior. Computing has never established a simple connection between the natural and the mathematical. Nowhere is this lack of a clear-cut connection clearer than when Ph.D. students select a problem for their thesis work; their dilemma is the key to understanding why computing represents a third place in the world of discourse—distinct from the natural and from the artificial of science and engineering.

Computing involves (virtual) systems that may never exist, either in nature or through human creation. Ph.D. students find it difficult to settle on a topic because the possibilities are endless and the topic may have no intersection with the real world, either in understanding a phenomenon or in creating an artifact. In trying to define the nature of computing I completely disagree with the late Nobel Prize physicist Richard Feynman.[1] Computing often results in a model of something. Although an object or process that interacts with or describes the real world may be the outcome, it does not have to be.[2]

Computing's disconnection from physical reality has an important consequence when explaining to the public what it is computer scientists do, whether to schoolchildren, noncomputing users in general, or funding agencies and decision makers. Unlike the artificial (the engineering end of the spectrum), some of what we do may not be obviously useful and therefore attractive to commerce and governments for optimizing social welfare or profit. Unlike the natural world (the scientific end of the spectrum), some of what we do may not necessarily be "for the advancement of pure knowledge" and therefore a priori worthwhile. In some sense, though, what we do underpins both of these engineering and scientific activities.

I am comfortable endorsing the claim that computing is less worldly than, say, cosmology. On the other hand, due to the possible use of computing as part of the foundation of practically any kind of system—whether physical or abstract—anyone is likely to build today, computer scientists can also claim that computing is inherently more useful than engineering.

Examples of the Virtual

To illustrate my argument, consider the following examples of the virtual I've selected from the history of computer science:

Virtualization. Within the discipline of computer science itself, the concept of virtualization represents a first-class tool. When confronted with intransigent engineering limitations of memory, processors, I/O, and networks, we've commonly taken the abstract approach. For example, we create virtual memory systems to replace one piece of hardware with another as needed to overcome capacity/performance problems and to choose when it's appropriate to do so; we replace inconvenient low-level processor interfaces (the instruction set) with virtual machines (such as VM, vmware, Xen, and Denali), to provide a more convenient (and stable) interface for systems programmers. We might provide a single API to all I/O devices, so programs need not worry whether, say, an MP3 file is being loaded from a tape, a magnetic disk, an optical disc, flash RAM, or even networked media. We also might replace a network with a virtual private network, allowing users to behave as if they were in an Internet of their own.

Virtual communities. In the emerging world of grid computing (notably in the U.K.'s e-Science program), we are creating virtual communities of scientists with virtual laboratories and computing resources dedicated to supporting "in silico" experiments, replacing the expensive, error-prone "in vivo" or "in vitro" experiments of the past. Here, we have virtualized natural systems, whether they involve fluids (such as the atmosphere, oceans, and plasma) or complex biological systems (such as genomes, proteins, and even whole ecologies).

Entertainment. The convergence of computer games and the movie industry represents the clearest evidence to support my view that computing is a wholly new discipline. The world of entertainment imposes no natural or artificial constraints on what a system may do. The only limit is the imagination of its creators, combined with knowledge and skills from the computing discipline. Constraints may be imposed from the discipline itself (such as computability, complexity, and plain affability) but may often be orthogonal to the goals (if any) of the computation.

Historically, simple examples of virtual worlds have been used in both games and online environments, as well as for playing with alternate realities (such as in artificial life), so this view is not something that has suddenly become true. It has always been one of the exciting but difficult aspects of working in computing that the bounds are not set from outside the field but by our own choice of what research projects we most want to work on and see developed.

Conclusion

Occupying a third place in human intellectual culture, computing is not bound by the need to describe what does exist (as in natural science) or what can be built in the real world (as in engineering). This place is the virtual. Although we computer scientists do not need to be complete, consistent, or correct, we have the tools to choose to be part of these categories whenever we wish our systems to be complete, consistent, or correct.

Notes

1. "Computer science also differs from physics in that it is not actually a science. It does not study natural objects. Neither is it, as you might think, mathematics; although it does use mathematical reasoning pretty extensively. Rather, computer science is like engineering; it is all about getting something to do something, rather than just dealing with abstractions, as in the pre-Smith geology." Richard Feynman, from the book *Feynman Lectures on Computation* (1970).

2. I am tempted to lay claim to the term "magic" [1]. A lot of what computer scientists do is now seen by the lay public as magical. Programmers (especially systems engineers) are often referred to as gurus, sorcerers, and wizards. Given the lofty goals of white magic, understanding the power of names and the value of pure thought, the power of labels is indeed attractive. However, many historically compelling reasons argue against this connotation, including the sad history of Isaac Newton's alchemical pursuit of the philosopher's stone and eternal life, and the religiously driven 17th century witch trials in Salem, MA, and other seemingly rational explanations for irrational behaviors.

Reference

Penrose, R. *The Road to Reality: A Complete Guide to the Laws of the Universe.* Jonathan Cape, London, U.K., 2004.

JON CROWCROFT (Jon.Crowcroft@cl.cam.ac.uk) is the Marconi Professor of Communications Systems in the Computer Laboratory at the University of Cambridge, Cambridge, U.K.

From *Communications of the ACM,* Vol. 48, No. 2, February 2005, pp. 19–20. Copyright © 2005 by Association for Computing Machinery, Inc. Reprinted by permission.

UNIT 2
The Economy

Unit Selections

Key Points to Consider

- The story of automatic underwriting software is not the first time that software has been blamed for problems in the financial services industry. Use the Internet to find another instance. How are the two stories related? Is the problem with the software or with those who use it? How much responsibility should be shared by those who developed the software?

- Two articles in the unit are about overly complex hardware and software. Is the software that you use overly complex? Do you think the two articles capture what is going on, or can you think of other reasons for the complexity in electronic gadgetry?

- Are you surprised to learn, as the author of "The Software Wars" asserts, that the software development can be unsystematic? Do you think this differs from the production of conventional engineering projects—a bridge, for example?

- What do you think of Google's decision to scan first and ask questions later?

- Intellectual property laws are a contested area. Some—those who engage in music sharing, for instance—would like to eliminate them. Others think they are necessary to encourage creativity. Use the Internet to find out about the Free Software Movement. What would motivate someone to create software and then give it away?

Student Web Site
www.mhcls.com/online

Internet References
Further information regarding these Web sites may be found in this book's preface or online.

CAUCE: Coalition Against Unsolicited Commercial Email
http://www.cauce.org

E-Commerce Times
http://www.ecommercetimes.com/

The End of Cash (James Gleick)
http://www.around.com/money.html

Fight Spam on the Internet
http://spam.abuse.net

The Linux Home Page
http://www.linux.org

The Rise of the Informediary
http://www.ait.unl.edu/crane/misgrad/sglee/informediary.htm

Smart Cards: A Primer
http://www.javaworld.com/javaworld/jw-12-1997/jw-12-javadev.html

Smart Card Group
http://www.smartcard.co.uk

Living in the United States in the beginning of the 21st century, it is hard to imagine that the accumulation of wealth once bordered on the disreputable. Listen to William Wordsworth, writing two hundred years ago:

> The world is too much with us; late and soon,
> Getting and spending, we lay waste our powers:
> Little we see in nature that is ours;
> We have given our hearts away, a sordid boon!

These are words that would quicken the pulse of any young protester of globalization. And no wonder. Wordsworth was writing a generation after James Watt perfected the steam engine. England was in the grips of the Industrial Revolution. Just as the developed world now appears to be heading away from an industrial towards a service economy, so Wordsworth's world was moving from an agrarian to an industrial economy. And just as the steam engine has become the emblem of that transformation, the computer has become the symbol of this one.

People, of course, did not stop farming after the Industrial Revolution, nor have they stopped producing steel and automobiles after the Information Revolution, though many commentators write as if this is exactly what happened. It is true that we in the United States have largely stopped working in factories. In the last three decades, the number of Americans employed has increased by over 50 million. During this same period, the number of manufacturing jobs declined by several hundred thousand. A large handful of these new workers are software developers, computer engineers, Web-site developers, manipulators of digital images—the glamour jobs of the information age. A much larger portion provide janitorial, health, food, and child care services, leading to the charge that the American economy works because we take in one another's laundry.

What else does this laundry consist of? Services, mostly, one of which is offered by companies that market loans to borrowers with weak credit ratings. Lynnley Browning tells this story in "The Subprime Loan Machine." Another service that Americans provide in abundance is advertising. One model in use on the Web is for businesses to pay their Internet hosts only when a potential buyer actually clicks on their site. Sounds good? Read about Martin Fleichmann (see "Click Fraud"), who calculates that invalid clicks have cost his company $100,000.

Now what of the decline in manufacturing? It is a rare week when the papers do not include coverage of a plant closure, the weakness of trade unions, or the drop in living wage manufacturing jobs. Some large part of this is due to plant relocations to countries with lower labor costs. To be convinced, take a look at where almost anything you purchase is made. It is impossible to imagine how a global manufacturing network could be coordinated without computers. Products manufactured abroad—with or without the productivity benefits of computers—pass through a bewildering array of shippers and distributors until they arrive on the shelves of a big box retailer in a Phoenix suburb, or just-in-time to be bolted to the frame of an automobile being assembled outside St. Louis. Or, imagine how Federal Express could track its parcels as they make their way from an office in a San Jose suburb to one in Manhattan. Not surprisingly,

The Mcgraw-Hill Companies,Inc./Christopher Kerrigan, Photographer

cities around the country are scrambling to provide uniform broadband access. "The Big Band Era" reports on a problem many are encountering. Even as cities like Philadelphia are working to transform the entire city into a wireless hot spot—with government as the Internet service provider of last resort—communications companies are fighting to keep local governments out of the broadband business.

Two articles in the unit describe an important and understudied topic: the complexity of computer hardware and software. Compare Google's home page with just about that of any large company. We have Marissa Mayers to thank for defending it against the natural urge to clutter it up with ads and features. On the other hand, many of us are also burdened by a universal remote: "So many buttons, so little time—and more complicated than the flight deck of the starship Enterprise" (see "The Beauty of Simplicity"). "The Software Wars" tells a personal tale of software development and its inefficiencies, while taking its own swipe at the almost willful complexity of the universal remote.

Libraries have been a part of Western culture since classical times. Public libraries, accessible to all, have been an American institution for over two centuries, beginning with the Free Library of Philadelphia, and passing through the many Carnegie-funded libraries that began to appear across America a century later. Now Google has a grander vision. It announced in 2004 that it would digitally scan the libraries at Harvard, Stanford, Michigan, Oxford, and New York City and make the contents searchable world-wide. It should surprise no one that authors and publishers are less than enthusiastic about Google's plan (see "Scan this Book!").

The Subprime Loan Machine

Automated underwriting software helped fuel a mortgage boom.

LYNNLEY BROWNING

Edward N. Jones, a former NASA engineer for the Apollo and Skylab missions, looked at low-income home buyers nearly a decade ago and saw an unexplored frontier.

Through his private software company in Austin, Tex., Mr. Jones and his son, Michael, designed a program that used the Internet to screen borrowers with weak credit histories in seconds. The software was among the first of its kind. By early 1999, his company, Arc Systems, had its first big customer: First Franklin Financial, one of the biggest lenders to home buyers with weak, or subprime, credit.

The old way of processing mortgages involved a loan officer or broker collecting reams of income statements and ordering credit histories, typically over several weeks. But by retrieving real-time credit reports online, then using algorithms to gauge the risks of default, Mr. Jones's software allowed subprime lenders like First Franklin to grow at warp speed.

By 2005, at the height of the housing boom, First Franklin had increased the number of subprime loan applications it processed sevenfold, to 50,000 every month. Since 1999, Mr. Jones's software has been used to produce $450 billion in subprime loans.

The rise and fall of the subprime market has been told as a story of a flood of Wall Street money and the desire of Americans desperate to be part of a housing boom. But it was the little-noticed tool of automated underwriting software that made that boom possible.

Automated underwriting software spawned an array of subprime mortgages, like those that required no down payment or interest-only payments. The software effectively helped move what was a niche product only a decade ago into the mainstream.

Automated underwriting "replaced the ways we used to extend credit," said Prof. Nicolas P. Retsinas, director of the Joint Center for Housing Studies at Harvard.

Underwriting software helped fuel the boom in subprime mortagages.

Automated underwriting is now used to generate as much as 40 percent of all subprime loans, according to Pat McCoy, a law professor at the University of Connecticut who has written on real estate lending.

The software itself, of course, cannot be blamed for lowered lending standards or lax controls. But critics say the push for speed influenced some lenders to take shortcuts, ignore warning signs or focus entirely on credit scores.

"Used properly, automated underwriting is a wonderful thing," Professor McCoy said. The problem, she said, comes when lenders customize it to approve the wrong borrowers.

During the housing boom, speed became something of an arms race, as software makers and subprime lenders boasted of how fast they could process and generate a loan. New Century Financial, second to HSBC in subprime lending last year and now on the brink of bankruptcy, promised mortgage brokers on its Web site that with its FastQual automated underwriting system, "We'll give you loan answers in just 12 seconds!"

A push for speed led some lenders to take shortcuts, critics say.

Dozens of little-known software companies compete with Arc Systems. They include MindBox of Greenbrae, Calif.; Metavante, in Milwaukee; Mortgage Cadence of Greenwood Village, Colo.; and Overture Technologies in Bethesda, Md.

With small staffs, the companies typically sell their software to home lenders with vast networks of call centers employing hundreds of thousands of loan officers. Some big Wall Street banks and housing lenders bought the software, then developed their own systems. First Franklin, which has been acquired by Merrill Lynch, said that it stopped using Arc Systems' software last year to create its own proprietary system.

Subprime lenders like automated underwriting because it is cheap and fast. A 2001 Fannie Mae survey found that automated underwriting reduced the average cost to lenders of closing a loan by $916. The software quickly weeds out the very riskiest of applicants and automatically approves the rest.

"You don't have to chase every lead—just greenlight 'em," Mr. Jones of Arc Systems said in an interview.

And greenlight them they did.

By mid-2004, Countrywide Financial, a major subprime lender, had used MindBox's automated underwriting system to double the number of loans it made, to 150,000 monthly.

"Without the technology, there is no way we would have been able to do the amount of business that we did and continue to do," Scott Berry, executive vice president for artificial intelligence at Countrywide Financial, told a trade publication, Bank Systems & Technology, in the summer of 2004. Countrywide now uses a proprietary system.

Early forms of automated underwriting were first developed and used in the 1970s to process car loans and credit card applications.

By the mid-1990s, software for home buyers with good credit had gone mainstream at Fannie Mae and Freddie Mac, the large government-sponsored mortgage finance companies, and big traditional lenders. But none had been developed for subprime lending, then a niche market.

There are no estimates of the sales volumes for this software niche, but companies like Arc Systems often have annual revenues in the tens of millions of dollars. Arc Systems, whose name is something of a pun—Mr. Jones's middle name is Noah—earns $10 to $30 each time a borrower submits a loan application.

Proponents say the software makes things fairer and more objective for risky borrowers.

"It takes the subjectivity out of the good ol' boy system in which Martha knows Joe, who approves the loan—then you end up with a bad decision," Mr. Jones said.

Samir Rohatgi, a vice president at MindBox, said that old system of manual underwriting actually encouraged loan officers working on commission to grant bad loans.

"Those people were feeling pressure because of the way their company's performing, so the decisions are sometimes biased," he said.

Mr. Jones said that because his program, LendTech, could parse credit reports for more than 3,000 risk variables, "we had better analytics than the trading desks" on Wall Street.

But some question whether such analysis gave comfort where it was not deserved.

"Automated underwriting put the credit score on such a pedestal that it obscured the other important things, like is the income actually there," said Professor Retsinas of Harvard. "Before there was A.U., down payment mattered a lot. Where we've crossed the line in recent years is to say, we don't need down payment."

Michael Perna, Arc Systems' marketing director, said that income "is supposed to be verified by a person."

Mr. Jones founded Arc Systems in 1984 to produce software for Suwannee County, Fla., which used it to track when policemen issued parking tickets and when jail wardens fed inmates. Then in 1992, a local subprime lender called Home Inc. asked Mr. Jones to develop a program to screen risky borrowers. In 1997, amid the adoption of the Internet, "we ditched that software and went Web-based," Mr. Jones said.

Since 1999, his software has been used by major subprime lenders including HSBC and its former Household subsidiary, Deutsche Bank and the Virginia Housing Development Authority. Lehman Brothers and the Ellington Management Group, a big seller of mortgage-backed securities, have used LendTech to analyze pools of billions of dollars of subprime loans that they sold to big institutional investors.

"We've had clients all along the food chain," Mr. Jones, who is 66, said.

An electrical engineer by training who worked at NASA in the 1960s and then Unisys, Mr. Jones keeps his NASA patches on a wall in his office. He likes to clear cedar and juniper brush on his 100-acre property near Austin. His wife, Gayle, a nurse by training, is the company's executive vice president. Arc Systems has 52 employees and at one point employed seven married couples.

"We like to have picnics and play softball," Mr. Jones said.

Since the subprime housing market began falling apart late last year, Arc Systems' sales have dropped 30 percent. Still, Mr. Jones sees a sparkling future for automated underwriting. "The smart money on Wall Street is now looking for the gems—and they'll use A.U. to find them."

Then he added, "You know that old symbol of the snake eating its own tail? Well, we've always thought the industry was that. And that's kind of where we're at right now."

Click Fraud

The Dark Side of Online Advertising

Brian Grow and Ben Elgin

Martin Fleischmann put his faith in online advertising. He used it to build his Atlanta company, MostChoice.com, which offers consumers rate quotes and other information on insurance and mortgages. Last year he paid Yahoo! Inc. and Google Inc. a total of $2 million in advertising fees. The 40-year-old entrepreneur believed the celebrated promise of Internet marketing: You pay only when prospective customers click on your ads.

Now, Fleischmann's faith has been shaken. Over the past three years, he has noticed a growing number of puzzling clicks coming from such places as Botswana, Mongolia, and Syria. This seemed strange, since MostChoice steers customers to insurance and mortgage brokers only in the U.S. Fleischmann, who has an economics degree from Yale University and an MBA from Wharton, has used specially designed software to discover that the MostChoice ads being clicked from distant shores had appeared not on pages of Google or Yahoo but on curious Web sites with names like insurance1472.com and insurance060.com. He smelled a swindle, and he calculates it has cost his business more than $100,000 since 2003.

Fleischmann is a victim of click fraud: a dizzying collection of scams and deceptions that inflate advertising bills for thousands of companies of all sizes. The spreading scourge poses the single biggest threat to the Internet's advertising gold mine and is the most nettlesome question facing Google and Yahoo, whose digital empires depend on all that gold.

The growing ranks of businesspeople worried about click fraud typically have no complaint about versions of their ads that appear on actual Google or Yahoo Web pages, often next to search results. The trouble arises when the Internet giants boost their profits by recycling ads to millions of other sites, ranging from the familiar, such as cnn.com, to dummy Web addresses like insurance1472.com, which display lists of ads and little if anything else. When somebody clicks on these recycled ads, marketers such as MostChoice get billed, sometimes even if the clicks appear to come from Mongolia. Google or Yahoo then share the revenue with a daisy chain of Web site hosts and operators. A penny or so even trickles down to the lowly clickers. That means Google and Yahoo at times passively profit from click fraud and, in theory, have an incentive to tolerate it. So do

smaller search engines and marketing networks that similarly recycle ads.

Slipping Confidence

Google and Yahoo say they filter out most questionable clicks and either don't charge for them or reimburse advertisers that have been wrongly billed. Determined to prevent a backlash, the Internet ad titans say the extent of click chicanery has been exaggerated, and they stress that they combat the problem

---

vigorously. "We think click fraud is a serious but manageable issue," says John Slade, Yahoo's senior director for global product management. "Google strives to detect every invalid click that passes through its system," says Shuman Ghosemajumder, the search engine's manager for trust and safety. "It's absolutely in our best interest for advertisers to have confidence in this industry."

That confidence may be slipping. A *BusinessWeek* investigation has revealed a thriving click-fraud underground populated by swarms of small-time players, making detection difficult. "Paid to read" rings with hundreds or thousands of members each, all of them pressing PC mice over and over in living rooms and dens around the world. In some cases, "clickbot" software generates page hits automatically and anonymously. Participants from Kentucky to China speak of making from $25 to several thousand dollars a month apiece, cash they wouldn't receive if Google and Yahoo were as successful at blocking fraud as they claim.

"It's not that much different from someone coming up and taking money out of your wallet," says David Struck. He and his wife, Renee, both 35, say they dabbled in click fraud last year, making more than $5,000 in four months. Employing a common scheme, the McGregor (Minn.) couple set up dummy Web sites filled with nothing but recycled Google and Yahoo advertisements. Then they paid others small amounts to visit the sites, where it was understood they would click away on the ads, says David Struck. It was "way too easy," he adds. Gradually, he says, he and his wife began to realize they were cheating unwitting advertisers, so they stopped. "Whatever Google and Yahoo are doing [to stop fraud], it's not having much of an effect," he says.

Spending on Internet ads is growing faster than any other sector of the advertising industry and is expected to surge from $12.5 billion last year to $29 billion in 2010 in the U.S. alone, according to researcher eMarketer Inc. About half of these dollars are going into deals requiring advertisers to pay by the click. Most other Internet ads are priced according to "impressions," or how many people view them. Yahoo executives warned on Sept. 19 that weak ad spending by auto and financial-services companies would hurt its third-quarter revenue. Share prices of Yahoo and Google tumbled on the news.

Google and Yahoo are grabbing billions of dollars once collected by traditional print and broadcast outlets, based partly on the assumption that clicks are a reliable, quantifiable measure of consumer interest that the older media simply can't match. But the huge influx of cash for online ads has attracted armies of con artists whose activities are eroding that crucial assumption and could eat into the optimistic expectations for online advertising. (Advertisers generally don't grumble about fraudulent clicks coming from the Web sites of traditional media outlets. But there are growing concerns about these media sites exaggerating how many visitors they have—the online version of inflating circulation.)

The success of Google and Yahoo is based partly on the idea that clicks are reliable

Most academics and consultants who study online advertising estimate that 10% to 15% of ad clicks are fake, representing roughly $1 billion in annual billings. Usually the search engines divide these proceeds with several players: First, there are intermediaries known as "domain parking" companies, to which the search engines redistribute their ads. Domain parkers host "parked" Web sites, many of which are those dummy sites containing only ads. Cheats who own parked sites obtain search-engine ads from the domain parkers and arrange for the ads to be clicked on, triggering bills to advertisers. In all, $300 million to $500 million a year could be flowing to the click-fraud industry.

Law enforcement has only lately started focusing on the threat. A cybercrime unit led by the FBI and U.S. Postal Inspection Service just last month assigned two analysts to examine whether federal laws are being violated. The FBI acted after noticing suspected cybercriminals discussing click fraud in chat rooms. The staff of the Senate Judiciary Committee has launched its own informal probe.

Many advertisers, meanwhile, are starting to get antsy. Google and Yahoo have each settled a class action filed by marketers. In late September a coalition of such major brands as InterActive Corp.'s Expedia.com travel site and mortgage broker LendingTree is planning to go public with its mounting unease over click fraud, *BusinessWeek* has learned. The companies intend to form a group to share information and pressure Google and Yahoo to be more forthcoming. "You can't blame the advertisers for being suspicious," says Robert Pettee, search marketing manager for LendingTree, based in Charlotte, N.C. "If it's your money that's going out the door, you need to be asking questions." He says that up to 15% of the clicks on his company's ads are bogus.

In June, researcher Outsell Inc. released a blind survey of 407 advertisers, 37% of which said they had reduced or were planning to reduce their pay-per-click budgets because of fraud concerns. "The click fraud and bad sites are driving people away," says Fleischmann. He's trimming his online ad budget by 15% this year.

Google and Yahoo insist there's no reason to fret. They say they use sophisticated algorithms and intelligence from advertisers to identify the vast majority of fake clicks. But the big search engines won't disclose the specifics of their methods, saying illicit clickers would exploit the information.

Some people who have worked in the industry say that as long as Google and Yahoo distribute ads to nearly anyone with a rudimentary Web site, fraud will continue. "Advertisers should be concerned," says a former Yahoo manager who requested anonymity. "A well-executed click-fraud attack is nearly impossible, if not impossible, to detect."

Although 5 feet 6 and 135 pounds, Marty Fleischmann is no one to push around. He barked orders at much bigger oarsmen while serving as coxswain on the varsity crew team at Yale in the mid-1980s. His shyness deficit surfaced again when he later played the role of Jerry Seinfeld in the student follies at Wharton. Married and the father of three children, he tends to pepper his conversation with jargon about incentives and efficiencies.

Follow the Money

Click fraud schemes vary and often involve a complicated chain of relationships. Here's one way the process can work:

1. XYZ Widgets signs up with Google or Yahoo to advertise on the Internet, agreeing to pay the search engine every time somebody clicks on an XYZ ad.
2. Google or Yahoo displays the ad on its own site but also recycles it to millions of affiliates, including "domain parking" companies.
3. Domain-parking outfits feed the Google or Yahoo ad to thousands of "parked" Web sites, some of which are nothing more than lists of ads.
4. A fraud artist who owns a parked site circulates it to "paid to read" (PTR) groups, whose members receive small payments to visit sites and click on ads.
5. When a PTR member clicks on the XYZ ad, the company is billed. Yahoo or Google shares the proceeds with the domain parker, the fraudster, and the clickers.

Before he and partner Michael Levy co-founded their financial-information company in 1999, Fleischmann worked in Atlanta at the management consulting firm A.T. Kearney Inc., advising major corporations in the shipping and pharmaceutical industries. One lesson he says he learned is that big companies are loath to cut off any steady source of revenue. Google and Yahoo are no different, he argues.

That cynicism several years ago contributed to MostChoice's assigning an in-house programmer to design a system for analyzing every click on a company ad: the Web page where the ad appeared, the clicker's country, the length of the clicker's visit to MostChoice's site, and whether the visitor became a customer. Few companies go to such lengths, let alone companies with only 30 employees and revenue last year of just $6.4 million.

To Fleischmann, the validity of his clicks, for which he pays up to $8 apiece, has become an obsession. Every day he pores over fresh spreadsheets of click analysis. "I told Yahoo years ago," he says, " 'If this was costing you money instead of making you money, you would have stopped this.' "

Google, he says, does a better job than Yahoo of screening for fraud. But neither adequately protects marketers, he argues. Until March, 2005, Google, based in Mountain View, Calif., charged advertisers twice for "double clicks," meaning those occasions when a user unnecessarily clicks twice in quick succession on an ad. Confirming this, Google's Ghosemajumder says that before the company made the change, it felt it had to focus "on issues of malicious behavior," though now it identifies double clicks and bills for only one.

Korean Clones

Fleischmann's daily immersion in click statistics fuels his indignation. How, he wants to know, did he receive traffic this summer from PCs in South Korea which are clicking on insurance1472. com and insurance060.com? The only content on these identical sites—and five other clones with similar names—are lists of Yahoo ads, which occasionally have included MostChoice promotions. Fleischmann's spreadsheets revealed, not surprisingly, that all of the suspected Korean clickers left his site in a matter of seconds, and none became customers. The two individuals registered as owning the mysterious insurance sites are based in South Korea. They didn't respond to requests for comment, and most of the sites disappeared in late summer, after MostChoice challenged Yahoo about them.

"If this was costing [Yahoo] money instead of making it," they would have stopped it

Fleischmann, like most other advertisers, has agreed to let Google and Yahoo recycle his ads on affiliated sites. The search engines describe these affiliates in glowing terms. A Google "help" page entitled "Where will my ads appear?" mentions such brand names as AOL.com and the Web site of *The New York Times*. Left unmentioned are the parked Web sites filled exclusively with ads and sometimes associated with click-fraud rings.

Google and Yahoo defend their practice of recycling advertising to domain-parking firms and then on to parked sites, saying that the lists of ads on the sites help point Internet surfers toward relevant information. Google notes that it allows advertisers to identify sites on which they don't want their ads to run.

But this Google feature doesn't apply to many parked sites, and Yahoo doesn't offer the option at all. In any event, excluding individual sites is difficult for marketers that don't do the sort of time-consuming research MostChoice does. Whether they know it or not, many other companies are afflicted in similar ways. At *BusinessWeek's* request, Click Forensics Inc., an online auditing firm in San Antonio, analyzed the records of its 170 financial-services clients and found that from March through July of this year, 13 companies had received clicks from Web sites identified as dubious by MostChoice.

Yahoo declined to comment on insurance1472, -060, and other suspect sites in its ad network. The Sunnyvale (Calif.) search giant stressed that in many cases it doesn't deal directly with parked sites; instead, it distributes its ads by means of domain-parking firms.

BusinessWeek's independent analysis of the MostChoice records turned up additional indications of click fraud. Over the past six months, the company received 139 visitors through an advertisement on the parked site healthinsurancebids.com, which offers only ads supplied by Yahoo. Most of these visitors were located in Bulgaria, the Czech Republic, Egypt, and

Taking the Search Engines to Court

Under pressure from advertisers, Google Inc. and Yahoo! Inc are adjusting the way they deal with click fraud. Several lawsuits filed on behalf of hundreds of advertisers have helped fuel the modest changes.

In June, Yahoo agreed to settle a class action filed in federal court in Los Angeles on behalf of advertisers alleging they had been billed for fake clicks. Without admitting wrongdoing, yahoo said it would grant refunds for bad clicks since January, 2004, that advertisers bring to its attention. The potential cost to Yahoo isn't clear. The company also agreed to appoint an in-house advocate to represent advertisers. The search engine said it would periodically invite marketers to inspect its now-secret fraud-detection systems. Separate from the settlement, Yahoo says that next year it will give marketers more control over where their ads appear.

Google reached its own settlement with unhappy advertisers in July in state court in Texarkana, Ark., where a judge approved a pact valued at $90 million. The agreement provides $30 million in cash for lawyers but only advertising credits for class members. Dissatisfied, a group of advertisers is seeking to challenge the settlement in appellate court. "The rot is so pervasive," says Clarence E. Briggs, III, a leader of the breakaway group. Briggs, a former Army

ranger, says his company, Advanced Internet Technologies in Fayetteville, N.C., has detected $90,000 of bad clicks on its Google ads.

Google, which denied any liability, has since announced it will pull back its cloak of secrecy and show individual advertisers the proportion of their clicks it has deemed invalid and for which they weren't billed.

—Ben Elgin and Brian Grow

Evolution of a Scam

The purpose of click fraud has changed in recent years

Version 1.0

Companies clicked on a rival's Internet advertisements, running up its ad bills and squeezing the competition. The ads in question typically appeared on Google, Yahoo and other search engine sites.

Version 2.0

Today click fraud is much more likely to occur on small Web sites that carry ads recycled from Yahoo and Google. Fraudsters arrange for fake clicks on the ads and split the resulting revenue with the search engines.

Ukraine. Their average stay on MostChoice.com was only six seconds, and none of them became a customer.

Healthinsurancebids.com offers a revealing entry point into the click-fraud realm. It is one of several parked sites registered to Roland Kiss of Budapest. Kiss also owns BestPTRsite.com. "PTR" refers to "paid to read." In theory, paid-to-read sites recruit members who agree to read marketing e-mails and Web sites tailored to their interests. PTR site operators pay members for each e-mail and Web site they read, usually a penny or less.

In reality, many PTR sites are click-fraud rings, some with hundreds or thousands of participants paid to click on ads. BestPTRsite says it has 977 members. On Aug. 23 its administrator sent an e-mail to members containing a list of parked sites filled with ads. One of these sites, mortgagebg.com, which is also registered to Kiss, has been a source of apparently bogus clicks on MostChoice. The e-mail instructed members to click on different links every day, a common means to avoid detection. Members were also told to cut and paste text from the Web pages they click as proof of their activity. "If you send us back always the same link you will get banned and not paid! So take care and visit everyday a new link," the e-mail said.

Reached by telephone, Kiss says that his registration name is false and declines to reveal the real one. He says he's the 23-year-old son of computer technicians and has studied finance. He owns about 20 paid-to-read sites, he says, as well as 200 parked sites stuffed with Google and Yahoo advertisements. But he says he will take down healthinsurancebids.com to avoid discovery. He claims to take in $70,000 in ad revenue a month, but

says that only 10% of that comes from PTRs. The rest, he says, reflects legitimate clicks by real Web surfers. He refrains from more PTR activity, he claims, because "it's no good for advertisers, no good for Google, no good for Yahoo." It's not unusual for people who are involved in PTR activity to profess that they restrict their behavior in some way for the good of advertisers and the big search engines.

After joining several PTR groups, *BusinessWeek* reporters received a torrent of e-mail showcasing hundreds of parked sites filled with Google and Yahoo ads. The groups urged participants to click aggressively on ads. "People don't click because they're interested in the subject," says Pam Parrish, a medical editor in Indianapolis who has participated in PTR sites. "They're clicking on ads to get paid."

Parrish, 52, says that when she started three years ago, PTR sites drew clickers like herself: potential customers looking to pick up a few spare dollars. At one point, she says she belonged to as many as 50 such sites but earned only about $200 all told. More recently, she says, most PTR sites have dropped the pretense of caring whether members are interested in the sites they visit. Parrish and others active on PTR sites say click fraud became more blatant as Google and Yahoo made their ads more widely available to parked sites.

Google and Yahoo say they filter out most PTR activity. "We manage that very well," says Google's Ghosemajumder. "It hasn't been an issue across our network, but it's something we take very seriously." Yahoo adds that PTR sites carrying its ads are in "very serious violation" of its standard distribution

Advertisers in China Are Getting Burned, Too

China has a reputation in the U.S. as a haven for click-fraud artists. Now, Chinese advertisers say they, too, have fallen victim to the proliferating racket.

In August, Chinese advertisers carrying placards even staged a small demonstration in front of the Beijing office of Baidu.com. China's top search engine. Leading the protest was Dr. Liu Wenhua, director of the Beijing Zhongbei Cancer Medical Research Center. Liu claims that his center, which advertises its services online, has suffered from fraudulent clicks on its ads on a Baidu-affiliated music and entertainment site. Baidu has offered a refund, Liu says, but he turned it down, preferring to take Baidu to court. "I'm not satisfied," the doctor says.

Zhang Xinwei, a partner with the Beijing Hetong Law Office, represents Liu and four other advertisers that also have sued Baidu, alleging fraud. "The problem is very serious," says Zhang. Another plaintiff, Land of Maples Tourism & Culture Exchange, a Beijing travel agency specializing in trips to Canada, has hired a different lawyer. Steven Donne, who runs the agency, says he became suspicious of a batch of 600 clicks this summer because they all came from one source. But Donne feared he wouldn't be able to prove click fraud, so his suit focuses on a claim that Baidu manipulates search results to punish certain advertisers. The legal cases are all in a preliminary stage.

Baidu officials declined to comment but provided a statement denying any impropriety. "Baidu places the highest priority on preventing fraudulent clicks," it said. "We have set up numerous measures both through automated technology and manual efforts to prevent fraudulent clicks and the effectiveness of which [has] been verified by [an] independent third party. . . . We are, however, continuing to invest aggressively in safeguarding measures which will help ensure that our customers and users continue to have the best possible experience."

Despite such assurances, advertisers say concern is spreading. Executives at Analysys International, an info tech researcher in Beijing, noted earlier this year that clicks on its ads on Baidu soared without any uptick in business. In April alone, Analysys burned through one-third of its modest yearly online marketing budget of $3,800. "It was like crazy," says CEO Edward Yu.

This spring, Analysys conducted a survey of 2,000 online advertiser in China and found that one-third believe they have been click-fraud victims. Yu continues to patronize. Google's Chinese affiliate, but he has stopped buying advertising from Baidu and Yahoo China, which is owned by Alibaba.com. Porter Erisman, a spokesman for Alibaba, said in an e-mail that "click fraud is a serious but manageable issue," adding that less than 0.01% of his company's customers have complained.

—Bruce Einhom

agreement. Yahoo says it scans its network for PTR activity, but declines to describe its methods.

PTR impresarios often don't fit the profile of an illicit kingpin. Michele Ballard runs a 2,200-member network called theOwl-Post.com from her home in the small town of Hartford, Ky. On disability since a 1996 car accident, Ballard, 36, lives with her ailing mother and her cat, Sassy. She says she works day and night running Owl-Post, a five-year-old group named after the postal system in the Harry Potter novels. Sometimes, Ballard says she takes a break at lunchtime to tend her vegetable garden or help her elderly neighbors with theirs.

She sends her members a daily e-mail containing links to parked Web pages, many of them filled with Google ads. Her e-mails, decorated with smiley faces, suggest to members: "If you could just give a click on something on each page." She owns some of the parked pages, so she gets a share of the revenue when ads on them are clicked. She claims her take amounts to only about $60 a month, noting that if she made more than $85, the government would reduce her $601 monthly disability check.

In August, Google cut off a domain parking firm that hosted some of Ballard's sites. Showing her resilience, she moved the sites to other domain parkers, although none of those currently distributes Google ads. "Google would prefer you not to send out ads on paid e-mails, because they get too much crappy traffic," she says in a phone interview. She realizes that advertisers would get angry "if they knew we were just sitting here, clicking and not interested" in their wares. But, she adds, "They haven't figured that out yet."

Despite these views, Ballard says she doesn't think she's doing anything improper, let alone illegal. While investigations of some Internet criminals have revealed evidence of click fraud, the activity itself hasn't been the subject of prosecution. Ballard says Owl-Post is "like a huge family" whose members sometimes help out colleagues in financial distress. She says the network includes people who have low incomes and are desperate to earn cash to pay their bills. "A lot of people would be hurt if [the PTR business] crashed," she says.

Google's Ghosemajumder says any operation inviting people to click on ads is encouraging fraud, but he expresses skepticism about the overall scale of PTR activity: "People have a great tendency to exaggerate when they say they can attack Google's service."

Networks of human clickers aren't the only source of fake Web traffic. Scores of automated clicking programs, known as clickbots, are available to be downloaded from the Internet and claim to provide protection against detection. "The primary use is to cheat advertising companies," says Anatoly Smelkov, creator of Clicking Agent, a clickbot he says he has sold to some 5,000 customers worldwide.

The brazen 32-year-old Russian software developer lives in the city of Novosibirsk in western Siberia and says he received a physics degree from the state university there. A fan of the British physicist and author Stephen W. Hawking, Smelkov says Clicking Agent is a sideline that generates about $10,000 a year for him; he also writes software for video sharing and other purposes.

"A lot of people would be hurt [if the paid-to-read business] crashed," says one organizer

Clickbots are popular among online cheats because they disguise a PC's unique numerical identification, or IP address, and can space clicks minutes apart to make them less conspicuous. Smelkov shrugs off his role in facilitating deception. He points out that the first four letters of the name of his company, Lote-Soft Co., stand for "living on the edge." Teasing, he asks: "You aren't going to send the FBI to me, are you?"

Past Media Scandals

Allegations that some publishers and TV companies deceive advertisers go back many decades. Now the problem has moved online:

Newspapers and Magazines

Outrage over circulation fraud, employed to boost ad rates, led to the 1914 creation of the Audit Bureau of Circulations. But that didn't stop some publishers from faking the numbers. In 2004 a scandal tainted Tribune's *Newsday* and its Spanish-language *Hoy*, Belo's *Dallas Morning News*, and Sun-Times Media's *Chicago Sun-Times*.

Television

Broadcasters set ad rates using surveys of how many people are tuned in during four "sweeps" periods a year. Advertisers complain that some networks and local stations use contests and other stunts to attract extra attention during sweeps. The American Association of Advertising Agencies says this practice "has been going on for decades."

Internet

Click fraud, generating bogus mouse clicks on an online ad, isn't the only way advertisers can get ripped off on the Internet. Some ads are priced according to "impressions," the number of Web surfers who see it, regardless of whether they click. Now there is concern that some media companies commit impression fraud by overstating the number of visitors to their sites.

Google and Yahoo say they can identify automated click fraud and discount advertisers' bills accordingly. Jianhui Shi, a Smelkov customer who goes by the name Johnny, says that for this very reason he steers away from Google and Yahoo ads. An unemployed resident of the booming southern Chinese city of Shenzhen, Jianhui says he has used Clicking Agent to click all sorts of ads on sites he controls, making about $20,000 a year from this activity. While he doesn't click on Google and Yahoo ads, he says that more skilled Chinese programmers modify Clicking Agent to outwit the American search engines. "Many in China use this tool to make money," he wrote in an e-mail to *BusinessWeek*.

Back at the bare-bones MostChoice offices in north Atlanta, Marty Fleischmann continues to demand recompense. He says he has received refunds from Google and Yahoo totaling only about $35,000 out of the $100,000 he feels he is owed. In one exchange, MostChoice e-mailed Google to point out 316 clicks it received in June from ZapMeta.com, a little-known search site. MostChoice paid an average of $4.56 a click, or roughly $1,500 for the batch. Only one converted into a customer. Google initially responded that "after a thorough manual review" some bad clicks were filtered out before MostChoice was charged. Refund request: denied.

But as clicks from ZapMeta kept arriving, Fleischmann demanded in an Aug. 7 e-mail to Google: "You should be trusting us and doing something about [ZapMeta] as a partner, instead of finding more ways to refute our data or requests." (*BusinessWeek's* e-mail to ZapMeta's site and its registered owner, Kevin H. Nguyen, elicited no response.)

Finally, on Aug. 8, Google admitted that clicks from ZapMeta "seem to be coming through sophisticated means." A Google employee who identified himself only as "Jason" added in an e-mail: "We are working with our engineers to prevent these clicks from continuing." MostChoice received a $2,527.93 refund that included reimbursement for suspect clicks from an additional site as well.

Google says it has refunded MostChoice for all invalid clicks and won't charge for any additional ZapMeta clicks until the situation is resolved. But Google also says it doesn't believe ZapMeta has done anything improper. As of late September, ZapMeta continued to carry ads that had been recycled from Google, although not MostChoice ads.

Randall S. Hansen, a professor of marketing at Stetson University in Deland, Fla., sees a larger lesson in tales of this sort. "We are just beginning to see more and more mainstream advertisers make the Internet a bigger part of their ad budget, and move dollars from print and TV," says Hansen, who has held marketing jobs at *The New Yorker* and *People* magazines. "But if we can't fix this click-fraud problem, then it is going to scare away the further development of the Internet as an advertising medium. If there is an undercurrent of fraud, then why should a large advertiser be losing $1 million, or maybe not know how much it is losing?"

With Moira Herbst

The Big Band Era

The quest for rapid and robust Internet access has cities grappling with how to bring the best of broadband to their businesses and residents.

CHRISTOPHER SWOPE

Talk to Chris O'Brien about broadband access, and the city of Chicago's technology chief will tell you that more Internet traffic flows through Chicago than anywhere else in the world. That's a difficult point to prove, a bit like saying that Chicago-style pizza is better than New York's. No matter. O'Brien knows that broadband means business, and that most companies can't survive today without superfast access to the Internet. So the Windy City has taken to selling itself as Broadband City—as much a national hub for Internet infrastructure as it's always been for railroads, highways and airports.

That claim is an easy one to believe from the vantage point of O'Brien's 27th-floor downtown office. Underneath the traffic-clogged streets below, private companies have buried miles of fiber-optic cable—an Internet backbone that is indeed as quick as any in the world. Here, big finance and technology firms that require huge amounts of bandwidth for the fastest Internet speeds don't have too much trouble getting it.

But you don't have to wander far from downtown to see how quickly Chicago's broadband prowess breaks down. In South Side neighborhoods and industrial corridors slated for economic development, fiber is much harder to find. Business customers have fewer broadband options here, and what they do have can be prohibitively expensive. For the modest bandwidth of a T-1 line, they can pay as much as $1,000 a month—more than the rent for some of them. Or they can look into two other broadband options: DSL and cable modem. Those are more limited still and aren't yet available in some pockets of the city.

The broadband landscape looks even more speckled over the city line. In the suburbs, researchers at federal laboratories and universities enjoy top-speed broadband at work but some can't get the modest speeds of DSL at home. The suburbs, however, are better off than the prairie towns that lie farther out. There, most computer users are making do with pokey dial-up Internet service that moves data along at a glacial pace.

Broadband access is an essential item for business, and it is quickly becoming one at home too, as everything digital, from e-mail to phone calls to "The Sopranos," tries to squeeze through the same Internet pipe. Yet as the Chicago region shows, the state of American broadband in 2005 ranges from Tiffany to the country store. This new digital divide—the broadband divide—leaves state and local officials facing a lot of tough questions. What's the best way to smooth out these disparities? And what's the proper role of the public sector? Should government build and own some of the infrastructure itself, as it does with highways? Or should broadband look more like the railroads, built and run by profit-seeking companies?

A Broad Reach

The current situation is cause for either hope or despair, depending on how one looks at it. As of last July, 63 million Americans were connecting to the Internet via broadband at home, according to Nielsen//NetRatings. Millions more use broadband at the office—DSL, T-1 or better—making workers more efficient and innovative. Entrepreneurs can now dream up new services to sell over broadband—founding new companies that create new jobs.

The bad news is that as quickly as broadband is catching on, the U.S. is a laggard compared with other nations. South Korea, Denmark, Japan and Canada have higher rates of residential broadband penetration. In fact, the U.S. is 11th in the world, according to the International Telecommunications Union in Geneva. Part of the problem is that Americans are more spread out than, say, the South Koreans, half of whom live in apartment buildings. But public policy also plays a big role. Japan and South Korea have national broadband strategies. The U.S. doesn't. Broadband deployment is largely up to the giant telephone and cable companies that currently compete with each other in the courtroom just as much as they slug it out in the marketplace. An upside of the American laissez-faire approach is innovation: Carriers have developed lots of technologies for delivering broadband, some using old existing wires, some requiring new lines and others using wireless. The downside is that they only deploy these products in markets where they believe they can turn a profit quickly.

There may be no national policy, but that doesn't mean cities, suburbs and rural communities are sitting on the sidelines.

In fact, localities are at the forefront of the broadband debate, stirring up controversy. For example, Philadelphia, like dozens of other cities, is looking at offering cheap broadband service by turning the whole city into a wireless "hot spot." Opponents of the idea, led by Verizon Communications, think that cities should stay out of broadband. They persuaded the Pennsylvania legislature in November to pass a law that makes it harder for cities to offer municipal broadband. (Verizon is letting Philadelphia proceed with its plans, however.)

Politics may be the least of local officials' worries. As they attack the broadband divide, they're finding that it's a terrifically complex problem, one that is only growing more complicated as technology advances and bandwidth needs grow. Realistically, they can't hope to "solve" the divide so much as manage it over time. Moreover, there's not just one broadband divide. There are at least four of them:

- **Access.** Millions of Americans still can't get basic DSL or cable modem service, or the local provider has a monopoly on the market.
- **Service.** There's lots of high-speed fiber in the ground in the U.S., but outside of dense business districts, the "last mile" problem of tapping into it is expensive to solve.
- **Cost.** Even where basic broadband is available, the monthly cost remains higher than many consumers are willing or able to pay.
- **Don't Need It.** More than one-third of U.S. households still don't have computers—let alone high-speed Internet. And many Internet users don't mind using slow dial-up service.

The Gatekeepers

You see a range of thinking about these issues across the Chicago region. The most controversial idea came from three cities on the western edge of the Chicago suburbs. Batavia, Geneva and St. Charles, also known as the Tri-Cities, are among the 2,000 U.S. cities that are in the electricity business. Public power has been pretty good for the Tri-Cities. Their electric rates are about 30 percent lower than neighboring towns. So it wasn't a stretch when they proposed getting into the broadband business as well.

The idea first came up two years ago. Comcast, the dominant cable company in the Chicago region, hadn't yet rolled out its cable modem service. The local phone company, SBC Communications, had started offering DSL—but large swaths of the Tri-Cities still couldn't get it.

The city governments held a trump card, however. Each owned a fiber-optic network—a valuable byproduct of running an electric utility. Officials began thinking that if they could build that fiber out directly to homes and businesses, it would be a huge draw for economic development. Municipal broadband—offering superfast Internet, cable TV and telephone—would compete directly with Comcast and SBC.

The towns put the question to a referendum in April 2003. Scared by the $62 million price tag, voters turned it down decisively. The plan went before voters again this past November with a new financing scheme. It got steam rolled again. Comcast and SBC waged an overwhelming campaign against the measure. They bused in employees to knock on doors, and Comcast even sent Hallmark greeting cards to voters' homes.

There was another factor at play. Not all residents saw the issue as a compelling one. As Jeffery Schielke, the mayor of Batavia, puts it, "When we put in sanitary sewers 100 years ago, a number of people said they'd prefer to go to the outhouse."

Proponents of municipal broadband are still bitter about the outcome. They argue that Comcast and SBC, by fighting the referendum, are holding back technology. "They think it's okay to give us limited bandwidth and charge us an arm and a leg for it," says Annie Collins, whose citizens' group was behind the second referendum. As Collins sees it, cities should view broadband as they do roads, sewers or any other essential infrastructure they provide. "Putting the infrastructure in place is just like pavement," she says. "It's basic infrastructure, and the cities should own it."

Comcast and SBC share a different view: Municipal broadband is a bad idea. "It's wrong of the government to get involved in areas where private corporations are offering choices," says Carrie Hightman, president of SBC Illinois. What about the argument that cities should provide broadband as basic infrastructure? "These aren't vital services," says Bob Ryan, a Comcast lobbyist. "They're nice services. But you're not going to die if you don't get video, data and telephony from the government."

All is not lost in the Tri-Cities. By the time of the second vote, Comcast and SBC had rolled out their networks almost ubiquitously there. Just two weeks before the election, SBC held a "digital ribbon-cutting" ceremony in Batavia. Both companies deny wooing voters by bumping the Tri-Cities up their to-do lists. But many observers in Illinois think that the squeaky wheel got the grease. "All of a sudden the Tri-Cities are getting better service," says Edward Feser, a University of Illinois professor who studies broadband. "Maybe the vote is looked at as a failure, but for the end-market consumer the whole effort has been a bonus."

At Your Service

Farther west, in the prairie town of Princeton, the broadband battle is playing out somewhat differently. A couple of years ago, manufacturers in town began complaining that the T-1 lines they used for broadband weren't fast or robust enough. Rural towns across Illinois have been hit hard lately by manufacturers going overseas. Princeton has fared pretty well so far. But officials there figured that if they could offer manufacturers more bandwidth, it might be all the more reason for companies to stay put.

Big cities have to show corporations that their broadband will stay on even if terrorists strike, says Chris O'Brien, Chicago's technology chief.

Princeton officials met with the local phone company—Verizon in this part of Illinois—to see if there was something it could do to upgrade service. But as Princeton's Jason Bird puts it, "at the end of the day, it came down to the fact that we needed to take on this endeavor ourselves." Princeton owns its electric utility, just as the Tri-Cities do. Unlike the Tri-Cities, however, Princeton is not proposing to go into the broadband business on a retail level. Instead, Princeton will build out the broadband infrastructure and let a local company called Connecting Point sell the service to customers.

Princeton's plan is to build fiber out to any customers who say they need it—most likely the big industrial users. Smaller customers and residential users will be handled differently. They'll be among the first in the nation to receive broadband over the same power lines that pump electricity into peoples' homes. This new technology is a convenient solution to the notorious "last mile" problem. Customers simply plug a box into a power outlet and plug their computers into the box. Bird thinks Princeton's approach to broadband represents a lighter touch to government intervention. "We have a partnership here," he says. "We didn't want to get into the business of being the provider. We didn't feel comfortable with that."

> **"Wireless really gives you the opportunity, on a relatively low-cost basis, to put technology into neighborhoods that could never afford it before."**
>
> —Bob Lieberman
> Center for Neighborhood Technology

But that distinction doesn't mean much to the big telephone and cable companies. The argue that any form of municipal broadband enjoys unfair advantages, such as tax-free bond financing. Comcast, SBC and other broadband providers are expected to lobby the legislature for a law similar to Pennsylvania's, either banning municipal broadband or severely restricting it. Similar laws have passed in 15 other states, and the U.S. Supreme Court recently found such bans constitutional. "This is an area where the powerful incumbents want to snuff out consumer option and choice," says Illinois Lieutenant Governor Pat Quinn. "They're snarling in Illinois. It looks like they'll try to wipe out the municipal option for our state this year. We'll see."

Broadband Browser

Technology	Speed	Consumer Cost	Upsides	Downsides
WIRED				
DSL	Moderate to fast	$25–$60/mo. for residential; $40–$300 for business	Uses existing copper telephone wires	Available only within 3 miles of the telephone company's switch
Cable modem	Moderate	$40–$70/mo.	Uses existing coaxial cable networks	Customers share bandwith, not as prevalent in commercial areas
Broadband over power lines (BPL)	Moderate	$25–$50/mo.	Uses existing power lines; just plug into a wall socket	Not widely available yet
T-1 line	Fast	$200–$1,000/mo. depending on location	Widely used by small businesses	Expensive to install; monthly charge can be more than the rent.
Fiber-optic lines	Fast to lightning fast	$35–$80/mo. for residential; varies widely for business	Fastest and most reliable for voice, data, video; huge capacity makes it "future proof"	Laying new fiber to the home or to business is expensive
WIRELESS				
Wi-Fi	Moderate	Free in public "hot spots"; $8–$10/day in private hot spots	Cheap and easy to deploy in libraries, parks, hotels and airports	Limited range; security remains a concern
Cellular broadband	Very slow to moderate	$30–$80/mo.	Rides off cell phone networks; better range than Wi-Fi	Available only in select cities
Satellite	Slow to moderate	$400–$800 for dish; $60–$150/mo. for service	The only option in many rural areas	Pricey start-up costs; slow uploads
WiMax	Very fast	Expected to be moderate	Future option in both cities and rural areas	Won't beat fiber, especially for online video

Chicago is more hesitant to use a heavy hand when it comes to broadband. Of course, the city also enjoys two luxuries: a dense downtown and a wealthy mix of corporations that broadband providers are hungry to serve. During the dot-com boom, lots of telecom companies trenched fiber-optic lines under downtown streets. It was a gold rush fueled by the exuberant Internet dreams of the age. Many of those companies later went bankrupt. But their fiber is still there, waiting to be used.

In the Loop, Chicago's busy downtown business section, the biggest broadband problem is figuring out where all the fiber is—and who owns it. That's an economic development issue: Businesses looking to tap into that fiber don't know whom to call. But it's increasingly a homeland security issue, too. After 9/11, many big corporations are queasy about locating critical operations such as data banks in big cities, fearing a terror attack. They want some assurance that their Internet traffic has redundant routes should disaster strike. "Corporate boards are asking whether it's dangerous to locate in a big city," Chris O'Brien says. "We have to prove to them that it's not."

Chicago's neighborhoods are a different story. Back in 2000, Chicago announced a big idea to wire the whole city for broadband. The plan was called CivicNet, and the idea was to aggregate all the public schools, firehouses and city offices into one massive telecom contract. In exchange for a 10-year deal, Chicago expected the winning bidder to lay broadband infrastructure to some 1,600 city facilities. It wouldn't wire the whole city, but since there's a police station, library or some city building in nearly every neighborhood, it would come pretty close.

CivicNet never happened. The telecom bust killed the industry's interest. And Chicago's budget bust killed the city's interest. The silver lining, as O'Brien sees it, is that Comcast and SBC have since pumped millions of dollars of their own into rolling out cable modem and DSL service across nearly all of Chicago. "The residential issue is not solved," O'Brien says. "But we're a lot closer to eliminating access as a problem because of cable modem and DSL." Of all the broadband divides, the one that now concerns O'Brien the most is level of access for small businesses that require more bandwidth than Comcast and SBC are offering. To target this problem, Chicago is considering a CivicNet Lite: a stripped-down version of the original broadband plan, targeted solely at six or seven underserved industrial corridors.

Wire Works

Others are more concerned about another of the broadband divides: cost. Comcast charges between $43 and $58 a month for cable Internet in Chicago. SBC charges between $27 and $37 a month for the most basic residential DSL. Bob Lieberman thinks that wireless broadband might be a cheaper alternative.

Lieberman heads the Center for Neighborhood Technology in Chicago, and is experimenting with wireless projects in three neighborhoods in the region. One is Lawndale, a predominantly African-American neighborhood west of the Loop. "The median household income in Lawndale is $22,000, so $600 a year for broadband is a big chunk," Lieberman says. "That's a lot of money for what is arguably entertainment."

The tallest building in Lawndale is an historic brick tower that rises 260 feet above an old Sears distribution center. "It's the first Sears Tower," Lieberman says. Just as the namesake skyscraper downtown is crowned with radio antennae, Lieberman has placed a small, barely visible antenna in the Lawndale tower. The antenna is wired to the Internet and beams a signal out to "nodes" scattered atop row houses in the neighborhood, which relay the signal back and forth to computers in peoples' homes. An unusual feature of this so-called "mesh" network is that the system actually becomes stronger and more reliable as more people use it.

The Lawndale project is up to 100 users, who for the time being are getting the service for free (the Center hooks people up with used computers, too). Lieberman thinks it could serve as a prototype for small cities or neighborhoods. He estimates the municipal cost of providing such a service would ring in at about $8 to $10 per month, per household. "Wireless really gives you the opportunity, on a relatively low-cost basis, to put technology into neighborhoods that could never afford it before," Lieberman says.

A lot of other cities are having exactly the same thought. The technology is cheap enough that Philadelphia thinks it could fill the air with a cloud of Internet signals for just about $10 million. And wireless technology is advancing quickly. A new generation of wireless broadband, called WiMax, is due out in the next year or so. WiMax will offer greater bandwidth than the current Wi-Fi does and work to a range of 30 miles. In other words, a single antenna could blanket entire cities, or large swaths of countryside, with broadband coverage.

A lot of people in city government around the country are very excited about wireless. Chicago has created Wi-Fi hot spots at all its city libraries, and in places where business travelers congregate, such as the airport and convention center. Yet Chris O'Brien is skeptical of taking on a broader, city-wide wireless project. Simply put, Chicago doesn't want to step on the private sector's turf. "Government needs to tread a very fine line," O'Brien says. "We could create a wireless network for the entire city if we wanted to. We own enough fiber that we could get into the telecom business, too. Figuring out where our leverage ends and where we leave it to the private sector is the tough issue."

CHRISTOPHER SWOPE can be reached at cswope@governing.com

The Beauty of Simplicity

I'm snuggled under the covers with Jon Stewart and the remote. The "Evolution/Schmevolution" skit is funny, but it's been a long day, and I'm fading fast. The promise of technology is that I'm one click away from slumberland. I hit the power button. The picture disappears, but the TV is still glowing a creepy blue that will haunt my dreams if I don't make it go away. I try the TV button. Nothing. The cable button. Nothing. What the %$*&?? I kick off the blankets and trudge over to turn off the miserable box at the source. I can't help but wonder, as I lie there, now wide awake, how it is that all the things that were supposed to make our lives so easy instead made them more complex. Why is so much technology still so hard?

LINDA TISCHLER

It is innovation's biggest paradox: We demand more and more from the stuff in our lives—more features, more function, more power—and yet we also increasingly demand that it be easy to use. And, in an Escher-like twist, the technology that's simplest to use is also, often, the most difficult to create.

Marissa Mayer lives with that conundrum every day. As Google's director of consumer Web products, she's responsible for the search site's look and feel. Mayer is a tall, blond 30-year-old with two Stanford degrees in computer science and an infectious laugh. She's also Google's high priestess of simplicity, defending the home page against all who would clutter it up. "I'm the gatekeeper," she says cheerfully. "I have to say no to a lot of people."

The technology that powers Google's search engine is, of course, anything but simple. In a fraction of a second, the software solves an equation of more than 500 million variables to rank 8 billion Web pages by importance. But the actual experience of those fancy algorithms is something that would satisfy a Shaker: a clean, white home page, typically featuring no more than 30 lean words; a cheery, six-character, primary-colored logo; and a capacious search box. It couldn't be friendlier or easier to use.

Here is how Mayer thinks about the tension between complexity of function and simplicity of design: "Google has the functionality of a really complicated Swiss Army knife, but the home page is our way of approaching it closed. It's simple, it's elegant, you can slip it in your pocket, but it's got the great doodad when you need it. A lot of our competitors are like a Swiss Army knife open—and that can be intimidating and occasionally harmful."

It would be lovely if Google's corporate mythology included an enchanting tale to account for the birth of this pristine marvel. But the original home-page design was dumb luck. In 1998, founders Sergey Brin and Larry Page were consumed with writing code for their engine. Brin just wanted to hack together something to send queries to the back end, where the cool technology resided. Google didn't have a Web master, and Brin didn't do HTML. So he designed as little as he could get away with.

The accident became an icon, of course, and a key reason the company enjoys a commanding lead. Google's design has been mimicked on the search pages of MSN and Yahoo, whose portals are messy throwbacks to the "everything but the kitchen sink" school of Web design. But they're poor imitations; according to Hitwise, Google controls 59.2% of the search market, up from 45% a year ago; MSN's share is down to 5.5% and Yahoo's is 28.8%.

No surprise that a site easy enough for a technophobe to use has caught the public imagination. Like desperate Gullivers, we're pinned down by too much information and too much stuff. By one estimate, the world produced five exabytes (one quintillion bytes) of content in 2002—the same amount churned out between 25,000 B.C. and A.D. 2000. Little wonder that *Real Simple* has been the most successful magazine launch in a decade, and the blogosphere is abuzz over the season's hottest tech innovation—the Hipster PDA: 15 index cards held together by a binder clip.

With Google's extraordinary trajectory and the stratospheric success of Apple's iPod—itself a marvel of simplicity and, with

The Simple, and the Simply Awful

A pantheon of technology products that marry great performance with simplicity of design—and those that miss the mark

Products we love . . .

TiVo, by TiVo. It's not often that owners refer to their pet technology as "life changing," but the ability to watch 24 at 3 A.M. surely counts as one of the decade's greatest humanitarian breakthroughs. The remote, the intuitive menus, the crisp instructions—everything about it can make even your parents feel smart.

iPod, by Apple. You don't have to be a hipster to love iPod, which plays Henry Mancini as easily as it blasts Cannibal Corpse.

Skype's Voice-over-Internet service. Cheap long distance? Without having to deal with the phone company? What's not to love?

Google's search engine. So good it's a verb. The real question is, How did we find anything in the pre-Google era?

BlackBerry by RIM. Love 'em or hate 'em, their ubiquity speaks for itself. Sure beats lugging around an eight pound laptop just to get e-mail.

. . . and love to hate

Universal remote. So many buttons, so little time—and more complicated than the flight deck of the starship *Enterprise.* If you're an engineering prof (or a 14-year-old), it's heaven on earth. For the rest of us, it's easier to haul our weary bodies out of the La-Z-Boy than to figure out how to turn of the TV with this thing.

PeopleSoft software. The product most likely to induce about of Tourette's syndrome in the office.

LG VX6100 cell phone. Why is it so hard to make it shut up? Finding the MUTE button requires digging through the innards of the user's manual.

HP Officejet 7110 printer. It does it all—printing, scanning, copying, faxing—and does it all badly.

Sony Synthesized Radio. One aggravated owner complained, "It's impossible to program. You can't get the clock to stop blinking . . . and the antenna is useless." But it looks cool.

20 million units sold, a staggering hit—we seem to be nearing a seminal moment. Whereas endless Sunday Styles stories may have failed to get its attention, the tech industry's interest is invariably galvanized by cash. If the equation T (technology) + E(ease of use) = $ can be proven, the time may be right for the voice of the technologically challenged who can't operate their remotes to be heard.

In a 2002 poll, the Consumer Electronics Association discovered that 87% of people said ease of use is the most important thing when it comes to new technologies. "Engineers say, 'Do you know how much complexity we've managed to build in here?' But consumers say, 'I don't care. It's just supposed to work!' " says Daryl Plummer, group vice president at Gartner Group.

It's often that tension—between the desire to cram in cool new features and the desire to make a product easy to use—that makes delivering on the simplicity promise so hard, particularly in companies where engineers hold sway. At Google, it's an ongoing battle. As developers come up with ever sexier services—maps! news alerts! scholarly papers!—the pressure to lard on links is fierce. Mayer holds them at bay with a smile and strict standards.

To make it to the home page, a new service needs to be so compelling that it will garner millions of page views per day. Contenders audition on the advanced-search page; if they prove their mettle—as image search did, growing from 700,000 page views daily to 2 million in two weeks—they may earn a permanent link. Few make the cut, and that's fine. Google's research shows that users remember just 7 to 10 services on rival sites. So Google offers a miserly six services on its home page. By contrast, MSN promotes more than 50, and Yahoo, over 60. And both sell advertising off their home pages; Google's is a commercial-free zone.

> **"I want to figure out how to combine simplicity, which is basic human life, with this thing—technology—that's out of control."**

So why don't those sites simply hit the DELETE button and make their home pages more Googlesque? Hewing to the simplicity principle, it turns out, is tougher than connecting with tech support, particularly if you try it retrospectively. "Once you have a home page like our competitors'," Mayer says, "paring it back to look like Google's is impossible. You have too many stakeholders who feel they should be promoted on the home page." (MSN says more than half its customers are happy with its home page—but it's experimenting with a sleeker version called "start.com.")

Google understands that simplicity is both sacred and central to its competitive advantage. Mayer is a specialist in artificial intelligence, not design, but she hits on the secret to her home page's success: "It gives you what you want, when you want it, rather than everything you could ever want, even when you don't."

That, says Joe Duffy, founder of the award–winning Minneapolis design firm Duffy & Partners and author of *Brand Apart,* is a pretty good definition of good design. He quotes a famous line from the eminent designer Milton Glaser: "Less isn't more; just enough is more." Just enough, says Duffy, contains an aesthetic component that differentiates one experience from another.

It's just that holding the line on what constitutes "just enough" is harder than it looks.

It's early September, and the streets of Cambridge, Massachusetts, are teeming with young technorati in flip-flops and shorts. But there is calm at the MIT Media Lab, just upstairs from the List Visual Arts Center, the university's preeminent gallery. It's a fitting juxtaposition, a place where art and technology seek common ground.

John Maeda runs the Media Lab's Simplicity Consortium. His goal is to find ways to break free from the intimidating complexity of today's technology and the frustration of information overload. He is a gentle, soft-spoken man, dressed elegantly in a crisp, white collarless shirt and black pants. And he is an unusual amalgam: having the mathematical wizardry of a computer geek with the soul of an artist. Indeed, in 1990, he left MIT for four years to study art. "My whole life changed," he says. "I thought, This is a great way to live." But rather than throwing over his digital life entirely, he conceived a mission. "I came back to MIT to figure out how you could combine simplicity, which is basic human life, with this thing—technology—that's out of control."

Maeda's ability to toggle back and forth between right brain and left affords him unusual insight into how we got stuck in this technological quagmire. On one level, he says, the problem is simply one of scale. Before computer technology, small things were simple; big things were more likely complex. But the microchip changed that. Now small things can be complex, too. But small objects have less room for instruction—so we get cell phones with tip calculators buried deep in submenus and user manuals the size of the Oxford English Dictionary to help us figure it all out.

Blame the closed feedback loop among engineers and industrial designers, who simply can't conceive of someone so lame that she can't figure out how to download a ringtone; blame a competitive landscape in which piling on new features is the easiest way to differentiate products, even if it makes them harder to use; blame marketers who haven't figured out a way to make "ease of use" sound hip. "It's easier," says Charles Golvin, principal analyst with Forrester Research, "to market technology than ease of use."

Across the river from MIT, in the Boston suburb of West Newton, Aaron Oppenheimer runs the product behavior group of Design Continuum, one of the country's preeminent design firms. He is the sympathetic counselor who gently points out that for each feature clients want to include—"Hey, if we've got a microprocessor in there, let's add an alarm clock!"—they're trading off a degree of ease of use. It's a never-ending battle. "I spend a lot of time talking clients out of adding features," he says with a sigh. "Every new feature makes things more complicated, even if you never use them."

In the past, he says, adding features usually meant adding costs. Put a sound system or power windows into a car, and you've upped the price, so you better make sure consumers really want what you're peddling. But in the digital world, that cost-benefit calculus has gone awry. "The incremental cost to add 10 features instead of one feature is just nothing," says Oppenheimer. "Technology is this huge blessing because we can do anything with it, and this huge curse because we can do anything with it."

But the issue is also our conflicted relationship with technology. We want the veneer of simplicity but with all the bells and whistles modern technology can provide. "The market for simplicity is complex," says Dan Ariely, a business-school professor who is spending a year off from MIT figuring out how to quantify the value of simplicity at Princeton's Institute for Advanced Study. "If I offer you a VCR with only one button, it's not all that exciting, even if when you use it, it's likely to be easier."

We also want our devices to talk to each other—cell phone to the Web, digital camera to printer. That requires a level of interoperability that would be difficult to attain in a perfect world, but is well nigh impossible in one where incompatibility is a competitive strategy. "In business, it's all about war," says Maeda. "I hate to sound like a hippie, but if there were just some sense of peace and love, products would be much better."

In his quiet way, Maeda hopes to right the balance between man and machine. He and his students are working on software, code-named OPENSTUDIO, that would create an "ecosystem of design"—connecting designers with customers on a broad scale. That could lead to bespoke products—a cell phone, for example, with 30 features for Junior, 3 for Gran. "You can't make the world simpler unless you can get in touch with design," he says, "and the only way you can do that is to get in touch with designers."

How do you make your company's products simpler? You can start by simplifying your company.

In the late 1990s, Royal Philips Electronics was a slow-footed behemoth whose products, from medical diagnostic imaging systems to electric shavers, were losing traction in the marketplace. By 2002, a new CEO, Gerard Kleisterlee, determined that the company urgently needed to address the dynamic global marketplace and become more responsive to consumers' changing needs.

Philips deployed researchers in seven countries, asking nearly 2,000 consumers to identify the biggest societal issue that the company should address. The response was loud and urgent. "Almost immediately, we hit on the notion of complexity and its relationship to human beings," says Andrea Ragnetti, Philips's chief marketing officer. Consumers told the researchers that they felt overwhelmed by the complexity of technology. Some 30% of home-networking products were returned because people couldn't get them to work. Nearly 48% of people had put off buying a digital camera because they thought it would be too complicated.

Strategists recognized a huge opportunity: to be the company that delivered on the promise of sophisticated technology without the hassles. Philips, they said, should position itself as a simple company. Ragnetti was dumbstruck. "I said, 'You must be joking. This is an organization built on complexity, sophistication, brainpower.'" But he and Kleisterlee responded with an even more audacious plan. Rather than merely retooling products, Philips would also transform itself into a simpler, more market-driven organization.

"The market for simplicity is complex. If I offer you a VCR with only one button, it's not all that exciting, even if when you use it, it's likely to be easier."

That initiative has been felt from the highest rungs of the organization to the lowest. Instead of 500 different businesses, Philips is now in 70; instead of 30 divisions, there are 5. Even things as prosaic as business meetings have been nudged in the direction of simplicity: The company now forbids more than 10 slides in any PowerPoint presentation. Just enough, they decided, was more.

The campaign, christened "Sense and Simplicity," required that everything Philips did going forward be technologically advanced—but it also had to be designed with the end user in mind and be easy to experience. That ideal has influenced product development from conception—each new product, like the ShoqBox, an MP3 mini-boom box, must be based on a user need that's tested and validated—to packaging. Philips invited 15 customers to its Consumer Experience Research Centre in Bruges, Belgium, to see how they unpacked and set up a Flat TV. After watching people struggle to lift the heavy set from an upright box, designers altered the packaging so the TV could be removed from a carton lying flat on the ground.

While many of the new products have yet to hit the market, early results of the business reorganization, particularly in North America, have been dramatic. Sales growth for the first half of 2005 was up 35%, and the company was named Supplier of the Year by Best Buy and Sam's Club. Philips's Ambilight Flat TV and GoGear Digital Camcorder won European iF awards for integrating advanced technologies into a consumer-friendly design, and the Consumer Electronics Association handed the company 12 Innovation Awards for products ranging from a remote control to a wearable sport audio player.

Maeda, who, as a member of Philips's Simplicity Advisory Board has had a front-row seat for this transformation, is impressed. "The best indication of their sincerity is that they're embracing the concept at a management level," says Maeda. "It isn't just marketing to them. That's quite a radical thing."

Designing products that are easy to use is nothing new for Intuit, the big tax- and business-software company. Indeed, it's been the mantra since founder Scott Cook developed Intuit's first product, Quicken, back in 1983 after listening to his wife complain about writing checks and managing bills.

But even by Intuit's standards, Simple Start, a basic accounting package that debuted in September 2004, was a leap. For one thing, the target market was tiny businesses that used no software at all. "These were people who said, 'I have a simple busi-

ness, and I don't want the complexity of having to learn this. I don't want to use the jargon, I don't want the learning curve, and besides, I'm afraid of it,' " says project manager Terry Hicks.

But the potential was huge: some 9 million microbusiness owners that Intuit wasn't reaching with its current line. So Hicks's team first tried a knockoff of Intuit's QuickBooks Basic, with a bunch of features turned off. Then they confidently took the product out for a test-drive with 100 potential customers.

And it bombed. It was still too hard to use, still riddled with accounting jargon, still too expensive. They realized they had to start from scratch. "We had to free ourselves and say, 'Okay, from an engineering point of view, we're going to use this code base, but we need to design it from a customer's point of view.' " says Lisa Holzhauser, who was in charge of the product's user interface.

The designers followed more customers home. They heard more complaints about complexity, but also anxiety that things in their business might be falling through the cracks. So the team distilled two themes that would guide their development: The product had to be simple, and it had to inspire confidence. Terms such as "aging reports" and "invoicing" were edited out, and the designers drew on the experience of the SnapTax division, which had hired an editor from *People* magazine to help translate accountant-speak into real-world language. Accounts receivable became "Money In," accounts payable, "Money Out." They pared back 125 setup screens to three, and 20 major tasks to six essentials. They spent days worrying about the packaging, knowing that to this audience, something labeled "Simple Accounting" was an oxymoron.

Above all, they subjected their work to the demanding standards of Intuit's usability lab, run by Kaaren Hanson. To get a product by her, users must be able, 90% of the time, to accomplish the tasks deemed most critical. It's a draconian standard. But "if our goal was to make it 'as easy as we can,' " Hanson says, "we wouldn't be as successful as if we had set a concrete number."

The Simple Start team thought they had nailed the user-interface problem after their third iteration of the product got rave reviews for its look and feel. But task completion results from the lab were dismal. The launch was delayed for months while the team reengineered the tools until they measured up.

The additional time was worth it. Simple Start—a product with 15 years of sophisticated QuickBooks code lurking behind an interface even a Luddite could love—sold 100,000 units in its first year on the market. Even better, reviews from target customers indicate that Intuit hit the mark. Ken Maples, owner of a tiny flight-instruction school in Cupertino, California, summed it up: "It's easy to use. It's got everything I need and nothing more." Ah . . . just enough. Good. Somewhere, Milton Glaser is smiling.

LINDA TISCHLER (ltischler@fastcompany.com) is a *Fast Company* senior writer. TiVo changed her life, but she can't find the MUTE button on her new phone. Jennifer Reingold contributed to this story.

The Software Wars

Why You Can't Understand Your Computer

PAUL DE PALMA

On a bright winter morning in Philadelphia, in 1986, my downtown office is bathed in sunlight. I am the lead programmer for a software system that my firm intends to sell to the largest companies in the country, but like so many systems, mine will never make it to market. This will not surprise me. If the chief architect of the office tower on whose twenty-sixth floor I am sitting designed his structure with the seat-of-the-pants cleverness that I am using to design my system, prudence would advise that I pack my business-issue briefcase, put on my business-issue overcoat, say good-bye to all that sunlight, and head for the front door before the building crumbles like a Turkish high-rise in an earthquake.

But I am not prudent; nor am I paid to be. Just the opposite. My body, on automatic pilot, deflects nearly all external stimuli. I can carry on a rudimentary conversation, but my mind is somewhere else altogether. In a book-length profile of Ted Taylor, a nuclear-weapons designer, that John McPhee wrote for *The New Yorker*, Dr. Taylor's wife tells McPhee a wonderful story about her husband. Mrs. Taylor's sister visits for the weekend. Taylor dines with her, passes her in the hall, converses. He asks his wife on Monday morning—her sister having left the day before—when she expects her sister to arrive. Mrs. Taylor calls this state "metaphysical absence." You don't have to build sophisticated weaponry to experience it. When my daughter was younger, she used to mimic an old John Prine song. "Oh my stars," she sang, "Daddy's gone to Mars." As you will see, we workaday programmers have more in common with weapons designers than mere metaphysical absence.

My mind reels back from Mars when a colleague tells me that the *Challenger* has exploded. The *Challenger*, dream child of NASA, complex in the extreme, designed and built by some of the country's most highly trained engineers, is light-years away from my large, and largely uninspired, piece of data-processing software. If engineering were music, the *Challenger* would be a Bach fugue and my system "Home on the Range." Yet despite the differences in technical sophistication, the software I am building will fail for many of the same reasons that caused the *Challenger* to explode seconds after launch nearly twenty years ago.

Software's unreliability is the stuff of legend. *Software Engineering Notes,* a journal published by the ACM, the largest professional association of computer scientists, is known mostly for the tongue-in-cheek catalogue of technical catastrophes that appears at the beginning of each issue. In the March 2001 issue—I picked this off my shelf at random—you can read about planes grounded in L.A. because a Mexican air-traffic controller keyed in too many characters of flight description data, about a New York database built to find uninsured drivers, which snared many of the insured as well, about Florida eighth graders who penetrated their school's computer system, about Norwegian trains that refused to run on January 1, 2001, because of a faulty Year 2000 repair. The list goes on for seven pages and is typical of a column that has been running for many years.

> **People often claim that one of every three large-scale software systems gets canceled midproject. Of those that do make it out the door, three-quarters are never implemented: some do not work as intended; others are just shelved.**

People often claim that one of every three large-scale software systems gets canceled midproject. Of those that do make it out the door, three-quarters are never implemented: some do not work as intended; others are just shelved. Matters grow even more serious with large systems whose functions spread over several computers—the very systems that advances in networking technology have made possible in the past decade. A few years ago, an IBM consulting group determined that of twenty-four companies surveyed, 55 percent built systems that were over budget; 68 percent built systems that were behind schedule; and 88 percent of the completed systems had to be redesigned. Try to imagine the same kind of gloomy numbers for civil engineering: three-quarters of all bridges carrying loads below specification; almost nine of ten sewage treatment plants, once completed, in need of redesign; one-third of highway projects canceled because technical problems have grown beyond the capacity of engineers to solve them. Silly? Yes. Programming has miles to go before it earns the title "software engineering."

In civil engineering, on the other hand, failures are rare enough to make the news. Perhaps the best-known example is the collapse of the Tacoma-Narrows Bridge. Its spectacular failure in 1940, because of wind-induced resonance, was captured on film and has been a staple of physics courses ever since. The collapse of the suspended walkway in the Kansas City Hyatt Regency in 1981 is a more recent example. It failed because structural engineers thought that verifying the design of connections joining the walkway segments was the job of their manufacturer. The manufacturer had a different recollection. The American Society of Civil Engineers quickly adopted a protocol for checking shop designs. These collapses are remarkable for two related reasons. First, bridge and building failures are so rare in the United States that when they do occur we continue to talk about them half a century later. Second, in both cases, engineers correctly determined the errors and took steps not to repeat them. Programmers cannot make a similar claim. Even if the cause of system failure is discovered, programmers can do little more than try not to repeat the error in future systems. Trying not to repeat an error does not compare with building well-known tolerances into a design or establishing communications protocols among well-defined players. One is exhortation. The other is engineering.

None of this is new. Responding to reports of unusable systems, cost overruns, and outright cancellations, the NATO Science Committee convened a meeting of scientists, industry leaders, and programmers in 1968. The term *software engineering* was invented at this conference in the hope that, one day, systematic, quantifiable approaches to software construction would develop. Over the intervening years, researchers have created a rich set of tools and techniques, from design practices to improved programming languages to techniques for proving program correctness. Sadly, anyone who uses computers knows that they continue to fail regularly, inexplicably, and, sometimes, wonderfully—*Software Engineering Notes* continues to publish pages of gloomy tales each quarter. Worse, the ACM has recently decided not to support efforts to license software engineers because, in its words, "there is no form of licensing that can be instituted today assuring public safety." In effect, software-engineering discoveries of the past thirty years may be interesting, but no evidence suggests that understanding them will improve the software-development process.

As the committee that made this decision surely knows, software-engineering techniques are honored mostly in the breach. In other words, business practice, as much as a lack of technical know-how, produces the depressing statistics I have cited. One business practice in particular ought to be understood. The characteristics of software often cited as leading to failure—its complexity, its utter plasticity, its free-floating nature, unhampered by tethers to the physical world—make it oddly, even paradoxically, similar to the practice of military procurement. Here is where the *Challenger* and my system, dead these twenty long years, reenter the story.

I n the mid-eighties I worked for a large management-consulting firm. Though this company had long employed a small group of programmers, mostly to support in-house systems, its software-development effort and support staff grew substantially, perhaps by a factor of ten, over a period of just a few years. A consulting firm, like a law firm, has a cap on its profits. Since it earns money by selling time, the number of hours its consultants can bill limits its revenue. And there is a ceiling to that. They have to eat and sleep, after all. The promise of software is the promise of making something from nothing. After development, only the number of systems that can be sold limits return on investment. In figuring productivity, the denominator remains constant. Forget about unhappy unions, as with cars and steel; messy sweatshops, as with clothing and shoes; environmental regulations, as with oil and petrochemicals. Software is a manufacturer's dream. The one problem, a very sticky problem indeed, is that it does not wear out. The industry responds by adding features, moving commercial software one step closer to military systems. More on this later. For now, just understand that my company, like so many others under the influence of the extraordinary attention that newly introduced personal computers were receiving at the time, followed the lure of software.

My system had one foot on the shrinking terra firma of large computers and the other in the roiling, rising sea of microcomputers. In fact, mine was the kind of system that three or four years earlier would have been written in COBOL, the language of business systems. It perhaps would have used a now obsolete database design, and it would have gone to market within a year. When told to build a similar system for a microcomputer, I did what I knew how to do. I designed a gray flannel system for a changing microcomputer market.

Things went along in a predictable if uninspired way until there was a shift in management. These changes occur so frequently in business that I had learned to ignore them. The routine goes like this. Everyone gets a new organization chart. They gather in conference rooms for mandatory pep talks. Then life goes on pretty much as before. Every so often, though, management decisions percolate down to the geeks, as when your manager arrives with a security officer and gives you five minutes to empty your desk, unpin your *Dilbert* comics, and go home. Or when someone like Mark takes over.

When that happened, I assumed falsely that we would go back to the task of producing dreary software. But this was the eighties. Junk bonds and leveraged buyouts were in the news. The arbitrageur was king. Business had become sexy. Mark, rumor had it, slept three hours a night. He shuttled between offices in New York, Philadelphia, and Montreal. Though he owned a house in Westchester County, now best known as the home of the Clintons, he kept an apartment in Philadelphia, where he managed to spend a couple of days each week. When Mark, the quintessential new manager ("My door is always open"), arrived, we began to live like our betters in law and finance. Great bags of bagels and cream cheese arrived each morning. We lunched in trendy restaurants. I, an erstwhile sixties radical, began to ride around in taxis, use my expense account, fly to distant cities for two-hour meetings. Life was sweet.

During this time, my daughter was an infant. Her 4:00 A.M. feeding was my job. Since I often had trouble getting back to sleep, I sometimes caught an early train to the office. One of these mornings my office phone rang. It was Mark. He sounded relaxed, as if finding me at work before dawn was no more surprising than bumping into a neighbor choosing apples at Safeway. This was a sign. Others followed. Once, Mark organized a dinner for our team in a classy hotel. When the time came for his speech, Mark's voice rose like Caesar's exhorting his troops before the Gallic campaign. He urged us to bid farewell to our wives and children. We would, he assured us, return in six months with our shields or upon them. I noticed then that a few of my colleagues were in evening dress. I felt like Tiresias among the crows. When programmers wear tuxedos, the world is out of joint.

Suddenly, as if by magic, we went from a handful of programmers producing a conventional system to triple that number, and the system was anything but conventional. One thing that changed was the programming language itself. Mark decided that the system would be splashier if it used a database-management system that had recently become commercially available for mainframes and was promised, shortly, for microcomputers. These decisions—hiring more people to meet a now unmeetable deadline; using a set of new and untested tools—represented two of the several business practices that have been at the heart of the software crisis. Frederick Brooks, in his classic book, *The Mythical Man-Month,* argues from his experience building IBM's System 360 operating system that any increased productivity achieved by hiring more people gets nibbled at by the increased complexity of communication among them. A system that one person can develop in thirty days cannot be developed in a single day by thirty people. This simple truth goes down hard in business culture, which takes, as an article of faith, the idea that systems can be decreed into existence.

The other practice, relying on new, untested, and wildly complex tools, is where software reigns supreme. Here, the tool was a relational database-management system. Since the late sixties, researchers have realized that keeping all data in a central repository, a database, with its own set of access techniques and backup mechanisms, was better than storing data with the program that used it. Before the development of database-management systems, it was common for every department in a company to have its own data, and for much of this data to overlap from department to department. So in a university, the registrar's office, which takes care of student records, and the controller's office, which takes care of student accounts, might both have copies of a student's name and address. The problem occurs when the student moves and the change has to be reported to two offices. The argument works less well for small amounts of data accessed by a single user, exactly the kind of application that the primitive microcomputers of the time were able to handle. Still, you could argue that a relational database-management system might be useful for small offices. This is exactly what Microsoft Access does. But Microsoft Access did not exist in 1986, nor did any other relational database-management system for microcomputers. Such systems had only recently become available for mainframes.

> **Something unique to software, especially new software: no experts exist in the sense that we might speak of an expert machinist, a master electrician, or an experienced civil engineer. There are only those who are relatively less ignorant.**

One company, however, an infant builder of database-management systems, had such software for minicomputers and was promising a PC version. After weeks of meetings, after an endless parade of consultants, after trips to Washington, D.C., to attend seminars, Mark decided to go with the new product. One of these meetings illustrates something unique to software, especially new software: no experts exist in the sense that we might speak of an expert machinist, a master electrician, or an experienced civil engineer. There are only those who are relatively less ignorant. On an early spring evening, we met in a conference room with a long, polished wood table surrounded by fancy swivel chairs covered in gorgeous, deep purple fabric. The room's walls turned crimson from the setting sun. As the evening wore on, we could look across the street to another tower, its offices filled with miniature Bartlebys, bent over desks, staring into monitors, leafing through file cabinets. At the table with representatives from our company were several consultants from the database firm and an independent consultant Mark had hired to make sure we were getting the straight scoop.

Here we were: a management-consulting team with the best, though still less than perfect, grasp of what the proposed system was supposed to do, but almost no grasp of the tools being chosen; consultants who knew the tools quite well, but nothing about the software application itself, who were fully aware that their software was still being developed even as we spoke; and an independent consultant who did not understand either the software or its application. It was a perfect example of interdependent parasitism.

My company's sin went beyond working with complex, poorly understood tools. Neither the tools nor our system existed. The database manufacturer had a delivery date and no product. Their consultants were selling us a nonexistent system. To make their deadline, I am confident they hired more programmers and experimented with unproven software from still other companies with delivery dates but no products. And what of *those* companies? You get the idea.

No one in our group had any experience with this software once we adopted it. Large systems are fabulously complex. It takes years to know their idiosyncrasies. Since the introduction of the microcomputer, however, nobody has had years to develop this expertise. Because software does not wear out, vendors must consistently add new features in order to recoup development costs. That the word processor you use today bears almost no resemblance to the one you used ten years ago has less to do with technological advances than with economic realities. Our company had recently acquired a smaller I company in the South. This company owned a mini computer for which a version of the database software had already been released. Mark decided that until the PC database was ready for release, we could develop our system on this machine, using 1,200-baud modems, a modem about one-fiftieth as fast as the one your cable provider tells you is too slow for the Web, and a whole lot less reliable.

Let me put this all together. We had a new team of programmers who did not understand the application, using ersatz software that they also did not understand, which was running on a kind of machine no one had ever used before, using a remote connection that was slow and unstable.

Weeks before, I had begun arguing that we could never meet the deadline and that none of us had the foggiest idea of how to go about building a system with the tools we had. This was bad form. I had been working in large corporations long enough to know that when the boss asks if something can be done, the only possible response is "I'm your boy." Business is not a Quaker meeting. Mark didn't get to be my boss by achieving consensus. I knew that arguing was a mistake, but somehow the more I argued, the more I became gripped by a self-righteous fervor that, while unattractive in anyone (who likes a do-gooder?), is suicide in a corporate setting. Can-do-ism is the core belief. My job was to figure out how to extend the deadline, simplify the requirements, or both—not second-guess Mark. One afternoon I was asked if I might like to step down as chief architect and take over the documentation group. This was not a promotion.

Sitting in my new cubicle with a Raskolnikovian cloud over my head, I began to look more closely at the database-management system's documentation. Working with yet another consultant, I filled a paper database with hypothetical data. What I discovered caused me to win the argument but lose the war. I learned that given the size of the software itself and the amount of data the average client would store, along with the overhead that comes with a sophisticated database, a running system would fill a microcomputer hard disk, then limited to 30 megabytes, several times over. If, by some stroke of luck, some effort of will, some happy set of coincidences that I had yet to experience personally, we were able to build the system, the client would run up against hardware constraints as soon as he tried to use it. After weeks of argument, my prestige was slipping fast. I had already been reduced to writing manuals for a system I had designed. I was the sinking ship that every clearheaded corporate sailor had already abandoned. My triumphant revelation that we could not build a workable system, even if we had the skill to do so, was greeted with (what else?) complete silence.

Late in 1986 James Fallows wrote an article analyzing the *Challenger* explosion for the *New York Review of Books*. Instead of concentrating on the well-known O-ring problem, he situated the failure of the *Challenger* in the context of military procurement, specifically in the military's inordinate fondness for complex systems. This fondness leads to stunning cost overruns, unanticipated complexity, and regular failures. It leads to Osprey aircraft that fall from the sky, to anti-missile missiles for which decoys are easy to construct, to FA-22 fighters that are fabulously over budget. The litany goes

on. What these failures have in common with the *Challenger* is, Fallows argues, "military procurement disease," namely, "over-ambitious schedules, problems born of too-complex design, shortages of spare parts, a 'can-do' attitude that stifles embarrassing truths ('No problem, Mr. President, we can lick those Viet Gong'), and total collapse when one component unexpectedly fails." Explanations for this phenomenon include competition among the services; a monopoly hold by defense contractors who are building, say, aircraft or submarines; lavish defense budgets that isolate military purchases from normal market mechanisms; the nature of capital-intensive, laptop warfare where hypothetical justifications need not—usually cannot—be verified in practice; and a little-boy fascination with things that fly and explode. Much of this describes the software industry too.

Fallows breaks down military procurement into five stages:

The Vegematic Promise, wherein we are offered hybrid aircraft, part helicopter, part airplane, or software that has more features than could be learned in a lifetime of diligent study. Think Microsoft Office here.

The Rosy Prospect, wherein we are assured that all is going well. I call this the 90 percent syndrome. I don't think I have ever supervised a project, either as a software manager overseeing professionals or as a professor overseeing students, that was not 90 percent complete whenever I asked.

The Big Technical Leap, wherein we learn that our system will take us to regions not yet visited, and we will build it using tools not yet developed. So the shuttle's solid-fuel boosters were more powerful than any previously developed boosters, and bringing it all back home, my system was to use a database we had never used before, running on a computer for which a version of that software did not yet exist.

The Unpleasant Surprise, wherein we learn something unforeseen and, if we are unlucky, calamitous. Thus, the shuttle's heat-resistant dies, all 31,000 of them, had to be installed at the unexpected rate of 2.8 days per tile, and my system gobbled so much disk space that there was scarcely any room for data.

The House of Cards, wherein an unpleasant surprise, or two, or three, causes the entire system to collapse. The Germans flanked the Maginot Line, and in my case, once we learned that our reliance on a promised database package outstripped operating-system limits, the choices were: one, wait for advances in operating systems; two, admit a mistake, beg for forgiveness, and resolve to be more prudent in the future; or, three, push on until management pulls the plug.

In our case, the first choice was out of the question. We were up against a deadline. No one knew when, or if, the 30 MB disk limit would be broken. The second choice was just as bad. The peaceable kingdom will be upon us, the lamb will lie down with the lion, long before you'll find a hard-driving manager admitting an error. These guys get paid for their testosterone, and for men sufficiently endowed, in the famous words of former NASA flight director Gene Kranz, "failure is not an option." We were left with the third alternative, which is what happened. Our project was canceled. Inside the fun house of corporate decision making, Mark was promoted—sent off to manage a growing branch in the South. The programmers left or were reassigned. The consultant who gave me the figures for my calculations was fired for reasons that I never understood. I took advantage of my new job as documentation chief and wrote an application to graduate school in computer science. I spent the next few years, while a student, as a well-paid consultant to our firm.

Just what is it about software, even the most conventional, the most mind-numbing software, that makes it similar to the classiest technology on the planet? In his book *Trapped in the Net,* the Berkeley physicist turned sociologist, Gene Rochlin, has this to say about computer technology:

Only in a few specialized markets are new developments in hardware and software responsive primarily to user demand based on mastery and the full use of available technical capacity and capability. In most markets, the rate of change of both hardware and software is dynamically uncoupled from either human or organizational learning logistics and processes, to the point where users not only fail to master their most recent new capabilities, but are likely to not even bother to try, knowing that by the time they are through the steep part of their learning curve, most of what they have learned will be obsolete.

To give a homey example, I spent the last quarter hour fiddling with the margins on the draft copy of this article. Microsoft Word has all manner of arcane symbols—Exacto knives, magnifying glasses, thumbtacks, globes—plus an annoying little paper clip homunculus that pops up, seemingly at random, to offer help that I always decline. I don't know what any of this stuff does. Since one of the best-selling commercial introductions to the Microsoft Office suite now runs to nearly a thousand pages, roughly the size of Shakespeare's collected works, I won't find out either. To the untrained eye, that is to say, to mine, the bulk of what constitutes Microsoft Word appears to be useful primarily to brochure designers and graphic artists. This unused cornucopia is not peculiar to Microsoft, nor even to microcomputer software. Programmers were cranking out obscure and poorly documented features long before computers became a consumer product.

Though the medium on which it is stored might decay, the software itself, because it exists in the same ethereal way as a novel, scored music, or a mathematical theorem, lasts as long as the ability to decode it.

But why? Remember the nature of software, how it does not wear out. Adding features to a new release is similar, but not identical, to changes in fashion or automobile styling. In those industries, a change in look gives natural, and planned, obsolescence a nudge. Even the best-built car or the sturdiest pair of jeans will eventually show signs of wear. Changes in fashion just speed this process along. Not so with software. Though the medium on which it is stored might decay, the software itself,

because it exists in the same ethereal way as a novel, scored music, or a mathematical theorem, lasts as long as the ability to decode it. That is why Microsoft Word and the operating systems that support it, such as Microsoft Windows, get more complex with each new release.

But this is only part of the story. While software engineers at Oracle or Microsoft are staying up late concocting features that no one will ever use, hardware engineers at Intel are inventing ever faster, ever cheaper processors to run them. If Microsoft did not take advantage of this additional capacity, someone else would. Hardware and software are locked in an intricate and pathological dance. Hardware takes a step. Software follows. Hardware takes another step, and so on. The result is the Vegematic Promise. Do you want to write a letter to your bank? Microsoft Word will work fine. Do you need to save your work in any one of fifteen different digital formats? Microsoft Word will do the job. Do you want to design a Web page, lay out a brochure, import clip art, or include the digitally rendered picture of your dog? The designers at Microsoft have anticipated your needs. They were able to do this because the designers at Intel anticipated theirs. What no one anticipated was the unmanageable complexity of the final product from the user's perspective and the stunning, internal complexity of the product that Microsoft brings to market. In another time, this kind of complexity would have been reserved for enterprises of true consequence, say the Manhattan Project or the *Apollo* missions. Now the complexity that launched a thousand ships, placed men on the moon, controlled nuclear fission and fusion, the complexity that demanded of its designers years of training and still failed routinely, sits on my desk. Only this time, developers with minimal, often informal, training, using tools that change before they master them, labor for my daughter, who uses the fruits of their genius to chat with her friends about hair, makeup, and boys.

As I say, accelerating complexity is not just a software feature. Gordon Moore, one of Intel's founders, famously observed, in 1965, that the number of transistors etched on an integrated circuit board doubled every year or so. In the hyperbolic world of computing, this observation, altered slightly for the age of microprocessors, has come to be called Moore's Law: the computing power of microprocessors tends to double every couple of years. Though engineers expect to reach physical limits sometime in the first quarter of this century, Moore has been on target for the past couple dozen years. As a related, if less glamorous example, consider the remote control that accompanies electronic gadgetry these days. To be at the helm of your VCR, TV, DVD player, stereo (never mind lights, fans, air-conditioning, and fireplace), is to be a kind of Captain Kirk of home and hearth. The tendency, the Vegematic Promise, is to integrate separate remote controls into a single device. A living room equipped with one of these marvels is part domicile, part mission control. I recently read about one fellow who, dazzled by the complexity of integrated remotes, fastened his many devices to a chunk of four-by-four with black electrical tape. I have ceded operation of my relatively low-tech equipment to my teenage daughter, the only person in my house with the time or inclination to decipher its runic symbols.

But software is different in one significant way. Hardware, by and large, works. When hardware fails, as early versions of the Pentium chip did, it is national news. It took a computer scientist in Georgia doing some fairly obscure mathematical calculations to uncover the flaw. If only software errors were so well hidden. Engineers, even electrical engineers, use well-understood, often off-the-shelf, materials with well-defined limits. To offer a simple example, a few years ago I taught a course in digital logic. This course, standard fare for all computer science and computer engineering majors, teaches students how to solve logic problems with chips. A common lab problem is to build a seven-segment display, a digital display of numbers, like what you might find on an alarm clock. Students construct it using a circuit board and chips that we order by the hundreds. These chips are described in a catalogue that lists the number and type of logical operations encoded, along with the corresponding pins for each. If you teach software design, as I do, this trespass into the world of the engineer is instructive. Software almost always gets built from scratch. Though basic sorting and string manipulation routines exist, these must be woven together in novel ways to produce new software. Each programmer becomes a craftsman with a store of tricks up his sleeve. The more experienced the programmer, the more tricks.

To be fair, large software-development operations maintain libraries of standard routines that developers may dip into when the need arises. And for the past ten years or so, new object-oriented design and development techniques have conceived of ways to modularize and standardize components. Unfortunately, companies have not figured out how to make money by selling components, probably for the same reason that the music industry is under siege from Napster's descendants. If your product is only a digital encoding, it can be copied endlessly at almost no cost. Worse, the object-oriented programming paradigm seems often to be more complex than a conventional approach. Though boosters claim that programmers using object-oriented techniques are more productive and that their products are easier to maintain, this has yet to be demonstrated.

Software is peculiar in another way. Though hardware can be complex in the extreme, software obeys no physical limits. It can be as feature-rich as its designers wish. If the computer's memory is too small, relatively obscure features can be stored on disk and called into action only when needed. If the computer's processor is too slow, just wait a couple of years. Designers want your software to be very feature-rich indeed, because they want to sell the next release, because the limits of what can be done with a computer are not yet known, and, most of all, because those who design computer systems, like the rich in the world of F. Scott Fitzgerald, are different from you and me. Designers love the machine with a passion not constrained by normal market mechanisms or even, in some instances, by managerial control.

On the demand side, most purchases are made by institutions, businesses, universities, and the government, where there is an obsessive fear of being left behind, while the benefits, just as in the military, are difficult to measure. The claims and their outcomes are too fuzzy to be reconciled. Since individual managers are rarely held accountable for decisions to buy yet more computing equipment, it should not surprise you that wildly complex technology is being underused. Thus: computer labs that no one knows what to do with, so-called smart classrooms that are obsolete before anyone figures out how to use them, and offices with equipment so complicated that every secretary doubles as a systems administrator. Even if schools and businesses buy first and ask questions later, *you* don't have to put up with this. You could tell Microsoft to keep its next Windows upgrade, your machine is working very nicely right now, thank you. But your impertinence will cost you. Before long, your computer will be an island where the natives speak a language cut off from the great linguistic communities. In a word, you will be isolated. You won't be able to buy new software, edit a report you wrote at work on your home computer, or send pictures of the kids to Grandma over the Internet. Further, a decision to upgrade later will be harder, perhaps impossible, without losing everything your trusted but obsolete computer has stored. This is what Rochlin means when he writes that hardware and software are "dynamically uncoupled from either human or organizational learning." To which I would add "human organizational need."

What if the massively complex new software were as reliable as hardware usually is? We still wouldn't know how to use it, but at least our screens wouldn't lock up and our projects wouldn't be canceled midstream. This reliability isn't going to happen, though, for at least three reasons. First, programmers love complexity, love handcrafted systems, with an ardor that most of us save for our spouses. You have heard about the heroic hours worked by employees of the remaining Internet start-ups. This is true, but true only partly so that young men can be millionaires by thirty. There is something utterly beguiling about programming a computer. You lose track of time, of space even. You begin eating pizzas and forgetting to bathe. A phone call is an unwelcome intrusion. Second, nobody can really oversee a programmer's work, short of reading code line by line. It is simply too complex for anyone but its creator to understand, and even for him it will be lost in the mist after a couple of weeks. The 90 percent syndrome is a natural consequence. Programmers, a plucky lot, always think that they are further along than they are. It is difficult to foresee an obstacle on a road you have never traveled. Despite all efforts to the contrary, code is handcrafted. Third—and this gets to the heart of the matter—system specifications have the half-life of an adolescent friendship. Someone—the project manager, the team leader, a programmer, or, if the system is built on contract, the client—always has a new idea. It is as if a third of the way through building a bridge, the highway department decided it should have an additional traffic lane and be moved a half mile downstream.

Notice that not one of the reasons I have mentioned for failed software projects is technical. Researchers trying to develop a discipline of software engineering are fond of saying that there is no silver bullet: no single technical fix, no single software-development tool, no single, yet-to-be-imagined programming technique that will result in error-free, maintainable software. The reason for this is really quite simple. The problem with software is not technical. Remember my project. It fell into chaos because of foolish business decisions. Had Mark resisted the temptation to use the latest software-development products, a temptation he succumbed to not because they would produce a better system, but because they would seem flashier to prospective clients, we might have gone to market with only the usual array of problems.

Interestingly, the geek's geek, Bruce Schneier, in his recent book, *Secrets and Lies*, has come to similar conclusions about computer security: the largest problems are not technical. A computer security expert, Schneier has recanted his faith in the impermeability of cryptographic algorithms. Sophisticated cryptography is as resistant as ever to massive frontal attacks. The problem is that these algorithms are embedded in computer systems that are administered by real human beings with all their charms and foibles. People use dictionary entries or a child's name as passwords. They attach modems to their office computers, giving hackers easy access to a system that might otherwise be more thoroughly protected. They run versions of Linux with all network routines enabled, or they surreptitiously set up Web servers in their dormitory rooms. Cryptographic algorithms are no more secure than their contexts.

> **Until computing is organized like engineering, law, and medicine through a combination of self-regulating professional bodies, government-imposed standards, and the threat of litigation, inviting a computer into your house or office is to invite complexity masquerading as convenience.**

Though the long march is far from over, we know a lot more about managing the complexity of software systems than we did twenty years ago. We have better programming languages and techniques, better design principles, clever software to keep track of changes, richly endowed procedures for moving from conception to system design to coding to testing to release. But systems still fail and projects are still canceled with the same regularity as in the bad old days before object-oriented

techniques, before software engineering becomes an academic discipline. These techniques are administered by the same humans who undermine computer security. They include marketing staff who decree systems into existence; companies that stuff yet more features into already overstuffed software; designers and clients who change specifications as systems are being built; programmers who are more artist than engineer; and, of course, software itself that can be neither seen, nor touched, nor measured in any significant way.

There is no silver bullet. But just as the *Challenger* disaster might have been prevented with minimal common sense, so also with software failure. Keep it simple. Avoid exotic and new programming techniques. Know that an army of workers is no substitute for clear design and ample time. Don't let the fox, now disguised as a young man with a head full of acronyms, guard the chicken coop. Make only modest promises. Good advice, certainly, but no one is likely to listen anytime soon. Until computing is organized like engineering, law, and medicine through a combination of self-regulating professional bodies, government-imposed standards, and, yes, the threat of litigation, inviting a computer into your house or office is to invite complexity masquerading as convenience. Given the nature of computing, even these remedies may fall short of the mark.

But don't despair. If software engineering practice is out of reach, you still have options. For starters, you could just say no. You could decide that the ease of buying plane tickets online is not worth the hours you while away trying to get your printer to print or your modem to dial. Understand that saying no requires an ascetic nature: abstinence is not terribly attractive to most of us. On the other hand, you could sign up for broadband with the full knowledge that your computer, a jealous lover, will demand many, many Saturday afternoons. Most people are shocked when they learn that their computer requires more care than, say, their refrigerator. Yet I can tell you that its charms are immeasurably richer. First among them is the dream state. It's almost irresistible.

PAUL DE PALMA is associate professor of mathematics and computer science at Gonzaga University. His essay "http://www.when_is_enough_enough?.com" appeared in the *Winter 1999* issue.

From *American Scholar*, Vol. 74, No. 1, Winter 2005, pp. 69–83. Copyright © 2005 by Paul De Palma. Reprinted by permission of the journal and Paul De Palma.

Scan This Book!

Kevin Kelly

In several dozen nondescript office buildings around the world, thousands of hourly workers bend over table-top scanners and haul dusty books into high-tech scanning booths. They are assembling the universal library page by page.

The dream is an old one: to have in one place all knowledge, past and present. All books, all documents, all conceptual works, in all languages. It is a familiar hope, in part because long ago we briefly built such a library. The great library at Alexandria, constructed around 300 B.C., was designed to hold all the scrolls circulating in the known world. At one time or another, the library held about half a million scrolls, estimated to have been between 30 and 70 percent of all books in existence then. But even before this great library was lost, the moment when all knowledge could be housed in a single building had passed. Since then, the constant expansion of information has overwhelmed our capacity to contain it. For 2,000 years, the universal library, together with other perennial longings like invisibility cloaks, antigravity shoes and paperless offices, has been a mythical dream that kept receding further into the infinite future.

Until now. When Google announced in December 2004 that it would digitally scan the books of five major research libraries to make their contents searchable, the promise of a universal library was resurrected. Indeed, the explosive rise of the Web, going from nothing to everything in one decade, has encouraged us to believe in the impossible again. Might the long-heralded great library of all knowledge really be within our grasp?

Brewster Kahle, an archivist overseeing another scanning project, says that the universal library is now within reach. "This is our chance to one-up the Greeks!" he shouts. "It is really possible with the technology of today, not tomorrow. We can provide all the works of humankind to all the people of the world. It will be an achievement remembered for all time, like putting a man on the moon." And unlike the libraries of old, which were restricted to the elite, this library would be truly democratic, offering every book to every person.

But the technology that will bring us a planetary source of all written material will also, in the same gesture, transform the nature of what we now call the book and the libraries that hold them. The universal library and its "books" will be unlike any library or books we have known. Pushing us rapidly toward that Eden of everything, and away from the paradigm of the physical paper tome, is the hot technology of the search engine.

1. Scanning the Library of Libraries

Scanning technology has been around for decades, but digitized books didn't make much sense until recently, when search engines like Google, Yahoo, Ask and MSN came along. When millions of books have been scanned and their texts are made available in a single database, search technology will enable us to grab and read any book ever written. Ideally, in such a complete library we should also be able to read any article ever written in any newspaper, magazine or journal. And why stop there? The universal library should include a copy of every painting, photograph, film and piece of music produced by all artists, present and past. Still more, it should include all radio and television broadcasts. Commercials too. And how can we forget the Web? The grand library naturally needs a copy of the billions of dead Web pages no longer online and the tens of millions of blog posts now gone—the ephemeral literature of our time. In short, the entire works of humankind, from the beginning of recorded history, in all languages, available to all people, all the time.

This is a very big library. But because of digital technology, you'll be able to reach inside it from almost any device that sports a screen. From the days of Sumerian clay tablets till now, humans have "published" at least 32 million books, 750 million articles and essays, 25 million songs, 500 million images, 500,000 movies, 3 million videos, TV shows and short films and 100 billion public Web pages. All this material is currently contained in all the libraries and archives of the world. When fully digitized, the whole lot could be compressed (at current technological rates) onto 50 petabyte hard disks. Today you need a building about the size of a small-town library to house 50 petabytes. With tomorrow's technology, it will all fit onto your *iPod*. When that happens, the library of all libraries will ride in your purse or wallet—if it doesn't plug directly into your brain with thin white cords. Some people alive today are surely hoping that they die before such things happen, and others, mostly the young, want to know what's taking so long. (Could we get it up and running by next week? They have a history project due.)

Technology accelerates the migration of all we know into the universal form of digital bits. Nikon will soon quit making film cameras for consumers, and Minolta already has: better think digital photos from now on. Nearly 100 percent of all contemporary recorded music has already been digitized, much of it by fans. About one-tenth of the 500,000 or so movies listed on the Internet Movie Database are now digitized on DVD. But because of copyright issues and the physical fact of the need to turn pages, the digitization of books has proceeded at a relative crawl. At most, one book in 20 has moved from analog to digital. So far, the universal library is a library without many books.

But that is changing very fast. Corporations and libraries around the world are now scanning about a million books per year. Amazon has digitized several hundred thousand contemporary books. In the heart of Silicon Valley, Stanford University (one of the five libraries collaborating with Google) is scanning its eight-million-book collection using a state-of-the-art robot from the Swiss company 4DigitalBooks. This machine, the size of a small S.U.V., automatically turns the pages of each book as it scans it, at the rate of 1,000 pages per hour. A human operator places a book in a flat carriage, and then pneumatic robot fingers flip the pages—delicately enough to handle rare volumes—under the scanning eyes of digital cameras.

Like many other functions in our global economy, however, the real work has been happening far away, while we sleep. We are outsourcing the scanning of the universal library. Superstar, an entrepreneurial company based in Beijing, has scanned every book from 900 university libraries in China. It has already digitized 1.3 million unique titles in Chinese, which it estimates is about half of all the books published in the Chinese language since 1949. It costs $30 to scan a book at Stanford but only $10 in China.

Raj Reddy, a professor at Carnegie Mellon University, decided to move a fair-size English-language library to where the cheap subsidized scanners were. In 2004, he borrowed 30,000 volumes from the storage rooms of the Carnegie Mellon library and the Carnegie Library and packed them off to China in a single shipping container to be scanned by an assembly line of workers paid by the Chinese. His project, which he calls the Million Book Project, is churning out 100,000 pages per day at 20 scanning stations in India and China. Reddy hopes to reach a million digitized books in two years.

The idea is to seed the bookless developing world with easily available texts. Superstar sells copies of books it scans back to the same university libraries it scans from. A university can expand a typical 60,000-volume library into a 1.3 million-volume one overnight. At about 50 cents per digital book acquired, it's a cheap way for a library to increase its collection. Bill McCoy, the general manager of Adobe's e-publishing business, says: "Some of us have thousands of books at home, can walk to wonderful big-box bookstores and well-stocked libraries and can get Amazon.com to deliver next day. The most dramatic effect of digital libraries will be not on us, the well-booked, but on the billions of people worldwide who are underserved by ordinary paper books." It is these underbooked—students in Mali, scientists in Kazakhstan, elderly people in Peru—whose lives will be transformed when even the simplest unadorned version of the universal library is placed in their hands.

2. What Happens When Books Connect

The least important, but most discussed, aspects of digital reading have been these contentious questions: Will we give up the highly evolved technology of ink on paper and instead read on cumbersome machines? Or will we keep reading our paperbacks on the beach? For now, the answer is yes to both. Yes, publishers have lost millions of dollars on the long-prophesied e-book revolution that never occurred, while the number of physical books sold in the world each year continues to grow. At the same time, there are already more than a half a billion PDF documents on the Web that people happily read on computers without printing them out, and still more people now spend hours watching movies on microscopic cellphone screens. The arsenal of our current display technology—from handheld gizmos to large flat screens—is already good enough to move books to their next stage of evolution: a full digital scan.

Yet the common vision of the library's future (even the e-book future) assumes that books will remain isolated items, independent from one another, just as they are on shelves in your public library. There, each book is pretty much unaware of the ones next to it. When an author completes a work, it is fixed and finished. Its only movement comes when a reader picks it up to animate it with his or her imagination. In this vision, the main advantage of the coming digital library is portability—the nifty translation of a book's full text into bits, which permits it to be read on a screen anywhere. But this vision misses the chief revolution birthed by scanning books: in the universal library, no book will be an island.

Turning inked letters into electronic dots that can be read on a screen is simply the first essential step in creating this new library. The real magic will come in the second act, as each word in each book is cross-linked, clustered, cited, extracted, indexed, analyzed, annotated, remixed, reassembled and woven deeper into the culture than ever before. In the new world of books, every bit informs another; every page reads all the other pages.

In recent years, hundreds of thousands of enthusiastic amateurs have written and cross-referenced an entire online encyclopedia called Wikipedia. Buoyed by this success, many nerds believe that a billion readers can reliably weave together the pages of old books, one hyperlink at a time. Those with a passion for a special subject, obscure author or favorite book will, over time, link up its important parts. Multiply that simple generous act by millions of readers, and the universal library can be integrated in full, by fans for fans.

In addition to a link, which explicitly connects one word or sentence or book to another, readers will also be able to add tags, a recent innovation on the Web but already a popular one. A tag is a public annotation, like a keyword or category name, that is hung on a file, page, picture or song, enabling anyone to search for that file. For instance, on the photo-sharing site Flickr, hundreds of viewers will "tag" a photo submitted by another user with their own simple classifications of what they think the picture is about: "goat," "Paris," "goofy," "beach party." Because tags are user-generated, when they move to the realm of books, they will be assigned faster, range wider and serve better than out-of-date schemes like the Dewey Decimal System, particularly in frontier or fringe areas like nanotechnology or body modification.

The link and the tag may be two of the most important inventions of the last 50 years. They get their initial wave of power when we first code them into bits of text, but their real transformative energies fire up as ordinary users click on them in the course of everyday Web surfing, unaware that each humdrum click "votes" on a link, elevating its rank of relevance. You may think you are just browsing, casually inspecting this paragraph or that page, but in fact you are anonymously marking up the Web with bread crumbs of attention. These bits of interest are gathered and analyzed by search engines in order to strengthen the relationship between the end points of every link and the connections suggested by each tag. This is a type of intelligence common on the Web, but previously foreign to the world of books.

Once a book has been integrated into the new expanded library by means of this linking, its text will no longer be separate from the text in other books. For instance, today a serious nonfiction book will usually have a bibliography and some kind of footnotes. When books are deeply linked, you'll be able to click on the title in any bibliography or any footnote and find the actual book referred to in the footnote. The books referenced in that book's bibliography will themselves be available, and so you can hop through the library in the same way we hop through Web links, traveling from footnote to footnote to footnote until you reach the bottom of things.

Next come the words. Just as a Web article on, say, aquariums, can have some of its words linked to definitions of fish terms, any and all words in a digitized book can be hyperlinked to other parts of other books. Books, including fiction, will become a web of names and a community of ideas.

Search engines are transforming our culture because they harness the power of relationships, which is all links really are. There are about 100 billion Web pages, and each page holds, on average, 10 links. That's a trillion electrified connections coursing through the Web. This tangle of relationships is precisely what gives the Web its immense force. The static world of book knowledge is about to be transformed by the same elevation of relationships, as each page in a book discovers other pages and other books. Once text is digital, books seep out of their bindings and weave themselves together. The collective intelligence of a library allows us to see things we can't see in a single, isolated book.

When books are digitized, reading becomes a community activity. Bookmarks can be shared with fellow readers. Marginalia can be broadcast. Bibliographies swapped. You might get an alert that your friend Carl has annotated a favorite book of yours. A moment later, his links are yours. In a curious way, the universal library becomes one very, very, very large single text: the world's only book.

3. Books: The Liquid Version

At the same time, once digitized, books can be unraveled into single pages or be reduced further, into snippets of a page. These snippets will be remixed into reordered books and virtual bookshelves. Just as the music audience now juggles and reorders songs into new albums (or "playlists," as they are called in iTunes), the universal library will encourage the creation of virtual "bookshelves"—a collection of texts, some as short as a paragraph, others as long as entire books, that form a library shelf's worth of specialized information. And as with music playlists, once created, these "bookshelves" will be published and swapped in the public commons. Indeed, some authors will begin to write books to be read as snippets or to be remixed as pages. The ability to purchase, read and manipulate individual pages or sections is surely what will drive reference books (cookbooks, how-to manuals, travel guides) in the future. You might concoct your own "cookbook shelf" of Cajun recipes compiled from many different sources; it would include Web pages, magazine clippings and entire Cajun cookbooks. Amazon currently offers you a chance to publish your own bookshelves (Amazon calls them "listmanias") as annotated lists of books you want to recommend on a particular esoteric subject. And readers are already using Google Book Search to round up minilibraries on a certain topic—all books about Sweden, for instance, or books on clocks. Once snippets, articles and pages of books become ubiquitous, shuffle-able and transferable, users will earn prestige and perhaps income for curating an excellent collection.

Libraries (as well as many individuals) aren't eager to relinquish ink-on-paper editions, because the printed book is by far the most durable and reliable backup technology we have. Printed books require no mediating device to read and thus are immune to technological obsolescence. Paper is also extremely stable, compared with, say, hard drives or even CD's. In this way, the stability and fixity of a bound book is a blessing. It sits there unchanging, true to its original creation. But it sits alone.

So what happens when all the books in the world become a single liquid fabric of interconnected words and ideas? Four things: First, works on the margins of popularity will find a small audience larger than the near-zero audience they usually have now. Far out in the "long tail" of the distribution curve—that extended place of low-to-no sales where most of the books in the world live—digital interlinking will lift the readership of almost any title, no matter how esoteric. Second, the universal library will deepen our grasp of history, as every original document in the course of civilization is scanned and cross-linked. Third, the universal library of all books will cultivate a new sense of authority. If you can truly incorporate all texts—past and present, multilingual—on a particular subject, then you can have a clearer sense of what we as a civilization, a species, do know and don't know. The white spaces of our collective ignorance are highlighted, while the golden peaks of our knowledge are drawn with completeness. This degree of authority is only rarely achieved in scholarship today, but it will become routine.

Finally, the full, complete universal library of all works becomes more than just a better Ask Jeeves. Search on the Web becomes a new infrastructure for entirely new functions and services. Right now, if you mash up Google Maps and Monster.com, you get maps of where jobs are located by salary. In the same way, it is easy to see that in the great library, everything that has ever been written about, for example, Trafalgar Square in London could be present on that spot via a screen. In the same way, every object, event or location on earth would "know" everything that has ever been written about it in any book, in any language, at any time. From this deep structuring of knowledge comes a new culture of interaction and participation.

The main drawback of this vision is a big one. So far, the universal library lacks books. Despite the best efforts of bloggers and the creators of the Wikipedia, most of the world's expertise still resides in books. And a universal library without the contents of books is no universal library at all.

There are dozens of excellent reasons that books should quickly be made part of the emerging Web. But so far they have not been, at least not in great numbers. And there is only one reason: the hegemony of the copy.

4. The Triumph of the Copy

The desire of all creators is for their works to find their way into all minds. A text, a melody, a picture or a story succeeds best if it is connected to as many ideas and other works as possible. Ideally, over time a work becomes so entangled in a culture that it appears to be inseparable from it, in the way that the Bible, Shakespeare's plays, "Cinderella" and the Mona Lisa are inseparable from ours. This tendency for creative ideas to infiltrate other works is great news for culture. In fact, this commingling of creations is culture.

In preindustrial times, exact copies of a work were rare for a simple reason: it was much easier to make your own version of a creation than to duplicate someone else's exactly. The amount of energy and attention needed to copy a scroll exactly, word for word, or to replicate a painting stroke by stroke exceeded the cost of paraphrasing it in your own style. So most works were altered, and often improved, by the borrower before they were passed on. Fairy tales evolved mythic depth as many different authors worked on them and as they migrated from spoken tales to other media (theater, music, painting). This system worked well for audiences and performers, but the only way for most creators to earn a living from their works was through the support of patrons.

That ancient economics of creation was overturned at the dawn of the industrial age by the technologies of mass production. Suddenly, the cost of duplication was lower than the cost of appropriation. With the advent of the printing press, it was now cheaper to print thousands of exact copies of a manuscript than to alter one by hand. Copy makers could profit more than creators. This imbalance led to the technology of copyright, which established a new order. Copyright bestowed upon the creator of a work a temporary monopoly—for 14 years, in the United States—over any copies of the work. The idea was to encourage authors and artists to create yet more works that could be cheaply copied and thus fill the culture with public works.

Not coincidentally, public libraries first began to flourish with the advent of cheap copies. Before the industrial age, libraries were primarily the property of the wealthy elite. With mass production, every small town could afford to put duplicates of the greatest works of humanity on wooden shelves in the village square. Mass access to public-library books inspired scholarship, reviewing and education, activities exempted in part from the monopoly of copyright in the United States because they moved creative works toward the public commons sooner,

weaving them into the fabric of common culture while still remaining under the author's copyright. These are now known as "fair uses."

This wonderful balance was undone by good intentions. The first was a new copyright law passed by Congress in 1976. According to the new law, creators no longer had to register or renew copyright; the simple act of creating something bestowed it with instant and automatic rights. By default, each new work was born under private ownership rather than in the public commons. At first, this reversal seemed to serve the culture of creation well. All works that could be copied gained instant and deep ownership, and artists and authors were happy. But the 1976 law, and various revisions and extensions that followed it, made it extremely difficult to move a work into the public commons, where human creations naturally belong and were originally intended to reside. As more intellectual property became owned by corporations rather than by individuals, those corporations successfully lobbied Congress to keep extending the once-brief protection enabled by copyright in order to prevent works from returning to the public domain. With constant nudging, Congress moved the expiration date from 14 years to 28 to 42 and then to 56.

While corporations and legislators were moving the goal posts back, technology was accelerating forward. In Internet time, even 14 years is a long time for a monopoly; a monopoly that lasts a human lifetime is essentially an eternity. So when Congress voted in 1998 to extend copyright an additional 70 years beyond the life span of a creator—to a point where it could not possibly serve its original purpose as an incentive to keep that creator working—it was obvious to all that copyright now existed primarily to protect a threatened business model. And because Congress at the same time tacked a 20-year extension onto all existing copyrights, nothing—no published creative works of any type—will fall out of protection and return to the public domain until 2019. Almost everything created today will not return to the commons until the next century. Thus the stream of shared material that anyone can improve (think "A Thousand and One Nights" or "Amazing Grace" or "Beauty and the Beast") will largely dry up.

In the world of books, the indefinite extension of copyright has had a perverse effect. It has created a vast collection of works that have been abandoned by publishers, a continent of books left permanently in the dark. In most cases, the original publisher simply doesn't find it profitable to keep these books in print. In other cases, the publishing company doesn't know whether it even owns the work, since author contracts in the past were not as explicit as they are now. The size of this abandoned library is shocking: about 75 percent of all books in the world's libraries are orphaned. Only about 15 percent of all books are in the public domain. A luckier 10 percent are still in print. The rest, the bulk of our universal library, is dark.

5. The Moral Imperative to Scan

The 15 percent of the world's 32 million cataloged books that are in the public domain are freely available for anyone to borrow, imitate, publish or copy wholesale. Almost the entire current scanning effort by American libraries is aimed at this 15 percent. The Million Book Project mines this small sliver of the pie, as does Google. Because they are in the commons, no law hinders this 15 percent from being scanned and added to the universal library.

The approximately 10 percent of all books actively in print will also be scanned before long. Amazon carries at least four million books, which includes multiple editions of the same title. Amazon is slowly scanning all of them. Recently, several big American publishers have declared themselves eager to move their entire backlist of books into the digital sphere. Many of them are working with Google in a partnership program in which Google scans their books, offers sample pages (controlled by the publisher) to readers and points readers to where they can buy the actual book. No one doubts electronic books will make money eventually. Simple commercial incentives guarantee that all in-print and backlisted books will before long be scanned into the great library. That's not the problem.

The major problem for large publishers is that they are not certain what they actually own. If you would like to amuse yourself, pick an out-of-print book from the library and try to determine who owns its copyright. It's not easy. There is no list of copyrighted works. The Library of Congress does not have a catalog. The publishers don't have an exhaustive list, not even of their own imprints (though they say they are working on it). The older, the more obscure the work, the less likely a publisher will be able to tell you (that is, if the publisher still exists) whether the copyright has reverted to the author, whether the author is alive or dead, whether the copyright has been sold to another company, whether the publisher still owns the copyright or whether it plans to resurrect or scan it. Plan on having a lot of spare time and patience if you inquire. I recently spent two years trying to track down the copyright to a book that led me to Random House. Does the company own it? Can I reproduce it? Three years later, the company is still working on its answer. The prospect of tracking down the copyright—with any certainty—of the roughly 25 million orphaned books is simply ludicrous.

Which leaves 75 percent of the known texts of humans in the dark. The legal limbo surrounding their status as copies prevents them from being digitized. No one argues that these are all masterpieces, but there is history and context enough in their pages to not let them disappear. And if they are not scanned, they in effect will disappear. But with copyright hyperextended beyond reason (the Supreme Court in 2003 declared the law dumb but not unconstitutional), none of this dark library will return to the public domain (and be cleared for scanning) until at least 2019. With no commercial incentive to entice uncertain publishers to pay for scanning these orphan works, they will vanish from view. According to Peter Brantley, director of technology for the California Digital Library, "We have a moral imperative to reach out to our library shelves, grab the material that is orphaned and set it on top of scanners."

No one was able to unravel the Gordian knot of copydom until 2004, when Google came up with a clever solution. In addition to scanning the 15 percent out-of-copyright public-domain books with their library partners and the 10 percent in-print books with their publishing partners, Google executives declared that they would also scan the 75 percent out-of-print books that no one else would touch. They would scan the entire book, without resolving its legal status, which would allow the full text to be indexed on Google's internal computers and searched by anyone. But the company would show to readers only a few selected sentence-long snippets from the book at a time. Google's lawyers argued that the snippets the company was proposing were something like a quote or an excerpt in a review and thus should qualify as a "fair use."

Google's plan was to scan the full text of every book in five major libraries: the more than 10 million titles held by Stanford, Harvard, Oxford, the University of Michigan and the New York Public Library. Every book would be indexed, but each would show up in search results in different ways. For out-of-copyright books, Google would show the whole book, page by page. For the in-print books, Google would work with publishers and let them decide what parts of their books would be shown and under what conditions. For the dark orphans, Google would show only limited snippets. And any copyright holder (author or corporation) who could establish ownership of a supposed orphan could ask Google to remove the snippets for any reason.

At first glance, it seemed genius. By scanning all books (something only Google had the cash to do), the company would advance its mission to organize all knowledge. It would let books be searchable, and it could potentially sell ads on those searches, although it does not do that currently. In the same stroke, Google would rescue the lost and forgotten 75 percent of the library. For many authors, this all-out campaign was a salvation. Google became a discovery tool, if not a marketing program. While a few best-selling authors fear piracy, every author fears obscurity. Enabling their works to be found in the same universal search box as everything else in the world was good news for authors and good news for an industry that needed some. For authors with books in the publisher program and for authors of books abandoned by a publisher, Google unleashed a chance that more people would at least read, and perhaps buy, the creation they had sweated for years to complete.

6. The Case Against Google

Some authors and many publishers found more evil than genius in Google's plan. Two points outraged them: the virtual copy of the book that sat on Google's indexing server and Google's assumption that it could scan first and ask questions later. On both counts the authors and publishers accused Google of blatant copyright infringement. When negotiations failed last fall, the Authors Guild and five big publishing companies sued Google. Their argument was simple: Why shouldn't Google share its ad revenue (if any) with the copyright owners? And why shouldn't Google have to ask permission from the legal copyright holder before scanning the work in any case? (I have divided loyalties in the case. The current publisher of my books is suing Google to protect my earnings as an author. At the same time, I earn income from Google Adsense ads placed on my blog.)

One mark of the complexity of this issue is that the publishers suing were, and still are, committed partners in the Google Book Search Partner Program. They still want Google to index and search their in-print books, even when they are scanning the books themselves, because, they say, search is a discovery tool for readers. The ability to search the scans of all books is good for profits.

The argument about sharing revenue is not about the three or four million books that publishers care about and keep in print, because Google is sharing revenues for those books with publishers. (Google says publishers receive the "majority share" of the income from the small ads placed on partner-program pages.) The argument is about the 75 percent of books that have been abandoned by publishers as uneconomical. One curious fact, of course, is that publishers only care about these orphans now because Google has shifted the economic equation; because of Book Search, these dark books may now have some sparks in them, and the publishers don't want this potential revenue stream to slip away from them. They are now busy digging deep into their records to see what part of the darkness they can declare as their own.

The second complaint against Google is more complex. Google argues that it is nearly impossible to track down copyright holders of orphan works, and so, it says, it must scan those books first and only afterward honor any legitimate requests to remove the scan. In this way, Google follows the protocol of the Internet. Google scans all Web pages; if it's on the Web, it's scanned. Web pages, by default, are born copyrighted. Google, therefore, regularly copies billions of copyrighted pages into its index for the public to search. But if you don't want Google to search your Web site, you can stick some code on your home page with a no-searching sign, and Google and every other search engine will stay out. A Web master thus can opt out of search. (Few do.) Google applies the same principle of opting-out to Book Search. It is up to you as an author to notify Google if you don't want the company to scan or search your copyrighted material. This might be a reasonable approach for Google to demand from an author or publisher if Google were the only search company around. But search technology is becoming a commodity, and if it turns out there is any money in it, it is not impossible to imagine a hundred mavericks scanning out-of-print books. Should you as a creator be obliged to find and notify each and every geek who scanned your work, if for some reason you did not want it indexed? What if you miss one?

There is a technical solution to this problem: for the search companies to compile and maintain a common list of no-scan copyright holders. A publisher or author who doesn't want a work scanned notifies the keepers of the common list once, and anyone conducting scanning would have to remove material that was listed. Since Google, like all the other big search companies—Microsoft, Amazon and Yahoo—is foremost a technical-solution company, it favors this approach. But the battle never got that far.

7. When Business Models Collide

In thinking about the arguments around search, I realized that there are many ways to conceive of this conflict. At first, I thought that this was a misunderstanding between people of the book, who favor solutions by laws, and people of the screen, who favor technology as a solution to all problems. Last November, the New York Public Library (one of the "Google Five") sponsored a debate between representatives of authors and publishers and supporters of Google. I was tickled to see that up on the stage, the defenders of the book were from the East Coast and the defenders of the screen were from the West Coast. But while it's true that there's a strand of cultural conflict here, I eventually settled on a different framework, one that I found more useful. This is a clash of business models.

Authors and publishers (including publishers of music and film) have relied for years on cheap mass-produced copies protected from counterfeits and pirates by a strong law based on the dominance of copies and on a public educated to respect the sanctity of a copy. This model has, in the last century or so, produced the greatest flowering of human achievement the world has ever seen, a magnificent golden age of creative works. Protected physical copies have enabled millions of people to earn a living directly from the sale of their art to the audience, without the weird dynamics of patronage. Not only did authors and artists benefit from this model, but the audience did, too. For the first time, billions of ordinary people were able to come in regular contact with a great work. In Mozart's day, few people ever heard one of his symphonies more than once. With the advent of cheap audio recordings, a barber in Java could listen to them all day long.

But a new regime of digital technology has now disrupted all business models based on mass-produced copies, including individual livelihoods of artists. The contours of the electronic economy are still emerging, but while they do, the wealth derived from the old business model is being spent to try to protect that old model, through legislation and enforcement. Laws based on the mass-produced copy artifact are being taken to the extreme, while desperate measures to outlaw new technologies in the marketplace "for our protection" are introduced in misguided righteousness. (This is to be expected. The fact is, entire industries and the fortunes of those working in them are threatened with demise. Newspapers and magazines, Hollywood, record labels, broadcasters and many hard-working and wonderful creative people in those fields have to change the model of how they earn money. Not all will make it.)

The new model, of course, is based on the intangible assets of digital bits, where copies are no longer cheap but free. They freely flow everywhere. As computers retrieve images from the Web or display texts from a server, they make temporary internal copies of those works. In fact, every action you take on the Net or invoke on your computer requires a copy of something to be made. This peculiar superconductivity of copies spills out of the guts of computers into the culture of computers. Many methods have been employed to try to stop the indiscriminate spread of copies, including copy-protection schemes, hardware-crippling devices, education programs, even legislation, but all have proved ineffectual. The remedies are rejected by consumers and ignored by pirates.

As copies have been dethroned, the economic model built on them is collapsing. In a regime of superabundant free copies, copies lose value. They are no longer the basis of wealth. Now relationships, links, connection and sharing are. Value has shifted away from a copy toward the many ways to recall, annotate, edit, authenticate, display, mark, transfer and engage a work. Authors and artists can make (and have made) their livings selling aspects of their works other than inexpensive copies of them. They can sell performances, access to the creator, personalization, add-on information, the scarcity of attention (via ads), sponsorship, periodic subscriptions—in short, all the many values that cannot be copied. The cheap copy becomes the "discovery tool" that markets these other intangible valuables. But selling things-that-cannot-be-copied is far from ideal for many creative people. The new model is rife with problems (or opportunities). For one thing, the laws governing creating and rewarding creators still revolve around the now-fragile model of valuable copies.

8. Search Changes Everything

The search-engine companies, including Google, operate in the new regime. Search is a wholly new concept, not foreseen in version 1.0 of our intellectual-property law. In the words of a recent ruling by the United States District Court for Nevada, search has a "transformative purpose," adding new social value to what it searches. What search uncovers is not just keywords but also the inherent value of connection. While almost every artist recognizes that the value of a creation ultimately rests in the value he or she personally gets from creating it (and for a few artists that value is sufficient), it is also true that the value of any work is increased the more it is shared. The technology of search maximizes the value of a creative work by allowing a billion new connections into it, often a billion new connections that were previously inconceivable. Things can be found by search only if they radiate potential connections. These potential relationships can be as simple as a title or as deep as hyperlinked footnotes that lead to active pages, which are also footnoted. It may be as straightforward as a song published intact or as complex as access to the individual instrument tracks—or even individual notes.

Search opens up creations. It promotes the civic nature of publishing. Having searchable works is good for culture. It is so good, in fact, that we can now state a new covenant: Copyrights must be counterbalanced by copyduties. In exchange for public protection of a work's copies (what we call copyright), a creator has an obligation to allow that work to be searched. No search, no copyright. As a song, movie, novel or poem is searched, the potential connections it radiates seep into society in a much deeper way than the simple publication of a duplicated copy ever could.

We see this effect most clearly in science. Science is on a long-term campaign to bring all knowledge in the world into one vast, interconnected, footnoted, peer-reviewed web of facts. Independent facts, even those that make sense in their own world, are of little value to science. (The pseudo- and parasciences are nothing less, in fact, than small pools of knowledge that are not connected to the large network of science.) In this way, every new observation or bit of data brought into the web of science enhances the value of all other data points. In science, there is a natural duty to make what is known searchable. No one argues that scientists should be paid when someone finds or duplicates their results. Instead, we have devised other ways to compensate them for their vital work. They are rewarded for the degree that their work is cited, shared, linked and connected

in their publications, which they do not own. They are financed with extremely short-term (20-year) patent monopolies for their ideas, short enough to truly inspire them to invent more, sooner. To a large degree, they make their living by giving away copies of their intellectual property in one fashion or another.

The legal clash between the book copy and the searchable Web promises to be a long one. Jane Friedman, the C.E.O. of HarperCollins, which is supporting the suit against Google (while remaining a publishing partner), declared, "I don't expect this suit to be resolved in my lifetime." She's right. The courts may haggle forever as this complex issue works its way to the top. In the end, it won't matter; technology will resolve this discontinuity first. The Chinese scanning factories, which operate under their own, looser intellectual-property assumptions, will keep churning out digital books. And as scanning technology becomes faster, better and cheaper, fans may do what they did to music and simply digitize their own libraries.

What is the technology telling us? That copies don't count any more. Copies of isolated books, bound between inert covers, soon won't mean much. Copies of their texts, however, will gain in meaning as they multiply by the millions and are flung around the world, indexed and copied again. What counts are the ways in which these common copies of a creative work can be linked, manipulated, annotated, tagged, highlighted, bookmarked, translated, enlivened by other media and sewn together into the universal library. Soon a book outside the library will be like a Web page outside the Web, gasping for air. Indeed, the only way for books to retain their waning authority in our culture is to wire their texts into the universal library.

But the reign of livelihoods based on the copy is not over. In the next few years, lobbyists for book publishers, movie studios and record companies will exert every effort to mandate the extinction of the "indiscriminate flow of copies," even if it means outlawing better hardware. Too many creative people depend on the business model revolving around copies for it to pass quietly. For their benefit, copyright law will not change suddenly.

But it will adapt eventually. The reign of the copy is no match for the bias of technology. All new works will be born digital, and they will flow into the universal library as you might add more words to a long story. The great continent of orphan works, the 25 million older books born analog and caught between the law and users, will be scanned. Whether this vast mountain of dark books is scanned by Google, the Library of Congress, the Chinese or by readers themselves, it will be scanned well before its legal status is resolved simply because technology makes it so easy to do and so valuable when done. In the clash between the conventions of the book and the protocols of the screen, the screen will prevail. On this screen, now visible to one billion people on earth, the technology of search will transform isolated books into the universal library of all human knowledge.

KEVIN KELLY is the "senior maverick" at Wired magazine and author of *Out of Control: The New Biology of Machines, Social Systems* and *the Economic World* and other books. He last wrote for the magazine about digital music.

UNIT 3
Work and the Workplace

Unit Selections

Key Points to Consider

- A guest worker program that provides seasonal and hard-to-find-labor is in the news. What are the pros and cons of such a program?

- What is an H1-B visa? Use the Internet to find out which companies favor the H1-B visa program. Does anyone oppose it? Why?

- How long do you spend answering e-mail every day? When managers claim that they spend two hours a day answering e-mail, do you think e-mail is helping or hurting productivity? What do you think they were doing with those two hours before the introduction of e-mail?

- Were you surprised to learn that there is no constitutional right to privacy at work? Find out how workplace privacy issues are handled in other Western democracies.

Student Web Site
www.mhcls.com/online

Internet References
Further information regarding these Web sites may be found in this book's preface or online.

American Telecommuting Association
  http://www.knowledgetree.com/ata-adv.html
Computers in the Workplace
  http://www.msci.memphis.edu/~ryburnp/cl/cis/workpl.html
InfoWeb: Techno-rage
  http://www.cciw.com/content/technorage.html
STEP ON IT! Pedals: Repetitive Strain Injury
  http://www.bilbo.com/rsi2.html
What About Computers in the Workplace
  http://law.freeadvice.com/intellectual_property/computer_law/computers_workplace.htm

Work is at the center of our lives. The kind of work we do plays a part in our standard of living, our social status, and our sense of worth. This was not always the case. Read some of the great Victorian novels, and you will find a society where paid employment, at least among the upper classes, does not exist. Even those men from the nineteenth century and before, whose discoveries and writings we study and admire, approached their work as an avocation. It is hard to imagine William Wordsworth, kissing his wife goodbye each morning, and heading off to the English Department where he will direct a seminar in creative writing before he gets to work on a sticky line in Ode Composed at Tintern Abbey. Or, think of Charles Darwin, donning a lab coat, and supervising an army of graduate students while he touches up his latest National Science Foundation proposal. A hundred or more years ago, there were a handful of professions—doctor, lawyer, clergyman, military office, a larger handful of craftsmen—joiner, miller, cooper, blacksmith, an army of agricultural workers, and an increasing number of displaced peasants toiling in factories, what William Blake called England's "dark Satanic mills."

The U.S. Census records tell us that there were only 323 different occupations in 1850, including the butcher, the baker, and the candlestick maker that children read about. The butcher is still with us, as well as the baker, but both of them work for national supermarket chains, using digitally-controlled tools and manage their 401k's online. The candlestick maker has morphed into a refinery worker, watching digital displays in petrochemical plants that light up the Louisiana sky. The Canadian National Occupational Classification lists more than 25,000 occupational titles. It was once feared that, first, machines in the early twentieth century and, then, computers in the later part would render work obsolete, transforming us into country gentlemen like Charles Darwin in the utopian view or nomadic mobs of starving proletarians in the distopian outlook.

It appears instead that fabulously productive farms and factories—as well as a third world willing to make our shoes, clothing, and electronics for pennies an hour—have opened up opportunities that did not exist in Darwin's time. We are now sales clerks, health care workers, state license examiners, light truck drivers, equal opportunity compliance officers, and, yes, also software engineers, database analysts, Web-site designers, and entrepreneurs.

Many of the lowest-paid jobs in the new economy are held by the foreign-born, some illegally, prompting the current immigration debate. That debate, in turn, has prompted some to propose a mechanism to determine who may and may not work in the United States. One proposal is a tamper-proof Social Security card, complete with biometric data (swee "National ID").

But immigrants hold many of the more interesting and better paid of the new jobs as well. AnnaLee Saxenian, observes in "Brain Circulation" that "more than a quarter of Silicon Valley's highly skilled workers are immigrant . . . ." This raises questions about whether the growth in numbers of foreign-born professionals displaces native workers, while at the same time draining talent from countries too poor to lose it.

As anyone knows who follows the doings in Silicon Valley, not all of the foreign-born tech workers live in the United States. Many live in Mumbai and Bangalore. Read "The New Face of the Silicon Age" and meet an Indian software engineer whose salary is $11,000 per year.

BananaStock Ltd

As a corrective, take a look at the piece from the Bureau of Labor Statistics, "Computer Software Engineers." There you will find that, all of the talk about outsourcing notwithstanding, "software engineers are projected to be one of the fasted-growing occupations from 2004 to 2014."

"The Computer Evolution" confirms what every working American has noticed, namely, that computers have spread throughout the workplace. It also confirms what many observers have long suspected: "the ability to use a computer is not a 'sufficient' condition for earning high wages, but it is increasingly a 'necessary' condition."

Just as necessary, is using the computer well. Most of us are fumbling about with a communications medium that did not exist a generation ago. "Making Yourself Understood" tells us what our English teachers have been telling us for years. Though the memo has become digitized, writing is still important. More than half of managers in one study report spending at least two hours a day answering e-mail. While communication is easier than ever, it has also "never been so easy to be misunderstood."

One of the more thought-provoking pieces in the unit is "Privacy, Legislation, and Surveillance Software." Here we learn that American employees have no constitutional right to privacy at work. Those who check stock quotes or send e-mail over a company computer, even if their account is password-protected, should read this article carefully.

National ID
Biometrics Pinned to Social Security Cards

RYAN SINGEL

The Social Security card faces its first major upgrade in 70 years under two immigration-reform proposals slated for debate this week that would add biometric information to the card and finally complete its slow metamorphosis into a national ID.

The leading immigration proposal with traction in Congress would force employers to accept only a very limited range of approved documents as proof of work eligibility, including a driver's license that meets new federal Real ID standards, a high-tech temporary work visa or a U.S. passport with an RFID chip. A fourth option is the notional tamper-proof biometric Social Security card, which would replace the text-only design that's been issued to Americans almost without change for more than 70 years.

A second proposal under consideration would add high-tech features to the Social Security card allowing employers to scan it with specially equipped laptop computers. Under that proposal, called the "Bonner Plan," the revamped Social Security card would be the only legal form of identification for employment purposes.

Neither bill specifies what the biometric would be, but it could range from a simple digital photo to a fingerprint or even an iris scan. The proposals would seem to require major changes to how Social Security cards are issued: Currently, new and replacement cards are sent in the mail. And parents typically apply for their children before they're old enough to give a decent fingerprint.

There are also logistical problems to overcome before forcing all of the nation's employers to verify a biometric card—given the nation has millions of employers, many of whom may not have computer equipment at all.

"This is an exact example of why IDs are so ludicrous as a form of security," American Civil Liberties Union legislative counsel Tim Sparapani said. "Do we really think the migrant workers are going to show up at the pickle farm and the farmer is going to demand ID and have a laptop in the field to check their ID?"

That's one of the problems that Rep. Zoe Lofgren (D-California), who heads a key House immigration subcommittee, says she's thinking about.

"There seems to be a fairly strong sentiment that there needs to be an easy way to reliably enforce whatever rules we adopt and the biometric is something being discussed in all the House bills," Lofgren told Wired News. "Obviously every small business isn't going to have a biometric card reader, but perhaps the post office might have a reader since every community in America has a post office."

The proposed biometric feature would apply to newly issued or replaced Social Security cards—you won't be asked to hand in your old one. Nevertheless, the plan doesn't sit well with privacy and civil liberties advocates like Sparapani. And immigrant-rights groups foresee rampant database errors, and an inevitable mission drift, with biometric cards—whether the Social Security card or one of the other cards pushed in the proposals—being used for purposes other than employment.

Currently, U.S. employers can accept a range of documents, including expired U.S. passports, tribal documents, refugee documents, birth certificates, driver's licenses and even school report cards, to establish an employee's eligibility for work.

Michele Waslin, the policy research director at the National Council of La Raza, a Latino civil rights group, supports immigration reform but emphasizes that employment-eligibility verification must be effective and have safeguards.

"This is one provision that would impact every single person that gets a job in the United States," Waslin said. "Given the inaccuracy of government databases, it is likely that some Americans will show documents and the answer will come back as a 'non-confirmation' and (they) could be denied employment based on a government mistake."

Waslin also fears that the existence of a document that proves immigration status will lead to widespread document checks, even from shop clerks.

"You can imagine arriving at a polling place and some people are being asked for a Real ID, while people who look 'American' aren't asked for a Real ID," Waslin said.

The controversy is likely to heat up this week. Senate Majority Leader Harry Reid is set to schedule two weeks of immigration-reform debate Tuesday, setting a deadline for a bipartisan panel of lawmakers to craft legislation that combines tighter border enforcement, avenues for current undocumented workers to earn legal status, and stringent employee-verification requirements for employers.

If they succeed, the bill will probably have roughly the same contours as the leading House bill, known as the *Strive Act*, co-authored by Reps. John Flake (R-Arizona) and Luis Gutierrez (D-Illinois).

The Strive Act would require employers to verify a new employee's credentials—by telephone or the internet—against databases maintained by the Social Security Administration and the Department of Homeland Security. If the answer comes back as a "non-confirmation," the new hire would have the opportunity to update any incorrect records.

The Strive Act's verification system is based on the Basic Pilot Program, a currently voluntary program that lets businesses verify new employees' work eligibility over the web. But that program relies on databases prone to inaccuracy, according to Tyler Moran, the employment policy director at the National Immigration Law Center.

"The Basic Pilot program has given more power to employers to oppress workers," Moran said. "It's the worker's burden to prove they are work-authorized, and employers are taking adverse action when there is a problem, such as demoting or firing workers before they have a chance to correct the database."

A recent report by the Social Security Administration's inspector general backs up Moran's criticism with findings that 17.8 million records in the government's employment databases contained inaccuracies that could initially and erroneously flag individuals as ineligible for employment.

From *Wired,* May 15, 2007. Copyright © 2007 by Condenet. Reprinted by permission of Wired Online.

Brain Circulation
How High-Skill Immigration Makes Everyone Better Off

AnnaLee Saxenian

Silicon Valley's workforce is among the world's most ethnically diverse. Not only do Asian and Hispanic workers dominate the low-paying, blue-collar workforce, but foreign-born scientists and engineers are increasingly visible as entrepreneurs and senior management. More than a quarter of Silicon Valley's highly skilled workers are immigrants, including tens of thousands from lands as diverse as China, Taiwan, India, the United Kingdom, Iran, Vietnam, the Philippines, Canada, and Israel.

Most people instinctively assume that the movement of skill and talent must benefit one country at the expense of another. But thanks to brain circulation, high-skilled immigration increasingly benefits both sides

Understandably, the rapid growth of the foreign-born workforce has evoked intense debates over U.S. immigration policy, both here and in the developing world. In the United States, discussions of the immigration of scientists and engineers have focused primarily on the extent to which foreign-born professionals displace native workers. The view from sending countries, by contrast, has been that the emigration of highly skilled personnel to the United States represents a big economic loss, a "brain drain."

Neither view is adequate in today's global economy. Far from simply replacing native workers, foreign-born engineers are starting new businesses and generating jobs and wealth at least as fast as their U.S. counterparts. And the dynamism of emerging regions in Asia and elsewhere now draws skilled immigrants homeward. Even when they choose not to return home, they are serving as middlemen linking businesses in the United States with those in distant regions.

In some parts of the world, the old dynamic of "brain drain" is giving way to one I call "brain circulation." Most people instinctively assume that the movement of skill and talent must benefit one country at the expense of another. But thanks to brain circulation, high-skilled immigration increasingly benefits both sides. Economically speaking, it is blessed to give *and* to receive.

"New" Immigrant Entrepreneurs

Unlike traditional ethnic entrepreneurs who remain isolated in marginal, low-wage industries, Silicon Valley's new foreign-born entrepreneurs are highly educated professionals in dynamic and technologically sophisticated industries. And they have been extremely successful. By the end of the 1990s, Chinese and Indian engineers were running 29 percent of Silicon Valley's technology businesses. By 2000, these companies collectively accounted for more than $19.5 billion in sales and 72,839 jobs. And the pace of immigrant entrepreneurship has accelerated dramatically in the past decade.

Not that Silicon Valley's immigrants have abandoned their ethnic ties. Like their less-educated counterparts, Silicon Valley's high-tech immigrants rely on ethnic strategies to enhance entrepreneurial opportunities. Seeing themselves as outsiders to the mainstream technology community, foreign-born engineers and scientists in Silicon Valley have created social and professional networks to mobilize the information, know-how, skill, and capital to start technology firms. Local ethnic professional associations like the Silicon Valley Chinese Engineers Association, The Indus Entrepreneur, and the Korean IT Forum provide contacts and resources for recently arrived immigrants.

Combining elements of traditional immigrant culture with distinctly high-tech practices, these organizations simultaneously create ethnic identities within the region and aid professional networking and information exchange. These are not traditional political or lobbying groups—rather their focus is the professional and technical advancement of their members. Membership in Indian and Chinese professional associations has virtually no overlap, although the overlap within the separate communities—particularly the Chinese, with its many specialized associations—appears considerable. Yet ethnic distinctions also exist within the Chinese community. To an outsider, the Chinese American Semiconductor Professionals Association and the North American Chinese Semiconductor Association are redundant organizations. One, however, represents Taiwanese, the other Mainland Chinese.

> **The most successful immigrant entrepreneurs in Silicon Valley today appear to be those who have drawn on ethnic resources while simultaneously integrating into mainstream technology and business networks.**

Whatever their ethnicity, all these associations tend to mix socializing—over Chinese banquets, Indian dinners, or family-centered social events—with support for professional and technical advancement. Each, either explicitly or informally, offers first-generation immigrants professional contacts and networks within the local technology community. They serve as recruitment channels and provide role models of successful immigrant entrepreneurs and managers. They sponsor regular speakers and conferences whose subjects range from specialized technical and market information to how to write a business plan or manage a business. Some Chinese associations give seminars on English communication, negotiation skills, and stress management.

Many of these groups have become important cross-generational forums. Older engineers and entrepreneurs in both the Chinese and the Indian communities now help finance and mentor younger co-ethnic entrepreneurs. Within these networks, "angel" investors often invest individually or jointly in promising new ventures. The Indus Entrepreneur, for example, aims to "foster entrepreneurship by providing mentorship and resources" within the South Asian technology community. Both the Asian American Manufacturers Association and the Monte Jade Science and Technology Association sponsor annual investment conferences to match investors (often from Asia as well as Silicon Valley) with Chinese entrepreneurs.

> **The long-distance networks are accelerating the globalization of labor markets and enhancing opportunities for entrepreneurship, investment, and trade both in the United States and in newly emerging regions in Asia.**

Although many Chinese and Indian immigrants socialize primarily within their ethnic networks, they routinely work with U.S. engineers and U.S.-run businesses. In fact, recognition is growing within these communities that although a start-up might be spawned with the support of the ethnic networks, it must become part of the mainstream to grow. The most successful immigrant entrepreneurs in Silicon Valley today appear to be those who have drawn on ethnic resources while simultaneously integrating into mainstream technology and business networks.

Transnational Entrepreneurship

Far beyond their role in Silicon Valley, the professional and social networks that link new immigrant entrepreneurs with each other have become global institutions that connect new immigrants with their counterparts at home. These new transnational communities provide the shared information, contacts, and trust that allow local producers to participate in an increasingly global economy.

Silicon Valley's Taiwanese engineers, for example, have built a vibrant two-way bridge connecting them with Taiwan's technology community. Their Indian counterparts have become key middlemen linking U.S. businesses to low-cost software expertise in India. These cross-Pacific networks give skilled immigrants a big edge over mainstream competitors who often lack the language skills, cultural know-how, and contacts to build business relationships in Asia. The long-distance networks are accelerating the globalization of labor markets and enhancing opportunities for entrepreneurship, investment, and trade both in the United States and in newly emerging regions in Asia.

Taiwanese immigrant Miin Wu, for example, arrived in the United States in the early 1970s to pursue graduate training in electrical engineering. After earning a doctorate from Stanford University in 1976, Wu saw little use for his new skills in economically backward Taiwan and chose to remain in the United States. He worked for more than a decade in senior positions at Silicon Valley–based semiconductor companies including Siliconix and Intel. He also gained entrepreneurial experience as one of the founding members of VLSI Technology.

By the late 1980s, Taiwan's economy had improved dramatically, and Wu decided to return. In 1989 he started one of Taiwan's first semiconductor companies, Macronix Co., in the Hsinchu Science-based Industrial Park. Wu also became an active participant in Silicon Valley's Monte Jade Science and Technology Association, which was building business links between the technical communities in Silicon Valley and Taiwan.

> **In this complex mix, the rich social and professional ties among Taiwanese engineers and their U.S. counterparts are as important as the more formal corporate alliances and partnerships.**

Macronix went public on the Taiwan stock exchange in 1995 and in 1996 became the first Taiwanese company to list on Nasdaq. It is now the sixth biggest semiconductor maker in Taiwan, with more than $300 million in sales and some 2,800 employees. Although most of its employees and its manufacturing facilities are in Taiwan, Macronix has an advanced design and engineering center in Silicon Valley, where Wu regularly recruits senior managers. A Macronix venture capital fund invests in promising start-ups in both Silicon Valley and Taiwan—not to raise money but to develop technologies related to their core business. In short, Miin Wu's activities bridge and benefit both the Taiwan and Silicon Valley economies.

A New Model of Globalization

As recently as the 1970s, only giant corporations had the resources and capabilities to grow internationally, and they did so primarily by establishing marketing offices or manufacturing plants overseas. Today, new transportation and communications technologies allow even the smallest firms to build partnerships with foreign producers to tap overseas expertise, cost-savings, and markets. Start-ups in Silicon Valley are often global actors from the day they begin operations. Many raise capital from Asian sources, others subcontract manufacturing to Taiwan or rely on software development in India, and virtually all sell their products in Asian markets.

The scarce resource in this new environment is the ability to locate foreign partners quickly and to manage complex business relationships across cultural and linguistic boundaries. The challenge is keenest in high-tech industries whose products, markets, and technologies are continually being redefined—and whose product cycles are exceptionally short. For them, first-generation immigrants like the Chinese and Indian engineers of Silicon Valley, who have the language, cultural, and technical skills to thrive in both the United States and foreign markets, are invaluable. Their social structures enable even the smallest producers to locate and maintain collaborations across long distances and gain access to Asian capital, manufacturing capabilities, skills, and markets.

These ties have measurable economic benefits. For every 1 percent increase in the number of first-generation immigrants from a given country, for example, California's exports to that country go up nearly 0.5 percent. The effect is especially pronounced in the Asia-Pacific where, all other things being equal, California exports nearly four times more than it exports to comparable countries elsewhere in the world.

Growing links between the high-tech communities of Silicon Valley and Taiwan, for example, offer big benefits to both economies. Silicon Valley remains the center of new product definition and of design and development of leading-edge technologies, whereas Taiwan offers world-class manufacturing, flexible development and integration, and access to key customers and markets in China and Southeast Asia. But what appears a classic case of the economic benefits of comparative advantage would not be possible without the underlying social structures, provided by Taiwanese engineers, which ensure continuous flows of information between the two regions.

The reciprocal and decentralized nature of these relationships is distinctive. The ties between Japan and the United States during the 1980s were typically arm's-length, and technology transfers between large firms were managed from the top down. The Silicon Valley-Hsinchu relationship, by contrast, consists of formal and informal collaborations among individual investors and entrepreneurs, small and medium-sized firms, and divisions of larger companies on both sides of the Pacific. In this complex mix, the rich social and professional ties among Taiwanese engineers and their U.S. counterparts are as important as the more formal corporate alliances and partnerships.

Silicon Valley-based firms are poised to exploit both India's software talent and Taiwan's manufacturing capabilities. Mahesh Veerina started Ramp Networks (initially Trancell Systems) in 1993 with several Indian friends, relatives, and colleagues. Their aim was to develop low-cost devices to speed Internet access for small businesses. By 1994, short on money, they decided to hire programmers in India for one-quarter of the Silicon Valley rate. One founder spent two years setting up and managing their software development center in the southern city of Hyderabad. By 1999 Ramp had 65 employees in Santa Clara and 25 in India.

Having used his Indian background to link California with India, Veerina then met two principals of a Taiwanese investment fund, InveStar, that folded in Taiwan. In less than three months, Veerina set up partnerships for high-volume manufacture of Ramp's routers with three Taiwanese manufacturers (it took nine months to establish a similar partnership with a U.S. manufacturer). The Taiwanese price per unit was about half what Ramp was paying for manufacturing in the United States, and Ramp increased its output one-hundred-fold because of relationships subsequently built by Veerina with key customers in the Taiwanese personal computer industry. Ramp also opted to use the worldwide distribution channels of its Taiwanese partners. And when Ramp designed a new model, the Taiwanese manufacturer was prepared to ship product in two weeks—not the six months it would have taken in the United States.

Veerina attributes much of his success to InveStar's partners and their network of contacts in Taiwan. In a business where product cycles are often shorter than nine months, the speed and cost savings provided by these relationships provide critical competitive advantages to a firm like Ramp. InveStar sees as one of its key assets its intimate knowledge of the ins and outs of the business infrastructure in Taiwan's decentralized industrial system. By helping outsiders (both Chinese and non-Chinese) negotiate these complicated networks to tap into Taiwan's cost-effective and high-quality infrastructure and capability for speedy and flexible integration, such firms provide their clients far more than access to capital.

Americans should resist viewing immigration and trade as zero-sum processes.

As Silicon Valley's skilled Chinese and Indian immigrants create social and economic links to their home countries, they simultaneously open foreign markets and identify manufacturing options and technical skills in Asia for the broader U.S. business community. Traditional Fortune 500 corporations as well as newer technology companies, for example, now increasingly turn to India for software programming and development talent. Meanwhile, information technology-related sectors in the United States rely heavily on Taiwan (and more recently China) for their fast and flexible infrastructure for manufacturing semiconductors and PCs, as well as their growing markets for advanced technology components. And these distant resources are now just as accessible to new start-ups like Ramp as to more established corporations.

These new international linkages are strengthening the economic infrastructure of the United States while providing new opportunities for once peripheral regions of the world economy. Foreign-born engineers have started thousands of technology businesses in the United States, generating jobs, exports, and wealth at home and also accelerating the integration of these businesses into the global economy.

A New Policy Environment

The Silicon Valley experience underscores far-reaching transformations of the relationship between immigration, trade, and economic development in the 21st century. Where once the main economic ties between immigrants and their home countries were remittances sent to families left behind, today more and more skilled U.S. immigrants eventually return home. Those who remain in America often become part of transnational communities that link the United States to the economies of distant regions. These new immigrant entrepreneurs thus foster economic development directly, by creating new jobs and wealth, as well as indirectly, by coordinating the information flows and providing the linguistic and cultural know-how that promote trade and investment with their home countries.

Analysts and policymakers must recognize this new reality. In the recent U.S. debate over making more H1-B visas available for highly skilled immigrants, discussion began—and ended—with the extent to which immigrants displace native workers. But these high-tech immigrants affect more than labor supply and wages. They also create new jobs here and new ties abroad. Some of their economic contributions, such as enhanced trade and investment flows, are difficult to quantify, but they must figure into our debates.

Economic openness has its costs, to be sure, but the strength of the U.S. economy has historically derived from its openness and diversity—and this will be increasingly true as the economy becomes more global. As Silicon Valley's new immigrant entrepreneurs suggest, Americans should resist viewing immigration and trade as zero-sum processes. We need to encourage the immigration of skilled workers—while simultaneously improving the education of workers here at home.

AnnaLee Saxenian is a professor of city and regional planning at the University of California at Berkeley.

The New Face of the Silicon Age

How India became the capital of the computing revolution.

Daniel H. Pink

Meet the pissed-off programmer. If you've picked up a newspaper in the last six months, watched CNN, or even glanced at Slashdot, you've already heard his anguished cry.

Now meet the cause of all this fear and loathing: Aparna Jairam of Mumbai. She's 33 years old. Her long black hair is clasped with a barrette. Her dark eyes are deep-set and unusually calm. She has the air of the smartest girl in class—not the one always raising her hand and shouting out answers, but the one who sits in back, taking it all in and responding only when called upon, yet delivering answers that make the whole class turn around and listen.

In 1992, Jairam graduated from India's University of Pune with a degree in engineering. She has since worked in a variety of jobs in the software industry and is now a project manager at Hexaware Technologies in Mumbai, the city formerly known as Bombay. Jairam specializes in embedded systems software for handheld devices. She leaves her two children with a babysitter each morning, commutes an hour to the office, and spends her days attending meetings, perfecting her team's code, and emailing her main client, a utility company in the western US. Jairam's annual salary is about $11,000—more than 22 times the per capita annual income in India.

Aparna Jairam isn't trying to steal your job. That's what she tells me, and I believe her. But if Jairam does end up taking it—and, let's face facts, she could do your $70,000-a-year job for the wages of a Taco Bell counter jockey—she won't lose any sleep over your plight. When I ask what her advice is for a beleaguered American programmer afraid of being pulled under by the global tide that she represents, Jairam takes the high road, neither dismissing the concern nor offering soothing happy talk. Instead, she recites a portion of the 2,000-year-old epic poem and Hindu holy book the Bhagavad Gita: "Do what you're supposed to do. And don't worry about the fruits. They'll come on their own."

This is a story about the global economy. It's about two countries and one profession—and how weirdly upside down the future has begun to look from opposite sides of the globe. It's about code and the people who write it. But it's also about free markets, new politics, and ancient wisdom—which means it's ultimately about faith.

Our story begins beside the murky waters of the Arabian Sea. I've come to Mumbai to see what software programmers in India make of the anti-outsourcing hubbub in the US. Mumbai may not have as many coders per square foot as glossier tech havens like Bangalore and Hyderabad, but there's a lot more real life here. Mumbai is India's largest city—with an official population of 18 million and an actual population incalculably higher. It's a sweltering, magnificent, teeming megalopolis in which every human triumph and affliction shouts at the top of its lungs 24 hours a day.

Jairam's firm, Hexaware, is located in the exurbs of Mumbai in a district fittingly called Navi Mumbai, or New Mumbai. To get there, you fight traffic thicker and more chaotic than rush hour in hell as you pass a staggering stretch of shantytowns. But once inside the Millennium Business Park, which houses Hexaware and several other high tech companies, you've tumbled through a wormhole and landed in northern Virginia or Silicon Valley. The streets are immaculate. The buildings fairly gleam. The lawns are fit for putting. And in the center is an outdoor café bustling with twenty-somethings so picture-perfect I look around to see if a film crew is shooting a commercial.

Hexaware's headquarters, the workplace of some 500 programmers (another 800 work at a development center in the southern city of Chennai, and 200 more are in Bangalore), is a silvery four-story glass building chock-full of blond-wood cubicles and black Dell computers. In one area, 30 new recruits sit through programming boot camp; down the hall, 25 even newer hires are filling out HR forms. Meanwhile, other young people—the average age here is 27—tap keyboards and skitter in and out of conference rooms outfitted with whiteboards and enclosed in frosted glass. If you pulled the shades and ignored the accents, you could be in Santa Clara. But it's the talent—coupled with the ridiculously low salaries, of course—that's luring big clients from Europe and North America. The coders here work for the likes of Citibank, Deutsche Leasing, Alliance Capital, Air Canada, HSBC, BP, Princeton University, and several other institutions that won't permit Hexaware to reveal their names.

Jairam works in a first-floor cubicle that's unadorned except for a company policy statement, a charcoal sketch, and a small statue of Ganesh, the elephant-headed Hindu god of knowledge and obstacle removal. Like most employees, Jairam rides to work aboard a private bus, one in a fleet the company dispatches throughout Mumbai to shuttle its workers to the office. Many days she eats lunch in the firm's colorful fourth-floor canteen. While Hexaware's culinary offerings don't measure up to Google's celebrity chef and gourmet fare, the food's not bad—chana saag, aloo gobi, rice, chapatis—and the price is right. A meal costs 22 rupees, about 50 cents.

After lunch one Tuesday, I meet in a conference room with Jairam and five colleagues to hear their reactions to the complaints of the pissed-off programmer. I cite the usual statistics: 1 in 10 US technology jobs will go overseas by the end of 2004, according to the research firm Gartner. In the next 15 years, more than 3 million US white-collar jobs, representing $136 billion in wages, will depart to places like India, with the IT industry leading the migration, according to Forrester Research. I relate stories of American programmers collecting unemployment, declaring bankruptcy, even contemplating suicide—because they can't compete with people willing to work for one-sixth of their wages.

DANIEL H. PINK (dp@danpink.com) is the author of *Free Agent Nation* and the forthcoming *A Whole New Mind*.

Computer Software Engineers

Significant Points

- Computer software engineers are projected to be one of the fastest growing occupations over the 2004–14 period.
- Very good opportunities are expected for college graduates with at least a bachelor's degree in computer engineering or computer science and with practical work experience.
- Computer software engineers must continually strive to acquire new skills in conjunction with the rapid changes that are occurring in computer technology.

Nature of the Work

The explosive impact of computers and information technology on our everyday lives has generated a need to design and develop new computer software systems and to incorporate new technologies into a rapidly growing range of applications. The tasks performed by workers known as computer software engineers evolve quickly, reflecting new areas of specialization or changes in technology, as well as the preferences and practices of employers. Computer software engineers apply the principles and techniques of computer science, engineering, and mathematical analysis to the design, development, testing, and evaluation of the software and systems that enable computers to perform their many applications. (A separate statement on Computer hardware engineers appears elsewhere in the *Handbook*.)

Software engineers working in applications or systems development analyze users' needs and design, construct, test, and maintain computer applications software or systems. Software engineers can be involved in the design and development of many types of software, including software for operating systems and network distribution, and compilers, which convert programs for execution on a computer. In programming, or coding, software engineers instruct a computer, line by line, how to perform a function. They also solve technical problems that arise. Software engineers must possess strong programming skills, but are more concerned with developing algorithms and analyzing and solving programming problems than with actually writing code. (A separate statement on computer programmers appears elsewhere in the *Handbook*.)

Computer applications software engineers analyze users' needs and design, construct, and maintain general computer applications software or specialized utility programs. These workers use different programming languages, depending on the purpose of the program. The programming languages most often used are C, C++, and Java, with Fortran and COBOL used less commonly. Some software engineers develop both packaged systems and systems software or create customized applications.

Computer systems software engineers coordinate the construction and maintenance of a company's computer systems and plan their future growth. Working with the company, they coordinate each department's computer needs—ordering, inventory, billing, and payroll recordkeeping, for example—and make suggestions about its technical direction. They also might set up the company's intranets—networks that link computers within the organization and ease communication among the various departments.

Systems software engineers work for companies that configure, implement, and install complete computer systems. These workers may be members of the marketing or sales staff, serving as the primary technical resource for sales workers and customers. They also may be involved in product sales and in providing their customers with continuing technical support. Since the selling of complex computer systems often requires substantial customization for the purchaser's organization, software engineers help to explain the requirements necessary for installing and operating the new system in the purchaser's computing environment. In addition, systems software engineers are responsible for ensuring security across the systems they are configuring.

Computer software engineers often work as part of a team that designs new hardware, software, and systems. A core team may comprise engineering, marketing, manufacturing, and design people, who work together until the product is released.

Working Conditions

Computer software engineers normally work in well-lighted and comfortable offices or laboratories in which computer equipment is located. Most software engineers work at least 40 hours a week; however, due to the project-oriented nature of the work, they also may have to work evenings or weekends to meet deadlines or solve unexpected technical problems. Like other workers who sit for hours at a computer, typing on a keyboard, software engineers are susceptible to eyestrain, back discomfort, and hand and wrist problems such as carpal tunnel syndrome.

As they strive to improve software for users, many computer software engineers interact with customers and coworkers. Computer software engineers who are employed by software vendors and consulting firms, for example, spend much of their time away from their offices, frequently traveling overnight to meet with customers. They call on customers in businesses ranging from manufacturing plants to financial institutions.

As networks expand, software engineers may be able to use modems, laptops, e-mail, and the Internet to provide more technical support and other services from their main office, connecting to a customer's computer remotely to identify and correct developing problems.

Training, Other Qualifications, and Advancement

Most employers prefer to hire persons who have at least a bachelor's degree and broad knowledge of, and experience with, a variety of computer systems and technologies. The usual degree concentration for applications software engineers is computer science or software engineering; for systems software engineers, it is computer science or computer information systems. Graduate degrees are preferred for some of the more complex jobs.

Academic programs in software engineering emphasize software and may be offered as a degree option or in conjunction with computer science degrees. Increasing emphasis on computer security suggests that software engineers with advanced degrees that include mathematics and systems design will be sought after by software developers, government agencies, and consulting firms specializing in information assurance and security. Students seeking software engineering jobs enhance their employment opportunities by participating in internship or co-op programs offered through their schools. These experiences provide the students with broad knowledge and experience, making them more attractive candidates to employers. Inexperienced college graduates may be hired by large computer and consulting firms that train new employees in intensive, company-based programs. In many firms, new hires are mentored, and their mentors have an input into the performance evaluations of these new employees.

For systems software engineering jobs that require workers who have a college degree, a bachelor's degree in computer science or computer information systems is typical. For systems engineering jobs that place less emphasis on workers having a computer-related degree, computer training programs leading to certification are offered by systems software vendors. Nonetheless, most training authorities feel that program certification alone is not sufficient for the majority of software engineering jobs.

Persons interested in jobs as computer software engineers must have strong problem-solving and analytical skills. They also must be able to communicate effectively with team members, other staff, and the customers they meet. Because they often deal with a number of tasks simultaneously, they must be able to concentrate and pay close attention to detail.

As is the case with most occupations, advancement opportunities for computer software engineers increase with experience. Entry-level computer software engineers are likely to test and verify ongoing designs. As they become more experienced, they may become involved in designing and developing software. Eventually, they may advance to become a project manager, manager of information systems, or chief information officer. Some computer software engineers with several years of experience or expertise find lucrative opportunities working as systems designers or independent consultants or starting their own computer consulting firms.

As technological advances in the computer field continue, employers demand new skills. Computer software engineers must continually strive to acquire such skills if they wish to remain in this extremely dynamic field. For example, computer software engineers interested in working for a bank should have some expertise in finance as they integrate new technologies into the computer system of the bank. To help them keep up with the changing technology, continuing education and professional development seminars are offered by employers, software vendors, colleges and universities, private training institutions, and professional computing societies.

Employment

Computer software engineers held about 800,000 jobs in 2004. Approximately 460,000 were computer applications software engineers, and around 340,000 were computer systems software engineers. Although they are employed in most industries, the largest concentration of computer software engineers—almost 30 percent—are in computer systems design and related services. Many computer software engineers also work for establishments in other industries, such as software publishers, government agencies, manufacturers of computers and related electronic equipment, and management of companies and enterprises.

Employers of computer software engineers range from start-up companies to established industry leaders. The proliferation of Internet, e-mail, and other communications systems is expanding electronics to engineering firms that are traditionally associated with unrelated disciplines. Engineering firms specializing in building bridges and powerplants, for example, hire computer software engineers to design and develop new geographic data systems and automated drafting systems. Communications firms need computer software engineers to tap into growth in the personal communications market. Major communications companies have many job openings for both computer software applications engineers and computer systems engineers.

An increasing number of computer software engineers are employed on a temporary or contract basis, with many being self-employed, working independently as consultants. Some consultants work for firms that specialize in developing and maintaining client companies' Web sites and intranets. About 23,000 computer software engineers were self-employed in 2004.

Job Outlook

Computer software engineers are projected to be one of the fastest-growing occupations from 2004 to 2014. Rapid employment growth in the computer systems design and related services industry, which employs the greatest number of computer software engineers, should result in very good opportunities for those college graduates with at least a bachelor's degree in computer engineering or computer science and practical experience working with computers. Employers will continue to seek computer professionals with strong programming, systems analysis, interpersonal, and business skills. With the software industry beginning to mature, however, and with routine software engineering work being increasingly outsourced overseas, job growth will not be as rapid as during the previous decade.

Employment of computer software engineers is expected to increase much faster than the average for all occupations, as businesses and other organizations adopt and integrate new technologies and seek to maximize the efficiency of their computer systems. Competition among businesses will continue to create an incentive for increasingly sophisticated technological innovations, and organizations will need more computer software engineers to implement these changes. In addition to jobs created through employment growth, many job openings will result annually from the need to replace workers who move into managerial positions, transfer to other occupations, or leave the labor force.

Demand for computer software engineers will increase as computer networking continues to grow. For example, the expanding integration of Internet technologies and the explosive growth in electronic commerce—doing business on the Internet—have resulted in rising demand for computer software engineers who can develop Internet, intranet, and World Wide Web applications. Likewise, expanding electronic data-processing systems in business, telecommunications, government, and other settings continue to become more sophisticated and complex. Growing numbers of systems software engineers will be needed to implement, safeguard, and update systems and resolve problems. Consulting opportunities for computer software engineers also should continue to grow as businesses seek help to manage,

upgrade, and customize their increasingly complicated computer systems.

New growth areas will continue to arise from rapidly evolving technologies. The increasing uses of the Internet, the proliferation of Web sites, and mobile technology such as the wireless Internet have created a demand for a wide variety of new products. As individuals and businesses rely more on hand-held computers and wireless networks, it will be necessary to integrate current computer systems with this new, more mobile technology. Also, information security concerns have given rise to new software needs. Concerns over "cyber security" should result in businesses and government continuing to invest heavily in software that protects their networks and vital electronic infrastructure from attack. The expansion of this technology in the next 10 years will lead to an increased need for computer engineers to design and develop the software and systems to run these new applications and integrate them into older systems.

As with other information technology jobs, employment growth of computer software engineers may be tempered somewhat as more software development is contracted out abroad. Firms may look to cut costs by shifting operations to lower wage foreign countries with highly educated workers who have strong technical skills. At the same time, jobs in software engineering are less prone to being sent abroad compared with jobs in other computer specialties, because the occupation requires innovation and intense research and development.

Earnings

Median annual earnings of computer applications software engineers who worked full time in May 2004 were about $74,980. The middle 50 percent earned between $59,130 and $92,130. The lowest 10 percent earned less than $46,520, and the highest 10 percent earned more than $113,830. Median annual earnings in the industries employing the largest numbers of computer applications software engineers in May 2004 were as follows:

Software publishers..$79,930
Management, scientific,
    and technical consulting services......................78,460
Computer systems design and related services.......76,910
Management of companies and enterprises............70,520
Insurance carriers..68,440

Median annual earnings of computer systems software engineers who worked full time in May 2004 were about $79,740. The middle 50 percent earned between $63,150 and $98,220. The lowest 10 percent earned less than $50,420, and the highest 10 percent earned more than $118,350. Median annual earnings in the industries employing the largest numbers of computer systems software engineers in May 2004 are as follows:

Scientific research and development services.......$91,390

Computer and peripheral equipment

    manufacturing..87,800

Software publishers...83,670

Computer systems design and related services.......79,950

Wired telecommunications carriers........................74,370

According to the National Association of Colleges and Employers, starting salary offers for graduates with a bachelor's degree in computer engineering averaged $52,464 in 2005; offers for those with a master's degree averaged $60,354. Starting salary offers for graduates with a bachelor's degree in computer science averaged $50,820.

According to Robert Half International, starting salaries for software engineers in software development ranged from $63,250 to $92,750 in 2005. For network engineers, starting salaries in 2005 ranged from $61,250 to $88,250.

Related Occupations

Other workers who use mathematics and logic extensively include computer systems analysts, computer scientists and database administrators, computer programmers, computer hardware engineers, computer support specialists and systems administrators, engineers, statisticians, mathematicians, and actuaries.

From *Occupational Outlook Handbook,* 2006/07 Edition (ONET codes 15-1031.00, 15-1032.00). Published by Bureau of Labor Statistics, U.S. Department of Labor. http://www.bls.gov/oco/

The Computer Evolution

Rob Valletta and Geoffrey MacDonald

Since the introduction of the IBM PC in 1981, desktop computers have become a standard fixture in most workplaces. Through their ubiquity and impact on how work is done, personal computers (PCs) arguably have transformed the workplace. At the same time, the use and impact of PCs varies across worker groups with different educational and skill levels. As a result, an extensive body of research suggests that the spread of computers, or perhaps increased workplace emphasis on skills that are closely related to computer use, has altered the distribution of wages as well. This process has been marked not so much by abrupt change as by slow and steady change—it is an "evolution" rather than a "revolution."

In this Economic Letter, we use data from five special surveys, covering the period 1984–2001, to examine two key aspects of the computer evolution: the spread of PCs at work and the evolving wage differentials between individuals who use them and those who do not. Although the spread of computers has been relatively uniform across labor force groups, the wage returns associated with computers tilted sharply in favor of the highly educated at the end of our sample frame. This finding appears consistent with the increase in trend productivity growth that occurred around the same time.

Computers and Workers

By the middle to late 1980s, the rapid expansion of computer power embodied in PCs, combined with software that enhanced the overall ease of PC use and application to common business tasks, suggested to researchers and casual observers alike that computers were playing an increasingly important role in the determination of worker productivity and wages. In the first systematic analysis of the impact of computer use on wages, Krueger (1993) used data for the years 1984 and 1989 to estimate standard wage regressions that included controls for computer use at work. As such his estimates reflect wage differences between workers who use and do not use computers, adjusted for other observable differences across such workers that are systematically related to wages as well (age, educational attainment, sex, etc.). His results suggested that workers who used computers earned about 10%–20% more than workers who did not. Moreover, Krueger found that differences between highly educated and less educated workers in the incidence of and returns to computer use could account for 40%–50% of the increased return to education during the 1980s.

Krueger's analysis tied in well with earlier work regarding the contribution of technological change to increased dispersion in the U.S. wage distribution. Since then, wage gaps have widened even further, intensifying the research focus on how equipment like computers can alter the wage distribution by altering the demand for workers with the skills to use such equipment effectively. In a notable recent piece, Autor, Levy, and Murnane (2003) argue that increased computer use can explain most of the increase in nonroutine job tasks, hence the advanced skill content of jobs, during the 1970s, 1980s, and 1990s, and as such can explain most of the increased relative demand for college-educated workers. Although Autor et al. do not directly address the question of computer effects on earnings, their results indirectly suggest that rising computer use also explains a substantial portion of the rising wage gaps between highly educated and less educated workers over these three decades.

PC Diffusion and Wage Effects

Given these existing findings about computer use, skill demand, and wages, an updated assessment of the returns to computer use is in order. To do so, we use the School Enrollment and the Computer and Internet Use Supplements to the federal government's Current Population Survey (CPS). The CPS covers about 60,000 households each month; the resulting sample of individuals serves as a primary source of information on U.S. employment, unemployment, and income patterns. The supplements we use were conducted in 1984, 1989, 1993, 1997, and 2001 (Krueger's work relied on the first two of these). In these surveys, the respondents were asked about computer use at home, work, and school. Although the exact content of the supplements changed over time (for example, Internet use was first addressed in 1997), the question about computer use at work has been essentially unaltered. We rely on samples of about 60,000 employed individuals in each survey to calculate rates of computer use at work; of these, information on wages and related variables is provided for a bit under one-fourth of the sample (about 12,000–14,000 individuals). We restrict the analysis to individuals age 18 to 65.

Figure 1 shows the time series of computer use rates for college graduates, nongraduates, and the combined population. Although the level of computer use is significantly higher for workers with a bachelor's degree (82.3% in 2001) than for those without it (42.7%), the diffusion over time has been relatively

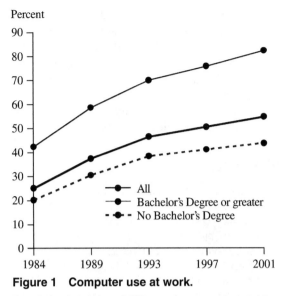

Figure 1   Computer use at work.

Note: Authors' tabulations of CPS computer use supplement data.

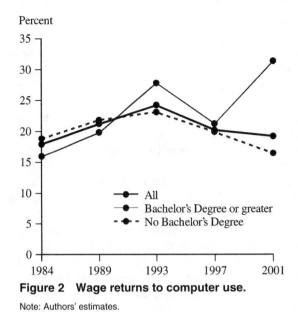

Figure 2   Wage returns to computer use.

Note: Authors' estimates.

uniform across these groups. Additional tabulations show a similar pattern of diffusion when the sample is broken down into narrower educational groups or by additional characteristics such as gender, race, age, geography, and occupation. In percentage terms, we find the sharpest increase in computer use at work for groups with low initial use, including older workers, part-time workers, blue-collar workers, and workers without a high school degree. Moreover, the diffusion of computer use at work slowed after 1993. These patterns are consistent with common models of technology diffusion, in which individuals and firms with the most to gain adopt the new technology first and the rate of diffusion slows as the group that has not yet adopted it shrinks.

To estimate the effect of computer use on wages, we use a regression model similar to Krueger's (1993). The model controls for observable characteristics that are systematically related to wages, including age, education, race, sex, marital status, veteran status, union status, part-time status, and geographic location (region and urban/rural residence), allowing us to isolate the effect of computer use on wages independent of the influence of these other characteristics. Given the potentially important interaction between computer use and education level, we also allow for separate estimates of the return to computer use for individuals who have attained at least a college degree versus those who have not. After applying an appropriate mathematical transformation based on the logarithmic regression function, we obtain the estimated percentage effect of computer use on wages.

Figure 2 plots how the estimated return to computer use at work has changed over time. For the full sample of workers, the return to computer use reached a peak in 1993, with a 24.2% wage advantage over otherwise similar workers. The estimated return to computer use for the full sample declined to 19.2% in 2001. However, the return for individuals with a college or graduate degree increased dramatically during the last period, reaching 31.4% in 2001. This sharp change is surprising, as it

conflicts with the general expectation, based on economic reasoning, that the return to scarce skills (those needed for computer use) should decline as that skill becomes less scarce. As shown in Figure 1, only about one in five college-educated workers did not use computers at work in 2001, which suggests that the skills needed to use computers are far from scarce among the highly educated.

Although the spread of computer skills suggests that the wage returns to computer use should decline, this argument ignores the possibility that production technology is changing rapidly and in ways that support increased rewards for workers with the skills needed for effective use of critical technologies such as computers. Available evidence suggests that rapid expansion of information technology capital (mainly computers and software) in the workplace accounts for a substantial portion of the increased growth in labor productivity during the period 1996–2001 (see for example Oliner and Sichel 2003). While computers make some tasks easier and reduce required skill levels, many advances in computer technology have enabled increasingly sophisticated applications that require complex analytical and evaluative skills. A leading reason to attend college is to acquire such skills. It appears that these skills commanded an increasing premium as workplace computer use intensified between 1997 and 2001, enabling college-educated workers to capture the largest benefits from the spread of computers in the workplace during this period.

Implications

Our findings confirm that workers who use computers earn more than otherwise similar workers who do not. We also find that this effect has been especially large for highly educated workers in recent years. Some researchers, however, have questioned whether the computer effect on wages is fundamentally meaningful in an economic sense. For example, DiNardo and Pischke (1997) have shown that workers who use simple office tools like pencils earn a wage premium similar to that estimated for computer users. This suggests the possibility that the estimated effect of computer use on wages reflects unobserved aspects of skilled workers and their jobs, such that these workers would earn higher wages even if they did not use computers. In other words, DiNardo and Pischke argue that computer use does not have an independent "causal" impact on wages but instead serves as a mediating or auxiliary factor, reflecting related skills that are more fundamental than the direct ability to use a computer.

Nevertheless, an abundance of evidence regarding close relationships among the use of advanced technology and the demand for and wages of skilled workers suggests an important causal role for computers and the skills needed to use them. In that regard, an emphasis on "causal" impacts may be misplaced. For many jobs, effective performance requires computer use, which suggests a close relationship between computer use and critical job skills. In technical parlance, the ability to use a computer probably is not a "sufficient" condition for earning high wages, but it is increasingly a "necessary" condition.

Overall, we interpret the evidence as suggesting that direct computer skills or skills that closely relate to computer use command a substantial premium in the labor market, especially in conjunction with a college degree. It remains to be seen whether the recent increase in returns to computer use for highly educated individuals will continue. However, the trend over the past few years suggests that U.S. productivity growth remains on (or even above) the accelerated growth path that was established during the late 1990s. Going forward, it is likely that these productivity gains will be largely reflected in wage gains for highly educated individuals who use computers, much as was the increase in the relative return to computer use for these individuals during the period 1997–2001.

References

Autor, David H., Frank Levy, and Richard J. Murnane. 2003. "The Skill Content of Recent Technological Change: An Empirical Exploration." *Quarterly Journal of Economics* 118(4) (November), pp. 1279–1333.

DiNardo, John, and Jörn-Steffen Pischke. 1997. "The Return to Computer Use Revisited: Have Pencils Changed the Wage Structure Too?" *Quarterly Journal of Economics* 112(1) (February), pp. 291–303.

Krueger, Alan. 1993. "How Computers Have Changed the Wage Structure: Evidence from Microdata, 1984–1989." *Quarterly Journal of Economics* 108(1) (February), pp. 33–60.

Oliner, Stephen D., and Daniel E. Sichel. 2003. "Information Technology and Productivity: Where Are We Now and Where Are We Going?" *Journal of Policy Modeling* 25(5) (July), pp. 477–503.

Reprinted with permission from the *FRBSF Economic Letter,* No. 2004-19, July 23, 2004, pp. 1–3, by Rob Valletta and Geoffrey MacDonald. The opinions expressed in this article do not necessarily reflect the views of the management of the Federal Reserve Bank of San Francisco, or of the Board of Governors of the Federal Reserve System.

Making Yourself Understood

In an age of technology, writing skills are more important than ever.

STUART CRAINER AND DES DEARLOVE

Business leaders have never had so many ways to communicate: e-mail, teleconferencing, text messaging, instant messaging, websites, weblogs, and satellite linkups—not to mention the old standbys. Your memos and directives and statements now can reach their intended recipients instantly, unfiltered by secretaries. You don't have to wait for a speech to be ghostwritten, scheduled, delivered, and reported; you don't have to wait for your annual-report opening statement to hit stockholders' desks; you don't have to wait for watercooler gossip to distribute a new policy.

But there's a dark lining to the new media and easy communication: It's never been so easy to be misunderstood. Your messages can be overlooked, misinterpreted, misused. Messages and memos that don't make a clear, immediate impact are likely to be lost in the deluge of information flooding the nation's inboxes.

In short, this may be a digital world, but the written word remains the fundamental tool of communication, and being able to write effectively and persuasively—whether creating a business plan, e-mail, report, appraisal, or positioning statement—is a core executive skill. Sure, America's e-mailers routinely infuriate grammarians by omitting punctuation and capitalization, and "like" is pervading spoken English, but when it comes to making yourself understood, language is critical.

While the PR or corporate-communications department is on call to help draft public documents for external audiences, executives must rely on their own literary devices for the multitude of internal documents that are increasingly grist to the management mill. The decline in secretarial support also means that the person who once tweaked the executive's grammar has typically been replaced by dubious spell-checking software. Be it purple or otherwise, the full glory of an executive's prose is likely to be exposed to the organization. If you can barely string together a sentence—let alone construct a pithy argument—your subordinates will know.

"There's a growing misconception that the proliferation of multimedia technology has diminished the need for strong writing skills, and this is just plain false," says Don Spetner, senior VP for global marketing at recruitment firm Korn/Ferry International. "At the core of all communications is content, which is a fancy word for good old-fashioned storytelling or straightforward, concise writing. We take a very critical eye toward a candidate's ability to write, whether it's in their resume, their cover letter, or the various samples of work product that reflect the quality of their skills."

The reality is that executives are spending ever more time writing in one form or another. Literary purists may regard e-mail as writing's poor cousin, but it has become the dominant form of corporate communication. A 2003 survey by Clearswift, the American Management Association, and The ePolicy Institute found that the average U.S. employee spends about one hour and forty-seven minutes a day dealing with e-mail. A Goizueta Business School study puts this even higher: Research among 1,200 managers found that more than half spend at least two hours per day answering e-mail at work, with 30 percent clocking an additional hour or more at home.

As philanthropist and former eBay president Jeff Skoll told us: "It's funny that in an age when e-mail has become such a dominant form of communication, people are writing more than they ever have. They spend so much time in front of the computer these days with written communication, and yet it seems that the art of that communication has declined over the same time."

Managers must increasingly rely on persuasion—and inspiration.

Of course, it's not just e-mail. Techno-savvy executives may keep up their own online commentary/diary weblogs, commonly known as blogs. Blogdex.net, part of an MIT-sponsored research project, estimates the number of blogs at one million and rising fast. And instant messaging, once associated with teenagers and chat rooms, is also rapidly finding its way into corporations—as a business tool. A year ago, Forrester Research estimated instant messaging's penetration in corporations at 45 percent, and the figure has certainly climbed since then. With IBM and Microsoft both adopting and pushing the technology, it is likely to become ubiquitous.

The Good, the Bad, and the Ugly

Business writing is riddled with literary nightmares. Take this job ad—please:

"The Senior Business Analyst will have primary responsibility to elicit, analyze, validate, specify, verify, and manage the real needs of the project stakeholders, including customers and end users. He/she will take the role of functional area manager, where he/she is the primary conduit between the customer community (the functional areas) and the software development and implementation team through which requirements flow."

The classic writing-by-committee approach tends to produce lists of verbs covering every eventuality and to introduce buzzwords such as *stakeholders, customer community,* and *implementation* at every opportunity.

Jargon is endemic and can render straightforward statements completely meaningless. One organization pronounced: "We continually exist to synergistically supply value-added deliverables such that we may continue to proactively maintain enterprise-wide data to stay competitive in tomorrow's world."

Beware of synergy in its many guises and value in its confusing array of valueless forms.

Another common mistake is to completely overlook the audience. A food company's annual report contained the following paragraph: "With the continued growth of hand-held foods, the commercialization of our patented sauce filling cold forming extrusion technology has attracted industry-wide interest for appetiser, hand-held and centre-of-plate applications."

Unfortunately, the audience for the company's annual report—investors, analysts, reporters, and so on—were unlikely to be knowledgeable about extrusion technology, meaning that the impact was therefore less than desired.

And then there is the writing-by-dictation approach, exemplified by that of business guru Tom Peters. At his best, Peters is insightful and enthusiastic. At his worst, his writing practically transcribes his seminar rants word-for-word. Take this example:

"Never—ever!—neglect 'community building.' WOW Projects feed on a growing web of supporters. You must—always!—be in the 'hustling' (suck up!) mode. Sure, your 'substantive'/operational duties could absorb the energy of a platoon. No matter. Make-the-damn-time-to-do-community-building. It's called politics . . . Building Bridges . . . Forging Alliances. Making Friends. Neutralizing Enemies. It's called WOW Project success!"

This is the literary equivalent of shouting. After a while—a short while—its impact wanes.

Luckily, there are plenty of examples of good business writing. Consider the opening of Gary Hamel and C.K. Prahalad's bestseller *Competing for the Future:*

"Look around your company. Look at the high-profile initiatives that have been launched recently. Look at the issues that are preoccupying senior management. Look at the criteria and benchmarks by which progress is being measured. Look at the track record of new business creation. Look into the faces of your colleagues and consider their dreams and fears. Look toward the future and ponder your company's ability to shape that future and regenerate success again and again in the years and decades to come."

This leads off a book about *strategy*. Despite their unpromising subject matter, Hamel and Prahalad write clearly, concisely, and effectively. Note the short sentences, the direct, personal tone, and the accessible language.

Or think of corporate slogans that manage to motivate and drive entire organizations with a few well-chosen words, such as Microsoft's call to arms, "A computer on every desk and in every home."

The quintessence of effective business writing comes in advertising. Whether it is IBM's Think or Budweiser's King of Beers, great ad slogans distill complex messages down to a few well-chosen words. Indeed, the addition of a single word—*new*—before a product routinely boosts sales. Written words are powerful tools. Handle them with care.

—Stuart Crainer and Des Dearlove

The Power of the Pen

The style of business writing is also changing. The rise of e-mail and other electronic channels has coincided with a growing need for executives to ensure that their communication is more direct, more personal. Flatter management structures mean that executives can no longer rely on hierarchical power to get things done. Issuing edicts is less often an option. Instead, managers must increasingly rely on persuasion—and inspiration. This requires a more sophisticated style of communication, one that is directed at the individual and imbued with emotional context as well as content. One survey of sixty executives found that the messages that get attention are those in which the message is personalized, evokes an emotional response, comes from a trustworthy or respected sender, and is concise.

Of course, great leaders have long been aware of this. They realize that while speeches can be inspirational, they are tran-

sient. At best, they are absorbed into an organization's oral history. But written communications—whether they boost morale, announce triumphs, acknowledge disasters, or spur employees to greater productivity—endure.

"Great business leaders, and those who aspire to the status, succeed in communicating well what is important," says Peter Knight, CEO of the London-based CEO Circle network. "Their writing stands out from the whirl of information. It memorably expresses the values, focuses, and thrusts necessary for their companies to prosper. It summarizes and reinforces the message of all their forms of communication."

The rise of instant messaging suggests that worse is to come.

Jack Welch habitually sent handwritten notes to GE workers at all levels, from part-time staff to inner-circle executives. Some even framed his letters, as tangible proof of their leader's appreciation.

From the handwritten to the homespun, Berkshire Hathaway CEO Warren Buffett is another exponent of the corporate missive. Each year, the sage of Omaha pens a letter that has become an annual media event, summarized in *Fortune* and dissected by stock analysts everywhere. Buffett's annual letter to his company's shareholders can move markets and make fortunes.

But it's not just the old guard that appreciates the power of writing. Jeff Skoll insists that writing laid the foundation of the eBay culture. When eBay was launched, many of its employees—in customer service, for example—were highly dispersed around the world, and communication was invariably by e-mail. "How do you build an organization, how do you build a culture, when your primary means of communication is written?" Skoll muses. "I guess the answer is that you have to be very thoughtful, and you have to be clear in your writing style. Both [founder] Pierre Omidyar and I put a lot of effort into getting our points across in writing."

The New Language of Business

While executives may recognize the importance of well-crafted writing, time pressures often conspire against quality. Jargon, obfuscation, poor punctuation, garbled syntax, and tortured grammar are facts of business life. Literary purists would be appalled to see much of what issues forth from executives' pens and keyboards.

Consultant and author Sam Hill, who has taught business-writing skills to fellow consultants at Booz Allen Hamilton and occasionally at Northwestern University, doesn't think business writing is necessarily getting worse. "I think it's always been terrible," he says. "But I do think tools like PowerPoint and e-mail, coupled with the organizational downsizing of secretaries, has given illiterate businesspeople the ability to send babble out unedited, and this has increased visibility of the problem."

E-mail hasn't improved matters. The medium that has done more than any other to elevate the importance of executive writing is often characterized by literary sloppiness and inattention to detail—a fact evidenced, painfully, by perhaps half of the messages currently in your Outlook inbox.

There are several reasons for this. E-mails are inherently more informal than letters, so the author tends to take less care with their construction and language. And dealing with an inbox full of e-mails is time-consuming, so executives, following the dubious example of the world's teenagers, take shortcuts. *Please* becomes *pls,* and it's a slippery slope down. Such linguistic contortions become trendy, and some e-mailers who adopt them out of convenience begin to do so self-consciously, to better appeal to Gen-X workers and managers.

If e-mail has corrupted the English language, the rise of instant messaging suggests that worse is to come. IM skips the drafting-and-rewriting stage that produces well-thought-out letters—indeed, that's the whole point. Together with texting, still a largely European phenomenon, it is the most lax of increasingly casual modes of communication.

"Most of us relax the rules of grammar and spelling when participating in a chat or instant-messaging situation, because the speed of this type of communication makes formatting difficult," observes Deborah Valentine of the Goizueta Business School Writing Center.

But despite the havoc wreaked on the conventions of writing—the use of the lowercase personal pronoun *i,* the wholesale omission of vowels, the mass abbreviation—does any of it really matter? Is this new writing *bad* writing?

John Patrick is president of Attitude LLC and former VP of Internet technology at IBM, where he worked for thirty-five years. Patrick, whose blogpatrickweb.com offers commentary on technology and its impact on business and society, believes effective writing to be a critical skill for the future—as it always has been. But he insists that we shouldn't blame the medium if the message is poorly constructed: "E-mail is a form of writing," he says. "Like with pen and paper, some people are good at it and some are not. Well-written e-mail is powerful and has numerous other positive attributes, including its ability to be sorted, archived, indexed, and so on. I also think blogging is grossly underestimated by just about everyone."

The Return of the Punctuators

A panda goes into a bar and orders some food. After finishing its meal, the panda produces a pistol and fires a shot into the ceiling before heading to the door. The barman catches up with the panda outside and asks for an explanation. "A panda eats, shoots, and leaves," the panda replies, thereby illustrating the power of the humble comma.

The Power of Words

The wrong words in the wrong place can prove costly. In 1983, computer manufacturer Coleco wiped $35 million off its balance sheet in one quarter. How? Customers swamped the company with returns of a new product line. There was nothing wrong with the product—the problem was that the manuals were unreadable. The firm went bust.

In another example, a major oil company sank hundreds of thousands of dollars of R&D into developing a new pesticide only to find that one of its own employees had invented the same product some time ago. Why did no one know? Because the report in which the discovery was written up was such heavy going that no one had bothered to read it all the way through.

One study of military-personnel researchers noted that officers took up to 23 percent less time to read clearly written documents. The researchers concluded that the Navy alone could save over $26.5 million in wasted man-hours if documents were written in a plain, easy-to-understand style. True, the Navy is unlikely to collapse due to a poorly written manual, but last time we checked, $30 million was real money.

—Stuart Crainer and Des Dearlove

There is a burgeoning back-to-basics movement. As we write, Lynne Truss's *Eats, Shoots & Leaves: The Zero Tolerance Approach to Punctuation* remains high on U.K. best-seller lists and is about to be published stateside. The book sold fifty thousand copies in the ten days after U.K. publication, and U.S. rights were sold for a six-figure sum. Proper punctuation is bizarrely fashionable these days.

Good writing, it seems, is reasserting itself. Sixty percent of Goizueta's surveyed executives claimed to prefer standard usage in business communication. This is, Valentine suggests, because traditional grammar and punctuation have developed over many centuries, and for a good reason: to guide the reader. "Paragraphs provide a visual break," she notes, "and punctuation slows or stops the reader at the appropriate place."

Valentine offers three reasons why the shortcuts characteristic of e-mail and instant messaging have little place in executive-level communication. First, not every recipient will understand the acronyms and abbreviations—time saved in the typing will likely be lost in the deciphering. Savvy executives, she says, write with their audiences' needs in mind. Second, clarity is essential and shortcuts can obscure meaning. (Warren Buffett has opined that if he doesn't understand something, he assumes that someone is trying to fool him.) Finally, careless e-mails can prove costly, as brokerage firm Merrill Lynch learned recently: After e-mails revealed analysts offhandedly disparaging stocks they were talking up in public, the embarrassed firm agreed to adopt conflict-of-interest reforms—and to a $100 million fine. It is best to remember, Valentine advises, that e-mail is forever. Bad writing habits, however, needn't be.

The Opportunity

For linguistically challenged executives, help is at hand. Growing recognition among executives of the importance of good writing is manifest in the growth in business-writing instruction. Executives and consultants are increasingly turning to communications experts, including journalists, for help. Says Peter Knight: "The whole purpose of The CEO Circle is to assist CEOs to improve their performance, to achieve greater success. To find better ways of expressing this was why I attended a writing workshop, and it certainly helped me. All I write is colored by my belief that well-written communication of what really matters helps produce the performance that makes companies and leaders great."

There is a profusion of writing coaches, classes, and ghost-writers ready to make sure that the message, whatever it is, is finely phrased. "Our clients—senior executives at technology and financial-services firms—understand the increasing importance of clear, persuasive writing in internal and external communications. The explosion of electronic information distribution over the Internet provides enormous opportunity and an enormous amount of content to be digested," says Write Effect co-founder Lynn Kearney, who has consulted on communications and orga-

---

12 Habits of Effective Writers

1. Get real: Writing is something we do all the time, so don't be precious about it. Think practical rather than poetical.
2. Distill it: What is your message in a nutshell? Effective writers are masters of distillation. Think of advertising slogans and newspaper headlines.
3. Think reader: Know your audience. Tune into your readers' world. What matters to them?
4. Prepare to write: Think before you write rather than writing before you think. Effective writers don't use the writing process to discover what they want to say. They have thought about it already and know what their point is.
5. Find the story: Effective writers—whether composing an e-mail, a report, or a newspaper article—decide on the angle. If you're writing an e-mail, fill in the subject box before you begin.
6. Don't reinvent the wheel: Seek out templates, style guides, and anything else that will make your life easier. Most organizations have these, but employees often are unaware of their existence.
7. Map it out: Good writers start with a structure. They think and write in modules—from the Ten Commandments to the four Ps of marketing.
8. Keep it simple: Effective writers aim for clarity. They know that an average sentence length of about eight words is the most readable and understandable. At fifteen words a sentence, comprehension falls to about 90 percent. At twenty words, it drops to 75 percent. At twenty-five words, it drops to 62 percent.
9. Make an impact: The first line counts no matter what you are writing.
10. Stay fresh: The clearer your mind, the clearer your writing.
11. Make it fit: Edit to length, and ask: Does it meet the brief? Does it fulfill its purpose?
12. Deliver and follow through: Make sure that what you have written arrives safely. Otherwise you have wasted your time.

—Stuart Crainer and Des Dearlove

---

nizational issues for more than two decades. "In years past, we have worked with corporate training and development managers to create business-writing courses. We now get calls directly from senior business-unit managers with specific requests for highly customized programs that include not just content but also guidance on how to package ideas that grab readers' attention. Increased competition for readers—clients—has alerted managers to the need for improved writing quality as a means to build and maintain client relationships."

Writer's block is a luxury that executives cannot afford.

Our own experience training executives and MBA students in effective business writing confirms that many veteran and fledgling managers recognize their deficiencies in this area. Many have similar issues and problems. For example, we are often asked about how to create effective messages for different audiences—say, internal and external stakeholders—and how to structure and present information in the most compelling way. Other requests include how to overcome blank-page syndrome or first-paragraph hell. Writer's block, we helpfully tell course participants, is a luxury that executives cannot afford.

While most executives recognize the difference between good and bad writing, they tend to accept poor writing—including their own—as a fact of business life. Yet improving the quality of writing is actually much easier, and less time-consuming, than people imagine. "Great writing is a state of mind as much as anything," says Gerry Griffin of the London-based Business Communication Forum, a media training organization. "Once I was reminded of the basic characteristics of good and bad writing, my own writing improved. Instead of taking it for granted, I began to think about writing more carefully, to think about my audience and so on."

Self-awareness about writing makes a significant difference to the quality of written output—and, potentially, your career. "Good writing is a wonderful way to differentiate yourself inside a company," Sam Hill says. "Back when I was competing with all those other aggressive young associates at Booz Allen, all of us in the same charcoal-gray Jos. A. Bank suits and faux Hermes ties, I used the ability to express myself clearly to get myself noticed. I used to work for hours at home secretly writing and rewriting reports until they were logical and stylistic masterpieces. The next afternoon, I'd drop them on my partner's desk casually and do my best to create the implication that I'd just dashed them off—and hopefully create the impression in his mind that I was effortlessly brilliant. It must have worked: I made partner." The write stuff works.

STUART CRAINER and **DES DEARLOVE** are the founders of *Suntop Media*. Their last article was *"Windfall Economics,"* the July/August 2003 cover story.

E-Monitoring in the Workplace

Privacy, Legislation, and Surveillance Software

Protecting the corporation while respecting employee privacy—an old puzzle made more complex with new software.

G. Daryl Nord, Tipton F. McCubbins, and Jeretta Horn Nord

"Through advanced computer technology, employers can now continuously monitor employees' actions without the employee even knowing he or she is being 'watched.' The computer's eye is unblinking and ever-present. Sophisticated software allows every minute of the day to be recorded and evaluated [1]."

Increasingly, personnel in institutions worldwide use email and the Internet on a daily basis at work. This daily reliance and dependency on technology has created new issues with respect to employee privacy in the workplace and has added new stress to the employer-employee relationship. Employee privacy, long considered a basic right, is often taken for granted by employees. However, as a result of technological monitoring, this view may be naïve.

According to the annual survey, *Workplace Monitoring and Surveillance Survey 2001* conducted by the American Management Association, more than three-quarters of all major U.S. firms (nearly double the 1997 survey results) are recording and/or reviewing the email messages, telephone calls, Internet connections, and computer files of their employees. Workplace monitoring has existed for a long time in one form or another and will undoubtedly continue to proliferate and become increasingly sophisticated as technology advances. This article examines the employer/employee workplace privacy relationship, identifies the existing federal and state law governing workplace privacy, and discusses the rapidly developing monitoring software market.

Workplace Privacy

Most U.S. citizens are accustomed to the expectation of privacy. Privacy, as defined by the Merriam-Webster dictionary is a: the quality or state of being apart from company or observation; b: freedom from unauthorized intrusion <one's right to *privacy*>. But in the workplace, to what degree can workers expect privacy and protection from observation and unauthorized intrusion? Workers may sometimes expect they have the same privacy rights at the office as they have at home. Others may assume that since they have an account number and password on their software and email system their individual privacy is protected and secure.

Do you know anyone who occasionally takes a moment out of his or her day to check a stock quote, sports score, or movie listing online at work? As of January 2002, approximately 55 million U.S. adults accessed the Internet at work, up from 43 million in March 2000. Fifty-five percent of those with Internet access at work went online on a typical day in 2001, compared to 50% in 2000, and many were going online more frequently throughout the day than they had in 2001 [10]. More than 72% of Internet users do more than just surf the Web. Popular Internet activities include instant messaging, downloading music, and watching video clips [9]. In another Internet work-related study, Yankelovich Partners discovered that 62% of workers go online at work for personal reasons at least once a day, while about 20% do so 10 or more times a day. In a 2002 study by the Computer Security Institute (CSI), 78% of polled enterprises reported employee abuse of Internet access privileges by workers, including downloading pirated software or pornography, shopping on the Internet, and inappropriate use of email systems. These studies readily show the escalating magnitude of non-work related Internet use at work.

Employers want to make sure their employees are using company time productively and not creating a legal liability for their business as a result of harassing or offensive communications. A recent study revealed that 10% of U.S. companies have received subpoenas resulting from employee email [5]. In addition, employers have security concerns relating to the intentional or accidental sending of sensitive data via email attachments as well as the ongoing concern of viruses entering the business from outside communications. Consequently, employers are monitoring employee's computer and Internet access to a greater degree than in the past. As illustrated in Table 1, the American Management Association surveys conducted from 1999 to 2001 and again in 2005, exposed the growing trend of employer monitoring of employees' computer files, email messaging, and Internet connections [2].

Table 1 Survey Results by AMA on Employee Monitoring

	1999	2000	2001	2005
Storage and review of computer files	21.4%	30.8%	36.1%	50%
Storage and review of email messages	27%	38.1%	46.5%	55%
Monitoring Internet connections	NA	54.1%	62.8%	76%

According to another recent AMA survey, the 2003 E-mail Rules, Policies and Practices Survey, over half (52%) of employers monitor email. Three-fourths of the 1,100 employers surveyed have put written email policies in place. And 22% have terminated an employee for violating email policy [3].

Federal Privacy Legislation in the Workplace

Most U.S.-based employees assume they have a constitutional right to privacy. However, constitutional rights to privacy are generally inferred through the U.S. Constitution's Fourth Amendment's rights to freedom from unreasonable search and seizure. These freedoms usually apply only to state actions. In an employment context, state actions are fairly narrowly limited to protecting federal, state, and municipal employees. Private-sector employees must look elsewhere for protection. Possible sources for such protection from employer snooping include federal legislation and state common law tort actions such as invasion of privacy [4].

The primary piece of federal legislation suggesting employee privacy interest is the Electronic Communications Privacy Act (ECPA). However, there are three exceptions under the ECPA that effectively eliminate any substantial expectation of privacy an employee might have with respect to his/her employer.

Workplace monitoring has existed for a long time in one form or another and will undoubtedly continue to proliferate and become increasingly sophisticated as technology advances.

The first of the ECPA exceptions is the "provider exception." If an employer actually owns and is providing the telephone, email, or Internet services to the employee being monitored, there is little doubt that the employer is protected from employee privacy claims. However, if the employer is merely providing email services through a third-party Internet provider, it is not as clear that the employer would enjoy the same protection. Nevertheless, given the fact the employer is "providing" the provider, coupled with the generous interpretation that most courts have granted employers, there is good reason to believe that even these providers of providers would enjoy protection from employee privacy suits [7].

The second exception is the "ordinary course of business" exception. It really provides an exception to the definition of an electronic device, and therefore excludes the employer's monitoring from the ECPA and the employee protections provided therein. Under this exception the employer may monitor employee communications to ensure such legitimate business objectives as assuring quality control, preventing sexual harassment, and preventing unauthorized use of equipment, such as excessive telephone or email usage.

However, the "course of business" language also implies a limitation on the extent of monitoring in the event the employer discovers he has accessed a personal conversation. In monitoring telephone conversations it is well established that employers can continue to listen only for so long as it takes to determine the conversation is in fact personal. At that point, the employer must cease the surveillance. The case setting the standard for this limitation is a 1983 case dealing with the use of the telephone. A thorough examination of the standard as it applies to email usage has not yet occurred, but a similar application should probably be expected. However, at least one case has suggested that no monitoring of an employee's personal email may be allowed without prior notification [8].

The third exception is the "consent" exception. If at least one party to the communication is either the party who intercepts the communication or gives consent to the interception then the ECPA has not been violated. The "consent" exception apparently applies even when the sender of the intercepted communication has been assured that all email communications would remain confidential and privileged. In *Smyth v. The Pillsbury Company,* Smyth sent his supervisor emails that contained inappropriate and unprofessional comments from Smyth's home computer. The supervisor received the email over Pillsbury's email system. The email included such statements such as "kill the backstabbing . . . " and referred to the company's holiday party as the "Jim Jones Koolaid affair." At a later date the company intercepted these email messages and terminated Smyth's employment based upon their content.

Although the court did not explain exactly how the interception took place, the email messages were apparently retrieved from storage with the supervisor's consent. As a result of the consent, even the prior promise of confidentiality did not provide the employee with privacy protection.

State Privacy Case Law

The common law tort of invasion of privacy is recognized by most states. The Restatement (Second) of Torts §652B defines invasion of privacy as: " . . . intentionally intruding, physically or otherwise, upon the solitude or seclusion of another . . . , if the intrusion would be highly offensive to a reasonable person." Employees have tried to use this tort as a protection for privacy in the workplace. Although it shows some potential for privacy protection, it has generally stumbled over two problems. The first is that the employee must have a reasonable expectation of privacy, and the second is that the intrusion would be highly offensive to the reasonable person.

Along with the ever-increasing exploitation of technology in the workplace has come the capability for employers to see and measure nearly every aspect of company usage.

In *McLaren v. Microsoft* (1999), Microsoft made available to McLaren, as part of his employment, use of an email system owned and administered by Microsoft. McLaren had the right and ability to store email he received either in the server-based "inbox" or in a "personal folder" protected by a personal store password. As part of a harassment investigation, Microsoft decrypted McLaren's personal store password and broke into his personal folder even though it had been specifically requested by McLaren not to do so.

McLaren argued that the password-protected personal folder was basically the same as a locked storage locker provided by a company for employees to store personal items in while at work. It has long been accepted that employees have a legitimate expectation of privacy with regard to such lockers. However, the court rejected this argument. It stated that because the email was first received and stored in the "inbox," which was subject to inspection, McLaren could have no expectation of privacy simply by moving it to a protected folder. How this is different from a telephone call that can only be monitored long enough to determine if it is of a business or personal nature the court did not explain. True, in this case, the fact that the email messages were pertinent to a harassment investigation would make them subject to legitimate business scrutiny. However, the court did not seem to rely on this fact in declaring a blanket open season on email monitoring. Second, although it is possible to distinguish between illicit information being carried through public space from the front door of a business to an employee's locked storage locker and an email message sitting in an inbox before being transferred to a protected personal folder, such distinctions are not so obvious as to deny a need for recognition. However the court seemed sufficiently confident in its analysis that it did not address the issue.

In determining that the intrusion was not highly offensive, the court properly recognized the importance of whether the intrusion was justified. The fact that McLaren was under investigation, and that he had notified Microsoft that the email was relevant to that investigation, clearly support the court's finding that Microsoft's actions were justified. Therefore, they were not highly offensive even though the actions had been specifically forbidden by McLaren and led to his dismissal.

Company Electronic Communications Policy

In a case [11] in which the California Appellant Court ruled in favor of the employer strictly on the basis of a signed electronic communications policy, the court stated that at a minimum the policy should contain a statement that:

1. Electronic communication facilities provided by the company are owned by the company and should be used solely for company business.
2. The company will monitor all employee Internet and email usage. It should state who may review the information, the purposes for which the information may be used, and that the information may be stored on a separate computer [6, 7].
3. The company will keep copies of the Internet and email passwords.
4. The existence of a separate password is not an assurance of the confidentiality of the communication or other "protected" material.

5. The sending of any discriminatory, offensive, or unprofessional message or content is strictly prohibited.
6. The accessing of any Internet site that contains offensive of discriminatory content is prohibited.
7. The posting of personal opinions on the Internet using the company's access is strictly prohibited. This is particularly true of, but not limited to, opinions that are political or discriminatory in nature.
8. Although not included in the court's list, the policy should clearly state potential repercussions to the employee for violating the policy [4].

Legally, these requirements are considered minimum standards that a sound policy should meet. They should be clear and unequivocal, and they should be read and signed by each employee. However, the employer should also remain aware of the employee's normal human desire for reasonable amounts of privacy. Therefore the employer should try to minimize unnecessary intrusion into this privacy expectation in order to reduce the negative impact on employee morale.

Monitoring Software

Along with the ever-increasing exploitation of technology in the workplace has come the capability for employers to see and measure nearly every aspect of company computer usage. The dilemma that employers must resolve is how to balance the obvious benefits of employee use of technological tools with the risks inherent in providing those tools to employees. As stated earlier, many employers have sought to achieve this balance by electronically monitoring the use that their employees make of email, the Internet, and other computer-related activities.

Monitoring software allows employers to see, measure, and manage employees' computer systems, monitors, disks, software, email, and Web and Internet access. The software can automatically archive all collected information into a corporate network server for review at a later time. The list in Table 2 illustrates the many capabilities of typical monitoring software readily available on the market today by companies such as Spectorsoft and DynaComm.

Conclusion

E-monitoring and employee workplace privacy are issues that will continue to present questions and problems for some time to come. In addition, it looks as if there will be ongoing efforts to balance employee workplace privacy with the need for employers to manage and protect company resources from non-productive, non-work related activities. Federal and state legislation governing monitoring and workplace privacy will undoubtedly continue to evolve and be tested in the court systems.

There are many legitimate reasons for organizations to want to know what is occurring on their computer systems. Those reasons range from workplace harassment, to loss of productivity, and even to company sabotage. Therefore, it is easy to understand why it would be prudent for companies to have such a strong incentive to find a healthy balance between employee privacy rights and organizational concerns.

Table 2 Surveillance Capabilities of Monitoring Software on the Market Today

The workplace end user types any keystroke in any window on his/her remote PC, that text appears on the network administrator's screen in real time or archived to a corporate server.

Typed text that is monitored may include email messages, online chat conversations, documents, passwords and all other keystrokes.

The network administrator can view the actual screen of the workplace desktops being monitored.

Internet usage can be monitored in real time and a log file recording of all Internet activity can be made.

A spy module can see and list software running on the remote PC and can view in real time the software applications and run executions.

A record and activity log for all workstations on the local or shared network location can be produced.

Monitoring software provides the ability to take snapshots of a remote PC screen or active window in specified time intervals and save them on the local or shared network location.

The workplace user's system can be turned off, restarted, and actually logged completely off the network.

The network administrator can run programs and execute commands on remote computers, open Web pages or documents, send instant messages for remote users, and terminate remote processes.

Files can be readily copied including logs and screenshots from the desktop computers. The administrator can have the same file access permissions, as a current user has on the workplace computer.

Multiple employee computers can simultaneously be monitored from a single workstation in the LAN.

Workplace surveillance software that runs on monitored computers is hidden and difficult for an employee to locate or even know that the software is present and monitoring their every keystroke. The monitoring software usually cannot be terminated without the network administrator's permission.

References

1. American Civil Liberties Union (ACLU). Workplace Rights on Electronic Monitoring, ACLU online archives; archive.aclu.org/issues/worker/legkit2.html.
2. American Management Association, AMA Research: Workplace Monitoring and Surveillance, 1999, 2000, 2001 and 2005; www.amanet.org/research/archive_2001_1999.htm.
3. American Management Association, Survey on Workplace E-Mail Reveals Disasters in the Making, May 28, 2003; www.amanet.org/press/amanews/Email_Survey2003.htm.
4. Bloom, E., Schachter, M., and Steelman, E. Justice in a Changing World: Competing Interests in the Post 9-11 Workplace: The New Line Between Privacy and Safety. 29 Wm. Mitchell L. Rev. 897 (2003).
5. Crimmins, J. Even federal judges come under surveillance when online. *Chicago Daily Law Bulletin 147,* 159 (Aug. 14, 2001).
6. *Deal v. Spears,* 980 F.2d 1153, 1155-1157 (8th Cir. 1992).
7. DiLuzio, S. Workplace E-Mail: It's Not as Private as You Might Think. 25 Del. J. Corp. L. 741 (2000).
8. Kopp, K. Electronic Communications in the Workplace: E-Mail Monitoring and the Right of Privacy. 8 Seaton Hall Const. L. J. 861 (1998).
9. Neilson//NetRankings, U.S. Online Population Internet Use. (Dec. 18, 2002); www.nielsen-netratings.com/pr/pr_021218.pdf.
10. Pew Internet & American Life, Getting Serious Online: As Americans Gain Experience, They Use the Web More at Work, Write Emails with More Significant Content, Perform More Online Transactions, and Pursue More Serious Activities, (Mar. 3, 2002); www.pewinternet.org/reports/toc.asp?Report555.
11. *TBG Insurance Services Corporation v. The Superior Court of Los Angeles Co.;* Robert Zieminski, Real Party in Interest, 96 Cal. App. 4th 443; 117 Cal. Rptr. 2d 155 (Cal. App. 2002).

G. DARYL NORD (daryl.nord@okstate.edu) is a professor of Management Science & Information Systems in the William S. Spears School of Business, at Oklahoma State University, Stillwater, OK. **TIPTON F. MCCUBBINS** (tipton.mccubbins@okstate.edu) is an associate professor of Legal Studies in Business in the William S. Spears School of Business, at Oklahoma State University, Stillwater, OK. **JERETTA HORN NORD** (jeretta.nord@okstate.edu) is a professor of Management Science & Information Systems and Associate Dean for Undergraduate Programs in the William S. Spears School of Business, at Oklahoma State University, Stillwater, OK.

From *Communications of the ACM,* 49(8), August 2006, pp. 73–77. Copyright © 2006 by Association for Computing Machinery, Inc. Reprinted by permission.

UNIT 4

Computers, People, and Social Participation

Unit Selections

Key Points to Consider

- The overview to this unit mentions de Tocqueville's observation that Americans tend to form civic associations and Putnam's argument that this tendency is declining. Do you think that computing has played any part in the decline? What does Putnam say? What do other scholars say about Putnam's work?

- Social scientists sometimes say that the likelihood of participating in civic life declines ten per cent for every ten miles one commutes. What is the source for this figure? Is there a similar figure relating civic participation to daily minutes spent on-line?

- Do you agree that "E-mail Is for Old People"?

- Who uses Internet dating services? Can you generalize about age, income, ethnicity, education, or religion?

- Find out more about the advance fee fraud. Do you think John Warner ("The Perfect Mark") should have gone to prison?

Student Web Site

www.mhcls.com/online

Internet References

Further information regarding these Web sites may be found in this book's preface or online.

Adoption Agencies
  http://www.amrex.org/

Alliance for Childhood: Computers and Children
  http://www.allianceforchildhood.net/projects/computers/index.htm

The Core Rules of Netiquette
  http://www.albion.com/netiquette/corerules.html

How the Information Revolution Is Shaping Our Communities
  http://www.plannersweb.com/articles/bla118.html

SocioSite: Networks, Groups, and Social Interaction
  http://www2.fmg.uva.nl/sociosite/topics/interaction.html

That early and astute observer of American culture, Alexis de Tocqueville (1805—1859), had this to say about the proclivity of Americans to form civic associations:

> Americans of all ages, all conditions, and all dispositions constantly form associations . . . , The Americans make associations to give entertainments, to found seminaries, to build inns, to construct churches, to diffuse books, to send missionaries to the antipodes; in this manner they found hospitals, prisons, and schools. If it is proposed to inculcate some truth or to foster some feeling by the encouragement of a great example, they form a society. Wherever at the head of some new undertaking you see the government in France, or a man of rank in England, in the United States you will be sure to find an associa-tion . . . ,. The first time I heard in the United States that a hundred thousand men had bound themselves publicly to abstain from spriritous liquors, it appeared to me more like a joke than a serious engagement, and I did not at once perceive why these temperate citizens could not content themselves with drinking water by their own firesides . . . ,. Nothing, in my opinion is more deserving of our attention than the intellectual and moral associations of America . . . ,. In democratic countries the science of association is the mother of science; the progress of all the rest depends upon the progress it has made (Tocqueville, 1945: v. 2, pp. 114–118)

De Tocqueville laid this tendency squarely at the feet of democracy. If all men—we're talking about the first half of the 19th century here—are equal before the law, then to do any civic good requires that these equal, but individually powerless, men band together.

A century and a half later, we have the technical means to communicate almost instantly, almost effortlessly across great distances. But we are banding together less. In 1995, Robert D. Putnam made the news with an article, later expanded into a book, called *Bowling Alone* (Putnam, 2000). He argued that the civil associations de Tocqueville had noticed so long ago were breaking down. Americans were not joining the PTA, the Boy Scouts, the local garden club, or bowling leagues in their former numbers. Putnam discovered that although more people are bowling than ever, participation in leagues was down by 40 percent since 1980. The consequences for a functioning democ-racy are severe.

Although the articles in this unit do not directly address the idea of civic participation, that topic is the necessary glue that holds them together. Do computers assist or detract from civic life? Another French social observer, Emile Durkheim (1858–1917), argued that a vital society must have members who feel a sense of community. Community is easily evident in pre-indus-trial societies where kinship ties, shared religious belief, and custom reinforce group identity and shared values. Not so in

Tom Grill/CORBIS

modern societies, particularly the United States, where a mobile population commutes long distances and retreats each evening to the sanctity and seclusion of individual homes. Contemporary visitors to the United States are struck by the cultural cafeteria available to Americans. They find a dizzying array of religions beliefs, moral and philosophical perspectives, modes of social interaction, entertainment venues and, now, networked com-puters. One need only observe a teenager frantically instant-messaging her friends from a darkened bedroom to know that while computer technology has surely given us great things, it has taken away something as well. The capacity to maintain friendships without face-to-face contact, the ability to construct a computer profile that edits anything not in line with one's inter-ests, seems to push society a step closer to self-interested individualism.

On the other hand, one can argue that the new communica-tions technologies permit relationships that were never before possible. To cite a large example, the organization moveon.org organized many thousands of people, in a matter of weeks, and entirely over the Internet, to oppose the invasion of Iraq in the spring of 2003. Immigration, always a wrenching experience, is less wrenching now, since immigrants to the United States can be in daily touch with their families across the globe. Or consider how the virtual bazaar, eBay, surely one of the extraordinary aspects of the Internet, puts Americans in touch with Japanese, Latvians, Montenegrans, peoples whom we might never have known. Recall Postman: "technology giveth and technology taketh away."

What technology seems to have "giveth" in the past few years is the ability to find love online. Christine Rosen's "Romance in the Information Age" provides a critical look at a practice that is not only becoming common but lucrative, as well. Revenue's from online dating services exceeded $302 million in 2002 with sites like Jdate.com (for Jewish dates), CatholicSingles.com and HappyBuddhist.com. Eager to distinguish themselves from the competition, some Internet dating sites have turned to social scientists to hone their matching skills. Chemistry.com, for instance, uses the services of Dr. Helen Fischer, a Rutgers anthropologist whose "research focuses on the brain physiology of romantic love and sexuality." Dr. Fisher tells us that if your ring finger is longer than your index finger you were exposed to elevated levels of fetal testosterone and are likely a director type as opposed to a negotiator (see "How Do I Love Thee").

The sad case of John Worley ("The Perfect Mark") is a cautionary tale for those who trust too completely in their on-line communities. An African con artist persuaded Worley, a Massachusetts psychotherapist, to join a money-laundering scheme. What was illegal at face value was actually a swindle. Most of us have received similar e-mails: "With regards to your trustworthiness and reliability, I decided to seek your assistance in transferring some money out of South Africa into your country, for onward dispatch and investment." Most of us have the good sense and cynicism to hit the delete button. But at fifty-five, Worley had not come of age with the Internet. Though he's a decorated war veteran, Worley appears disarmingly naïve. What has technology taken here, beyond money and two years of a man's life? And what has it given in return?

It should surprise no one that entering freshmen, who grew up using the Internet, should turn to university-sponsored blogs to ease the transition to college life. "Back-to-School Blogging" tells the story of blogs at Davidson College and Washington University. Here's a sample posting that some faculty might take issue with:

> Squirrelhanded (August 15, 10:18 P.M.): here's a piece of advice . . . .
> If you have a choice between having an incredible talk with a good friend in the hallway or getting 3 extra hours of sleep . . . take the talk. If it's between ANOTHER 5-point math assignment and a midnight magical mystery trek through town . . . go crazy. Have a good time.
> don't get me wrong, academics are priority. They're the reason we're all here in the first place . . . but choose your memories. Make them lasting ones.

Once they arrive on campus, these same freshmen seem to be turning their backs on e-mail, much to the dismay of colleges who are increasingly using e-mail as a cost-saving measure (see "E-Mail is for Old People").

References

Tocqueville, Alexis de. (1945). *Democracy in America.* New York: Vintage Books, 1945.
Putnam, Robert D. (2000). *Bowling Alone: The Collapse and Revival of American Community.*
New York: Simon & Schuster, 2000.

Romance in the Information Age

Christine Rosen

When Samuel F. B. Morse sent his first long-distance telegraph message in 1844, he chose words that emphasized both the awe and apprehension he felt about his new device. "What hath God wrought?" read the paper tape message of dots and dashes sent from the U.S. Capitol building to Morse's associates in Baltimore. Morse proved prescient about the potential scope and significance of his technology. In less than a decade, telegraph wires spread throughout all but one state east of the Mississippi River; by 1861, they spanned the continent; and by 1866, a transatlantic telegraph cable connected the United States to Europe.

The telegraph, and later, the telephone, forever changed the way we communicate. But the triumph wrought by these technologies was not merely practical. Subtly and not so subtly, these technologies also altered the range of ways we reveal ourselves. Writing in 1884, James Russell Lowell wondered a bit nervously about the long-term consequences of the "trooping of emotion" that the electric telegraph, with its fragmented messages, encouraged. Lowell and others feared that the sophisticated new media we were devising might alter not just how we communicate, but how we feel.

Rapid improvement in communication technologies and the expansion of their practical uses continue unabated. Today, of course, we are no longer tethered to telegraph or telephone wires for conversation. Cell phones, e-mail, Internet chatrooms, two-way digital cameras—we can talk to anyone, anywhere, including those we do not know and never see. The ethical challenges raised by these new communication technologies are legion, and not new. Within a decade of the invention of the telephone, for example, we had designed a way to wiretap and listen in on the private conversations flourishing there. And with the Internet, we can create new or false identities for ourselves, mixing real life and personal fantasy in unpredictable ways. The "confidence man" of the nineteenth century, with his dandified ruses, is replaced by the well-chosen screen name and false autobiography of the unscrupulous Internet dater. Modern philosophers of technology have studied the ethical quandaries posed by communication technologies—questioning whether our view of new technologies as simply means to generally positive ends is naïve, and encouraging us to consider whether our many devices have effected subtle transformations on our natures.

But too little consideration has been given to the question of how our use of these technologies influences our emotions. Do certain methods of communication flatten emotional appeals, promote immediacy rather than thoughtful reflection, and encourage accessibility and transparency at the expense of necessary boundaries? Do our technologies change the way we feel, act, and think?

Love and E-Mail

There is perhaps no realm in which this question has more salience than that of romantic love. How do our ubiquitous technologies—cell phones, e-mail, the Internet—impact our ability to find and experience love? Our technical devices are of such extraordinary practical use that we forget they are also increasingly the primary medium for our emotional expression. The technologies we use on a daily basis do not merely change the ways, logistically, we pursue love; they are in some cases transforming the way we think and feel about what, exactly, it is we should be pursuing. They change not simply how we find our beloved, but the kind of beloved we hope to find. In a world where men and women still claim to want to find that one special person—a "soul mate"—to spend their life with, what role can and should we afford technology and, more broadly, science, in their efforts?

Love After Courtship

The pursuit of love in its modern, technological guise has its roots in the decline of courtship and is indelibly marked by that loss. Courtship as it once existed—a practice that assumed adherence to certain social conventions, and recognition of the differences, physical and emotional, between men and women—has had its share of pleased obituarists. The most vigorous have been feminists, the more radical of whom appear to take special delight in quelling notions of romantic love. Recall Andrea Dworkin's infamous equation of marriage and rape, or Germaine Greer's terrifying rant in *The Female Eunuch:* "Love, love, love—all the wretched cant of it, masking egotism, lust, masochism, fantasy under a mythology of sentimental postures, a welter of self-induced miseries and joys, blinding and masking the essential personalities in the frozen gestures of courtship, in the kissing and the dating and the desire, the compliments and the quarrels which vivify its barrenness." Much of this work is merely an unpersuasive attempt to swaddle basic human bitterness in the language of female empowerment. But such sentiments have had their effect on our culture's understanding of courtship.

More thoughtful chroniclers of the institution's demise have noted the cultural and technological forces that challenged courtship in the late nineteenth and early twentieth century, eroding the power of human chaperones, once its most effective guardians. As Leon Kass persuasively argued in an essay in *The Public Interest,* the obstacles to courtship "spring from the very heart of liberal democratic society and of modernity altogether." The automobile did more for unsupervised sexual exploration than many technologies in use today, for example, and by twentieth century's end, the ease and availability of effective contraceptive devices, especially the birth control pill, had freed men and women to pursue sexual experience without the risk of pregnancy. With technical advances came a shift in social mores. As historian Jacques Barzun has noted, strict manners gave way to informality, "for etiquette is a barrier, the casual style an invitation."

Whether one laments or praises courtship's decline, it is clear that we have yet to locate a successful replacement for it—evidently it is not as simple as hustling the aging coquette out the door to make way for the vigorous debutante. On the contrary, our current courting practices—if they can be called that—yield an increasing number of those aging coquettes, as well as scores of unsettled bachelors. On college campuses, young men and women have long since ceased formally dating and instead participate in a "hooking up" culture that favors the sexually promiscuous and emotionally disinterested while punishing those intent on commitment. Adults hardly fare better: as the author of a report released in January by the Chicago Health and Social Life Survey told CNN, "on average, half your life is going to be in this single and dating state, and this is a big change from the 1950s." Many men and women now spend the decades of their twenties and thirties sampling each other's sexual wares and engaging in fits of serial out-of-wedlock domesticity, never finding a marriageable partner.

In the 1990s, books such as *The Rules,* which outlined a rigorous and often self-abnegating plan for modern dating, and observers such as Wendy Shalit, who called for greater modesty and the withholding of sexual favors by women, represented a well-intentioned, if doomed, attempt to revive the old courting boundaries. Cultural observers today, however, claim we are in the midst of a new social revolution that requires looking to the future for solutions, not the past. "We're in a period of dramatic change in our mating practices," Barbara Dafoe Whitehead told a reporter for *U.S. News & World Report* recently. Whitehead, co-director of the National Marriage Project at Rutgers University, is the author of *Why There are No Good Men Left,* one in a booming mini-genre of books that offer road maps for the revolution. Whitehead views technology as one of our best solutions—Isolde can now find her Tristan on the Internet (though presumably with a less tragic finale). "The traditional mating system where people met someone in their neighborhood or college is pretty much dead," Whitehead told

CBS recently. "What we have is a huge population of working singles who have limited opportunities to go through some elaborate courtship."

Although Whitehead is correct in her diagnosis of the problem, neither she nor the mavens of modesty offer a satisfactory answer to this new challenge. A return to the old rules and rituals of courtship—however appealing in theory—is neither practical nor desirable for the majority of men and women. But the uncritical embrace of technological solutions to our romantic malaise—such as Internet dating—is not a long-term solution either. What we need to do is create new boundaries, devise better guideposts, and enforce new mores for our technological age. First, however, we must understand the peculiar challenges to romantic success posed by our technologies.

Full Disclosure

Although not the root cause of our romantic malaise, our communication technologies are at least partly culpable, for they encourage the erosion of the boundaries that are necessary for the growth of successful relationships. Our technologies enable and often promote two detrimental forces in modern relationships: the demand for total transparency and a bias toward the over-sharing of personal information.

To Google or Not to Google

With the breakdown of the old hierarchies and boundaries that characterized courtship, there are far fewer opportunities to glean information about the vast world of strangers we encounter daily. We can little rely on town gossips or networks of extended kin for background knowledge; there are far fewer geographic boundaries marking people from "the good part of town"; no longer can we read sartorial signals, such as a well-cut suit or an expensive shoe, to place people as in earlier ages. This is all, for the most part, a good thing. But how, then, do people find out about each other? Few self-possessed people with an Internet connection could resist answering that question with one word: Google. "To google"—now an acceptable if ill-begotten verb—is the practice of typing a person's name into an Internet search engine to find out what the world knows and says about him or her. As one writer confessed in the *New York Observer,* after meeting an attractive man at a midtown bar: "Like many of my twenty-something peers in New York's dating jungle, I have begun to use Google.com, as well as other online search engines, to perform secret background checks on potential mates. It's not perfect, but it's a discreet way of obtaining important, useless and sometimes bizarre information about people in Manhattan—and it's proven to be as reliable as the scurrilous gossip you get from friends."

That is—not reliable at all. What Google and other Internet search engines provide is a quick glimpse—a best and worst list—of a person, not a fully drawn portrait. In fact, the transparency promised by technologies such as Internet search engines is a convenient substitute for something we used to assume would develop over time, but which fewer people today seem willing to cultivate patiently: trust. As the single Manhattanite writing in the *Observer* noted, "You never know. He seemed nice that night, but he could be anyone from a rapist or murderer to a brilliant author or championship swimmer."

In sum, transparency does not guarantee trust. It can, in fact, prove effective at eroding it—especially when the expectation of transparency and the available technological tools nudge the suspicious to engage in more invasive forms of investigation or surveillance. One woman I interviewed, who asked that her name not be revealed, was suspicious that her live-in boyfriend of two years was unfaithful when her own frequent business trips took her away from home. Unwilling to confront him directly with her doubts, she turned to a technological solution. Unbeknownst to him, she installed a popular brand of "spyware" on his computer, which recorded every keystroke he made and took snapshots of his screen every three minutes—information that the program then e-mailed to her for inspection. "My suspicions were founded," she said, although the revelation was hardly good news. "He was spending hours online looking at porn, and going to 'hook-up' chatrooms seeking sex with strangers. I even tracked his ATM withdrawals to locations near his scheduled meetings with other women."

She ended the relationship, but remains unrepentant about deploying surveillance technology against her mate. Considering the amount of information she could find out about her partner by merely surfing the Internet, she rationalized her use of spyware as just one more tool—if a slightly more invasive one—at the disposal of those seeking information about another person. As our technologies give us ever-greater power to uncover more about each other, demand for transparency rises, and our expectations of privacy decline.

The other destructive tendency our technologies encourage is over-sharing—that is, revealing too much, too quickly, in the hope of connecting to another person. The opportunities for instant communication are so ubiquitous—e-mail, instant messaging, chatrooms, cell phones, Palm Pilots, BlackBerrys, and the like—that the notion of making ourselves unavailable to anyone is unheard of, and constant access a near-requirement. As a result, the multitude of outlets for expressing ourselves has allowed the level of idle chatter to reach a depressing din. The inevitable result is a repeal of the reticence necessary for fostering successful relationships in the long term. Information about another person is best revealed a bit at a time, in a give-and-take exchange, not in a rush of overexposed feeling.

The Bachelor

Perhaps the best example of this tendency is reality TV and its spawn. Programs like *The Bachelor* and *The Bachelorette,* as well as pseudo-documentary shows such as *A Dating Story* (and *A Wedding Story* and *A Baby Story*) on The Learning Channel, transform the longings of the human heart into top Nielsen ratings by encouraging the lovelorn to discuss in depth and at length every feeling they have, every moment they have it, as the cameras roll. Romances begin, blossom, and occasionally end in the space of half an hour, and audiences—privy to even the most excruciatingly staged expressions of love and devotion—nevertheless gain the illusion of having seen "real" examples of dating, wedding, or marriage.

On the Internet, dating blogs offer a similar sophomoric voyeurism. One dating blogger, who calls himself Quigley, keeps a dreary tally of his many unsuccessful attempts to meet women, peppering his diary with adolescent observations about women he sees on television. Another dating blogger, who describes herself as an "attractive 35-year old," writes "A Day in the Life of Jane," a dating diary about her online dating travails. Reflecting on one of her early experiences, she writes: "But what did I learn from Owen? That online dating isn't so different from regular dating. It has its pros and cons: Pros—you learn a lot more about a person much more quickly, that a person isn't always what they seem or what you believe them to be, that you have to be really honest with yourself and the person you are communicating with; Cons—uh, same as the pros!"

BadXPartners.com

Successful relationships are not immune to the over-sharing impulse, either; a plethora of wedding websites such as SharetheMoments.com and TheKnot.com offer up the intimate details of couples' wedding planning and ceremonies—right down to the brand of tie worn by the groom and the "intimate" vows exchanged by the couple. And, if things go awry, there are an increasing number of revenge websites such as BadXPartners.com, which offers people who've been dumped an opportunity for petty revenge. "Create a comical case file of your BadX-Partners for the whole world to see!" the website urges. Like the impulse to Google, the site plays on people's fears of being misled, encouraging people to search the database for stories of bad exes: "Just met someone new? Think they are just the one for you? Well remember, they are probably someone else's X. . . . Find out about Bill from Birmingham's strange habits or Tracy from Texas' suspect hygiene. Better safe than sorry!"

Like the steady work of the wrecking ball, our culture's nearly-compulsive demand for personal revelation, emotional exposure, and sharing of feelings threatens the fragile edifice of newly-forming relationships. Transparency and complete access are exactly what you want to avoid in the early stages of romance. Successful courtship—even successful flirtation—require the gradual peeling away of layers, some deliberately constructed, others part of a person's character and personality, that make us mysteries to each other.

Among Pascal's minor works is an essay, "Discourse on the Passion of Love," in which he argues for the keen "pleasure of loving without daring to tell it." "In love," Pascal writes, "silence is of more avail than speech . . . there is an eloquence in silence that penetrates more deeply than language can." Pascal imagined his lovers in each other's physical presence, watchful of unspoken physical gestures, but not speaking. Only gradually would they reveal themselves. Today such a tableau seems as arcane as Kabuki theater; modern couples exchange the most intimate details of their lives on a first date and then return home to blog about it.

"It's difficult," said one woman I talked to who has tried—and ultimately soured on—Internet dating. "You're expected to be both informal and funny in your e-mails, and reveal your likes and dislikes, but you don't want to reveal so much that you appear desperate, or so little so that you seem distant." We can, of course, use these technologies appropriately and effectively in the service of advancing a relationship, but to do so both people must understand the potential dangers. One man I interviewed described a relationship that began promisingly but quickly took a technological turn for the worse. After a few successful dates, he encouraged the woman he was seeing, who lived in another city, to keep in touch. Impervious to notions of technological etiquette, however, she took this to mean the floodgates were officially open. She began telephoning him at all hours, sending overly-wrought e-mails and inundating him with lengthy, faxed letters—all of which had the effect not of bringing them closer together, which was clearly her hope, but of sending him scurrying away as fast as he could. Later, however, he became involved in a relationship in which e-mail in particular helped facilitate the courtship, and where technology—bounded by a respect on the part of both people for its excesses—helped rather than harmed the process of learning about another person. Technology itself is not to blame; it is our ignorance of its potential dangers and our unwillingness to exercise self-restraint in its use that makes mischief.

The Modern-Day Matchmaker

Internet dating offers an interesting case study of these technological risks, for it encourages both transparency and oversharing, as well as another danger: it insists that we reduce and market ourselves as the disembodied sum of our parts. The woman or man you might have met on the subway platform or in a coffee shop—within a richer context that includes immediate impressions based on the other person's physical gestures, attire, tone of voice, and overall demeanor—is instead electronically embalmed for your efficient perusal online.

And it is a booming business. Approximately forty percent of American adults are single, and half of that population claims to have visited an online dating site. Revenue for online dating services exceeded $302 million in 2002. There is, not surprisingly, something for the profusion of tastes: behemoth sites such as Match.com, Flirt.com, Hypermatch.com, and Matchmaker.com traffic in thousands of profiles. Niche sites such as Dateable.org for people with disabilities, as well as sites devoted to finding true love for foot fetishists, animal lovers, and the obese, cater to smaller markets. Single people with religious preferences can visit Jdate.com (for Jewish dates), CatholicSingles.com, and even HappyBuddhist.com to find similarly-minded spiritual singles. As with any product, new features are added constantly to maintain consumer interest; even the more jaded seekers of love might quail at Match.com's recent addition to its menu of online options: a form of "speed dating" that offers a certain brutal efficiency as a lure for the time-challenged modern singleton.

A Case Study

One woman I interviewed, an attractive, successful consultant, tried online dating because her hectic work schedule left her little time to meet new people. She went to Match.com, entered her zip code, and began perusing profiles. She quickly decided to post her own. "When you first put your profile on Match.com," she said, "it's like walking into a kennel with a pork chop around your neck. You're bombarded with e-mails from men." She received well over one hundred solicitations. She responded to a few with a "wink," an electronic gesture that allows another person to know you've seen their profile and are interested—but not interested enough to commit to sending an e-mail message. More alluring profiles garnered an e-mail introduction.

After meeting several different men for coffee, she settled on one in particular and they dated for several months. The vagaries of online dating, however, quickly present new challenges to relationship etiquette. In her case, after several months of successful dating, she and her boyfriend agreed to take their Match.com profiles down from the site. Since they were no longer "single and looking," but single and dating, this seemed to make sense—at least to her. Checking Match.com a week later, however, she found her boyfriend's profile still up and actively advertising himself as available. They are still together, although she confesses to a new wariness about his willingness to commit.

The rapid growth of Internet dating has led to the erosion of the stigma that used to be attached to having "met someone on the Internet" (although none of the people I interviewed for this article would allow their names to be used). And Internet dating itself is becoming increasingly professionalized—with consultants, how-to books, and "expert" analysis crowding out the earlier generation of websites. This February, a "commonsense guide to successful Internet dating" entitled *I Can't Believe I'm Buying This Book* hit bookstores. *Publishers Weekly* describes the author, an "Internet dating consultant," as "a self-proclaimed online serial dater" who "admits he's never sustained a relationship for more than seven months," yet nevertheless "entertainingly reviews how to present one's self on the Web."

Designing the "dating software" that facilitates online romance is a science all its own. *U.S. News & World Report* recently described the efforts of Michael Georgeff, who once designed software to aid the space shuttle program, to devise similar algorithms to assess and predict people's preferences for each other. "Say you score a 3 on the introvert scale, and a 6 on touchy-feely," he told a reporter. "Will you tend to like somebody who's practical?" His weAttract.com software purports to provide the answer. On the company's website, amid close-ups of the faces of a strangely androgynous, snuggling couple, weAttract—whose software is used by Match.com—encourages visitors to "Find someone who considers your quirks adorable." Fair enough. But the motto of weAttract—"Discover your instinctual preferences"—is itself a contradiction. If preferences are instinctual, why do you need the aid of experts like weAttract to discover them?

We need them because we have come to mistrust our own sensibilities. What is emerging on the Internet is a glorification of scientific and technological solutions to the challenge of finding love. The expectation of romantic happiness is so great that extraordinary, scientific means for achieving it are required—or so these companies would have you believe. For example, Emode, whose pop-up ads are now so common that they are the Internet equivalent of a swarm of pesky gnats, promotes "Tickle Matchmaking," a service promising "accurate, Ph.D. certified compatibility scores with every member!"

EHarmony.com

The apotheosis of this way of thinking is a site called eHarmony. com, whose motto, "Fall in love for the right reasons," soothes prospective swains with the comforting rhetoric of professional science. "Who knew science and love were so compatible?" asks the site, which is rife with the language of the laboratory: "scientifically-proven set of compatibility principles," "based on 35 years of empirical and clinical research," "patent-pending matching technology," "exhaustively researched" methods, and "the most powerful system available." As the founder of eHarmony told *U.S. News & World Report* recently, we are all too eager—desperate, even—to hustle down the aisle. "In this culture," he said, "if we like the person's looks, if they have an ability to chatter at a cocktail party, and a little bit of status, we're halfway to marriage. We're such suckers." EHarmony's answer to such unscientific mating practices is a trademarked "Compatibility Matching System" that promises to "connect you with singles who are compatible with you in 29 of the most important areas of life." As the literature constantly reminds the dreamy romantics among us, "Surprisingly, a good match is more science than art."

EHarmony's insistence that the search for true love is no realm for amateurs is, of course, absurdly self-justifying. "You should realize," their website admonishes, after outlining the "29 dimensions" of personality their compatibility software examines, "that it is still next to impossible to correctly evaluate them on your own with each person you think may be right for you." Instead you must pay eHarmony to do it for you. As you read the "scientific" proof, the reassuring sales pitch washes over you: "Let eHarmony make sure that the next time you fall in love, it's with the right person."

In other words, don't trust your instincts, trust science. With a tasteful touch of contempt, eHarmony notes that its purpose is not merely dating, as it is for megasites such as Match.com. "Our goal is to help you find your soul mate." Four pages of testimonials on the website encourage the surrender to eHarmony's expertise, with promises of imminent collision with "your" soul mate: "From the minute we began e-mailing and talking on the phone, we knew we had found our soul mate," say Lisa and Darryl from Dover, Pennsylvania. "It took some time," confessed Annie of Kansas City, Missouri, "but once I met John, I knew that they had made good on their promise to help me find my soul mate."

Some observers see in these new "scientific" mating rituals a return to an earlier time of courtship and chaperoned dating. *Newsweek* eagerly described eHarmony as a form of "arranged marriage for the digital age, without the all-powerful parents," and Barbara Dafoe Whitehead argues that the activities of the Internet love seeker "reflect a desire for more structured dating." Promoters of these services see them as an improvement on the mere cruising of glossy photos encouraged by most dating sites, or the unrealistic expectations of "finding true love" promoted by popular culture. Rather, they say, they are like the chaperones of courtship past—vetting appropriate candidates and matching them to your specifications.

Not Real Matchmakers

As appealing as this might sound, it is unrealistic. Since these sites rely on technological solutions and mathematical algorithms, they are a far cry from the broader and richer knowledge of the old-fashioned matchmaker. A personality quiz cannot possibly reveal the full range of a person's quirks or liabilities. More importantly, the role of the old-fashioned matchmaker was a social one (and still is in certain communities). The matchmaker was embedded within a community that observed certain rituals and whose members shared certain assumptions. But technological matchmaking allows courtship to be conducted entirely in private, devoid of the social norms (and often the physical signals) of romantic success and failure.

Finally, most Internet dating enthusiasts do not contend with a far more alarming challenge: the impact such services have on our idea of what, exactly, it is we should be seeking in another person. Younger men and women, weaned on the Internet and e-mail, are beginning to express a preference for potential dates to break down their vital stats for pre-date perusal, like an Internet dating advertisement. One 25-year old man, a regular on Match.com, confessed to *U.S. News & World Report* that he wished he could have a digital dossier for all of his potential dates: "It's, 'OK, here's where I'm from, here's what I do, here's what I'm looking for. How about you?' " One woman I spoke to, who has been Internet dating for several years, matter-of-factly noted that even a perfunctory glance at a potential date's résumé saves valuable time and energy. "Why trust a glance exchanged across a crowded bar when you can read a person's biography in miniature before deciding to strike up a conversation?" she said. This intolerance for gradual revelation increases the pace of modern courtship and erodes our patience for many things (not the least of which is commencement of sexual relations). The challenge remains the same—to find another person to share your life with—but we have allowed the technologies at our disposal to alter dramatically, even unrecognizably, the way we go about achieving it.

The Science of Feeling

This impulse is part of a much broader phenomenon—the encroachment of science and technology into areas once thought the province of the uniquely intuitive and even the ineffable. Today we program computers to trounce human chess champions, produce poetry, or analyze works of art, watching eagerly as they break things down to a tedious catalog of techniques: the bishop advances, the meter scans, the paintbrush strokes across the canvas. But by enlisting machines to do what once was the creative province of human beings alone, we deliberately narrow our conceptions of genius, creativity, and art. The *New York Times* recently featured the work of Franco Moretti, a comparative literature professor at Stanford, who promotes "a more rational literary history" that jettisons the old-fashioned reading of texts in favor of statistical models of literary output. His dream, he told reporter Emily Eakin, "is of a literary class that would look more like a lab than a Platonic academy."

Yet this "scientific" approach to artistic work yields chillingly antiseptic results: "Tennyson's mind is to be treated like his intestines after a barium meal," historian Jacques Barzun noted with some exasperation of the trend's earlier incarnations. Critic Lionel Trilling parodied the tendency in 1950 in his book, *The Liberal Imagination.* By this way of thinking, Trilling said, the story of Romeo and Juliet is no longer the tragic tale of a young man and woman falling in love, but becomes instead a chronicle of how, "their libidinal impulses being reciprocal, they activated their individual erotic drives and integrated them within the same frame of reference."

What Barzun and Trilling were expressing was a distaste for viewing art as merely an abstraction of measurable, improvable impulses. The same is true for love. We can study the physiological functions of the human heart with echocardiograms, stress tests, blood pressure readings, and the like. We can examine, analyze, and investigate ad nauseum the physical act of sex. But we cannot so easily measure the desires of the heart. How do you prove that love exists? How do we know that love is "real"? What makes the love of two lovers last?

There is a danger in relying wholly or even largely on science and technology to answer these questions, for it risks eroding our appreciation of the ineffable things—intuition and physical attraction, passion and sensibility—by reducing these feelings to scientifically explained physiological facts. Today we catalog the influence of hormones, pheromones, dopamine, and serotonin in human attraction, and map our own brains to discover which synapses trigger laughter, lying, or orgasm. Evolutionary psychology explains our desire for symmetrical faces and fertile-looking forms, even as it has little to tell us about the extremes to which we are taking its directives with plastic surgery. Scientific study of our communication patterns and techniques explains why it is we talk the way we do. Even the activities of the bedroom are thoroughly analyzed and professionalized, as women today take instruction from a class of professionals whose arts used to be less esteemed. Prostitutes now run sex seminars, for example, and a recent episode of Oprah featured exotic pole dancers who teach suburban housewives how to titillate their husbands by turning the basement rec room into a simulacrum of a Vegas show girl venue.

Science continues to turn sex (and, by association, love and romance) into something quantifiable and open to manipulation and solution. Science and technology offer us pharmaceuticals to enhance libido and erectile function, and popular culture responds by rigorously ranking and discussing all matters sexual—from the disturbingly frank talk of female characters on Sex and the City to the proliferation of "blind date" shows which subject hapless love-seekers to the withering gaze of a sarcastic host and his viewing audience. "What a loser!" cackled the host of the reality television program Blind Date, after one ignominious bachelor botched his chance for a good night kiss. "The march of science," Barzun wrote, "produces the feeling that nobody in the past has ever done things right. Whether it's teaching or copulation, it has 'problems' that 'research' should solve by telling us just how, the best way."

Test-Driving Your Soul Mate

Why is the steady march of science and technology in these areas a problem? Shouldn't we be proud of our expanding knowledge and the tools that knowledge gives us? Not necessarily. Writing recently in the journal Techné, Hector Jose Huyke noted the broader dangers posed by the proliferation of our technologies, particularly the tendency to "devalue the near." "When a technology is introduced it, presumably, simply adds options to already existing options," he writes. But this is not how technology's influence plays out in practice. In fact, as Huyke argues, "as what is difficult to obtain becomes repeatedly and easily accessible, other practices and experiences are left out—they do not remain unchanged." The man who sends an e-mail to his brother is not merely choosing to write an e-mail and thus adding to his range of communication options; he is choosing not to make a phone call or write a letter. A woman who e-mails a stranger on the Internet is choosing not to go to a local art exhibit and perhaps meet someone in person. "Communications technologies indeed multiply options," says Huyke. "An increase in options, however, does not imply or even serve an advance in communications." Technologies, in other words, often make possible "what would otherwise be difficult to obtain." But they do so by eliminating other paths.

Personal Ads

Love and genuine commitment have always been difficult to attain, and they are perhaps more so today since it is the individual bonds of affection—not family alliance, property transfer, social class, or religious orthodoxy—that form the cornerstone of most modern marriages. Yet there remains a certain grim efficiency to the vast realm of love technologies at our disposal. After a while, perusing Internet personal ads is like being besieged by an aggressive real estate agent hoping to unload that tired brick colonial. Each person points out his or her supposedly unique features with the same banal descriptions ("adventurous," "sexy," "trustworthy") never conveying a genuine sense of the whole. Machine metaphors, tellingly, crop up often, with women and men willingly categorizing themselves as "high maintenance" or "low maintenance," much as one might describe a car or small kitchen appliance. As an executive of one online dating service told a reporter recently, "If you want to buy a car, you get a lot of information before you even test-drive. There hasn't been a way to do that with relationships."

But we have been "test driving" something: a new, technological method of courtship. And although it is too soon to deliver a final verdict, it is clear that it is a method prone to serious problems. The efficiency of our new techniques and their tendency to focus on people as products leaves us at risk of understanding ourselves this way, too—like products with certain malfunctioning parts and particular assets. But products must be constantly improved upon and marketed. In the pursuit of love, and in a world where multiple partners are sampled before one is selected, this fuels a hectic culture of self-improvement—honing the witty summary of one's most desirable traits for placement in personal advertisements is only the beginning. Today, men and women convene focus groups of former lovers to gain critical insights into their behavior so as to avoid future failure; and the perfection of appearance through surgical and non-surgical means occupies an increasing amount of people's time and energy.

Our new technological methods of courtship also elevate efficient communication over personal communication. Ironically, the Internet, which offers many opportunities to meet and communicate with new people, robs us of the ability to deploy one of our greatest charms—nonverbal communication. The emoticon is a weak substitute for a coy gesture or a lusty wink. More fundamentally, our technologies encourage a misunderstanding of what courtship should be. Real courtship is about persuasion, not marketing, and the techniques of the laboratory cannot help us translate the motivations of the heart.

The response is not to retreat into Luddism, of course. In a world where technology allows us to meet, date, marry, and even divorce online, there is no returning to the innocence of an earlier time. What we need is a better understanding of the risks of these new technologies and a willingness to exercise restraint in using them. For better or worse, we are now a society of sexually liberated individuals seeking "soul mates"—yet the privacy, gradualism, and boundaries that are necessary for separating the romantic wheat from the chaff still elude us.

Alchemy

Perhaps, in our technologically saturated age, we would do better to rediscover an earlier science: alchemy. Not alchemy in its original meaning—a branch of speculative philosophy whose devotees attempted to create gold from base metals and hence cure disease and prolong life—but alchemy in its secondary definition: "a power or process of transforming something common into something precious." From our daily, common interactions with other people might spring something precious—but only if we have the patience to let it flourish. Technology and science often conspire against such patience. Goethe wrote, "We should do our utmost to encourage the Beautiful, for the Useful encourages itself." There is an eminent usefulness to many of our technologies—e-mail and cell phones allow us to span great distances to communicate with family, friends, and lovers, and the Internet connects us to worlds unknown. But they are less successful at encouraging the flourishing of the lasting and beautiful. Like the Beautiful, love occurs in unexpected places, often not where it is being sought. It can flourish only if we accept that our technologies and our science can never fully explain it.

CHRISTINE ROSEN is a senior editor of *The New Atlantis* and resident fellow at the Ethics and Public Policy Center. Her book *Preaching Eugenics: Religious Leaders and the American Eugenics Movement* was just published by Oxford University Press.

How Do I Love Thee?

A growing number of Internet dating sites are relying on academic researchers to develop a new science of attraction. A firsthand report from the front lines of an unprecedented social experiment

LORI GOTTLIEB

I'd been sitting in Dr. Neil Clark Warren's office for less than fifteen minutes when he told me he had a guy for me. It wasn't surprising that the avuncular seventy-one-year-old founder of eHarmony.com, one of the nation's most popular online dating services, had matchmaking on his mind. The odd thing was that he was eager to hook me up without having seen my eHarmony personality profile.

I'd come to the eHarmony headquarters in Pasadena, California, in early October to learn more about the site's "scientifically proven" and patented Compatibility Matching System. Apparently, the science wasn't working for me. The day before, after I'd taken the company's exhaustive (and exhausting) 436-question personality survey, the computer informed me that of the approximately 9 million eHarmony members, more than 40 percent of whom are men, I had zero matches. Not just in my city, state, region, or country, but in the entire world. So Warren, who looks like Orville Redenbacher and speaks with the folksy cadence of Garrison Keillor, suggested setting me up with one of his company's advisory board members, whom he described as brilliant, Jewish, and thirty-eight years old. According to Warren, this board member, like me, might have trouble finding a match on eHarmony.

"Let me tell you why you're such a difficult match," Warren said, facing me on one of his bright floral sofas. He started running down the backbone of eHarmony's predictive model of broad-based compatibility, the so-called twenty-nine dimensions (things like curiosity, humor, passion, intellect), and explaining why I and my prospective match were such outliers.

"I could take the nine million people on our site and show you dimension by dimension how we'd lose people for you," he began. "Just on IQ alone—people with an IQ lower than 120, say. Okay, we've eliminated people who are not intellectually adequate. We could do the same for people who aren't creative enough, or don't have your brilliant sense of humor. See, when you get on the tails of these dimensions, it's really hard to match you. You're too bright. You're too thoughtful. The biggest thing you've got to do when you're gifted like you are is to be patient."

After the over-the-top flattery wore off—and I'll admit, it took an embarrassingly long time—I told Warren that most people I know don't join online dating sites to be patient. Impatience with real-world dating, in fact, is precisely what drives many singles to the fast-paced digital meat market. From the moment Match.com, the first such site, appeared in 1995, single people suddenly had twenty-four-hour access to thousands of other singles who met their criteria in terms of race, religion, height, weight, even eye color and drinking habits.

Nearly overnight, it seemed, dozens of similar sites emerged, and online dating became almost de rigueur for busy singles looking for love. According to a recent Pew survey, 31 percent of all American adults (63 million people) know someone who has used a dating Web site, while 26 percent (53 million people) know someone who has gone out with a person he or she met through a dating Web site. But was checking off boxes in columns of desired traits, like an à la carte Chinese take-out menu, the best way to find a soul mate?

Enter eHarmony and the new generation of dating sites, among them PerfectMatch.com and Chemistry.com. All have staked their success on the idea that long-term romantic compatibility can be predicted according to scientific principles—and that they can discover those principles and use them to help their members find lasting love. To that end they've hired high-powered academics, devised special algorithms for relationship-matching, developed sophisticated personality questionnaires, and put into place mechanisms for the long-term tracking of data. Collectively, their efforts mark the early days of a social experiment of unprecedented proportions, involving millions of couples and possibly extending over the course of generations. The question at the heart of this grand trial is simple: In the subjective realm of love, can cold, hard science help?

Although eHarmony was the first dating site to offer science-based matching, Neil Clark Warren seems like an unlikely pioneer in the field. Even though he earned a Ph.D. in clinical psychology from the University of Chicago, in 1967, he never had much of a passion for academic research—or an interest in couples. "I was scared to death of adults," he told me. "So I did child therapy for a while." With a master's degree in divinity from Princeton Theological Seminary, he went on to Fuller Theological Seminary's Graduate School of Psychology, in southern California, where he taught and practiced humanistic psychology (what he calls "client-centered stuff") in the vein of his University of Chicago mentor, Carl Rogers. "I hated doing research," he admitted, before adding with a smile, "In fact, I was called 'Dr. Warm.'"

Fittingly, it was Warren's family, not academia, that piqued his interest in romantic compatibility. "When my daughters came along, that was a big pivot in my life in thinking about how do two people get together," he told me. "I started reading in the literature and realizing what a big chance they had of not having a satisfying marriage. I started trying to look into it."

Soon he began a private practice of couples therapy—with a twist. "People have always thought, wrongly, that psychotherapy is a place to go deal with problems," he said. "So when a couple would come in, I'd say, 'Tell me how you fell in love. Tell me the funniest thing that's happened in your marriage.' If you want to make a relationship work, don't talk about what you find missing in it! Talk about what you really like about it."

Warren is a big proponent of what he likes to call "folksy wisdom." One look at the shelves in his office confirms this. "I've been reading this little book about the Muppets—you know, Jim Henson," he said. "And I've been reading another book about Mister Rogers. I mean, Mister Rogers was brilliant beyond belief! He got a hold of concepts so thoroughly that he could transmit them to six-year-old kids! Do you know how much you have to get a hold of a concept to transmit it simply? His idea of simple-but-profound has had a profound influence on me."

The basis of eHarmony's matching system also sounds simple but profound. In successful relationships, Warren says, "similarities are like money in the bank. Differences are like debts you owe. It's all right to have a few differences, as long as you have plenty of equity in your account."

He leaned in and lowered his voice to a whisper. "Mister Rogers and Jim Henson," Warren continued, "they got a hold of the deep things of life and were able to put them out there. So that's what we want to do with our products. We want to put them out there in a way that you'd say, 'This is common sense. This seems right, this seems like it would work.' Our idea of broad-based compatibility, I put it out there in front of you. Does that seem right?"

Whether or not it seems right on an intuitive level is almost beside the point. After all, eHarmony's selling point, its very brand identity, is its scientific compatibility system. That's where Galen Buckwalter comes in.

A vice president of research and development for the company, Buckwalter is in charge of recruiting what he hopes will be twenty to twenty-five top relationship researchers away from academia—just as he was lured away by Warren nine years ago. A former psychology graduate student at Fuller Theological Seminary (his dissertation was titled "Neuropsychological Factors Affecting Survival in Malignant Glioma Patients Treated with Autologous Stimulated Lymphocytes"), Buckwalter had become an assistant professor at the University of Southern California, where he was studying the effects of hormones on cognition, when he got the call from Warren.

"Neil knew I lived and breathed research, and he had this idea to try to develop some empirically based model to match people," Buckwalter said when I visited him at his office at eHarmony. He wore a black T-shirt and wire-rimmed glasses, and had a hairstyle reminiscent of Einstein's. "He wasn't necessarily thinking, over the Internet—maybe a storefront operation like Great Expectations." Relationships weren't Buckwalter's area, but he welcomed the challenge. "A problem is a problem, and relationships are a good problem," he said. "In the research context, it's certainly an endlessly fascinating question."

With the help of a graduate student, Buckwalter reviewed the psychological literature to identify the areas that might be relevant in predicting success in long-term relationships. "Once we identified all those areas, then we put together a questionnaire—just a massively long questionnaire," he said. "It was probably close to a thousand questions. Because if you don't ask it, you're never gonna know. So we had tons of questions on ability, even more on interest. Just every type of personality aspect that was ever measured, we were measuring it all."

The question is simple: In the subjective realm of love, can cold, hard science help?

Because it wasn't practical to execute a thirty-year longitudinal study, he and Warren decided to measure existing relationships, surveying people who were already married. The idea was to look for patterns that produce satisfaction in marriages, then try to reproduce them in the matching of singles.

Buckwalter's studies soon yielded data that confirmed one of Warren's longtime observations: namely, that the members of a happy couple are far more similar to each other than are the members of an unhappy couple. Compatibility, in other words, rests on shared traits. "I can't tell you how delighted I was," Warren said, "when the factor-analytic studies started bringing back the same stuff I'd seen for years."

But could this be true across the board? I told Warren that my most successful relationships have been with men who are far less obsessive than I am. Warren assured me that's not a similarity their system matches for. "You don't want two obsessives," he explained. "They'll drive each other crazy. You don't find two control freaks in a great marriage. So we try to tweak the model for that. Fifty percent of the ball game is finding two people who are stable."

For Warren, a big question remained: What should be done with these findings? Originally, he had partnered with his son-in-law, Greg Forgatch, a former real-estate developer, to launch the business. Their first thought was to produce educational videotapes on relationship compatibility. After all, Warren had recently written his book, *Finding the Love of Your Life*.

"We tried so hard to make videotapes and audiotapes," Warren said. "I went into the studio and made lists. We came up with a hundred things singles need. But singles don't want education; they want flesh! They want a person. So that's when, in 1997, we said, 'We've gotta help people find somebody who would be good for them. Some *body*.'"

To connect singles and create a data pool for more research, the Internet seemed the best option. Based on a study of 5,000 married couples, Warren put together the compatibility model that became the basis for eHarmony. "We got encouraged by everybody, 'Get out there, get out there! The first person to market is going to be the most successful,'" Warren recalled. But he insisted on getting the matching system right before launching the site—and that didn't happen until August of 2000, during the dot-com bust. By 2001 he was contemplating declaring bankruptcy.

"And then," Warren recalled, "we found an error in our matching formula, so a whole segment of our people were not getting matched. It was an error with all the Christian people on the site."

This is a sensitive topic for Warren, who bristles at the widely held opinion that eHarmony is a Christian dating site. The company's chief operating officer, he offered by way of rebuttal, is Jewish, and Buckwalter, who became a quadriplegic at age sixteen after jumping into a river and breaking his neck, is agnostic. And while Warren describes himself as "a passionate Christian" and proudly declares, "I love Jesus," he worried about narrowing the site with too many questions about spiritual beliefs. Which is where the error came in.

"We had seven questions on religion," he explained, "and we eliminated four of them. But we forgot to enter that into the matching formula! These were seven-point questions. You needed twenty-eight points to get matched with a Christian person, but there was no way you could get them! We only had three questions! So every Christian person who had come to us had zero matches."

Fortunately, a wave of positive publicity, featuring married couples who'd met through eHarmony and the naturally charismatic Warren, turned things around. Still, Warren said of the innocent mistake, "you kind of wonder how many relationships fall apart for reasons like this—how many businesses?"

Today, eHarmony's business isn't just about using science to match singles online. Calling itself a "relationship-enhancement service," the company has recently created a venture-capital-funded think tank for relationship and marital research, headed up by Dr. Gian Gorizaga, a scientist from the well-known marriage-and-family lab at the University of California at Los Angeles. The effort, as Gorizaga put it to me recently, is "sort of like a Bell Labs or Microsoft for love."

An energetic, attractive thirty-five-year-old, Gonzaga thought twice about leaving the prestige of academia. "It seemed cheesy at first," he said. "I mean, this was a dating service." But after interviewing with Warren, he realized that conducting his research under the auspices of eHarmony would offer certain advantages. He'd be unfettered by teaching and grant-writing, and there would be no sitting on committees or worrying about tenure. More important, since his research would now be funded by business, he'd have the luxury of doing studies with large groups of ready subjects over many years—but without the constraints of having to produce a specific product.

"We're using science in an area most people think of as inherently unscientific," Gonzaga said. So far, the data are promising: a recent Harris Interactive poll found that between September of 2004 and September of 2005, eHarmony facilitated the marriages of more than 33,000 members—an average of forty-six marriages a day. And a 2004 in-house study of nearly 300 married couples showed that people who met through eHarmony report more marital satisfaction than those who met by other means. The company is now replicating that study in a larger sample.

"We have massive amounts of data!" Warren said. "Twelve thousand new people a day taking a 436-item questionnaire! Ultimately, our dream is to have the biggest group of relationship psychologists in the country. It's so easy to get people excited about coming here. We've got more data than they could collect in a thousand years."

But how useful is this sort of data for single people like me? Despite Warren's disclaimer about what a tough eHarmony match I am, I did finally get some profiles in my inbox. They included a bald man with a handlebar moustache, who was fourteen inches taller than me; a five-foot-four-inch attorney with no photos; and a film editor whose photo shows him wearing a kilt—and not in an ironic way. Was this the best science could do?

When I asked Galen Buckwalter about this, he laughed, indicating that he'd heard the question before. "The thing you have to remember about our system is we're matching on these algorithms for long-term compatibility," he said. "Long-term satisfaction is not the same as short-term attraction. A lot of people, when they see their initial matches, it's like, 'This is crap!'"

In ads and on his Web site. Warren talks about matching people "from the inside out." Was eHarmony suggesting that I overlook something as basic as romantic chemistry? "When we started out," Buckwalter said, "we were almost that naive." But now, he added, eHarmony is conducting research on the nature of physical attraction.

"We're trying to find out if we can predict physical chemistry with the same degree of statistical certainty that we've used to predict long-term satisfaction through our compatibility matching. In general, people seem to be attracted to people who share their physical attributes," Buckwalter explained, noting that he has found some exceptions, like height preference. "There's a lot of variability on that dimension," he said. "A person's height, it turns out, is not a consistent predictor of short-term attraction." Meanwhile, Buckwalter's team is in the process of testing new hypotheses.

"We're still convinced that our compatibility-matching process is essential for long-term satisfaction, so we're not going to mess with that," he insisted. "But if we can fit a short-term attraction model on top of that, and it's also empirically driven, that's the Holy Grail."

Over at Chemistry.com, a new site launched by Match.com, short-term attraction is already built into the system. This competitor of eHarmony's was developed with help from Match.com's chief scientific adviser, Dr. Helen Fisher, an anthropologist at Rutgers University, whose research focuses on the brain physiology of romantic love and sexuality. Chemistry.com is currently assembling a multidisciplinary group of psychologists, relationship counselors, sociologists, neuroscientists, and sexologists to serve as consultants.

The company sought out Fisher precisely because its market research revealed that although a large segment of singles wanted a scientific approach, they didn't want it to come at the expense of romantic chemistry. "On most of the other sites, there's this notion of 'fitness matching,'" Fisher said from her office in New York City. "You may have the same goals, intelligence, good looks, political beliefs. But you can walk into a room, and every one of those boys might come from the same background, have the same level of intelligence, and so on, and maybe you'll talk to three but won't fall in love with any of them. And with the fourth one, you do. What creates that chemistry?"

It's a constellation of factors, Fisher told me. Sex drive, for instance, is associated with the hormone testosterone in both men and women. Romantic love is associated with elevated activity of the neurotransmitter dopamine and probably also another one, norepinepherine. And attachment is associated with the hormones oxytocin and vasopressin. "It turns out," she said, "that seminal fluid has all of these chemicals in it. So I tell my students, 'Don't have sex if you don't want to fall in love.'"

Romantic love. Fisher maintains, is a basic mating drive—more powerful than the sex drive. "If you ask someone to go to bed with you, and they reject you," she says, "you don't kill yourself. But if you're rejected in love, you *might* kill yourself."

For Chemistry.com's matching system, Fisher translated her work with neurotransmitters and hormones into discrete personality types. "I've always been extremely impressed with Myers-Briggs," she said, referring to the personality assessment tool that classifies people according to four pairs of traits: Introversion versus Extroversion, Sensing versus Intuition, Thinking versus Feeling, and Judging versus Perceiving. "They had me pinned to the wall when I took the test, and my sister, too. So when Chemistry.com approached me, I said to myself, 'I'm an anthropologist who studies brain chemistry, what do I know about personality?'"

Turns out she knew quite a bit: Genes for the activity of dopamine are associated with motivation, curiosity, anxiety, and optimism. Genes for the metabolism of serotonin, another neurotransmitter, tend to modulate one's degree of calm, stability, popularity, and religiosity. Testosterone is associated with being rational, analytical, exacting, independent, logical, rank-oriented, competitive, irreverent, and narcissistic. And the hormone estrogen is associated with being imaginative, creative, insightful, humane, sympathetic, agreeable, flexible, and verbal.

"So I had these four sheets of paper," Fisher continued. "And I decided to give each a name. Serotonin became the Builder. Dopamine, the Explorer. Testosterone, the Director. And estrogen—I wish I'd called it the Ambassador or Diplomat, but I called it the Negotiator." Myers-Briggs, she says, "clearly knew the four types but didn't know the chemicals behind them."

The 146-item compatibility questionnaire on Chemistry.com correlates users' responses with evidence of their levels of these various chemicals. One question, for instance, offers drawings of a hand, then asks:

Which one of the following images most closely resembles your left hand?

Index finger slightly longer than ring finger

Index finger about the same length as ring finger

Index finger slightly shorter than ring finger

Index finger significantly shorter than ring finger

The relevance of this question might baffle the average online dater accustomed to responding to platitudes like, "How would you describe your perfect first date?" But Fisher explains that elevated fetal testosterone determines the ratio of the second and fourth finger in a particular way as it simultaneously builds the male and female brain. So you can actually look at someone's hand and get a fair idea of the extent to which they are likely to be a Director type (ring finger longer than the index finger) or a Negotiator type (index finger longer or the same size).

Another question goes like this:

How often do you vividly imagine extreme life situations, such as being stranded on a desert island or winning the lottery?

Almost never

Sometimes

Most of the time

All the time

"Someone who answers 'All the time' is a definite Negotiator," Fisher said. "High estrogen activity is associated with extreme imagination."

While other sites gather data based on often unreliable self-reports ("How romantic do you consider yourself to be?"), many of the Chemistry.com questions are designed to translate visual interpretation into personality assessment, thus eliminating some of the unreliability. In one, the user is presented with a book's jacket art. We see a woman in a sexy spaghetti-strapped dress gazing at a man several feet away in the background, where he leans on a stone railing. The sky is blue, and they're overlooking an open vista. "What is the best title for this book?" the questionnaire asks, and the choices are as follows:

A Spy in Rimini

Anatomy of Friendship: A Smart Guide for Smart People

A Scoundrel's Story

Things Left Unsaid

According to Fisher, each response is correlated with one of the four personality types: Choice A corresponds to Explorer, B to Builder, C to Director, and D to Negotiator.

Even sense of humor can be broken down by type, with questions like "Do you sometimes make faces at yourself in the mirror?" (people with a sense of humor do) and "At the zoo, which do you generally prefer to watch?" (the reply "monkeys and apes" indicates more of a funny bone than "lions and tigers"). According to Fisher, a Director likes people to laugh at his or her jokes; a Negotiator likes to be around someone funny so he or she can laugh at that person's jokes; an Explorer is spontaneous and laughs at just about anything; and a Builder, she suspects, generally isn't as funny as the others.

But how to match people up according to Fisher's four personality types, and under what circumstances, isn't so straightforward. Another question, for instance, presents four smiling faces and asks:

Take a look at the faces below. Are their smiles sincere?

Fisher says that people with high levels of estrogen—usually women—have better social skills, and are better at reading other people. So users who choose the correct "real" smiles will be the Negotiators. This, Fisher says, is an area where "complementarity" might be important. The problem with sites like eHarmony, she believes, is that they place too much emphasis on similarity, whereas, in her view, falling in love depends on two elements: similarity and complementarity. "We also want someone who masks our flaws," she explained. "For example, people with poor social skills sometimes gravitate toward people with good social skills. I'm an Explorer, so I don't really need a partner who is socially skilled. That's not essential to me. But it may be essential to a Director, who's generally less socially skilled."

Chemistry.com's compatibility questionnaire also examines secondary personality traits. To illustrate, Fisher cited her own relationship. "I'm currently going out with a man," she said, "and of course I made him take the test instantly. We're both Explorers and older. I'm not sure two Explorers want to raise a baby together, because nobody will be home. But in addition, I'm a Negotiator and he's a Director type. Our dominant personality is similar, but underneath, we're complementary."

Determining which works best—similarity or complementarity—may change with the circumstances. A young woman who's an Explorer, Fisher said, might be attracted to a Builder, someone who's more of a homebody, loyal, dependable, and protective. But the pair will be more compatible if their secondary personalities match—maybe they're both Negotiators underneath.

"Nobody is directly locked into any one of these temperament types," Fisher said. "That's why we provide each person

with both a major and a minor personality profile. Do Explorers go well together? Do likes attract likes? Sometimes they do and sometimes they don't."

If this sounds a bit, well, unscientific, Fisher is the first to admit it. "I have theories about what personality type a person would be most ideally suited with," she told me, "but I also trust people to tell me what they are looking for. All throughout the questionnaire are checks and balances to what are just Helen Fisher's theories."

This is why she decided to include an item on the Chemistry.com questionnaire that asks about the traits of a person's partner in his or her most successful former relationship: Was that person an Explorer, a Builder, a Director, a Negotiator? "Anybody can match somebody for values. But I'm hoping to create a system so that five years later they still fascinate each other."

At the same time, Fisher wants couples to be fascinated by each other early on. In other words, why waste time e-mailing back and forth to get to know a potential match over the course of several weeks, as eHarmony encourages its users to do, if there won't be any chemistry when they finally meet? Chemistry.com's guided 1-2-3-Meet system provides a step-by-step structure to get couples face to face as soon as possible for that all-important "vibe check." Then there's a post-meeting "chemistry check," where each person offers feedback about the date.

The goal is to incorporate this information into the algorithm to provide better matches, but it can also serve as an accuracy check of the data. Say, for instance, that Jack describes himself as a fashionable dresser, but Jill reports that he showed up for their date in flip-flops, cut-offs, and a do-rag. If the feedback from a number of Jack's first meetings indicates the same problem, Chemistry.com will send him an e-mail saying, "Jack, wear a pair of trousers."

When I asked Helen Fisher how the site's scientific algorithm might change based on this user feedback, she said that perhaps the computer could pick up cues about a person's physical type based on the people he or she finds attractive or unattractive, then send that person closer matches. Or, it might know better than to match me—an avid reader attracted to literary types—with the guy whose personality assessment indicates a literary bent but whose essay reads as follows:

> While I do read books, I have a notoriously short attention span for them. As a result, partially read copies of numerous really good (so I'm told) books are scattered around my apartment. When these get set aside, it's because I've gotten sucked into magazines . . . Every few days, the magazines lose out to DVDs.

It's also possible that user feedback could change the matching formula completely. "We always look at data," Fisher said. "If we find that Explorer/Builder to Director/Negotiator is working for more people, if we find the biochemistry is stronger, we'll adjust that in the formula." Fisher acknowledged that the system right now is mostly a learning tool—a way to collect large amounts of data, look for patterns, and draw conclusions based on the findings.

Still, even a thoroughly researched biochemical model won't prevent glitches in the matching system. In Fisher's view, for example, no scientifically based site would pair her with the men she's dated, because, as she put it, "they're all better-looking than me."

"It would be preposterous for anyone to say they can create a formula that works perfectly," she said emphatically. "But I do believe that science can help us get close, and that there's a lot more to be learned."

"This test doesn't pretend to be about chemistry," said Dr. Pepper Schwartz—who developed the Duet Total Compatibility System in conjunction with the two-year-old site PerfectMatch.com. She was speaking by cell phone from San Francisco, where she had just attended a meeting of the National Human Sexuality Resource Center, on whose board she sits. "The chemistry test at Match—that's not about chemistry either. If I could concoct a test for chemistry, I'd make a zillion dollars."

A sociologist at the University of Washington in Seattle, Schwartz is PerfectMatch.com's hipper version of Neil Clark Warren: the accessible, empathic, media-savvy love doctor who guides users through the treacherous dating trenches and onto the path of true compatibility.

According to the site—which calls her by the cutesy moniker "Dr. Pepper"—Schwartz is "the leading relationship expert in the nation," a woman who "holds the distinction of being the only relationship expert on the Web who's a published authority, as well as a professor at a major U.S. university." Oh, and then there are her appearances on *Oprah, The Today Show,* and *Good Morning America,* the fourteen books she's written, and her regular column for LifetimeTV.com.

Unlike Warren, however, she neither founded the company (she was brought in by PerfectMatch's Duane Dahl), nor follows Warren's credo of simplicity. In fact, the nifty-sounding Duet Compatibility Profiler takes some complex deconstruction. This makes sense, given that Schwartz has been studying gender relations since the early 1970s, when she was a sociology graduate student at Yale and wrote a Ph.D. thesis on how people hooked up in the college mixer system.

My matches included a film editor wearing a kilt—and not in an ironic way. Was this the best science could do?

Like Helen Fisher, the Rutgers anthropologist, Schwartz believes that both similarity and complementarity are integral to romantic compatibility. But while Fisher has more of an "it depends" attitude on the question of which of the two makes sense for a particular couple under particular circumstances, Schwartz has a more elaborately defined system, which she outlines in her latest book, *Finding Your Perfect Match.*

Schwartz's Duet model consists of a mere forty-eight questions and focuses on eight specific personality characteristics: romantic impulsivity, personal energy, outlook, predictability, flexibility, decision-making style, emotionality, and self-nurturing style. On the first four, she believes, a well-suited couple should be similar; on the last four, however, a couple can thrive on either similarity or difference—provided that both people know themselves well enough to determine which works best.

"My first thought was, *Know yourself*," Schwartz said of how she created PerfectMatch's system. "How can you pick somebody else if you have no insight into yourself?"

Her questionnaire, she believes, will help users to think in a conscious way about who they are. As an example of the kind of introspection she hopes for, Schwartz cites the area of money. "It's a very important thing," she said, "and there's very little research on it, because nobody wants to talk about money. I can ask people if they're orgasmic, and they'll tell me in a second. But ask a subject about money, and they're embarrassed."

When it comes to money, PerfectMatch asks users to get specific—and honest—about how important it is to them. "I want them to think about things like, Should parents pay for college education no matter what it costs? Do you feel you need to make extravagant purchases every once in a while?" Other tests generally stop at innocuous questions about whether people consider themselves fiscally responsible, but Schwartz ventures into un-PC territory with true-or-false statements like, "All other things being equal, I tend to respect people who make a lot of money more than people who have modest incomes"; "I could not love a person who doesn't make enough money to help me live the lifestyle I need in order to be happy"; and "I would very much prefer to be with someone who did not have major economic responsibilities to children or parents unless they had a lot of money and these responsibilities did not affect our life together."

Like Chemistry.com's system. Duet has its roots in the Myers-Briggs Type Indicator. But, Schwartz explained, Duet is different from Myers-Briggs in several ways. It has eight characteristics to Myers-Briggs's four; it uses two personality profiles—similarity and complementarity—instead of one; and it relies on studies from a number of fields, rather than just psychology, to determine how these personality characteristics combine in romantic situations, as opposed to general workplace or team-building ones.

"If, say, I'm rigid in my tastes but I have a sense of humor," Schwartz explained, "you can work with me. But if I'm rigid and very earnest, it's going to be difficult. So in our test it's not just, 'Is this person rigid?' Because rigidity can co-exist with humor or earnestness, and which one of those traits is present makes a big difference. It's important how these traits are put together."

I took the Duet test and was classified on the similarity scale as X, A, C, and V—that is, Risk Averse, High Energy, Cautious, and Seeks Variety. The site then interpreted the findings, which, to my surprise, rather accurately captured my personality:

You are careful about entering a relationship. You have a cautious side to your personality on more than one dimension, and so it takes you awhile to believe in love and romance with someone you are dating. Nonetheless, you are a high energy, intense kind of person. Once you believe in a relationship, you can be a good partner. IF you give it enough time. You demand a lot from the world and you take on a lot. You probably want someone who does the same, or at least supports your own high energy, explorative approach to life.

Yet the complementarity section of my test results—those traits on which my best match might be similar or different—reflected my temperament on only two of the four parameters. I was characterized as S, C, T, and E—that is, Structured, Compromiser, Temperate, and Extrovert—but I'm neither a C nor a T.

Schwartz wasn't ruffled by these inaccuracies. "PerfectMatch is the only scientific site out there that's completely transparent and user-operated," she said. "If you disagree with me, you can retake the test anytime and get a different profile that more accurately reflects the subtleties we may have missed. Or you can keep the same profile, but in addition to the matches we provide for you, you can do a search on your own. Say I think a passionate person would want another passionate person. But maybe you know about yourself that you're passionate, but want a calm person, someone who stops the escalation of things. I don't care if what you think is theoretically sound; if it doesn't work for you, you can search using your own criteria."

This, she said, distinguishes PerfectMatch from eHarmony and Chemistry.com. "In the Chemistry test," said Schwartz, who is a friend of Helen Fisher's and a fan of her work, "there was a question about where you'd like to live. And I chose the country. And I *would*—but the people I tend to prefer are in the city. So they sent me people from Bass Breath, Arizona. And there was no way I could change it! At PerfectMatch, we don't overdetermine people's answers that way."

What Schwartz is referring to, of course, is the bugaboo of all these compatibility-matching systems: nuance. "Even if a site lets you choose physical characteristics like height," she said, "there's no way it's going to guess your physical template. It could be lankiness in one case, it could be somebody's eyes in another. We can't get that out of a questionnaire. Nobody can. So we say, 'Go look at the pictures on our site, see who you find attractive, then look at their personality types and see if they're compatible [with you]. You have that option on PerfectMatch.'"

The advantage to scientific matching, she says, isn't to come up with some foolproof formula for romantic connection. Instead, the science serves as a reality check, as a way of not letting that initial rush of attraction cloud your judgment when it comes to compatibility.

"I went out with a man for about a year who, if I'd taken the test with him—we both would have known we should have stopped early on," Schwartz said. "But, of course, I was attracted to him, and probably to the characteristics that were wrong for me, for the wrong reasons. That's what attraction can do. But if you're also armed with information about compatibility—or lack of compatibility—from the very beginning, you might think twice before getting involved, before you make the mistake of e-mailing the cute guy in the picture, like you might on Match."

All the Lonely People

Findings from a recent Pew study on American online dating habits—the first national study of its kind

One in three respondents was unattached . . .

. . . but just 7% were actively looking for partners . . .

. . . and only 4% had been on a date in the last three months.

Of those singles looking for partners, 37% had tried online dating sites . . .

. . . roughly half of those had actually gone on dates as a result . . .

. . . about a third of whom had formed long-term relationships.

Survey of 3,215 American adults by the pew internet and American life project, 2005

Schwartz, who had been married for twenty-three years before she reentered the dating pool, empathizes with Perfect-Match users. "I know what dating is like," she said. "I'm doing it, too. You start to burn out, and you need to find a certain amount of positive reinforcement. So if we can cut down the really inappropriate personalities for you, we can help out."

Of course, before the days of Myers-Briggs and PerfectMatch and academic departments devoted to deconstructing romantic relationships, there were matchmakers. And today, despite the science, they're still thriving. One of the West Coast's largest matchmaking agencies is called Debra Winkler Personal Search, and its slogan is the opposite of scientific: "The art of the perfect match." Indeed, in the FAQ section of the company's Web site, the reply to "How do you go about matching members?" reads as follows:

Our matchmakers use a combination of tools—including experience and intuition—when matching members. We start with basic demographic information such as age, religion, location, physical requirements and other preferences. Personality profiles are also used but not relied upon exclusively. In the end, however, it comes down to your personal matchmaker.

They hand-select the individuals for you to meet. And it is not based on some absolute, statistical formula. It's more like a feeling, gained from years of experience, that tells them you and another person would be great for each other.

Winkler founded the company eighteen years ago and sold it in 2003, leaving its day-to-day operations to Annie Ahlin, who worked with Winkler for fourteen years and until November was the company's president.

"Intuition is a big part of determining long-term compatibility," Ahlin told me. She said many of the agency's clients are people who have tried scientific matching online but had no luck. Ahlin believes she knows why. "When you're reading a profile online, or looking at a photo, it's one-dimensional," she explained. "It's that person's PR for themselves." There's no substitute, she believes, for sitting down with a person one-on-one to get the full picture.

"When we meet our clients, we get a multifaceted impression," she said. "I may read on your profile that you love cats, but when I ask you about it, I learn that you had a beloved cat when you were three and now you're allergic to them. Or, I'll read a personality profile, but when I sit down with this person, I'll think, *Wow, I didn't know she had this kind of energy*. It wasn't reflected on the page."

While the Winkler clients fill out personality profiles similar to the ones found online, the difference, Ahlin believes, is the hour-and-a-half interview. Some of these matchmakers have a psychological background, but others are recruited for different reasons. "We go for people who have a heart, are good listeners, are empathetic, and who just have a feel for matching people for the long term," Ahlin told me. "On resumes, we look for evidence of good people skills—PR, customer service, nursing. It's not necessarily about an intellectual understanding. People either get it or they don't."

Ahlin estimates the agency's success rate at 70 percent—meaning that 70 percent of clients either end up in a relationship engineered by their matchmakers or get engaged to someone they've met through the agency. But unlike the studies being done at eHarmony, there's no follow-up to determine how long these relationships or marriages last, or how satisfying they are down the line. Besides, Ahlin admitted, other variables may play a role in the high number of pairings. "When you pay eight or ten thousand dollars for a service like ours," she said, "you seriously want to find someone. It puts the notion 'I'm really ready' into your subconscious."

Ahlin and her matchmakers use feedback forms like those on Chemistry.com to learn how a match went after two clients have met in person. But whereas the Chemistry.com people classify this step as part of their scientific research, Ahlin says simply, "This way, you know what it is that works so you can get closer the next time—it helps us with intuition."

Often when Ahlin talks about intuition, she describes the same principles that the scientists I spoke with use in their empirically based matching systems. For instance, in matching couples, she follows what is essentially the similarity-complementarity model. "For a match to be successful," Ahlin said, "a couple's goals have to be the same, they have to want the same things in life." But, she added, "that doesn't mean they should be the same person. On the one hand, it's good if they have the same experiences, but sometimes having experiences that are different adds energy to the relationship."

No Ordinary Love

Found Object

While Web sites like eHarmony.com and Chemistry.com attempt to help people of all sorts find potential mates, a number of other online matchmaking services target smaller populations. Herewith a sampling of some of the more specific niche offerings, as they describe themselves:

Conservative Match (www.conservativematch.com)—"Sweethearts not bleeding hearts"

Liberal Hearts (www.liberalhearts.com)—"Uniting Democrats, Greens, animal lovers & environmentalists who are like in mind and liberal in love"

Good Genes (www.goodgenes.com)—"[Helping] Ivy Leaguers and similarly well-educated graduates and faculty find others with matching credentials"

MillionaireMatch (www.millionairematch.com)—"Where you can add a touch of romance to success and achievement!"

The Atlasphere (www.theatlasphere.com)—"A place where admirers of Ayn Rand's novels can meet, 365 days a year, to network, find shared interests, and perhaps . . . even fall in love"

May–December (www.maydecember.net)—"Years apart, coming together"

Golfmates (www.golfmates.com)—"The world's premier online dating service designed specifically for the golfing community"

Riders2Love (www.riders2love.com)—"Bringing Bikers Together . . . For a Ride or For a Lifetime"

EquestrianCupid (www.equestriancupid.com)—"The best dating site in the world for friends and singles who are horse lovers"

CowboyCowgirl (www.cowboycowgirl.com)—"Join thousands of singles that share your love for the country way of life"

GothicMatch (www.gothicmatch.com)—"Where gothic friends and singles feel at home!"

Single FireFighters (www.singlefirefighters.com)—"The ONLY place to meet firefighters without calling 911!"

Positive Love (www.positivelove.com)—"Don't let STDs control your Love Life"

Singles with Scruples (www.singleswithscruples.com)—"[Emphasizing] integrity and good character"

Private Affairs (www.philanderers.com)—"Discreet Extramarital Personal Ads exclusively for discriminating men and women seeking an Extramarital Affair"

Asexual Pals (www.asexualpals.com)—"Because there is so much more to life!"

Like Helen Fisher and Pepper Schwartz, Annie Ahlin believes that similarity and complementarity are situational models. "Each person is unique and contradictory," she told me, "and you can't just group people into big categories, the way the personality profiles do. So one person who is a Type A may be attracted to Type A in the beginning, but then we send them out and find out they need a Type B. So we adjust along the way. We're always adjusting. It's not a scientific process, it's an intuitive one."

Gian Gonzaga, the UCLA researcher hired by eHarmony, doesn't dismiss matchmakers. "I wouldn't be surprised if the basic constructs they're measuring are the exact same ones [that scientists measure]," he said. "Those who are good at matchmaking are the ones who get that four or five things are really critical."

I asked Gonzaga what those four or five things are, and he let out a long sigh.

"Oh, I don't know," he said, sheepishly. "It's funny enough, but I don't know. A similar sense of values. Other things, like agreeableness or warmth, are probably fairly important in terms of people matching up. You want two people who are relatively similar on wanting to cuddle, or things like that."

At the word "cuddle," I raised an eyebrow.

"It's kind of an unscientific term," he said, "but . . ."

I asked Gonzaga if using science to try to find lasting love might be too lofty a goal—a method that seems promising in theory but that turns out to be no more effective than consulting a matchmaker or cruising at your local bar. He disagreed.

"Imagine being in a bar," he said, "and how hard it would be to find five people you might connect with. If you actually match those people in the beginning, you're increasing your odds of meeting someone. Also, some people go to a bar to have a drink, some to meet people. We put people seriously looking for a relationship in one place, at the same time. So I think it's both the medium and it's the scale. And a matchmaker only knows so many people, but there are eight million or ten million users on eHarmony."

Moreover, in the future, science-based dating sites will evolve in ways that mimic real-world situations. Galen Buckwalter, eHarmony's research-and-development head, said that rather than relying on self-reports to assess how comfortable a person feels in social situations, his group is developing a model that will use computer simulation to immerse people in scenarios—a bar, a party, an intimate dinner—where variables like gender composition can be altered. "How does this person interact differently as the variables change?" Buckwalter asked. "I don't think we'll be relying on self-report twenty years from now. I think not only will data collection advance, but so will our analysis. We're just at the beginning, really."

Indeed, it may well take a generation before we learn whether the psychological, anthropological, or sociological model works best. Or maybe an entirely different theory will emerge. But at the very least, these dating sites and the relationships they spawn will help us to determine whether science has a place, and if so, how much of a place, in affairs of the heart.

Meanwhile, until these sites start sending me better dating prospects, I figured I'd take Neil Clark Warren up on his offer to introduce me to the thirty-eight-year-old single board member he thought would be such a good match for me. But when I asked a company spokesman about him, I was told that he had recently begun seeing someone. Did they meet through eHarmony? My potential soul mate declined to answer.

LORI GOTTLIEB is the author of Stick Figure (2000) and a co-author of the forthcoming *I Love You, Nice to Meet You.*

The Perfect Mark

How a Massachusetts psychotherapist fell for a Nigerian e-mail scam.

Mitchell Zuckoff

L ate one afternoon in June, 2001, John W. Worley sat in a burgundy leather desk chair reading his e-mail. He was fifty-seven and burly, with glasses, a fringe of salt-and-pepper hair, and a bushy gray beard. A decorated Vietnam veteran and an ordained minister, he had a busy practice as a Christian psychotherapist, and, with his wife, Barbara, was the caretaker of a mansion on a historic estate in Groton, Massachusetts. He lived in a comfortable three-bedroom suite in the mansion, and saw patients in a ground-floor office with walls adorned with images of Jesus and framed military medals. Barbara had been his high-school sweetheart—he was the president of his class, and she was the homecoming queen—and they had four daughters and seven grandchildren, whose photos surrounded Worley at his desk.

Worley scrolled through his in-box and opened an e-mail, addressed to "CEO/Owner." The writer said that his name was Captain Joshua Mbote, and he offered an awkwardly phrased proposition: "With regards to your trustworthiness and reliability, I decided to seek your assistance in transferring some money out of South Africa into your country, for onward dispatch and investment." Mbote explained that he had been chief of security for the Congolese President Laurent Kabila, who had secretly sent him to South Africa to buy weapons for a force of élite bodyguards. But Kabila had been assassinated before Mbote could complete the mission. "I quickly decided to stop all negotiations and divert the funds to my personal use, as it was a golden opportunity, and I could not return to my country due to my loyalty to the government of Laurent Kabila," Mbote wrote. Now Mbote had fifty-five million American dollars, in cash, and he needed a discreet partner with an overseas bank account. That partner, of course, would be richly rewarded.

Mbote's offer had the hallmarks of an advance-fee fraud, a swindle whose victims are asked to provide money, information, or services in exchange for a share of a promised fortune. Countless such e-mails, letters, and faxes are sent every year, with a broad variety of stories about how the money supposedly became available (unclaimed estate, corrupt executive, and dying Samaritan being only a few of the most popular). Worley, who had spent his adult life advocating self-knowledge and introspection, seemed particularly unlikely to be fooled. He had developed a psychological profiling tool designed to reveal a person's "unique needs, desires and probable behavioral responses." He promised users of the test, "The individual's understanding of self will be greatly enhanced, increasing the potential for a fulfilled and balanced life." And Worley was vigilant against temptation. Two weeks before the e-mail arrived, he had been the keynote speaker at his eldest granddaughter's graduation from the First Assembly Christian Academy in Worcester, Massachusetts. He cautioned the students about Satan, telling them, "He's going to be trying to destroy you every inch of the way."

Still, Worley, faced with an e-mail that would, according to federal authorities, eventually lead him to join a gang of Nigerian criminals seeking to defraud U.S. banks, didn't hesitate. A few minutes alter receiving Mbote's entreaty, he replied, "I can help and I am interested." His only question was how Mbote had found him, and he seemed satisfied with the explanation: that the South African Department of Home Affairs had supplied his name. When Worley attributed this improbable event to God's will, Mbote elaborated on the story to say that Worley's name was one often that he had been given, and that it had been pulled from a hat after much prayer by someone named Pastor Mark. (A more likely possibility is that his e-mail address was plucked from an Internet chain letter, which he received and passed on, that promised a cash reward from Microsoft to anyone who forwarded the letter to others.) In e-mails, phone calls, faxes, and letters during the ensuing weeks, Mbote laid out the plan: If Worley would pay up-front costs, such as fees to a storage facility where the cash was being kept, and possibly travel to South Africa to collect the money, he would receive thirty per cent, or more than sixteen million dollars.

Worley told Mbote that he lived his life with the "utmost integrity" and didn't want to jeopardize that. He also said that he couldn't fund the operation. (Though he would report nearly a hundred and forty thousand dollars in income in 2001, he had declared personal bankruptcy in the early nineties, had relatively little saved for retirement, and wanted to help his grandchildren through college.) No problem, Mbote answered; "investors" would provide up to a hundred and fifty thousand dollars for airfare and other expenses needed to move the money to the United States, while Worley would act as middleman and curator of the funds.

As promised, in late August, 2001, Worley received a check for forty-seven thousand five hundred dollars, purportedly from one such investor. It was from an account belonging to the Syms Corporation, the discount-clothing chain whose slogan is "An Educated Consumer Is Our Best Customer." Worley was wary. He called the Fleet Bank in Portland, Maine, where the check had been drawn. The bank told him it was an altered duplicate of a check that Syms had paid to the Maryland office of an international luggage manufacturer.

Every swindle is driven by a desire for easy money; it's the one thing the swindler and the swindled have in common. Advance-fee fraud is an especially durable con. In an early variation, the Spanish Prisoner Letter, which dates to the sixteenth century, scammers wrote to English gentry and pleaded for help in freeing a fictitious wealthy countryman who was imprisoned in Spain. Today, the con usually relies on e-mail and is often called a 419 scheme, after the anti-fraud section of the criminal code in Nigeria, where it flourishes. (Last year, a Nigerian comic released a song that taunted Westerners with the lyrics "I go chop your dollar. I go take your money and disappear. Four-one-nine is just a game. You are the loser and I am the winner.") The scammers, who often operate in crime rings, are known as "yahoo-yahoo boys," because they frequently use free Yahoo accounts. Many of them live in a suburb of Lagos called Festac Town. Last year, one scammer in Festac Town told the Associated Press, "Now I have three cars, I have two houses, and I'm not looking for a job anymore."

According to a statement posted on the Internet by the U.S. State Department, 419 schemes began to proliferate in the mid-nineteen-eighties, when a collapse in oil prices caused severe economic upheaval in Nigeria. The population—literate, English-speaking, and living with widespread government corruption—faced poverty and rising unemployment. These conditions created a culture of scammers, some of them violent. Marks are often encouraged to travel to Nigeria or to other countries, where they fall victim to kidnapping, extortion, and, in rare cases, murder. In the nineteen-nineties, at least fifteen foreign businessmen, including one American, were killed alter being lured to Nigeria by 419 scammers. Until recently, Nigerian officials tended to blame the marks. "There would be no 419 scam if there are no greedy, credulous and criminally-minded victims ready to reap where they did not sow," the Nigerian Embassy in Washington said in a 2003 statement. The following year, Nuhu Ribadu, the chairman of Nigeria's Economic & Financial Crimes Commission, noted that not one scammer was behind bars. Last November, however, Ribadu's commission convicted two crime bosses who had enticed a Brazilian banker to spend two hundred and forty-two million dollars of his employer's money on a fictitious airport-development deal. (Prosecutions by U.S. authorities are rare; most victims don't know the real names of their "partners," and 419 swindlers are adept at covering their tracks.)

Despite Nigeria's efforts, the schemes have reached "epidemic proportions," according to a publication by the U.S. Federal Trade Commission. The agency received more than fifty-five thousand complaints about them last year, nearly six times as many as in 2001. The increase is due in part to the Internet, which makes it easy for scammers to reach potential marks in wealthier countries. "If we educate the public to the point where nobody falls for it, then they'll go out of business," Eric Zahren, a spokesman for the Secret Service, the lead U.S. agency in investigating advance-fee frauds, says. The agency estimates that 419 swindlers gross hundreds of millions of dollars a year, not including losses by victims too embarrassed to complain. In February, the son of a prominent California psychiatrist named Louis A. Gottschalk—he identified what turned out to be early signs of Alzheimer's in Ronald Reagan alter analyzing his speech—filed suit seeking to remove his father from control over a family partnership, claiming that Gottschalk had lost more than a million dollars to Nigerian scammers. Some victims try to pass along their losses. The former Iowa congressman Edward Mezvinsky, who had refashioned himself as an international businessman, was caught up in a 419 scam, and during the nineteen-nineties stole from his law clients, friends, and even his mother-in-law to cover his losses. He is serving more than six years in prison after pleading guilty to thirty-one counts of fraud.

Robert B. Reich, the former Labor Secretary, who has studied the psychology of market behavior, says, "American culture is uniquely prone to the 'too good to miss' fallacy. 'Opportunity' is out favorite word. What may seem reckless and feckless and hapless to people in many parts of the world seems a justifiable risk to Americans." But appetite for risk is only part of it. A mark must be willing to pursue a fortune of questionable origin. The mind-set was best explained by the linguist David W. Maurer in his classic 1940 book, "The Big Con": "As the lust for large and easy profits is fanned into a hot flame, the mark puts all his scruples behind him. He closes out his bank account, liquidates his property, borrows from his friends, embezzles from his employer or his clients. In the mad frenzy of cheating someone else, he is unaware of the fact that he is the real victim, carefully selected and fatted for the kill. Thus arises the trite but none the less sage maxim: 'You can't cheat an honest man.' "

Born in the small town of Zanesville, Ohio, Worley joined the Army after high school. He served for a year as a staff sergeant with the 101st Airborne Division in Vietnam, earning decorations that included a Bronze Star. In 1976, after fifteen years in the military, he was convicted of driving a car for a fellow-serviceman who held up a store; nevertheless, Worley received an honorable discharge and was later pardoned for his role in the robbery. He went to college and divinity school, and got a Ph.D. in psychology through correspondence courses from the Carolina University of Theology, then in Mount Holly, North Carolina. A. Erven Burke, a Baptist pastor who has known Worley for nearly thirty years, has called him a man of "integrity and honesty," dedicated to helping others.

In the early nineteen-nineties, Worley developed a sixty-item questionnaire that he called Worley's Identity Discovery Profile, or W.I.D.P., which sought to quantify a person's temperament in three areas: social and vocational, leadership, and relationships. W.I.D.P. assigned labels to each: Introverted Sanguine, Sanguine, Phlegmatic, Melancholy, or Choleric, or a blend, such as Phlegmatic Introverted Sanguine. People whose "living patterns" were primarily focussed on fulfilling a temperament need were labelled Compulsive. Over rime, Worley built a successful business selling W.I.D.P. to churches, businesses, schools, individuals, and other counsellors.

Worley's own profile was Melancholy Compulsive in the social-vocational realm, Choleric Compulsive in leadership, and Introverted Sanguine in personal relationships: inward, headstrong, needy. The combination, he said later, made him ripe for scamming. He had abundant time to Strategize with Nigerian partners, he tended to ignore warnings, and he yearned for his family's approval. (Anticipating his fortune, he asked his daughters to list all their debts, which he promised to pay.) But Worley's egotism also may have made him think he could gain the Upper hand. When Mbote asked him to fly to South Africa to collect the money, he agreed—but only if Mbote reimbursed him for lost wages. Worley set the price at thirty-five thousand dollars a week.

After the Syms check proved false and Mbote failed to send a replacement, Worley told him that their partnership was over. A few days later, though, he began receiving e-mails from someone claiming to be Mohammed Abacha, the eldest surviving son of Nigeria's late dictator General Sani Abacha, who reputedly stole billions from the Nigerian treasury. Mohammed Abacha told Worley that Joshua Mbote had been operating surreptitiously on the Abacha family's behalf, but had bungled so badly that Abacha decided to step forward. He told Worley that the story about buying weapons had been a ruse to protect the Abacha family, and their money, which, he said, was actually hidden in Ghana. Soon Worley was put in touch with someone claiming to be the General's widow, Maryam Abacha. In a torrent of phone calls and e-mails, she appealed to Worley: "I learned you wanted to hear from me," she wrote. "Here I am. Help me." In his e-mails, Worley seemed invigorated by this new scenario; he apparently believed that he was on the verge of becoming rich while rescuing a woman in distress.

In late November of 2001, Worley spent several thousand dollars on an attorney who specialized in international tax planning. The attorney warned him against the seeming opportunity, as did Barbara Worley. She knew little about her husband's "project," as he called it, but she didn't like it. Barbara lived a life that revolved, as she put it, "around God and family." In some ways, she still looked to her husband for guidance, as she had when they were in high school; she expressed her opinion, but deferred to his judgment.

Worley dismissed these warnings; now that he had committed money to the partnership, he had a vested interest. By the end of 2001, he was telling the Abachas that he had investigated ways to ship the cash secretly and had searched a half-dozen countries for a bank that would accept a huge deposit without alerting authorities. He reassured them that they had chosen the right partner, and begged for patience: "I am a smart man and very cautious and do not want anything to go wrong." He settled on the Bermuda-based Bank of Butterfield, and in late January, 2002, he told Mrs. Abacha that be had spent forty-three hundred dollars to open an account there. There will be no trail back to the U.S. and no tax to be paid," he wrote.

Worley's partners soon persuaded him to wire more than eight thousand dollars to retain a Nigerian lawyer and "to cover the bank fees and late fees" that supposedly were the last barriers to the transfer. But, after more delays and growing doubts, Worley told them that he would not travel abroad—the money, they said, had been moved to Amsterdam—to collect the cash. They couldn't change his mind, so they tried a different approach. Mrs. Abacha asked him for help in claiming forty-five million dollars that she told him was hidden in an account of the Federal Ministry of Aviation at the Central Bank of Nigeria. It was a textbook 419 tactic. When Worley doubted Mbote, he disappeared; when Worley wouldn't travel for one treasure, they found another. He sent more money.

Under this new plan, Worley allowed his partners to file false documentation claiming that he was a private aviation contractor to whom the Nigerian government owed forty-five million dollars. At the end of February, Worley crossed another line when a patient named Jennifer Morlock came to his home office for a counselling session. She had barely arrived when he told her he was engaged in a business venture with partners in Nigeria. Violating his profession's code of ethics, he asked to borrow fifteen thousand dollars. Morlock went home, spoke with her husband, and agreed. By noon, Worley was at her door to collect the money. The same day, he went to a nearby liquor store with a Western Union outlet and wired all fifteen thousand dollars to Nigeria. He soon repaid Morlock, with interest, by borrowing on his credit card.

Meanwhile, Worley was growing more and more distressed. The number of correspondents was increasing—at one point, he counted nine—and the spelling of their names kept changing. He complained of receiving letters from "Maram Abacha," "Mariam Abacha," and "Mrs. Maryam S. Abacha." "I would think that everyone would know how to spell their own real name," he wrote testily. "Obviously, someone does not." When he still seemed no closer to receiving the payment he'd been promised, he made a bid for sympathy, falsely telling his partners that he had been given a diagnosis of cancer. That didn't work, so he told them that he was abandoning the project: "To date, I have lost nearly fifty thousand dollars chasing a rainbow with a pot of gold at the end of it. I cannot go any further. It will take me two years to recover from this, and I will probably be dead by then." Mrs. Abacha's reassurances wrung thirteen thousand dollars more from Worley, but in April, 2002, he swore he was through, writing, "I must stop this financial torment and anguish and pray that God forgives me for my pursuit of money, simply put, greed."

For five months, Worley didn't correspond with the Nigerians. Then, in September, 2002, a fax arrived from someone calling herself Mercy Nduka, who claimed to be a confidential secretary at the Central Bank of Nigeria. Nduka told Worley that the Aviation Ministry funds were still waiting for him, and that she was secretly working with the Abacha family. She said that they needed five hundred thousand dollars to bribe five Nigerian bank officials who had the power to release the forty-five million; plus, she said, they needed another eighty-five thousand to cover fees. Worley refused to send more money, so Nduka and her boss, Usman Bello, said that they would borrow it from investors. Worley would pass along the investors' money and then receive the fortune on behalf of the Abachas, with shares going to him, Nduka, and Bello for their services.

Soon men who claimed to be investors began calling Worley from New York and Washington, asking him to provide credit references and requesting that he put up collateral for the loans they were considering making to him. He refused to offer collateral, but that was never the point. The investors' questions and demands made him feel more secure, as though they were truly weighing whether to lend him money. In late November, 2002, Worley received a check for ninety-five thousand dollars, drawn on an account of the Robert Plan Corporation, a Long Island-based insurance company. Without verifying it, as he had done with the Syms check, he deposited it at a branch of Fleet Bank. In fact, the check was fraudulent, but a novice employee at the insurance company approved Fleet's payment inquiry. When the money appeared in Worley's account, Nduka told him to wire eighty-five thousand dollars to a bank in Latvia, which he did. He wired another thirty-eight hundred dollars when Bello said that he needed to buy a Rolex watch to bribe a bank official. Although the Robert Plan employee had approved the check and Fleet had paid it, Worley, according to federal law, was responsible for repayment. (If a fraudulent check is passed deliberately, a depositor can face felony charges.) About a month later, the Nigerians sent Worley a check for some four hundred thousand dollars from a Michigan marketing company. This check was real, but it had been stolen and altered to make Worley the payee. When Worley deposited it at a branch of Citizens Bank near his home, it cleared; following Nduka's instructions, he wired the money to an account in a Swiss bank.

In the meantime, the Nigerians had ensnared the wife of a Mississippi car dealer, a woman named Marcia Cartwright. In October, 2002, she had received a 419 e-mail from a man saying he was desperate to get his money out of Nigeria. Two months later, Cartwright received a check made out to her for nearly a hundred and nine thousand dollars, drawn on the account of a Texas advertising firm, and deposited it at the Farmers & Merchants Bank of Booneville, Mississippi. It cleared, and, on orders from Nigeria, she sent Worley a cashier's check for a hundred and six thousand dollars, keeping the remainder for herself. He deposited the money in his Citizens account on January 15, 2003. The next day, he wired a hundred thousand dollars to the Swiss account.

Worley told Nduka and Bello that he was certain they now had more than enough to bribe the bankers and cover other expenses. Nduka, ever polite, said that they were not quite there. She sympathized with his frustration, and Worley promised to be patient. She asked for another six thousand dollars—the balance of Cartwright's cashier's check—to bribe the telex operators who would execute the transfer. Worley hesitated, but soon sent that money, too. Finally, Nduka told him what he longed to hear: "All is set for the final release of your fund."

That day, the president of the Farmers & Merchants Bank learned that the check Marcia Cartwright had deposited a month earlier had been returned as fraudulent. Bank officials called federal and state authorities, and Citizens Bank, where Worley had deposited Cartwright's cashier's check, was also notified. An investigator for Citizens, a former police lieutenant named Michael Raymond, told Worley what had happened and said that he was investigating potentially fraudulent activity. Worley sent frantic e-mails and made repeated calls to Nigeria, begging for a replacement check. Nduka answered with bad news: Bello had been attacked by robbers and was comatose. But, she wrote, "I have reached an agreement with them for your fund to be released as planned on Friday." All she needed was a thousand dollars to bribe another telex operator.

Worley seemed on the verge of panicking. "If you are my friend, then make it happen tomorrow," he pleaded. "Why are you badgering me with this $1,000? I have gone

as far as I will go with this. I am desperate and have nothing else to say at this rime. I am emotionally, spiritually, and financially drained." Nduka answered humbly, calling herself "an ordinary woman" who struggled on four hundred dollars a month. Worley responded that Nduka had "touched my heart." He wired the thousand dollars on January 30, 2003.

The next day, Raymond told Worley that the other check he had deposited at Citizens, the check from Michigan for four hundred thousand dollars, was also phony. Worley knew what that meant, and, according to Raymond, disclosed his suspicion that the Robert Plan check was probably fake, too. When Worley got off the phone with Raymond, be was enraged. "I hate being taken advantage of by you evil bastards," he wrote to Nduka. "This is all lies?" He went on, "Your day will come that you will be judged by God, and so will I. And I am ashamed, and shamed, and an embarrassment to my family, who are so precious and Godly people. What a terrible model of a Christian that I am. Thoughts of suicide are filling my mind, and I am full of rage at you despicable people. I hate living right now, and I want to die. My whole life is falling apart, my family, my ministry, my reputation and all that I have worked for all my life. Dear God, help me. I am so frightened."

In May, 2005, Worley went on trial in U.S. District Court in Boston on charges of bank fraud, money laundering, and possession of counterfeit checks. Worley's overseas correspondents, whose real identities he never knew, disappeared, and were never located or charged. With them went more than forty thousand dollars of Worley's money and nearly six hundred thousand dollars from the checks. Including credit-card interest, money-wiring fees, long-distance telephone charges, and the tax lawyer's bills, Worley's losses may have been closer to eighty thousand dollars.

The prosecutor, an Assistant U.S. Attorney named Nadine Pellegrini, urged the jury to reject suggestions that Worley had simply been scammed. At best, she said, Worley "got in over his head." Pellegrini portrayed Worley as the puppeteer, not the puppet, and said that he knowingly passed bad checks, in the belief that he was entering into a "mutually beneficial arrangement." She focussed Oh Worley's recognition at various points that he was dealing with liars, and said that he displayed "willful blindness" by ignoring the warning signs of their criminality and his own. Pellegrini said that Worley's claims of innocence were undermined by consistent bad conduct—lying to his wife, borrowing from a patient, plotting to avoid taxes, posing as an aviation contractor, claiming to have cancer, and agreeing to bribe Nigerian bank officials. She was unsparing during her cross-examination. "So you don't have any integrity either, do you, Dr. Worley?" she asked. He answered, "No, I don't."

"Ladies and gentlemen," she told the jury, "it's clear John Worley understands behavior of people and motivation of people, and he could and he can manipulate both behavior and reaction. . . . There is only one story here, and that's the story of John Worley's greed."

Worley's lawyer, a former prosecutor named Thomas Hoopes, cast him as a childlike man who was tricked by sophisticated con artists into a check-cashing scheme. Hoopes stressed that Fleet and Citizens had approved payment on the checks, which, he said, reasonably led Worley to believe they were legitimate. He urged the jury to focus on the final thousand dollars that Worley had sent after he knew an investigation was under way—this was evidence, he said, of Worley's gullibility. He likened Worley to Marcia Cartwright, whom the government viewed as a victim despite her also having passed a bad check. (Cartwright made partial restitution, testified for the prosecution, and was not charged.) Mostly, Hoopes urged the jury to view Worley's acts as foolish, not criminal. Hoopes emphasized that Worley had lost heavily in the scam. "It's not willful blindness," Hoopes said. "It is blind trust."

In addition to witness testimony and lawyers' arguments, the jury was given hundreds of e-mails between Worley and the Nigerians which told a story of their own, about a man transformed by his pursuit of riches. Reading the e-mails, in which Worley displays both cunning and credulousness—sometimes in the same message—it is clear that the Nigerians were able to take advantage of his religious convictions, his stubbornness, and his desire to be a hero to Mrs. Abacha and to his family. Patiently and persistently, the Nigerians turned Worley's skepticism into suspension of disbelief, to the point where he seemed to worry that they might not trust him. They made Worley the perfect mark.

The trial took six days, and the jury found Worley guilty on all counts. On February 15th, Worley, now sixty-two, returned to the federal courthouse at the edge of Boston Harbor to face sentencing. Accompanied by more than three dozen family members and friends, be arrived wearing a charcoal suit with a support-the-troops pin on the lapel. U.S. District Judge George O'Toole, Jr., acknowledging the "ordeal" that Worley had been through, said

that he was nevertheless bound by the jury's finding. He sentenced Worley to two years in prison, plus restitution of nearly six hundred thousand dollars, and gave him five weeks to turn himself in. Outside the courtroom, Barbara Worley, a stout woman with blond hair, said they would appeal. (They eventually decided not to.) "My husband is the victim here," she said. "It's an atrocity."

One morning a week later, I drove past acres of winter-brown fields to the Worleys' large, blue-gray house, which was owned by a trust created by the Lawrence family, one of Massachusetts's nineteenth-century industrial dynasties. (The Worleys, looking for an inexpensive place to live after John left the Army, believe that divine guidance delivered them to the Lawrences, who needed the home restored and overseen.) Barbara, in a white bathrobe, let me in, saying she thought the meeting had been rescheduled. The house was dark, and the hallways were filled with packing boxes: Worley was preparing for prison, and Barbara was moving to a small house in a nearby town.

Barbara led the way upstairs to a living room with a brass plaque on the door. "As for me and my house, we will serve the Lord," it read. Worley entered, wearing a red-white-and-blue robe with an eagle on the back. He sat in a green leather chair, and fed treats to Pancake, the family cat. He seemed stunned by his misadventures of the past five years. "The communications that I had with those people were so convincing that I really believed that they were real, they were true," he said. "I would question them and they would come back with a response that was adequate to cover my concerns each and every time." Despite everything, he insisted that he still believed he had been dealing with the real Maryam and Mohammed Abacha. "I think they were legitimately trying to use me and my resources to get their funds out of Nigeria into a safe place where they could have access to them," he said. Worley wasn't sure whom to blame for the bad checks, though Nduka was suspect. "Somehow there was a buy-off, a payoff, or something that went on there, and then it got switched to the point where I was then dealing with fraudsters," he said.

When I asked Worley what he wished he had done differently, he didn't answer directly. Instead, he spoke about hoping that the Abachas would get back in touch with him. However, before they could resume work on the multimillion-dollar transfer, he expected them to send the six hundred thousand dollars that he needs for restitution.

"What if they sent you a check?" Barbara demanded. "Would you put it in the bank to see if it cleared again?"

"Yeah."

"John!" she said.

"I don't know," Worley said finally, sounding defeated. "I have to have time to think about what I would do in that situation."

"My husband is naïve," she explained to me. "He trusts people."

A month later, moments after dropping off Worley at a federal prison in Pennsylvania, Barbara called me in tears. "They knew they couldn't go after the Nigerians, so they just get the person they can reach. They're trying to stop people in America from getting involved in it by making an example of my husband," she said. "Why don't they assign an F.B.I. agent to go after the people who scammed my husband? Where's the justice?"

An enduring trait of Nigerian letter scammers—indeed, of most con artists—is their reluctance to walk away from a mark before his resources are exhausted. On February 5, 2003, several days after the checks were revealed as phony, after Worley was under siege by investigators, after his bank account had been frozen, after he had called his partners "evil bastards," Worley received one more e-mail from Mercy Nduka.

"I am quite sympathetic about all your predicaments," she wrote, "but the truth is that we are at the final step and I am not willing to let go, especially with all of these amounts of money that you say that you have to pay back." She needed just one more thing from Worley and the millions would be theirs: another three thousand dollars.

"You have to trust somebody at times like this," she wrote. "I am waiting your response."

Back-to-School Blogging

Web logs help new students prepare for campus life.

BROCK READ

Like almost any student preparing to move into a freshman dormitory, Nora Goldberger spent much of the summer batting around questions about college life: Would she struggle to make friends? Which courses should she take, and which ones should she avoid? How would she get her laundry done?

Such concerns are the stuff that precollege apprehension is made of. But Ms. Goldberger, a Philadelphia native who is beginning her studies at Davidson College, says she feels more at ease than most of her friends. Credit for that, she says, goes to her computer.

Throughout the summer she joined her peers in posting questions on a Web log, or blog, for students at the North Carolina college. Using the informal discussion forum, maintained by students at Davidson, she chatted with her soon-to-be-classmates and hit up wizened upperclassmen for advice on the coming year.

When Ms. Goldberger wondered if she could trust the university's laundry service—which collects students' dirty clothes and washes them at no cost—she asked her fellow bloggers. Within a day, several upperclassmen had given her a consensus opinion: Don't be afraid to use the service, but wash delicate items yourself.

When she wanted to know how much she should expect to pay for a semester's worth of textbooks, she quickly got a number of estimates. And after she mentioned offhandedly that she'd been listening to a song by the band Sister Hazel, she compared notes with two other students who owned all of the cult group's albums.

The popularity of blogs is helping students across the country meet their dorm mates, form study groups, and make friends before they set foot on their new campuses.

Free, Web-based tools like Xanga and LiveJournal, which allow users to easily create their own blogs, have attracted a large following among high-school and college students. At institutions like Davidson, enterprising students have used the popularity of the medium to create thriving communities in which incoming freshmen meet to exchange practical questions, personal information, movie recommendations, and jokes.

Administrators say the sites constitute an important new trend: Students who grow up using the Web as a social tool can now ask their peers, instead of college officials, for counseling on the process of preparing for college. The colleges aren't about to get rid of their orientation sessions, but officials say freshmen who use the Internet for college planning may become more self-reliant students.

Meanwhile, students like Ms. Goldberger relish the chance to get a head start on college socializing. "This has definitely made me feel more excited and better about coming here," she says. "I have friendly faces and people to look out for, and I'm just a little bit better informed."

Flood of Questions

The success of the Davidson students' Web log (http://www.livejournal.com/community/davidson college) has exceeded the expectations of its creator, Emily McRae, a sophomore.

Ms. McRae started the site—a group journal that allows anyone to post comments—this summer after speaking to an incoming freshman who found her own blog inundated with questions about Davidson from people she'd never met.

The flood of questions, Ms. McRae says, proves that first-year students are eager to touch base with their peers—and that information travels quickly among bloggers. A Web log, she reasoned, would let incoming freshmen share questions about Davidson among a broad pool of college-age bloggers.

The blog is hosted on LiveJournal, a free service. Anyone can see the postings, but only those who have signed up with the service can contribute. On pages that resemble discussion boards, users with pseudonymous screen names like "onenoisygirl" and "atrain14" post questions or comments, and others respond.

At first the site was popular with freshmen who logged on to do little more than introduce themselves and post their course schedules. But soon upperclassmen happened onto the Web log and made their presence known. Students began asking about cafeteria food, required courses, dorm-room accouterments, and other concerns of campus life, and the community took off.

"I think freshmen became really interested when there were upperclassmen giving sage advice on classes, orientation, and living in Davidson," says Peter Benbow, a sophomore who regularly contributes to the site as "crazydcwildcat7."

"We know what it's like to come wide-eyed and mystified onto a college campus," he says.

The site now has almost 80 users, including alumni and prospective students. "The alumni get to reconnect, the freshmen get to ask advice, the upperclassmen get to consult one another, and the prospectives get lots of answers for 'Why did you come to Davidson?'" says Ms. McRae.

The site has a generally earnest tone, with posts that range from informational to motivational. During the week before freshmen headed to campus for orientation activities in August, students sought tips for decorating their rooms and updated classmates on their packing progress. One first-year student tried to set up a knitting party, a sophomore offered an inspirational poem, another student asked her classmates for help in choosing a gym class, and an alumnus reminded frantic packers to bring cold medicine.

The site has caught on with upperclassmen and alumni because they remember how daunting the transition to dormitory life can be, says Rachel Andoga, a sophomore who helps run the LiveJournal blog and posts regularly under the name "rachigurl5." "I imagine that if I'd had something like this when I came to college, I wouldn't have been as insanely nervous about starting out," she says. "Everyone's so friendly on the site."

Ms. Andoga hopes that the blog will survive the start of the academic year and become an informal bulletin board where first-year students can organize study sessions and publicize extracurricular activities. The bonds that students have formed on the site are real, she says. She expects to drop in on several freshman bloggers to see how they are adjusting to college, and she is helping to plan a party for all the Davidson students who joined the LiveJournal community.

Lurking Administrators

Davidson administrators, too, have been tuning in to the blog—even though they had no part in its creation—in an effort to determine what issues freshmen are most worried about.

"I think I've spent as much time on the site as the students have," jokes Leslie Marsicano, director of residence life at the college. "It's been riveting and addicting for me."

She has recommended the site to students and parents who called her office with niggling questions about bedsheets and laundry arrangements. Some students have speculated that she had recruited upperclassmen to log on and serve as mentors to incoming students.

To the contrary, she says: She's strictly a watcher of the blog. "I think if we tried to encourage the site we'd spoil it," she says. "It works so much better because it comes from the grass roots, and there's no administration figures for students to be suspicious of."

But Davidson officials do have a vested interest in the online gathering. For many prospective students, Ms. Marsicano says, the Web log may be a more effective form of advertisement than a glossy brochure or even a college visit. High-school students

---

Chemistry 115, Midnight Treks, and Knitting: Online Reassurance at Davidson College

Users who post messages on Davidson College's student-run Web log, or blog, discuss a wide range of topics, including course schedules, extracurricular activities, and their views of college life. A sampling of comments:

sleeprocker (August 13, 1:27 A.M.): I signed up for Organic Chemistry, but now I think I want to drop back to Chem 115. The course schedule says that all the sections are full right now. How likely is it that I can make the switch?

nayetter (August 13, 7:17 A.M.): Go to the 115 class on the first day (or both 115 classes, if you can) and talk to the professor, and explain your situation to him. He won't be able to raise the ceiling beyond how many students can fit in the lab at once, but if you talk to him then he'll do his best to accommodate your needs.

Also, watching the "add/drop" page like a hawk is a good idea.

squirrelhanded (August 15, 10:18 P.M.): Here's a piece of advice. . . . If you have the choice between having an incredible talk with a good friend in the hallway or getting 3 extra hours of sleep . . . take the talk. If it's between ANOTHER 5-point math assignment and a midnight magi-

cal mystery trek through town. . . . go crazy. Have a good time.

Don't get me wrong, academics are priority. They're the reason we're all here in the first place. . . . but choose your memories. Make them lasting ones.

rachigurl5 (August 16, 8:28 A.M.): Exactly. Education isn't limited to the classroom . . . God, if I had a nickel for every Great Thing I've learned from long midnight talks . . . le sigh!

superluci (August 18, 3:23 A.M.): I haven't been able to find out anything about this online. I'm a knitter, and I'm looking for yarn stores in the Davidson area. Are there any stores selling yarn and knitting supplies near the college? I'm stocked up reasonably well coming in but I doubt my supply will last long. I love knitting with other people so if anybody wants to knit with me or have stitch & bitch parties that would be awesome! See you all. . . . TODAY!: Belk 243, come by and chat!

advice_and_ice (August 18, 6:51 A.M.): There's a knitting store on main street. would a crocheter be welcome occasionally?

choosing between Davidson and its competitors are adept at tracking down student Web logs and are likely to trust them to provide an unfiltered view of college life, she says.

Davidson is lucky: The blog has been consistently cheery and cordial. But Ms. Marsicano says she'd be unhappy if she felt that students were misrepresenting the institution. "When parents call me to ask how long the beds are, they're really asking if there's some nice person who will look after their baby," she says. "I'd like to be able to keep pointing to this site to say, 'The kids can take care of each other.'"

Bonding Online

Blogs are not the only online forums that have developed to help incoming students break the ice with classmates. Many students are using e-mail lists and social-networking sites like Friendster and Thefacebook to make bonds before arriving on the campus.

For Anna Dinndorf, a freshman at Washington University in St. Louis, a personal Web log and an online discussion group led to romance. Last spring she mentioned her early-admission acceptance in her online journal, a daily blog she maintains on the popular Web site Diaryland. Another blogger who had been admitted to Washington spotted the entry and invited Ms. Dinndorf to join a growing group of incoming students in a discussion forum that makes use of a free service by Yahoo, the popular search site.

"I had never spoken to her before, and I never spoke to her after that, but she clued me in, and for that I'm very thankful," Ms. Dinndorf says.

In the Yahoo group, users not only post questions about courses and dorm preparations at Washington, but contribute to a database of students' contact information, exchange screen names so they can chat on instant-messaging software, and create informal polls that ask their peers to comment on matters both political and personal. For example, almost none of the incoming freshmen approve of the Bush administration's proposed Constitutional amendment to ban gay marriage. On a lighter note, most students said they order soft drinks by asking for "soda" instead of "pop" or "Coke."

Chattier Comments

With more than 200 students registered, the discussion at Washington is chattier and less focused than the Davidson blog. It's also a bit franker: Some students grouse about their housing assignments or other matters. But the incoming students, by and large, seem to have few quibbles with Washington, and administrators surfing the site would find little to worry about.

For most students, the site is more about socializing than it is for airing serious concerns. Ms. Dinndorf says she's spent much of her time on the site just meeting people, including a fellow freshman whom she now calls her boyfriend. The pair, it turns out, have met only once in real life, but they've gotten to know each other through posts on the discussion board and on AOL Instant Messenger chats.

"We started out talking online and things developed, and then we met in person when I went to Washington for a weekend in July," says Ms. Dinndorf. "It's so great to be going down to school and already have all these connections."

The connections, she says, are forged by jokes and gossip as much as by serious conversations. Some students took notice when a rumor popped up on the board that the radio "shock jock" Howard Stern's daughter would be part of the Class of 2008 at Washington, but, ultimately, the claim was debunked.

For Ms. Dinndorf, that light touch is a welcome distraction from the often tense process of preparing to move away from home. "Basically, the site has been like a sounding board for all the precollege jitters and worries and questions and everything that everyone goes through at this point," she says. "And I'm really addicted to it."

E-Mail Is for Old People

As students ignore their campus accounts, colleges try new ways of communicating

DAN CARNEVALE

Maurice Johnson, a freshman studying interior design at Harcum College, spends hours each day online, both for work and play. One thing he rarely does, though, is open his campus e-mail account. "I check it about every other month," he says.

Moe, as his friends call him, has his own fashion label and regularly corresponds with other designers through his MySpace page. He chats with friends through instant messaging. He also has a few commercial e-mail accounts that he checks daily.

But his Harcum account lies dormant. Not only does he prefer other means of communication, but the college e-mail addresses—created by a combination of a student's first and last names plus part of the student's identification number—are too complicated to give out to friends or to check online. "I don't like the Harcum e-mail," he says. "It's too confusing."

Mr. Johnson is not alone in his disdain for campus e-mail. College officials around the country find that a growing number of students are missing important messages about deadlines, class cancellations, and events sent to them by e-mail because, well, the messages are sent to them by e-mail.

In response, some institutions require that students check their college e-mail accounts so they do not miss announcements, holding students responsible for official information that comes through that medium. Other institutions are attempting to figure out what technology students are using to try to reach them there.

A 2005 report from the Pew Internet and American Life Project called "Teens and Technology" found that teenagers preferred new technology, like instant messaging or text messaging, for talking to friends and use e-mail to communicate with "old people." Along the same lines, students interviewed for this article say they still depend on e-mail to communicate with their professors. But many of the students say they would rather send text messages to friends, to reach them wherever they are, than send e-mail messages that might not be seen until hours later.

Students have not given up on e-mail altogether. In fact, a survey of more than 1,300 students at the University of Illinois at Chicago earlier this year found that 86 percent of them still use campus e-mail regularly. Eszter Hargittai, an assistant professor of communication studies and sociology at Northwestern University who conducted the survey, says students often ignore messages coming from their colleges, considering them a form of spam.

Brian Niles, chief executive officer of TargetX, a company that helps colleges use technology to recruit new students, says colleges need to branch out and find new ways to connect with students.

"It's not that they don't read e-mail," Mr. Niles says. "It's that they have their own world, and you need to know how to reach them in that world."

'Big Family'

Harcum, a two-year college outside Philadelphia, enrolls about 900 students. It is the type of institution where the college president's wife can be found tending to the plants in front of campus buildings. "Harcum's a very big family," says Lisa A. Mixon, assistant director of public relations and marketing.

Ms. Mixon created the college's MySpace page (http://myspace.com/harcumcollege) after she realized that many students were missing important messages. They were paying no attention to the college e-mail newsletter. They were not even showing up for ice-cream socials—and everyone likes ice cream.

It seemed clear that students were not ignoring their MySpace pages, though. Some students here have more than one such page. Some have MySpace pages for their pet snakes.

A key feature of MySpace and other social-networking sites is the ability to link with another user by designating him or her a "friend." Friends are able to send each other messages and announcements, and view pictures and items that are blocked from other users.

After the college put up its site in August, Ms. Mixon searched online for Harcum students with MySpace pages and found more than 200 of them. She contacted the students individually, over the course of a few weeks, and asked each of them to become a friend of the college. So far, more than 160 have said yes.

Joseph J. Diorio, Harcum's director of public relations and marketing, who admits that he relies on Ms. Mixon to keep him "hip," says he finds the online service to be a good way for the college and its students to get to know each other better.

Using MySpace is like "being able to walk into a residence hall and everybody's door is open," says Mr. Diorio. "We knew that's where students were going."

Harcum keeps its MySpace page lively, with photos of students on the campus. Officials have also posted a picture of a cartoon rabbit with the caption: "College prepares you for the real world, which also sucks."

"We thought, What the heck, it's not the official Harcum Web page," Mr. Diorio says.

A student also writes a weekly blog for the college MySpace page. Current blog posts include some complaints about cafeteria food interjected in discussions about forthcoming events. Ms. Mixon plans to invite additional students to write for the blog, letting them vent honestly about anything on their minds.

Reaching Students

As some students reduce their use of e-mail in favor of other means of communication, colleges are trying new technologies to reach them. Among the new techniques:

Cellphone Text Messages

Students live and die by their cellphones. A few colleges now provide information, including snow closures and sports scores, to students instantly, wherever they are.

Instant Messages

Some professors now make themselves available to students via instant-messaging software, especially during office hours. And some admissions counselors use it to answer questions from prospective students faster, and through a medium in which many students are most comfortable.

MySpace and Facebook

Some colleges have begun using the popular social-networking services to provide information to their students, including calendars of events, deadlines, and other announcements. College officials also use the services to present a lighter side of an institution—something different from the stuffy main Web page.

"They like Harcum," she says, "but they'd be honest about things they didn't like."

'Not as Formal'

In addition, the Harcum MySpace page includes dates of important events, such as volleyball games and alumni weekends. It also allows students to pose general questions to college officials, if they are not sure whom they need to talk to. "If they have a question and they can't get to the right person," Ms. Mixon says, "they have someplace to go."

Ashley M. Elliott, a veterinary-technology student in her second year at Harcum, says the Harcum MySpace page shows the college is making an effort to reach students. "It's down to the student's level," she says. "It's not as formal as the Web site."

Becoming MySpace friends with a college may seem lame to some students. But Steven J. Arnone, another veterinary-technology student in his second year at Harcum, wants to convince his classmates that all the cool kids are doing it.

"I'm spreading the word that it's not stupid," Mr. Arnone says. "To be honest, I'm proud. It's like slapping a college sticker on the back of your car."

The MySpace service asks users to rank their friends, which could put Harcum in the awkward position of seeming to play favorites. Ms. Mixon says she picks the college's top friends randomly. "I just keep rotating them," she says.

She says that the college may have a contest to determine who deserves to be listed as Harcum's favorite friend, possibly judging how much school spirit a student displays on his or her MySpace page.

While Harcum has convinced a good portion of its student population to be its friends, some friends are closer than others.

"I'm a friend, but I've never actually been to the site," says Shay Curry, who is in her first year studying early-childhood education at Harcum.

Ms. Curry says she felt obligated to befriend Harcum when the request came in—even though the invitation did not indicate that it was mandatory to do so.

Matthew J. Roane, a Harcum psychology major who has four e-mail accounts, says he never uses his Harcum account or the college MySpace page. He finds out about announcements and events the old-fashion way—from printed fliers.

Trying Too Hard?

Just because students use new means of communication does not mean that colleges should, however.

Some students at the University of Maryland at College Park, for instance, say they would rather keep talking to professors and campus officials through e-mail.

"I like to separate my personal life from my school life," says Amanda J. Heilman, a freshman studying animal sciences at the university.

Emily Diehl, another freshman majoring in animal sciences, agrees. "It would be weird if all your professors had Facebook," she says.

But even the students who use their campus e-mail accounts will sometimes not open messages that appear to be from the college.

"These students are walking spam filters," says Paul Lehmann, the director of student activities at Utica College. "They are masters of multiple forms of communication and have perfected the skill of cutting through the multiple forms of communication that they are bombarded with to find what they are interested in and want to reply to."

The result, he says, is that no matter how important the message from the college, students will often choose to ignore it.

"Students receive multiple 'official' messages a day, with information that runs the gamut of importance," says Stephanie Dupaul, director of undergraduate business admissions at Southern Methodist University's business school. "A reminder that there is a free movie in the student center on Friday night hits their in boxes with the same level of urgency as an announcement of registration deadlines or changes in official university policies."

Pennsylvania State University has been trying different ways to use technology to reach students, including podcasts, RSS feeds, and Web video clips.

The university's latest attempt is to use cellphone text messaging, by setting up a service that can blast announcements to students using the technology.

Subscribers to the service can let the university know what types of messages they want to receive. Many choose to get updates on emergency announcements, such as school closures, and some also want to be notified about upcoming concerts or sports scores, which are available seconds after a Nittany Lions game has ended.

Bill Mahon, assistant vice president for university relations at Penn State, says many students use text messaging more than e-mail. So administrators expected the plan to be popular with the students.

"We thought maybe in a year we'd get 2,000 people," Mr. Mahon says of the program, which started in August. "As it turns out, in the first three weeks or so we have 1,000 subscribers."

Mr. Mahon says the service will really come in handy in the winter, when snow can create havoc on campus. And the service has already proved useful, he says. Not long ago, a road near the campus was closed because of an oil spill. Penn State officials were able to let subscribers know immediately, so they could plan an alternate route.

"In the old days, we couldn't do that," Mr. Mahon says. "We just let thousands of people drive on that road to find policemen sending them in a different direction."

Not all students want the cell-phone service, he says. It is best to give them many options. "The key is, you can't do just one thing," he says.

Web Portals

Harrisburg University of Science and Technology, a new institution that began enrolling students last year, has already run into difficulties communicating with students.

Because many students do not check their e-mail, officials are creating a Web portal for students. James B. Young, associate vice president for information services at the university, says the portal will be a place that lets students register for courses and find out about upcoming events, and that provides other services.

But, he says, it will be much more informal than the main university Web page. He hopes to put a "youthful edge to it."

"We're brand new and we're pushing habits early," Mr. Young says. "Hopefully MyHU will become an indispensable space."

The University of South Carolina Upstate, on the other hand, is sticking with campus e-mail accounts. Officials have informed students that e-mail is the official means of communication and that they must check it.

In the past, any student could send a message via campus e-mail to the entire student population. Students used the capability to find roommates and for other informal matters, but it also led to many unwanted messages for students.

"So they stopped checking it," says Laura Puckett-Boler, assistant vice chancellor for student and diversity affairs. "They were missing announcements."

So the university set up an electronic newsletter, called E-blast, that is sent out once a week with students' informal announcements and requests. Now only certain administrators can send bulk e-mail.

Despite the requirement, not everybody on the campus uses their university e-mail accounts, she says. But students manage to get by, either by forwarding the information to another account, or just learning what they need to know through friends.

"They're still responsible for the information," Ms. Puckett-Boler says. "Students figure out what to do."

UNIT 5

Societal Institutions: Law, Politics, Education, and the Military

Unit Selections

Key Points to Consider

- The overview to this unit mentions that civil institutions were overlooked in the excitement after the collapse of the former Soviet Union. Find on the Internet and read Francis Fukuyama's essay, "The End of History." Do you agree with his arguments? Does computing have any role to play in the development of civil institutions?

- Find out how profitable some big-city U.S. papers are. Are you surprised at the results?

- Use the Internet to find out if commentators have anything to say about the difficulty of managing complex weaponry in outposts around the globe.

- How has high-tech weaponry fared in the Iraq war?

- Do you read political blogs? Why would someone read a political blog rather than *The New Statesman* (on the right) or *The Nation* (on the left)?

Student Web Site

www.mhcls.com/online

Internet References

Further information regarding these Web sites may be found in this book's preface or online.

ACLU: American Civil Liberties Union
 http://www.aclu.org
Information Warfare and U.S. Critical Infrastructure
 http://www.twurled-world.com/Infowar/Update3/cover.htm
Living in the Electronic Village
 http://www.rileyis.com/publications/phase1/usa.htm
Patrolling the Empire
 http://www.csrp.org/patrol.htm
United States Patent and Trademark Office
 http://www.uspto.gov/
World Intellectual Property Organization
 http://www.wipo.org/

After the collapse of the Soviet Union, many Americans believed that democracy and a market economy would develop in short order. Commentators seemed to have taken a cue from Francis Fukuyama's imposingly entitled essay, "The End of History," that appeared in *The National Interest* in 1989. "What we may be witnessing," he wrote, is "not just the end of the Cold War, or the passing of a particular period of post-war history, but . . . the universalization of Western liberal democracy as the final form of human government." Fukuyama, deputy director of the State Department's planning staff in the elder Bush administration, hedged a bit. He was careful to argue that the victory of liberal capitalism "has occurred primarily in the realm of ideas or consciousness and is as yet incomplete in the real or material world."

We have grown wiser since those heady times. The events of September 11 showed Americans, in the most brutal fashion, that not everyone shares their values. More importantly, the political and economic chaos that has been so much a part of Russian life for the past decade, has led many commentators to conclude that liberal democracy and a market economy require more than "the realm of ideas or consciousness." They need, above all else, institutions that govern political and economic relationships. They require mechanisms for business contracts and land use, courts to adjudicate disputes, government agencies to record titles and regulate resources, and, not just a mechanism but a tradition of representative government. In a phrase, democracy and a market economy require the institutions of civil society.

We in the United States and Western Europe have long traditions of civil society, in some cases reaching back hundreds of years. The French sociologist, Emile Durkheim (1858–1917), hoped that as traditional societies gave way to urban industrial societies, rule by contract and law would provide the glue for social cohesion. To a very large extent this has been the case in the United States. The room in which I am writing is part of a house that sits on a small piece of property that belongs to me. I am confident that my title to this property is part of the public record. Were someone to appear on my doorstep with a claim to my property, a procedure exists to adjudicate our dispute. If I do not personally understand the rule, I can hire a lawyer, a specialist in civil procedures, to make my case before an independent judiciary.

But the rapid introduction of information technology over the past decade has proven problematic for the orderly resolution of disputes. It has been difficult for legislators to formulate laws for a set of relationships—those mediated by a computer—that are not well understood. Even if laws are successfully enacted, their existence does not guarantee compliance, especially in the absence of an enforcement mechanism. As Jonathan Band points out in "The Copyright Paradox," "the problem with piracy

DOD Photo by SSgt T R Tolley, USAF

is not the inadequacy of existing laws, but the high cost of enforcing any law against the large universe of infringers." Still, the computer and recording industry tries. The Digital Millennium Copyright Act of 1998 provides severe penalties for both piracy and for publicizing ways to circumvent security mechanisms. Not severe enough for students, it appears. Those who have read their university's computer-use policies are more likely to violate them (see "Piracy, Computer Crime, and IS Misuse at the University").

Education is yet another piece of civil society. American students in public schools study the mechanism of government, recite the pledge of allegiance, and learn to revere the sacred texts of American democracy: the Declaration of Independence, the Constitution, and the Bill of Rights. One task of American public education is to instill a common ideal of citizenship into a diverse and changing population. The contribution of computing to education—if not always uncontroversial—has been substantial. From educational software, to wired college campuses, to Internet-mediated distance education, computing has been a part of education since the introduction of personal computers in the early eighties. If you throw in mass, standardized testing, an enterprise nearly unthinkable without computers, computing has been a part of American education since the fifties.

Consider the job of a university president. Leading a college in the age of the Internet requires sifting through e-mail, reading blogs, and fending off criticism the volume of which would be inconceivable without networked computers. According to Jeffrey Selingo ("Facing Down the E-Maelstrom"), "many universities' Web sites list the e-mail address of every employee from the president on down, enabling unencumbered access to all of them."

No civil institution is more sacred in a democracy than the way it chooses public officials. Liberals have been envious ever since Richard Viguerie's computer-generated mailing lists—an innovation at the time—contributed to Ronald Reagan's victory in 1980. At a time when even Senate Majority Leader Harry Reid has a blog, some Democrats hope that the computer is finally on their side. According to Lakshmi Chaudry ("Can Blogs Revolutionize Progressive Politics"), "if television made politics more elitist and less substantive, blogs . . . have the potential to become engines of truly democratic, bottom-up, issue-rich political participation." The history of computing, for all that it has delivered, is littered with shards of broken promises. Only time will tell about this one.

A civil society is unimaginable without a free press. Yet in the United States, the readership of newspapers is declining, along with the numbers watching TV news, the very medium that did away with so many afternoon papers not long ago. While TV news has added the aggressive editorializing of Lou Dobbs and Bill O'Reilly, large newspapers have developed Web sites to generate readership and revenue. "Center Stage" tells the story of several online newsrooms. Here we learn that "with many people posting and without fixed schedules, it is impractical to funnel all content through a copy desk. So a fair amount of copy produced by the Web staff gets little or no editing, and few items get the multiple reads that are routine in print."

Strictly speaking, the military is not part of civil society. Yet since civilians control the U.S. military by constitutional mandate, we can consider it a civil institution without stretching the meaning of the term terribly. As of this writing, the war in Iraq is front-page news. On the eve of the Iraq war in April, 2003, *Business Week Online* ran a pair of articles illustrating what one called the "doctrine of digital warfare," a doctrine that stresses air power, agile ground forces, and computer communication over lethal firepower and a large infantry. Sophisticated military systems take years to develop and deploy. Despite some tough going in Iraq, the U.S. commitment to a high-tech battlefield has not waned. Steve Featherstone ("The Coming Robot Army") describes the Army's Future Combat System "as the costliest program in history." The individual soldier is still part of the vision, "but he has been reconfigured as a sort of plug-and-play warrior, a node in what is envisioned as a sprawling network of robots, manned vehicles, ground sensors, satellites, and command sensors." Featherstone's piece makes it clear that military hardware is the result of a partnership between the engineering talent of the private sector and the very deep pockets of the American military.

The Copyright Paradox

Fighting Content Piracy in the Digital Era

JONATHAN BAND

The Internet has given rise to a puzzling copyright paradox. To hear the recording industry tell it, the copyright world as we know it is coming to an end. Between Gnutella and Napster-like sites, fans can easily exchange music files over the Internet, sending CD sales plummeting. Copyright law is powerless to halt the onslaught of Internet piracy, which will soon remove any economic incentive for creative activity.

At the same time, libraries, universities, and content user groups, voicing their helplessness before ever-strengthening copyright legal protections, insist that the content provider community is better positioned than ever to eliminate traditional user privileges. Historically, for example, the fair use doctrine has allowed academic users to reproduce without payment parts of copyrighted works for purposes such as criticism and classroom use. But, say these users, the new Uniform Computer Information Transactions Act (UCITA), adopted by the National Conference of Commissioners on Uniform State Laws in 1999, and the technological measures protected by the 1998 Digital Millennium Copyright Act (DMCA) will soon enable content providers to create the "pay-per-use" environment they have long sought.

Who's Right?

At first blush, it would seem that the content providers and the content users—the Recording Industry Association of America and the libraries and universities (hereafter the library community)—can't both be right. We can't possibly be living in both the best of times and the worst of times for copyright protection. One of these two communities must be exaggerating.

Indeed, the available facts suggest that the recording industry may be overstating the harm caused by Napster and Gnutella. Although CD sales in record stores near university campuses have fallen (college students are among the biggest users of Napster and Gnutella), CD sales overall have grown 8 percent since last year. The group 'N Sync recently broke the one-week record for CD sales, ringing up more than 2.5 million. Beyond these hard numbers, anecdotal evidence suggests that people sample music on Napster and then buy the higher-quality CD if they like what they hear. So Napster-like sites may actually spur CD sales.

Moreover, the content community seems to be on a winning streak. The recording industry secured a preliminary injunction against Napster (at this writing, the injunction was stayed pending appeal). A judge imposed the largest amount of statutory damages in copyright history—more than $100 million—on MP3.com. The major sports leagues shut down IcraveTV. And the motion picture studios won an injunction against DeCSS, software that unlocks the encryption protecting DVDs.

Still, there is no question that the Internet facilitates piracy by allowing the widespread dissemination of lawful copies with no degradation in quality. Further, technologies like Gnutella do not require a central server, as does Napster or a typical pirate web site, making it hard to detect infringers. In short, the Internet does seem to pose an increasing threat to providers of copyrighted content.

At the same time, technological measures like encryption or copy controls encoded in software will prevent a teacher from making digital copies of an article for classroom use, and the DMCA has banned devices that enable users to circumvent such measures. The net effect will be less fair use, and the de facto extension of the copyright term, as works remain technologically protected long after the copyright expires. (This assumes, of course, that the DMCA will survive the constitutional challenges now being mounted against it.)

The content community fears too little copyright protection; the library community fears too much. How can this be?

Similarly, UCITA validates the enforceability of shrink-wrap licenses (which appear on software packages) and click-on licenses (which appear on screen and which users must click to install software or access a web site) and will accelerate their use to prohibit fair use by contract. The circuit courts are split as to whether such license terms are preempted by federal law, and it may take years for the Supreme Court to resolve the issue. And if the Supreme Court decides that federal law does not preempt such license terms, licensees will be at the mercy of the licensors.

Which brings us back to the copyright paradox: both the content community and the library community appear to have legitimate, yet opposite, concerns about the future of copyright in the digital era. The content community fears too little protection, the library community too much. How can this be?

Of Ends and Means

The paradox is rooted in a mismatch between the stated ends of the content community and the means employed to reach them. The content industries have responded to the threat of Internet piracy by pushing for more legislation, such as the DMCA and UCITA. But although new legislation is the most expedient response to the threats posed by new technologies, it probably will not hinder Internet piracy because the problem with piracy is not the inadequacy of existing laws, but the high cost of enforcing any law against the large universe of infringers. Each of the hundreds of millions of computers attached to the Internet is a potential distributor of unlawful copies. Although of limited use against this large universe of potential individual pirates, the new legislation ensnares the libraries—the most public of our institutions.

The following examples demonstrate the disparate impact of UCITA and the DMCA. A software firm markets a CD-ROM subject to a shrink-wrap license that prohibits the further distribution of the CD-ROM or its contents. If a consumer acquires the CD-ROM, copies it onto his hard drive, and e-mails it to a dozen friends, the publisher is unlikely to find out about the breach of contract, much less prosecute it. If, however, a library acquires the CD-ROM and lends it out in accordance with copyright's first-sale doctrine, the publisher almost certainly will sue the library for breach of contract. While the shrink-wrap license (validated by UCITA) cannot stop infringing activity by the consumer, it can stop otherwise legitimate lending activity by the library.

Similarly, the DMCA probably would not discourage a college student from finding a circumvention utility somewhere on the Internet and using it to elude the technological protection on his favorite CD so that he could make the sound recordings on it available to his friends. But the DMCA would prevent a library from acquiring the utility through legitimate channels to make a preservation copy permitted under Section 108 of the Copyright Act. The DMCA flatly bans almost all circumvention devices, even those capable of noninfringing uses. Put differently, the DMCA would do little to deter unlawful conduct, but much to deter conduct that is otherwise lawful.

In short, libraries (and other high-profile entities such as universities and large corporations) are likely to obey the laws and contractual terms that apply to them because they are law-abiding institutions and because they know they probably would be sued if they did not follow the law. In contrast, individual infringers are not likely to obey the law because they are not law-abiding and because they know they are unlikely to get caught. Seen in this light, the copyright paradox makes sense. Because the new laws do not meaningfully address Internet piracy, the content community remains vulnerable to piracy, but libraries are kept from engaging in historic library activities. The new laws also interfere with legitimate corporate activities. UCITA, for example, allows a software company to prohibit a business from selling copies of software when it sells a subsidiary even though copyright's first-sale doctrine permits the transfer.

The logical next question is whether this discontinuity between means and ends, and the resultant collateral damage, is inadvertent or intentional. The charitable view is that the content community really believes that this legislation will help reduce piracy and has no intention of stifling library and educational activities. A more cynical perspective is that the content community pursued this legislation in part because it allowed the rollback of fair use, first-sale, and other user privileges the content community has always opposed. Indeed, conspiracy theorists believe that the libraries were the real target of the legislation, and Internet piracy served as a convenient pretext. Although generally I am not a conspiracy theorist, I am reminded of the following aphorism: "Just because you're paranoid doesn't mean they're not out to get you."

Piracy, Computer Crime, and IS Misuse at the University

Who commits software misuse? Knowing the answer to this question will help organizations protect their information systems.

TIMOTHY PAUL CRONAN, C. BRYAN FOLTZ, AND THOMAS W. JONES

"Professor, can you help me? I installed software on my computer from my friend's CD and it doesn't work anymore. My friend is gone and I don't have the original CD. What should I do?"

Does this statement sound familiar? If so, you are not alone. Many students openly admit to illegally installing software on home computers or otherwise misusing computer information systems. Other studies have examined characteristics of students (and non-students) who admit to committing information systems misuse, piracy, and computer crime. We used a survey to examine demographic characteristics of students as well as their awareness of university computer usage policies.

Thirty-four percent (34%) of students responding to this survey admit to committing some form of software misuse or piracy and 22% admit to committing data misuse during their lifetimes. Knowing that students commit information systems misuse is not new [10]. However, today's students are tomorrow's professionals. As such, an understanding of the demographic factors common to those students who commit misuse could help both university information systems departments and organizations better protect their information systems.

An amazing number of students in this study report committing some form of information systems misuse or computer crime. As mentioned, 34% and 22% of respondents admit committing software misuse and data misuse during their lifetimes, respectively. Software misuse in this study means destroying or copying software, using copied software, or distributing copied software without permission. Data misuse means accessing, modifying, or copying data stored on a computerized information system without authorization. Behaviors characteristic of misuse were located in the literature and condensed into these two areas. This study examines these responses by years of experience with computers, academic classification (underclassmen, upperclassmen), major, gender, and age.

Familiarity with computers. As expected, students who are more familiar with computers report committing more misuse. Upperclassmen, students with more experience, and students in computer-related majors all report committing more misuse than others. An interesting trend appears (Table 1) when broken down by academic classification. Underclassmen (freshmen and sophomores) report the least amount of software misuse (18%), while upperclassmen (juniors and seniors) report notably larger amounts (37%). Overall, 34% of respondents report software misuse; 7% report 10 or more occurrences. A similar pattern also is observed for data misuse, although fewer incidents of misuse are reported (underclassmen, 12%; upperclassmen, 25%). Overall, 22% of respondents report data misuse; 3% report 10 or more occurrences.

Further, of greater concern, individuals who indicate reading the computer usage policies also report more software misuse and data misuse. For example, of underclassmen who read the computer usage policies, 39% committed software misuse and 8% admit 10 or more occurrences. Of underclassmen who had not read the policies, 15% committed software misuse and 2% report this level of misuse. This unexpected and troubling result can be observed for both software misuse and data misuse in most academic classifications.

Years of experience with computers also are thought to influence misuse [10]. As seen in Table 2, respondents with greater experience report greater numbers of misuse. For example, all individuals with less than one year experience indicate no software misuse during their lifetimes, whereas 41% of individuals with more than 14 years experience make the same claim. Also, 78% of individuals with less than one year experience indicate never engaging in data misuse. This percentage drops to 61% for individuals with more than 14 years experience.8

Table 1 Classification and Familiarity with the University Computer Usage Policy

Software Misuse: How many times have you destroyed or copied *software*, used copied *software*, or distributed copied *software* without permission during your lifetime?

Usage Policy	Class	Ten or More	Seven to Nine	Four to Six	One to Three	Never	N
	Under	3.1%		1.5%	13.8%	81.5%	65
	Upper	8.5%	3.6%	7.5%	17.3%	63.1%	388
All	Masters	4.3%	6.5%	4.3%	15.2%	69.6%	46
	Other	5.9%		5.9%	41.2%	47.1%	17
	Overall	7.4%	3.3%	6.4%	17.4%	65.5%	516
	Under	7.7%		7.7%	15.4%	69.2%	13
	Upper	16.0%	6.0%	9.0%	17.0%	52.0%	100
Read Policy	Masters		20.0%	10.0%	30.0%	40.0%	10
	Other					100.0%	1
	Overall	13.7%	6.5%	8.9%	18.5%	52.4%	124
	Under	1.9%			13.5%	84.6%	52
	Upper	5.9%	2.8%	6.9%	17.4%	67.0%	288
Did Not Read Policy	Masters	5.6%	2.8%	2.8%	11.1%	77.8%	36
	Other	6.3%		6.3%	37.5%	50.0%	16
	Overall	5.4%	2.3%	5.6%	17.1%	69.6%	392

Data Misuse: How many times have you accessed, modified, or copied *data* stored on a computerized information system without authorization during your lifetime?

Usage Policy	Class	Ten or More	Seven to Nine	Four to Six	One to Three	Never	N
	Under	1.5%		3.1%	7.7%	87.7%	65
	Upper	3.4%	2.6%	4.4%	14.5%	75.2%	387
All	Masters	4.3%	2.2%		8.7%	84.8%	46
	Other	5.6%		5.6%	11.1%	77.8%	18
	Overall	3.3%	2.1%	3.9%	13.0%	77.7%	516
	Under			7.7%	15.4%	76.9%	13
	Upper	7.1%	5.1%	5.1%	17.2%	65.7%	99
Read Policy	Masters		10.0%		20.0%	70.0%	10
	Other					100.0%	1
	Overall	5.7%	4.9%	4.9%	17.1%	67.5%	123
	Under	1.9%		1.9%	5.8%	90.4%	52
	Upper	2.1%	1.7%	4.2%	13.5%	78.5%	288
Did Not Read Policy	Masters	5.6%			5.6%	88.9%	36
	Other	5.9%		5.9%	11.8%	76.5%	17
	Overall	2.5%	1.3%	3.6%	11.7%	80.9%	393

Upperclassmen, students with more experience, and students in computer-related majors all report committing more misuse than others.

Misuse by major is presented in Table 3. As one might expect, computer information systems (CIS) majors report the most software misuse with 24% of CIS majors performing 10 or more instances within their lifetimes. This percentage does not exceed 8% for another major. Examining the percentages of individuals who report no misuse presents a similar view. Forty-nine percent of CIS majors indicate they never committed software misuse, while 57% of arts and science majors and 71% of business and economics majors make the same claim. Further, 73% of CIS majors, 78% of business and economics majors, and 83% of arts and sciences majors deny ever committing data misuse.

Gender and age. Other factors examined by this research include gender and age. As anticipated, males commit more misuse than females, while individuals in their twenties and thirties commit more misuse than other age groups. Gender often is associated with increased misuse [10]. Fifty-five percent of

Table 2 Experience with Computers

Software Misuse: How many times have you destroyed or copied *software*, used copied *software*, or distributed copied *software* without permission during your lifetime?

Years of Experience	Ten or More	Seven to Nine	Four to Six	One to Three	Never	N
less than 1					100.0%	9
1 to 2	2.1%	2.1%	2.1%	16.7%	77.1%	48
3 to 6	5.0%	1.0%	6.0%	20.1%	67.8%	199
7 to 10	7.8%	7.2%	7.2%	15.0%	62.7%	153
11 to 14	7.0%	3.5%	7.0%	17.5%	64.9%	57
more than 14	24.4%	2.4%	9.8%	22.0%	41.5%	41
not sure				14.3%	85.7%	7

Data Misuse: How many times have you accessed, modified, or copied *data* stored on a computerized information system without authorization during your lifetime?

Years of Experience	Ten or More	Seven to Nine	Four to Six	One to Three	Never	N
less than l			11.1%	11.1%	77.8%	9
1 to 2		4.2%		6.3%	89.6%	48
3 to 6	2.5%		3.5%	14.5%	79.5%	200
7 to 10	3.3%	3.9%	4.6%	12.4%	75.8%	153
11 to 14	1.8%	3.6%	3.6%	14.3%	76.8%	56
more than 14	14.6%	2.4%	7.3%	14.6%	61.0%	41
not sure					100.0%	7

males and 76% of females report no instances of software misuse, and 13% of males and only 2% of females report committing 10 or more software misuses. Further, 69% of males and 86% of females never committed data misuse, while 6% of males and less than 1% of females report committing 10 or more data misuses. However, the aforementioned percentages change dramatically when broken down by familiarity with computer usage policies. For example, of respondents who read the policies, the percentage committing 10 or more software misuses increases to 18% of males and 5% of females. Whereas, of those who do not read the policies, only 10% of males and 2% of females report this much software misuse. And, of those who read the policies, the percentage committing 10 or more data misuses increases to 7% of males and 2% of females. Of respondents who do not read the policies, these percentages are 5% of males and less than 1% of females.

The final demographic factor examined in this study is age. Thirty-five percent of respondents under 40 and 39% of respondents 40 and older report committing software misuse during their lifetimes, while 22% of respondents under 40 and 17% of respondents 40 and older report committing data misuse. However, the highest frequency of misuse occurs within the younger groups. Nine percent of respondents under 20 and 8% aged 21 to 29 report committing 10 or more lifetime software misuses, as compared to 4% each of respondents 30 to 39 and 40 and older. (Of the 509 usable responses to this question, only 23 respondents are 40 and older.) For data misuse, 3%, 3%, 2%, and 9% of respondents less than 20, 21 to 29, 30 to 39, and 40 and older, respectively, report 10 or more instances. However,

these results must be interpreted with caution as this survey was administered to college students, and thus is biased toward younger respondents.

A Widespread Problem

Other studies have evaluated the prevalence of information systems misuse and computer crime by university students. A recent study notes 40% of students surveyed at two universities admitted to committing software piracy [3]. Further, none of these students were worried about punishment for their actions [3]. In a survey of 581 students at a southern university, 41% "knowingly used, made, or gave to another person a 'pirated' copy of commercially sold computer software" at some time in the past, while 34% did so during the past year [10]. Further, 18% "accessed another's computer account or files without his or her knowledge or permission just to look at the information or files," while 7% "added, deleted, changed, or printed" information from another's files without permission. Finally, 21% guessed passwords in attempting to access another student's accounts or files. In another study, 10% of respondents committed software misuse during the prior semester [5]. These misuse figures are very close to those generated within the present research, which indicate 34% of respondents committed software misuse during their lifetimes, while 22% committed data misuse sometime during their lifetimes.

The demographic results of the present study are also very similar to the results of past research. For example, males over 22 years old, enrolled as seniors or graduate students, were most likely to report committing misuse [5]. Further, misuse was especially common among majors dealing with forestry, engineering, business, liberal arts, and the sciences [5]; and misuse was more prevalent among computer science and engineering students, especially those in upper-level classes [3]. As previously noted, this research suggests males commit more misuse than females, as do students majoring in CIS.

Although the three universities discussed within this article publicly post computer usage policies (two of the universities insist students read these policies before email accounts are activated), only 24% of the respondents report having actually read the computer usage policies. Of these, 62% indicate reading the policies more than one year before the survey. Also, respondents who indicate reading the policies report higher levels of misuse.

These findings present an interesting challenge to universities: should additional resources be expended to familiarize all students with the university computer usage policies? The majority of students are unfamiliar with the university computer usage policies; however, students who are familiar with the policies report committing more misuse. Although an explanation of this unexpected result is beyond the scope of the current research, some possible explanations can be identified. For example, students who commit misuse could be more interested in reading the university computer usage policies than students not committing misuse. A second alternative might involve the university computer usage policies acting as a challenge to students and thus increasing the performance of misuse.

Until further research clarifies this matter, university computer security administrators must reconsider the methods used to educate students as to acceptable and unacceptable uses of university computing resources. This research clearly demonstrates that the majority of students are unfamiliar with the rules guiding their usage of university computing equipment. Perhaps repeated exposure would be more effective.

These unexpected results challenge the long-held belief that university computer usage policies prevent or limit the performance of misuse. Since organizations also utilize computer usage policies, the concern generated from these findings must be extended from the university setting to the organizational setting.

Although the use of student samples raises questions of representativeness and generalizability, in this case the students are valid users of the computing resources of these organizations. Users are defined as "individuals who interact with the system regularly" [11]; students utilizing university computers meet this definition of a user. From a technological standpoint, universities and other organizations share the same types of technology and the same risk factors. Universities must utilize the same methods as other organizations to protect themselves. In addition, universities may face even greater threats than the typical business organization. Since the computers in a classroom or lab are open for public use, tracking an instance of misuse usually leads back to the computer rather than the user. Further, university networks are often more vulnerable than corporate networks due to the need for collaboration and easy access to data [8].

The target population for this study is university students. The sample consists of 519 students enrolled in junior- and senior-level business courses at three Midwestern U.S. universities.

Table 3 Misuse by Major

Software Misuse: How many times have you destroyed or copied *software*, used copied *software*, or distributed copied *software* without permission during your lifetime?

Major	Ten or More	Seven to Nine	Four to Six	One to Three	Never	N
Arts and Science	4.3%	2.2%	8.7%	28.3%	56.50%	46
Business and Economics	3.9%	3.3%	6.1%	15.6%	71.1%	360
CIS	24.4%	2.6%	3.8%	20.5%	48.7%	78
Other	7.7%	7.7%	15.4%	19.2%	50.0%	26
Undecided				33.3%	66.7%	3

Data Misuse: How many times have you accessed, modified, or copied *data* stored on a computerized information system without authorization during your lifetime?

Major	Ten or More	Seven to Nine	Four to Six	One to Three	Never	N
Arts and Science	5.0%		2.5%	10.0%	82.5%	40
Business and Economics	1.9%	1.9%	4.4%	14.2%	77.7%	367
CIS	9.1%	3.9%	2.6%	11.7%	72.7%	77
Other		3.8%	3.8%	7.7%	84.6%	26
Undecided					100.0%	3

The universities (and courses) were selected based upon the willingness of colleagues to participate in the study. Although this sample does not represent all students enrolled at these universities, this sample was deliberately chosen to maximize the potential for reported misuse conducted by the subject students. Students from arts and science colleges, business and economics colleges, and engineering colleges commit more misuse than other students [5].

All three universities utilize computer usage policies that outline acceptable and unacceptable use of computer systems. Each university also posts the policies on its Web site; two universities require their students to read these policies before email accounts are issued. The use of such policies has been linked to lower levels of misuse, while failing to use them has been linked to misunderstanding of correct use and thus to misuse [12].

The survey questionnaire was constructed by combining Straub's Computer Security Model Victimization Instrument [12] and items from instruments focusing on Ajzen's Theory of Planned Behavior [1]. The items based on Ajzen's Theory of Planned Behavior were customized to two specific areas of interest: software misuse and data misuse.

Conclusion

Although concern with information systems misuse and computer crime is not new [10], it is of growing concern to commercial organizations [4] and the military [9]. Moreover, information systems misuse, piracy, and computer crime are international in scope. Reports suggest that the frequency of misuse is increasing rapidly [2]. Further, the cost of misuse is extremely high. A recent survey reports that respondents estimated losses of $141,496,560 during 2004. However, only 269 of 494 respondents were willing to report estimated dollar losses [4]. The actual loss is probably greater than stated since estimates only include recognized losses, and many organizations elect not to report losses for fear of negative publicity [4, 7].

Many organizations are so dependent upon their information systems that disruptions or failures often result in severe consequences that range from inconveniences to catastrophes such as complete organizational failure [6]. In addition, access to organizational information systems through networks and dial-in accounts leads to an extremely vulnerable environment [6]. This same situation may be found in universities around the country. Campus networks are becoming "an alluring target for hackers" and, possibly, terrorists [8].

Several researchers have reported that three-fourths or more of computer security violations by humans could be attributed to insiders or other trusted individuals, although current research suggests this trend may be changing. The 2004 CSI/FBI Computer Crime and Security Survey notes that about half of all reported incidents originate within the company, while half are external [4].

This research confirms past conclusions: students commit misuse and pirate software. Students possessing greater familiarity with computers report committing greater amounts of misuse. Individuals with certain majors, such as CIS, tend to commit more misuse than others. In addition, individuals with more computer experience tend to commit greater amounts of misuse than novices. Also, more misuse occurs by upperclassmen than by underclassmen. Finally, males commit more misuse than females, and individuals in their twenties and thirties report more misuse than other age groups.

However, the results of this research also suggest university computer usage policies are not effective in preventing students from committing misuse. First, the majority of respondents never read the computer usage policies at their universities. Second, students who read the policies report committing more misuses than those who do not read the policies. This unexpected result, which disagrees with past findings, suggests the need for continued research in this area.

Both of these results are particularly concerning as many organizations utilize written policy statements to explain proper and improper use of organizational information systems. It is thought such policies reduce the occurrence of misuse within an organization. Future research should address the issue of familiarity with computer usage policies. Given that the majority of respondents have not read the policies despite being required to do so by their respective universities, a method to enforce exposure to computer usage policies must be found.

Controlling misuse has been a concern in the MIS literature since the early 1960s [10], however, many organizations and critical systems are still vulnerable, especially as the modern computer environment incorporates ever-increasing amounts of networking and Internet connectivity. Existing research suggests organizations can defend themselves against such misuse by using computer usage policies. Unfortunately, the results herein, as well as simple observations of ever-increasing amounts of misuse, suggest these policies are ineffective. As a result, organizations need to consider other methods of protecting themselves. The first problem noted in the current research is a lack of familiarity with computer usage policies. Perhaps organizations need to enforce exposure, rather than relying on the user to read the policies. Further, repeated exposure could increase user retention of computer usage policies. The second problem noted in this research is the ineffectiveness of such policies at stopping misuse. While this could be a result of lack of familiarity with organizational computer usage policies, organizations must consider the possibility that such policies are simply ineffective in today's environment. This suggests other approaches should be explored, especially more active approaches, such as password protection and encryption.

The results of this research also suggest university computer usage policies are not effective in preventing students from committing misuse.

It is clear that additional means are necessary for every member of an organization to develop greater appreciation of, to understand, and to comply with computer usage policies. Unfortunately, simply having a company-wide computer usage policy in place does not correspondingly lead to the practice that the policy will be observed (or even enforced by the organization).

> **These results are particularly concerning as many organizations utilize written policy statements to explain proper and improper use of organizational information systems.**

Future research should examine the impact of multiple exposures to those policies and should explore the relationship between repeated exposure to computer usage policies and reported instances of misuse as well as the implementation, communication, and enforcement of such policies. In order to reduce the cost and frequency of information systems misuse, piracy, and computer crime in today's environment, the authors recommend that an organization's (university's) employee (student) orientation program must include discussion of correct and incorrect computer usage, penalties imposed for violations, moral appeals, and methods of enforcement along with tougher enforcement policies.

References

1. Ajzen, I. *Attitudes, Personality, and Behavior.* The Dorsey Press, Chicago, IL, 1988.
2. Anthes, G.H. Hack attack: Cyberthieves siphon millions from U.S. firms. *Computerworld 30*, 16 (1996), 81.
3. Carnevale, D. Software piracy seems rampant among students in a survey at 2 universities. *The Chronicle of Higher Education: Daily News* (March 4, 2002).
4. Gordon, L., Loeb, M., Lucyshyn, W., and Richardson, R. *2004 Ninth Annual CSI/FBI Computer Crime and Security Survey,* Computer Security Institute, 2004.
5. Hollinger, R.C. Crime by computer: Correlates of software piracy and unauthorized account access. *Security Journal 2*, 1 (1992), 2–12.
6. Loch, K.D., Carr, H.H., and Warkentin, M.E. Threats to information systems: Today's reality, yesterday's understanding. *MIS Quarterly 16*, 2 (1992), 173–186.
7. McAdams, A.C. Security and risk management: A fundamental business issue. *The Information Management Journal 38*, 4 (2004), 36–44.
8. Olsen, F. The growing vulnerability of campus networks. *The Chronicle of Higher Education 48*, 27 (March 15, 2002), A35–A36.
9. Schwartz, K.D. Hackers are ubiquitous, malicious, and taken far too lightly, experts say. *Government Computer News 16,* 23 (1997), 81–82.
10. Skinner, W.F. and Fream, A.M. A social learning theory analysis of computer crime among college students. *The Journal of Research in Crime and Delinquency 34*, 4 (1997), 495–518.
11. Stair, R.M. and Reynolds, G.W. *Principles of Information Systems: A Managerial Approach, 3E.* Course Technologies, Cambridge, MA, 1998.
12. Straub, D.W. Deterring computer abuse: The effectiveness of deterrent countermeasures in the computer security environment. Dissertation, Indiana University Graduate School of Business, 1986.

TIMOTHY PAUL CRONAN (cronan@uark.edu) is a professor and the M.D. Matthews Chair in Information Systems in the Sam M. Walton College of Business at the University of Arkansas. **C. BRYAN FOLTZ** (foltzc@utm.edu) is an assistant professor in the computer science and information systems deparment, College of Business, at the University of Tennessee, Martin, TN. **THOMAS W. JONES** (twjones@uark.edu) is a professor of Information Systems in the Sam M. Walton College of Business at the University of Arkansas.

From *Communications of the ACM,* 49(6), June 2006, pp. 85–89. Copyright © 2006 by Association for Computing Machinery, Inc. Reprinted by permission.

Facing Down the E-Maelstrom

**When every campus dispute has the potential to explode—
thanks to e-mail and blogs—presidents are never off the hot seat**

JEFFREY SELINGO

By San Francisco state university standards, it was a small protest. Early last month some 100 students turned out at a campus career fair to demonstrate against the presence of military recruiters. A few protesters were removed by university police officers for allegedly violating the student-conduct code on rallies.

Ten years ago such an incident might have received a mention in the student newspaper, and that would have been that. But times have changed. Within hours of the protest, the university's president, Robert A. Corrigan, had received two dozen e-mail messages, mostly from people off the campus, criticizing the administration for allowing students to march against the military. Then, about a week later, while Mr. Corrigan was traveling, his in-box was flooded with about 200 more messages, many from out of state, demanding that he not censure the students involved.

The deluge of messages left Mr. Corrigan wondering how so many people had found out about such a small skirmish on his campus. So his assistant poked around on the Web and discovered that six days after the protest, a liberal blog (http://sf.indymedia.org) run by the San Francisco Independent Media Center had posted an article headlined "Defend Free Speech Rights at San Francisco State University" that included Mr. Corrigan's e-mail address.

It was not the first time that Mr. Corrigan has been electronically inundated after a campus incident. Three years ago he received 3,000 e-mail messages after a pro-Israel rally was held at the university.

"Every time something happens on campus, an organized group goes after you," he says. "The president becomes the conduit for all this hate stuff, for the political polarization in this country, and electronic communication spreads it everywhere."

Among college leaders, Mr. Corrigan is hardly alone in his frustration. It used to take days or weeks, if ever, for an incident simmering on a campus to ignite into a full-fledged controversy. But now, thanks to e-mail—and, more recently, blogs—news about even minor campus dust-ups is disseminated much more quickly, and well beyond the bounds of the college or local community. The president, as the institution's public face, must deal with the resulting flood of interest in his campus's doings.

Compounding the problem of dealing with the sheer volume of responses is the fact that the e-mail or blog reports of the initial clash are frequently taken out of context or just plain wrong—often purposely so, to advance political agendas.

"Campuses are no longer places for civil public discourse," says Robert Zemsky, chairman of the Learning Alliance for Higher Education, a think tank at the University of Pennsylvania that advises college leaders on management issues. "They've become places for political campaigns that are getting sourer and sourer. People are no longer willing to fight their battles without trying to muster allies outside of campus."

For campus CEO's accustomed to responding to nearly everything that happens at their institutions, this new environment has left them not only fatigued, but also wondering how best to handle a situation before they become the next Lawrence H. Summers or Elizabeth Hoffman.

Few campus leaders have figured out how to manage the huge volume of e-mail they receive when their campuses are thrust into the spotlight. Presidents who pick and choose which messages to respond to know that they do so at their own peril, since they never can be sure which dispute will draw the attention of well-to-do donors or influential politicians.

And the many leaders who have just given up and pushed the situation off on assistants face another danger: "There is something about having as many tentacles out there as possible," says Mr. Corrigan, of San Francisco State. "The notion that you are available to lots of people can help you manage the enterprise better. It's too bad if we're forced to cut ourselves off."

Everyone Has a Beef

Conflicts on campuses are nothing new, of course. But colleges today are no longer viewed as ivory towers. Institutions of all sizes and types are under greater scrutiny than ever before from lawmakers, parents, taxpayers, students, alumni, and especially political partisans. Empowered by their position or by the fact that they sign the tuition checks, they do not hesitate to use any available forum to complain about what is happening at a particular institution.

In this Internet age, information travels quickly and easily, and colleges have become more transparent, says Collin G. Brooke, an assistant professor of writing at Syracuse University, who studies the intersection between rhetoric and technology. Many universities' Web sites list the e-mail addresses of every employee, from the president on down, enabling unencumbered access to all of them.

"That was not possible 10 years ago," Mr. Brooke says. "Maybe I'd go to a library, find a college catalog, and get an address. Then I'd have to write a letter. Now it's easy to whip off a couple of sentences in an e-mail when it takes only a few seconds to find that person's address."

And no subject is off limits. Last year the Board of Trustees of Rice University was blitzed with hundreds of e-mail messages by alumni and others as it weighed a decision on downgrading its athletics program from the National Collegiate Athletic Association's top tier, Division I-A. The messages flooded in even though the university had set up a Web site for just such input. The volume of e-mail was such that the trustees did not even attempt to respond (most of the messages were against the move, and the trustees eventually decided to stay put).

E-mail is just one part of the growing communications nightmare facing presidents. In the past year or so, a new electronic tool has accelerated the flow of information from campuses: blogs. There are now an estimated 10 million Web logs in cyberspace, many with loyal followings and widespread readership. E-mail messages about campus contretemps that once got forwarded to maybe a dozen people now get posted on blogs for anyone to see. Blogs link to other blogs and get picked up by popular group blogs like Metafilter. In the blogosphere "there is no gatekeeper," says Barry Toiv, director of communications and public affairs at the Association of American Universities.

"Now everybody and anybody with a keyboard in front of them has the ability to have his reporting or his views or some combination heard or read," says Mr. Toiv, who worked in the White House press office during the Clinton administration. "As soon as higher education became a vehicle for partisan politics, this became inevitable. Nonevents become problems, and problems become crises."

A Hate-Mail Folder

Take an incident at Tufts University in October 2001, less than a month after the September 11 terrorist attacks. Editors of a conservative campus magazine decided to paint an American flag on a cannon in the middle of the campus. (It is a Tufts tradition for students to redecorate the cannon, often nightly, with birthday wishes, promotions for sporting events, or political statements.) One of the editors ended up getting into a tussle with three peace activists. The editor filed a complaint with the judicial-affairs office at Tufts, and the three pacifists were eventually sentenced to probation by a student judicial board.

The university's president, Lawrence S. Bacow, says the panel's decision should have been the end of the story. But one of the magazine editors wrote an article about the confrontation, saying conservative students at Tufts were under assault. It was posted on a conservative Web site (http://www.frontpagemag.com) run by David Horowitz, president of the Los Angeles-based Center for the Study of Popular Culture.

Almost immediately, Mr. Bacow's e-mail box started filling up with messages from off-campus sources attacking him for the light sentence given to the three peace activists. Liberals also weighed in. Over the course of the next few weeks, the president says he received hundreds of e-mail messages. He saved some of them in a file called "hate mail."

The subject lines include "American Flag disgraced," "What Kind of Left Wing Show Are You People Running," and "The endless and continuing sixties—another bubba legacy." One message promised that Republicans would "cut off all tax money to leftist universities like yours." Another wondered when Tufts would be moving to another country, "more friendly to its 'America is always wrong' viewpoint." Some writers were personal, calling Mr. Bacow a "coward" with "no common sense."

In the end, the e-mail barrage did nothing to change the outcome of the judicial hearing. But Mr. Bacow says the constant flow of messages was disruptive: "It makes it all that much more difficult to pay attention to legitimate events." The president eventually answered the most thoughtful and courteous messages, he says, although he never received any responses in return. (He objects to form responses because, he says, they tend to stimulate yet another round of e-mail.)

Like a Never-Ending Campaign

The conservatives, liberals, and activists of every kind who publicize political controversies like those at Tufts and San Francisco State rarely do so because they have any affinity for the institution in question. More often they do it for their own purposes, particularly fund raising. The result, college administrators say, is that the ideological and scholarly debates that were once a mainstay of campus classrooms and academic quads have largely turned into a partisan free-for-all that at times feels like a grueling election-year campaign. When yet another issue on another campus pops up, the outsiders move on.

"The others who enter the fray have absolutely no interest long term in the civility of the debate," Mr. Bacow says. "We are a community, and what kind of community we are when this is done depends on how we treat this issue and each other. People on campus understand that. Those from the outside have no such interest."

One of those outsiders is Mr. Horowitz, who is leading a national campaign to get state legislatures and Congress to adopt an "academic bill of rights." It enumerates several principles that colleges should follow in making tenure decisions, developing course curricula, and selecting campus speakers in order to foster a variety of political and religious beliefs.

While Mr. Horowitz laughs at the suggestion that he is the root cause of the e-mail traffic to college administrators in response to postings on his Web site, he says that if presidents are complaining, then those who write to them are indeed making a difference. "They deserve all the criticism they can get," he says. "These people are not hired to disrespect their conservative students. They pay $40,000 a year at some of these universities, and they are second-class citizens."

How much longer people either off campus or on will be able to quickly reach a college's president by e-mail, though, is unclear. While some presidents, like Mr. Bacow and Mr. Corrigan, still have just one e-mail address, many others have added a second address that is not publicly available. It wasn't just the political e-mail that was getting out of hand. Presidents were fielding suggestions from boosters about how to improve the football team, complaints from students about tuition increases, and pleas from parents for more financial aid. At many of those colleges, messages now sent to the president's public e-mail address are read by an assistant or the public-affairs office.

Since 2001 Graham B. Spanier, president of Pennsylvania State University, has had his public-affairs staff send him summaries of the e-mail in his public in-box (occasionally he asks to see certain messages). The change was prompted by a surge of messages, up to 500 on some days. "We'd have thousands of people writing telling him how to change the BCS formula," says Stephen J. MacCarthy, vice president for university relations. (Mr. Spanier is a conference representative in college football's Bowl Championship Series.)

No Single Strategy

In an era when news of campus incidents spreads so quickly that another dispute may erupt before campus leaders have had a chance to respond to the first, there seems to be no single, agreed-upon strategy for helping presidents cope.

For years, college leaders dealing with a crisis have followed a script borrowed from their days as academics: Examine the incident, talk to all sides, develop a response, and then vet that statement with other administrators. Such an approach would sometimes take days or even weeks. Now a response from the university is needed immediately, says Christopher Simpson, president of Simpson Communications, a public-relations firm in Williamsburg, Va., that works with colleges.

"If you subscribe to the theory that you can wait to gather all the facts, the opposition will eat your lunch," says Mr. Simpson, who was recently hired by the University of Colorado System to repair its public image in the wake of recent scandals. "You need to be able to work in minutes and hours, not in days and weeks, to resolve these issues."

But speed should not always be the first priority in putting out a response, says Terry Shepard, vice president for public affairs at Rice University. It's more important, he says, to get the facts right. "Given that the folks attacking you can say what they want, the only thing we have is our credibility," he says. "If your credibility starts crumbling under your desire to act quickly, then you lose the higher ground."

A response is sometimes necessary even if the issue at hand seems too ridiculous to warrant one, public-relations experts say. San Francisco State, for example, sent form responses to many of the people who e-mailed the president after the military-recruiting protest.

One reason to respond is that college officials never know which cyberspace rumor will gain traction. Last fall, using blogs and e-mail, conservative groups took aim at universities that offered speaking engagements to the controversial filmmaker Michael Moore. At Penn State, Mr. Moore was invited by the College Democrats, who also paid for his appearance, but the story making the rounds over the Internet was that the university was sponsoring the event. Penn State officials acted quickly to refute that account; Mr. MacCarthy says he spent three weeks doing little else but replying to e-mail messages about Michael Moore. "If we didn't address the facts in the minds of angry alumni," he says, "conservative donors would walk away from the university, and we can't let that happen."

Correcting such inaccuracies, however, is usually difficult because the source of the information is so often unknown, he adds. "In the days when you got your news from three networks, if something was wrong, you could go to the source and get it fixed quickly," he says. "Now there are thousands of sources."

And with advances in technology, campus officials fear that the problems they face today are only going to get worse.

"If there is a saturation point," says Mr. Toiv, of the Association of American Universities, "we haven't reached it yet."

Can Blogs Revolutionize Progressive Politics?

LAKSHMI CHAUDHRY

We have no interest in being anti-establishment," says Matt Stoller, a blogger at the popular Web site MyDD .com. "We're going to be the establishment."

That kind of flamboyant confidence has become the hallmark of blog evangelists who believe that blogs promise nothing less than a populist revolution in American politics. In 2006, at least some of that rhetoric is becoming reality. Blogs may not have replaced the Democratic Party establishment, but they are certainly becoming an integral part of it. In the wake of John Kerry's defeat in the 2004 presidential elections, many within the Democratic leadership have embraced blog advocates' plan for political success, which can be summed up in one word: netroots.

This all-encompassing term loosely describes an online grassroots constituency that can be targeted through Internet technologies, including e-mail, message boards, RSS feeds and, of course, blogs, which serve as organizing hubs. In turn, these blogs employ a range of features—discussion boards, Internet donations, live e-chat, social networking tools like MeetUp, online voting—that allow ordinary citizens to participate in politics, be it supporting a candidate or organizing around a policy issue. Compared to traditional media, blogs are faster, cheaper, and most importantly, interactive, enabling a level of voter involvement impossible with television or newspapers.

No wonder, then, that many in Washington are looking to blogs and bloggers to counter the overwhelming financial and ideological muscle of the right—especially in an election year. Just 18 months ago, the *New York Times Magazine* ran a cover story depicting progressive bloggers as a band of unkempt outsiders, thumbing their nose at party leadership. But now, it's the party leaders themselves who are blogging. Not only has Senate Minority leader Harry Reid started his own blog—Give 'em Hell Harry—and a media "war room" to "aggressively pioneer Internet outreach," he's also signed up to be the keynote speaker at the annual conference of the top political blog, Daily Kos.

Stoller predicts that as an organizing tool, "blogs are going to play the role that talk radio did in 1994, and that church networks did in 2002."

An Internet-fueled victory at the polls would certainly be impressive—no candidate backed by the most popular progressive blogs has yet won an election. But electoral success may merely confirm the value of blogs as an effective organizing tool to conduct politics as usual, cementing the influence of a select group of bloggers who will likely be crowned by the media as the new kingmakers.

Winning an election does not, however, guarantee a radical change in the relations of power. Technology is only as revolutionary as the people who use it, and the progressive blogosphere has thus far remained the realm of the privileged—a weakness that may well prove fatal in the long run.

In 2006, the biggest question facing blogs and bloggers is: Will their ascendancy empower the American people—in the broadest sense of the word—or merely add to the clout of an elite online constituency?

The Birth of a Revolution

Alienation may not have been the mother of blogging technology, but it most certainly birthed the "political blogosphere." The galvanizing cause for the rapid proliferation of political blogs and their mushrooming audience was a deep disillusionment across the political spectrum with traditional media—a disillusionment accentuated by a polarized political landscape.

In the recent book *Blog! How the Newest Media Revolution Is Changing Politics, Business and Culture,* Web guru Craig Shirky links the rise of political blogs to the sharpening Red/ Blue State divide. Both 9/11 and the Iraq war reminded people that "politics was vitally important," and marked the "moment people were looking for some kind of expression outside the bounds of network television," or, for that matter, cable news or the nation's leading newspapers.

Progressives were angry not just with the media but also with Democratic Party leaders for their unwillingness to challenge the Bush administration's case for war. That much-touted liberal rage found its expression on blogs like Eschaton, Daily Kos and Talking Points Memo, and continues to fuel the phenomenal growth of the progressive blogosphere. Like the rise of right-wing talk radio, this growth is directly linked to an institutional failure of representation. Finding no mirror for their views in the media, a large segment of the American public turned to the Internet to speak for themselves—often with brutal, uncensored candor.

As blogs have grown in popularity—at the rate of more than one new blog per second—they've begun to lose their vanguard edge. The very institutions that political bloggers often criticize have begun to adopt the platform, with corporate executives, media personalities, porn stars, lawyers and PR strategists all jumping into the fray. That may be why Markos Moulitsas Zúniga, the founder and primary voice of Daily Kos, thinks the word "blog" is beginning to outlive its usefulness. "A blog is merely a publishing tool, and like a tool, it can be used in any number of ways," he says.

But for many, to rephrase director Jean Renoir, a blogs are still a state of mind. To their most ardent advocates, blogs are standard-bearers of a core set of democratic values: participation, egalitarianism and transparency. Books like Dan Gillmor's *We the Media,* Howard Rheingold's *Smart Mobs,* James Surowiecki's *The Wisdom of Crowds,* and Joe Trippi's *The Revolution Will Not Be Televised* have become the bibles of progressive politics. Taken together, they express the dream of Internet salvation: harnessing an inherently democratic, interactive and communal medium, with the potential to instantaneously tap into the collective intellectual, political and financial resources of tens of millions of fellow Americans to create a juggernaut for social change.

According to Moulitsas, "The word 'blog' still implies a certain level of citizen involvement, of giving power to someone who is not empowered"—especially to progressives who, according to a study released last year by the New Politics Institute, have overtaken conservatives as the heavyweights of the political blogosphere.

Vox Populi

Political blogs have often been most effective as populist fact-checkers, challenging, refuting and correcting perceived errors in news coverage.

"Independent bloggers have challenged the mainstream media and held them accountable, whether it's with Judy Miller or Bob Woodward," says Huffington Post founder Arianna Huffington. The most significant effect of this "we can fact-check your ass" credo has not been merely to put journalists on notice, but to change the way public knowledge is produced on a daily basis. "It's hard now for an important story to hit the front page of the *New York Times* and just die there," says Huffington. A news article is now merely the beginning of a public conversation in the blogosphere, where experts, amateurs and posers alike dissect its merits and add to its information, often keeping it alive long after journalists have moved on.

Popular understanding of what blogs are and what they can do has been muddled by an inevitably hostile relationship between political bloggers and traditional media. Writing in the Dec. 26 issue of *The New Republic,* Franklin Foer took bloggers to task for nursing "an ideological disdain for 'Mainstream Media'—or MSM, as it has derisively (and somewhat adolescently) come to be known." But Foer, like so many traditional journalists who criticize blogs, failed to grasp the very nature of his intended target.

Blogs are literally vox populi—or at the least the voice of the people who post entries and comments, and, to a lesser extent, of their devoted readers. Telling bloggers that they're wrong or to shut up is somewhat like telling respondents to an opinion survey to simply change their mind. When journalists reject bloggers as cranks or wingnuts, they also do the same to a large segment of the American public who see blogs as an expression of their views. Such dismissals feed the very alienation that makes blogs and bloggers popular.

The irony is that bloggers are most powerful when they work in tandem with the very media establishment they despise. "Bloggers alone cannot create conventional wisdom, cannot make a story break, cannot directly reach the vast population that isn't directly activist and involved in politics," says Peter Daou, who coordinated the Kerry campaign's blog outreach operations. Blogs instead exert an indirect form of power, amplifying and channeling the pressure of netroots opinion upwards to pressure politicians and journalists. "It's really a rising up," says Daou.

Can this online rebellion lead to real political change? The prognosis thus far is encouraging, but far from definitive.

Can the Netroots Grow the Grassroots?

If television made politics more elitist and less substantive, blogs—and more broadly, netroots tools—have the potential to become engines of truly democratic, bottom-up, issue-rich political participation.

Blogs allow rank-and-file voters to pick the candidate to support in any given electoral race, influence his or her platform, and volunteer their time, money and expertise in more targeted and substantive ways. Democratic candidates in the midterm elections are already busy trying to position themselves as the next Howard Dean, vying for a digital stamp of approval that will bring with it free publicity, big money and, just maybe, a whole lot of voters.

When Rep. Sherrod Brown (D-Ohio) decided to take on Iraq veteran Paul Hackett in the Democratic primary for the Senate race in Ohio, he moved quickly to neutralize his opponent's advantage as the unquestioned hero of the progressive bloggers. The ace up Brown's sleeve: Jerome Armstrong, founder of the influential MyDD.com and veteran of Howard Dean's online campaign. Brown's next move was a blog entry on The Huffington Post titled, "Why I am a Progressive."

But not everyone is convinced that blogs can be as influential in a midterm election, when there are a large number of electoral contests spread across the country. "Raising money at a nationwide level for a special election is one thing," Pew scholar Michael Cornfield says, "but raising it and developing a core of activists and all the ready-to-respond messages when you have to run hundreds of races simultaneously—which is what will happen in 2006—is another thing." Moreover, the ability of the Internet to erase geographical distances can become a structural weakness in elections where district lines and eligibility are key.

An effective netroots strategy in 2006 will have to master the failings of Howard Dean's campaign, which stalled because it couldn't grow his support base beyond his online constituency.

An effective netroots strategy in 2006 will also have to master the shortcomings of the Dean's campaign, which stalled mainly because it failed to grow his support base beyond his online constituency—antiwar, white and high-income voters. In contrast, the Bush/Cheney operation used the Internet to coordinate on-the-ground events such as house parties, and rallies involving church congregations.

Cornfield describes the Republican model as, "one person who is online and is plugged into the blogosphere. That person becomes an e-precinct captain, and is responsible for reaching out offline or any means necessary for ten people."

This time around, Armstrong is determined to match the GOP's success. GrowOhio.org, which he describes as "a community blog for Democratic Party activists," will coordinate field operations for not just Brown but all Democratic candidates in each of Ohio's 88 counties. Its primary goal is to reach rural voters in areas where the campaign cannot field organizers on the ground.

"This isn't just about using the net for communications and fundraising, but for field organizing," Armstrong says.

What is also new in 2006 is the effort to redirect attention from the national to the local. "It's not just about focusing the national blogosphere on Ohio, but about building from the ground up in Ohio," Armstrong says. "Over 90 percent of our signups on GrowOhio.org are Ohio activists, and we will soon have Internet outreach coordinators in all 88 counties."

But many like Daou remain skeptical about the power of blogs to directly impact politics at the grassroots level. "You're not going to go out there and mobilize a million people and have them all come to the polls and donate money. Blogs will never do that," he says

And they may be even less effective in areas that are traditionally not as internet-savvy as the rest of the country, be it the rural red states or impoverished inner cities. Creating a virtual "community center" is unlikely to compensate for the Democrats' disadvantage on the ground. Due to the eroding presence of unions, Democrats no longer possess a physical meeting place where they can target and mobilize voters—unlike Republicans, who rely on a well-organized network of churches, gun clubs and chambers of commerce.

What is clear is that the 2006 elections will test the claim of blog evangelists that online activism can radically transform offline politics—a claim that is central to their far more ambitious vision for the future. In their book *Crashing the Gate* (to be released in April), Moulitsas and Armstrong envision blogs as the centerpiece of a netroots movement to engineer an imminent and sweeping transformation of the Democratic Party:

We are at the beginning of a comprehensive reformation of the Democratic Party—driven by committed progressive out-

siders. Online activism on a nationwide level, coupled with offline activists at the local level . . . can provide the formula for a quiet, bloodless coup that can take control of the party. Money and mobilization are the two key elements of all political activity, and if the netroots have their way, the financial backbone of the Democratic Party will be regular people.

Whether a truly decentralized and "leaderless" netroots can function like a political party is debatable, but the latest wave of technological innovation does offer unprecedented opportunities for constructing a progressive movement for the digital age. Such an outreach effort would use the Internet very much like conservatives such as Richard Viguerie used direct mail to build a powerful political force. But in order to craft a genuinely democratic form of politics, the progressive blogosphere will have to overcome its greatest weakness: lack of diversity.

The Rise of the Blogerati

In *Newsweek,* Simon Rosenberg, a beltway insider who lost the DNC chair to Dean, described the progressive blogosphere as the new "Resistance" within the Democratic Party, engaged in a civil war to wrest power from a craven and compromised beltway leadership. According to Rosenberg, the leaders of this "resistance" are the top progressive bloggers, more specifically the most popular and increasingly influential Moulitsas. Rosenberg told the *Washington Monthly,* "Frankly I don't think there's anyone who's had the potential to revolutionize the Democratic Party that Markos does."

Yet both the progressive blogosphere and the "revolutionaries" who dominate its ranks look a lot like the establishment they seek to overthrow.

The report by the New Politics Institute—which was launched by Rosenberg's New Democracy Network—notes: "Clearly, blogging is a world with a handful of haves, and a nearly uncountable number of have-nots. There are likely a few hundred thousand blogs in this country that talk about politics, but less than one-tenth of one percent of them account for more than 99 percent of all political blogging traffic."

For better or worse, traffic numbers have become an endorsement of the political agenda of specific individuals. While A-list bloggers repeatedly deny receiving any special treatment, the reality is that both the media and political establishment pay disproportionate attention to their views, often treating them as representative of the entire progressive blogosphere.

In a *Foreign Policy* article, political scientists Daniel Drezner and Henry Farrell cheerfully note, "The skewed network of the blogosphere makes it less time-consuming for outside observers to acquire information. The media only need to look at elite blogs to obtain a summary of the distribution of opinions on a given political issue." Why? Because the "elite blogs" serve as a filtering mechanism, deciding which information offered up by smaller blogs is useful or noteworthy. In effect, A-list blogs get to decide what issues deserve the attention of journalists and politicians, i.e., the establishment.

The past two years have also marked the emergence of a close relationship between top bloggers and politicians in Washington. A number of them—for example, Jesse Taylor at Pandagon, Tim Tagaris of SwingStateProject, Stoller and Armstrong—have been hired as campaign consultants. Others act as unofficial advisers to top politicos like Rep. Rahm Emmanuel (D-Ill.), who holds conference calls with preeminent bloggers to talk strategy. When the Senate Democrats invite Moulitsas to offer his personal views on netroots strategy—treating him, as a *Washington Monthly* profile describes, "a kind of part-time sage, an affiliate member"—the perks of success become difficult to deny.

Armstrong sees the rise of the blogger-guru—or "strategic adviser," as he puts it—as a positive development. Better to hire a blogger who is personally committed to the Democratic cause than a D.C.-based mercenary who makes money irrespective of who wins.

But the fact that nearly all these "advisers" are drawn from a close-knit and mostly homogenous group can make them appear as just a new boys' club, albeit one with better intentions and more engaged politics. Aside from notable exceptions like Moulitsas, who is part-Salvadoran, and a handful of lesser-known women who belong to group blogs, top progressive bloggers tend to be young, well-educated, middle class, male and white.

Reach, Representation and Credibility

The lack of diversity is partly a function of the roots of blogging in an equally homogenous tech-geek community. Nevertheless, women and people of color constitute the fastest rising segment of those joining the blogosphere. Feminist and female-authored political blogs like Feministing, Bitch Ph.D, Echidne of the Snakes, and Salon's Broadsheet made considerable gains in traffic and visibility in 2005, as did Latino Pundit, Culture Kitchen, and Afro-Netizen. Better yet, they're forging networks and alliances to help each other grow. There is no doubt the membership of the blogosphere is changing, and will look very different five years from now. "We're just a step behind, just like any other area," says Pandagon's Amanda Marcotte.

But while the growth of the blogosphere may increase the actual traffic to a greater number of blogs, it also makes visibility far more scarce and precious for each new blogger. As one of the top women bloggers, Chris Nolan, noted on the PressThink blog, "The barrier to entry in this new business isn't getting published; anyone can do that. The barrier to entry is finding an audience."

Elite bloggers can play a key role in generating that audience. As Marcotte points out, "A lot more women are moving up in the Technorati rankings" (Technorati is a search engine for the blogosphere) because A-listers like Duncan Black and Kevin Drum in 2005 made it a priority to promote female bloggers. But when someone like Moulitsas decides to stop linking to other blogs—as he has recently done because he doesn't want to play "gatekeeper"—or when top bloggers repeatedly cite their fellow A-listers, it has enormous consequences. "It's pretty darn hard today to break in to the A-list if the other

A-listers aren't linking to you," says Global Voices co-founder Rebecca MacKinnon.

If blogs derive their credibility from being the "voice of the people," surely we should be concerned about which opinions get attention over others. The question of representation affects not just who is blogging—and with great success—but also the audience of these blogs. What kind of democratic consensus does the blogosphere reflect when the people participating in it are most likely to be white, well-educated men?

Yet when it comes to issues of diversity, A-list bloggers like Moulitsas and Stoller can get defensive, and at times, dismissive. "Take a look at what you have today. Take a look at the folks who're leading the party, dominating the media, or even within corporations. Do you think the top ranks of any of those

---

A Blog for the Other Six Billion of Us

Want to know about the upcoming cricket match between India and China? The recent arrests of human rights activists in Cambodia? Or why Bolivian president Evo Morales wears the same damned sweater for all his international photo-ops? You can find answers to these and other pressing questions on Global Voices, a gateway to the whole, wide virtual world that lies outside the confines of the American blogosphere. A project of the Berkman Center for Internet and Society at the Harvard Law School, the meta-blog is assembled by an international team of "blogger-editors" who serve as guides to conversations taking place on blogs in their corner of the world.

"If as an American you wanted to know what an ordinary Iranian or Bangladeshi or Chinese person thinks about what's happening in their country or their daily life, you had to wait for CNN to interview them or *New York Times* to quote them in an article," says Global Voices co-founder Rebecca MacKinnon. Now all you have to do is point on the country or region of your choice to find someone who can tell you, for example, just why the South African government is cozying up to Iran.

The Web site—which receives 10 to 12 thousand visitors a day—is in large part a response to the myopic reporting that passes for international news coverage in the mainstream media. The kind of reporting that MacKinnon was expected to deliver as the Asia correspondent for CNN USA, a job she quit in 2004. "I was told to cover my region more like a tourist, and that my expertise was getting in the way of doing the kind of story they wanted," she says.

But it's not just the media that are self-absorbed. Global Voices also offers an important corrective to the equally U.S.-centric focus of American political bloggers who seem as likely to forget that there are more pressing issues in this world than who wins what congressional seat in Colorado.

http://cyber.law.harvard.edu/globalvoices/

institutions is any more representative?" responds Stoller, his voice rising in indignation.

Where Stoller openly acknowledges the problem—describing blogs in one of his posts as "a new national town square for the white progressive base of the Democratic party"—and the need to take steps to tackle the disparity, Moulitsas is less generous. In his view, it's simply absurd to demand what he sarcastically describes as an "affirmative action of ideas" within an inherently meritocratic medium such as the blogosphere: "I don't see how you can say, 'Well, let's give more voice to African American lesbians.' Create a blog. If there's an audience, great. If there isn't, not so great." Besides, he suggests, if a Salvadoran war refugee—in his words, a "political nobody"—like him can make it on the Internet, there's nothing stopping anyone else from doing the same.

As for the relative paucity of top female progressive bloggers, Moulitsas is indifferent: "I haven't given it a lot of thought. I find it totally uninteresting. What I'm interested in is winning elections, and I don't give a shit what you look like." It's an odd and somewhat disingenuous response from an advocate of blogging as the ultimate tool of democratic participation.

Keith Jenkins, who authors Good Reputation Sleeping and works a day job as the picture editor at the *Washington Post,* says the low barriers to entry do not in themselves offer a sufficient guarantee of equal participation. "It's less about actively stopping and standing in the way and more about affirmatively enabling access, which was the underlying argument of civil rights movements and freedom movements across the board," he says. "It's about affirmatively making it possible for everybody to have a seat at the table, which benefits not only the people who are sitting down, but also the people who are already seated."

"We need to be encouraging a more diverse group of people to blog," agrees Global Voices' MacKinnon. "But we also need to be linking to them and giving them traffic so that they have a chance to make it to the A-list."

While the organic growth of the blogosphere may resolve issues of race and gender over time, it will do little to address its overwhelming bias toward urban professionals. And that can't be good news for a party that is already being punished at the polls for its weak connection to working-class Americans.

"For me the greatest problem is low-income people," Cornfield says. "The irony is that it's not because they don't have money to get a laptop—especially with the $100 laptop now. It's that people who are poor don't have the civic skill sets and motivation to go online and do these sorts of things. That will take a concerted effort."

At a time when the visible digital divide may be shrinking as increasing numbers of Americans come online, it may be replaced by an invisible version that benefits those who are well-educated, well-connected and organized.

Stoller does not think that it's important for blogs to reach a less-affluent audience: "Not everybody has to be part of that conversation. If someone wants to have access to those discussions, they should be able to do that. But for the most part, people—like that person working two shifts—will go on with their lives knowing that good people are making good decisions and policies on their behalf." Bloggers like Moulitsas—who is equally unconcerned that his blog will never reach "someone working at the DMV"—are likely betting that the cadre of activists they reach will be able to form connections across those differences within their community.

Perhaps sites like GrowOhio.org will prove them to be right if it manages to mobilize a constituency—e.g. rural voters—that is least likely to be wired, and in a region where the party's on-the-ground resources are weak. But any such strategy is unlikely to work if those in charge of crafting it—be they bloggers, politicians or so-called netizens—show little interest in expanding the reach of the progressive blogosphere to include the largest, most diverse audience possible. If the blogs are unable to bridge the class divide online, there is no reason to think they can create a grassroots movement that can do so in the real world.

"If you do make an active effort, it is easier to accomplish through the Internet than through pretty much any other medium including direct mail," Cornfield says. "But it will not happen on its own. It has to be a concerted effort." Social movements are built by people not ghosts in some virtual machine.

The *Washington Monthly* profile of Moulitsas included a revealing quote, in which he expressed disappointment at not being able to fulfill his dream of making it big in the tech industry back in 1998: "Maybe at some time, Silicon Valley really was this democratic ideal where the guy with the best idea made a billion dollars, but by the time I got there at least, it was just like anything else—a bunch of rich kids who knew each other running around and it all depended on who you knew."

The danger is that many may come to feel the same way about the blogosphere in the coming years.

LAKSHMI CHAUDHRY has been a reporter and an editor for independent publications for more than six years, and is a senior editor at *In These Times,* where she covers the cross-section of culture and politics.

Center Stage

The Internet has become an integral part of the way newspapers distribute their content, a phenomenon that's only going to increase. AJR's senior editor takes a firsthand look at four papers' Web operations.

Carl Sessions Stepp

It's only 9 A.M. and today's Houston Chronicle has barely hit people's doorsteps, but Sylvia Wood, the Chronicle's online local news editor, already is working a breaking, and heartbreaking, story.

A 15-year-old boy has been killed playing with a pistol with three friends. As seems so common, the boys thought the gun was unloaded. They pulled the trigger once. A harmless click. The second time, the ninth grader was shot in the chest.

Wood has posted a brief on chron.com. She has a Chronicle reporter on the way to the scene and is scrambling to locate a yearbook photo of the victim. She's also juggling two more spot stories while around her, in a newsroom as quiet as a library, print colleagues shuffle in sipping from their Starbucks cups and grunting their good mornings.

> **"The chance for error probably soars. On the other hand, you can correct those errors immediately and forever."**

It is a scene repeated more and more often as mainstream newsrooms adjust to becoming two worlds in one. The roller-coaster rhythm of print—the steady early climb followed by the precipitous plunge to deadline—is being joined, and may soon be overtaken, by the Web's all-out, all-day, all-night news cycle. Like the arrival of a gigantic planet next door, online newsrooms have begun exerting a culture-changing gravitational pull.

What do online newsrooms look like? How do they work? How are they affecting their print neighbors? I recently visited online newsrooms of various sizes and interviewed journalists within and outside the online world. The results were enlightening, and sometimes surprising.

First, at places large enough to have separate online newsrooms, they look similar to their print counterparts, except they are cleaner, quieter and younger. You see the usual rows of desks grouped into pods, with executives occupying glass offices. But things tend to look newer and sleeker, with carpet still unstained. There seem to be more twentysomethings. And because Web journalists mostly post copy gathered by others, there is less reporting going on and thus less noise.

Organizationally, online newsrooms are arranged by section. But you also find TV studios and mysterious hideaways where technical wizardry takes place (one at washingtonpost.com is known as The Cave). Titles vary. Online journalists are as likely to be called producers or news directors as editors.

A vital difference: With many people posting and without fixed schedules, it is impractical to funnel all content through a copy desk. So a fair amount of copy produced by the Web staff gets little or no editing, and few items get the multiple reads routine in print.

Design isn't a daily concern. Most homepages have a standard look, with a low-tech tool or template that lets editors post easily. Covering breaking news—especially crime, a role that had been appropriated by broadcast—is making a comeback. The running spot-news blog seems especially popular.

Most striking are two clear, probably transforming trends: a move toward merging online and print newsrooms, and a surge toward producing news almost around the clock. These changes may well revolutionize newsrooms, and they raise important questions. Who will produce the volumes of copy required? How will quality be monitored without the overlapping layers of editing? What will be stressed in hiring? How will all this affect the enduring and ingrained newsroom culture?

To explore all this, a good place to start is the sprawling operations of the Houston Chronicle and chron.com.

Dean Betz, chron.com's online news editor and in effect its managing editor, is hurrying to the newsroom's 4 P.M. meeting when he encounters, in an elevator, Dudley Althaus, a Mexico City correspondent on a home visit.

The reporter has heard the paper wants him to start a blog. Betz nods. The reporter wonders how you balance news and opinion in a blog. Let's discuss it with your editor, Betz replies. In the hallway, the Chronicle's reader representative, James Campbell, buttonholes Betz. He's already blogging. They chat about it as they enter the news meeting, a huge affair involving more than 35 people. Betz sets up an online connection projected onto a big screen.

He's called on right away by Editor Jeff Cohen. Betz describes what chron.com and its competitors have been posting.

Some key financial reports are due today, and Cohen presses for quick online publication. "We have got to be getting these stories up the second they come in," Cohen says. Then he announces, to predictable titters, that the Web site will be partnering in some unspecified way with a local Web-based dating service.

From blogs to business data to dating, Web activity is seizing center stage in Houston.

Betz, 44, says the goal is "making the newspaper and the Web site one thing. That's the only way newspapers have any chance of making things work—not thinking they are newspaper companies, but that they are news companies."

Editor Cohen, 51, is a convert. His print newsroom has about 350 staffers, and the paper's daily circulation is about 520,000. As at most newspapers, circulation and penetration have dropped, but Cohen says "we have more than made up for it on the Web." With 20 editorial staffers, the Web site draws some 2.9 million unique viewers a month and makes a profit. "It's obvious you have to start devoting more of your resources to the Web," Cohen says.

For now, most Web staffers work from the paper's 10th floor. Only Sylvia Wood sits in the fifth-floor city room. But all that is going to change.

Cohen opens a binder to show his online goals for 2006: to generate more content from readers, develop more Spanish content and "further integrate the Web and the newsroom."

He leads a brisk tour of space being remodeled to bring Web journalists onto the newsroom floor. "In order for it to be clear what we're doing," he says, "they've got to be close—in sight, in mind, not out of sight, out of mind."

Environmental reporter Dina Cappiello, 32, understands. "Psychologically, the physical presence says, 'This is important. This isn't going to be an afterthought.'"

The one Web editor inside the newsroom, Wood, sits with other assistant city editors at the center of the action. Here, she says, "You're pretty much clued in as to what the reporters are doing."

Wood, 39, works a 7 A.M. to 4 P.M. shift. She takes a handoff from an overnight editor, sits in on the morning news meeting, trolls early for updates and spot news, and tries to post about eight local items a day. "My goal," Wood says, "is to get as much as we can up before the 12 o'clock news."

The morning flurry stems in part from the fact that visits to chron.com spike as people arrive at work. The entire morning paper "rolls over" onto the Web around 12:30 A.M., but the site evolves all day. There are updates and Web-only features from sports and entertainment as well as news, plus numerous discussion forums and blogs by staff members and readers.

TV News Online

The police chase breaks out at 2:20 P.M., just as Jim Thompson, KHOU-TV's Web site manager, is saying, "Our bread and butter is immediacy, breaking news, delivering content as it happens."

On cue, both Channel 11, a CBS affiliate, and its partner, KHOU.com, go straight to live chase video from the station's helicopter. Web Deputy Editor Michelle Homer streams it online, while KHOU reporters provide TV voice-over. The chase runs live for more than an hour until its dramatic end. The runaway driver crashes into a car occupied by a grandmother, mother and 8-month-old girl. As cameras roll and police close in, the mother leaps from her car and pounds furiously on the offending vehicle.

With about 350,000 unique visitors a month and a full-time staff of four, Belo-owned KHOU.com is smaller than its Houston Chronicle competitor. But it aggressively tracks local news, especially stories with hot video.

The KHOU newsroom resembles a small newspaper, with reporters' desks lining one side. The room is dominated by a power triangle: the TV assignment desk, the TV producers' pod and the Web pod, which benefits from the proximity. "Anyone who has worked in a newsroom knows," Thompson says, "that about 50 percent of what you get you overhear."

The police chase electrifies the room. All four assignment desk editors are simultaneously barking into phones and pounding keyboards. A news meeting comes to a standstill as Executive News Director Keith Connors follows the action. Thompson's group staffs the Web site six days a week, changing the lead story at least every three hours or so. The set-up is similar to newspaper sites, but far more preoccupied with video.

"If on TV we don't get video, we don't have a story," Thompson, 38, says. "So whenever a story breaks, our team is out the door. And that plays great for the Web site."

The Web also lends itself to footage that might not suit TV, Thompson says. "We don't want it to be a polished TV stand-up. We want it to be rough and raw. We want you the viewer to know what's it's like to be there. Sometimes it's not going to be pretty, but it's going to be the fastest, most accurate news you can get."

Connors plans to double the Web staff this year. "To be in this game, you have to get in totally," he says. "We are not wading in the kiddie pool. We need to jump totally in."

—Carl Sessions Stepp

Legal reporter Mary Flood, 52, a Web enthusiast who has covered Enron-related stories for three years, says she has filed as many as 12 updates a day from important court cases. "It's simultaneously made things more exciting and more exhausting," she says.

Online Favorites

Most viewed newspaper Web sites in February

Unique visitors

nytimes.com	12,702,000
USAToday.com	10,372,000
washingtonpost.com	8,244,000
latimes.com	4,865,000
SFGate.com (San Francisco Chronicle)	4,602,000
wsj.com (Wall Street Journal)	3,937,000
Boston.com (Boston Globe)	3,525,000
nydailynews.com	3,026,000
chicagotribune.com	2,942,000
chron.com (Houston Chronicle)	2,916,000

Source: *Nielsen//NetRatings*

Wood, Flood and practically everyone else acknowledge that with speed and continuous posting come risks. "The chance for error probably soars," says Flood, who urges sources to look for mistakes and alert her. "On the other hand, you can correct those errors immediately and forever."

Most Web content does get edited, although blurbs, headlines and short items may be posted directly by one person, and some contributors' blogs are unedited.

Cohen stresses that "I would prefer to have it completely accurate, vetted and dead-solid perfect rather than racing to get it up. If there are five editors that read every story before the newspaper version, there may be just two or three who vet it for the Web site. But still they are acutely aware of the accuracy issues."

Scott Clark, 46, the Web site's vice president and editor, says Web producers want better quality control. They consult wire service veterans about handling the fast pace. "We're jumping into stories in progress, and we get things wrong, the natural errors that come from the fog of news," Clark says. "We talk about knowing when to 'vague it up' and wait for the facts to settle. People on the Web recognize that they're seeing a flow and not the newspaper end product. They expect to come back and see that the story has changed. But the standards of journalism on the Web are the same as in print."

Almost everybody also agrees that the 24-7 cycle stretches resources.

Science writer Eric Berger, 32, is another big Web fan. As a reporter and SciGuy blogger, his is a familiar byline online. He tells about covering the launch of the shuttle Discovery last July. He rose before dawn and blogged from 4:55 A.M. through the 9:39 A.M. launch until 11 A.M., then wrote a print story for the next morning's front page. He isn't complaining, Berger stresses, but it's clear the Web adds work.

Reporter Cappiello underlines the point. "Industrywide, not just here, the Web requires more labor," she says. "I'm a little concerned how a reporter who covers cops is going to not only file, file, file for the Web, but report the print story and do the Sunday enterprise story."

Cohen does foresee his Web staff growing this year. Still, extra work and all, these journalists and others increasingly welcome the chance to revitalize their work. Blogging has been a big incentive; all those writers who wanted to be columnists now have the chance. You still encounter some skeptics, but it seems that a corner has been turned.

"There are people who think this is a ridiculous extension of their job," Flood says. "I look at this as my new job. It's the future of news. I love it."

This will also be the year of print-online integration at USA Today, where Editor Ken Paulson wants "a single 24-hour news organization." He's even moved the site's top executive, Kinsey Wilson, to the paper's masthead as an executive editor. For now, the online newsroom still occupies it own floor in USA Today's gleaming McLean, Virginia, skyscraper. But Paulson says that "culturally, we're merged," and over the coming months many sports, business, features and other online staffers will move side by side with their print counterparts.

On the day I visit, the Web staff is gathering for its 8:15 A.M. "cabinet meeting," so called because the nine editors huddle around a row of metal filing cabinets.

USAToday.com staffs its homepage around the clock, although less gets posted once the newspaper's contents are uploaded by midnight. Today's homepage editor, Brett Molina, 30, has been on duty since 6 A.M., updating stories about a mine fire and an Osama bin Laden tape.

The news meeting, one of several daily, resembles the typical print get-together, except more attention goes to multimedia and special effects. For example, Chet Czarniak, 55, the online managing editor who presides, expresses concern about live coverage of the mining disaster. "If raw video comes in," he warns, "be careful what we use."

Another exchange highlights the costs and benefits of immediacy. An editor has spotted what he calls a classic dumb headline, "Flawed coin was a mistake." Unlike in a print edition where it would live forever, the head is quickly rewritten.

With more than 10 million unique visitors a month, USAToday.com has 75 editorial staffers, with a funky combination of titles, some from print, some from broadcast. They face an unusual mission, since they don't produce local news. Their national audience spills over several time zones. Viewers come for assorted news, sports and the special packages and surprises associated with the USA Today brand.

USAToday.com puts less emphasis on breaking-news updates from its reporters than on special stories, imaginative packaging and Web-only features. "I'd rather have their 'breaking analysis' than chasing the basics," says Executive Producer Jody Brannon, 46. "What we're trying to do online," she adds, "is celebrate a new way of storytelling that leverages our expertise in visuals, graphics and multimedia." For example, video editor David Freer, 22, is fixing up an on-site TV studio and plans to "pump up this site" with video.

The action seems nonstop, with the homepage changing at least every 15 or 20 minutes. "The pace is just incredible," Czarniak says. "Saturday at 11 P.M. is just as important as Monday at 11 A.M. Speed to market is vital. It's not even a deadline a minute. There are constant deadlines. Our train is always leaving the station."

News Editor Randy Lilleston, 46, sees print people learning "broadcast sensibilities." "Stories are not permanent," he says. "They evolve. The story you read now is not the same as the one you'll read in two hours."

Lilleston, too, worries about balancing accuracy and speed. "Do you get the vetting you get in a newspaper? No, you do not," he says. But he adds crisply, "I reject the idea that online is an excuse for sloppiness. One of my goals is to knock down the idea that it is OK to be temporarily wrong. It is not OK."

Lilleston sees progress toward online safeguards. For example, most items posted directly are short, so typos and errors may be relatively easy to spot. Without a copy desk, editors are expected to turn to the person sitting next to them for a "second set of eyes." They constantly read behind one another, before and after postings.

News Director Patty Michalski, 33, who oversees the homepage, advises, "Get it right the first time. If it means taking two seconds longer, so be it." Michalski also stresses those small but all-important headlines, subheads (known as "chatter") and blurbs. Those few words often determine readership. She pushes posters to seek suggestions from others and to consider "anything to make it a teensy bit more specific."

Across the sites I visited, editors are emphasizing journalistic skills over technical know-how. A few years ago, Czarniak says, hiring priorities were something like 60 percent technical skills, 40 percent journalistic. "Now we're going the other way. The tools are much improved. It's easier to publish now. What we're looking for most are people who know good storytelling."

Even at USA Today, where the newspaper helped revolutionize design, the look of the homepage remains relatively constant. Too much change, says Brannon, "complicates the experience for the user." Except for mammoth stories, the homepage sticks to two or three "standard looks," with templates for easy posting.

Nor did I find many signs of the totally converged reporter, prowling for news with notebook, tape recorder and digital camera and wearing a videocam as headgear. Increasingly, reporters do take photos and provide audio, and some sites are experimenting with giving reporters, especially abroad, cell phones that allow video feeds. But few yet have the time, or capability, to function as multimedia do-it-alls. "I've seen their video," laughs video editor Freer, "and I don't like it."

For now, the big step is consolidation, a culture shock in itself. Czarniak says merging makes sense for production, quality and content. "The ultimate vision is that there are conversations about content among everyone," he says. "You're not concerned about the platform. You're concerned about how to tell the story."

Other major papers are moving toward consolidation, including the New York Times and the Los Angeles Times. But merging news operations can be complicated. In some places, the print newsroom is unionized while the online newsroom is not. Sometimes more than one corporate structure is involved. Besides, independence has its own advantages.

So not everyone is consolidating. A prime exception is washingtonpost.com, located across the Potomac River, in Virginia, four miles from its print sibling.

Technically, it's a separate company: Washington Post-Newsweek Interactive. Post Ombudsman Deborah Howell, in a column last December titled "The Two Washington Posts," quoted Post Co. CEO Donald Graham as saying that, while the two versions obviously must cooperate, each is a full-time, stand-alone operation.

The action seems nonstop, with the homepage changing at least every 15 or 20 minutes.

Many Web staffers privately believe being closer would help. But there also is a sense that separate status lets the Web site flourish outside the shadow of the magisterial printed Post.

"Whether it is the Web or print or handhelds, the future is giving people news when they want it and how they want it."

In February, the Newspaper Association of America named washingtonpost.com as the best overall news site among large publications.

Staff members also point out that coordination by phone, e-mail and instant messaging is easy. In addition, a seven-person Continuous News Desk inside the Post's print newsroom provides copy and liaison.

Here, too, the online newsroom resembles that of a newspaper, except that the architecture is more modernistic, the tones more subdued. It's a jeans and sneakers environment, but less rowdy than many city rooms.

Executive Editor and Vice President Jim Brady, 38, says it sometimes feels like an insurance office, and he goads people to walk rather than e-mail across the room.

A big challenge, Brady says, is "getting a newsroom to move at lightning speed." But he sees somewhat less pressure here because, with stories constantly being posted, "there isn't the big run-up to deadline and then a sigh of relief."

The site, with about 65 full-time editorial staff and 20 to 24 part-timers, received 8.2 million unique visitors in February, according to Nielsen//NetRatings. About 80 percent are not from the Washington area, so the homepage is "bifurcated." A computer reads the ZIP codes of incoming viewers and directs them to either the local or the national homepage.

Dominating the room is the newsdesk, a semicircular command center occupied by a homepage editor, breaking news producer and photo editor. They work facing 10 monitors tuned to local and national news and weather. Two people have overnight duty, but the action picks up with the 5:30 A.M. arrival of a dayside homepage editor. Regular news meetings take place at 7 A.M., noon, 3 P.M. and 7 P.M.

Deputy Editor Meghan Collins Sullivan, 31, oversees the homepage and what she calls "the constant decision-making process." Rarely do more than a few minutes pass between updates, and the site gets frequent feeds from the Continuous News Desk's writers and other Post reporters. "There's a different sense of urgency here because we are on constant deadline," Sullivan says. "We don't have a limited amount of space. We have an infinite amount. So you can always be doing new things."

Sullivan and homepage editor Kenisha Malcolm, 28, convene the noon news meeting, similar to those at other Web sites. On this day, about 15 people take part, including, via conference call from the Post, Lexie Verdon, 51, from Continuous News. There's the usual discussion of upcoming stories, plus attention to audio, video, special features and the explosively popular blogs and online discussions.

Brady's second in command, Editor Howard Parnell, 45, grew up in nearby Falls Church, Virginia, and delivered the Post as a kid. He spent more than a decade working in print and the past 11 years online. Parnell agrees that the biggest difference online is the 24-7 pace. But he also sees across-the-board similarities.

"The managing people part is similar," he says, "and the emphasis on storytelling, on getting it right, and, just as it was in my newspaper days, the idea that this is a public trust."

Consolidation's not that big an issue at the Daily Times in Salisbury, Maryland, where the "online newsroom" consists pretty much of City Editor Joe Carmean posting from his desk when he has time.

This morning's Web lead is about the newspaper itself, where a press breakdown has delayed delivery for hours. Papers are being printed at another Gannett paper up the road, and many won't be delivered until after lunch. With regular carriers unavailable, Executive Editor Greg Bassett and other honchos have been drafted to run delivery routes. The phone is ringing ceaselessly, and people wander into the lobby scouting for copies.

Ironically, the print version's front page can be found only one place this morning: on the Web site (delmarva.com), which regularly links to a pdf version of page one.

Bassett, 45, in the office since 4 A.M. and out on his route since 9, finally makes it back around 2 P.M., having just delivered his last 50 copies to subscribers at a local jail. He edits his hometown paper, which is unusual in this mobile age. In fact, he was born in the hospital directly across the street.

The paper has 28 editorial staffers, about 29,000 in circulation and 130,000 unique Web visitors a month. It's a small, community-oriented operation, but Bassett sees the future as clearly as anyone else, and he embraces the Web's potential.

"We write for online and update for print," he recites, echoing a refrain heard often around Gannett. "The only time I'm happy is when I have a newspaper in front of me and a tuna sandwich in my hand. But my 9-year-old son is going to get all his news from his cell phone."

When corporate executives solicited his training priorities for this year, Bassett specified "how to set up a 24-hour newsroom" and "how to write for online."

For now, only a handful of newsroom staffers can post, including Bassett, Carmean and Managing Editor Erick Sahler. More are being trained, and Bassett hopes to hire a full-time "online champion" this year.

Contents from the paper and several affiliated weeklies are automatically uploaded through Gannett's Digital Production Center, and Gannett provides additional Web packages. Wire news is also automatically updated. The Web site does relatively little with local sports, has no discussion groups or blogs (though one is planned), and offers only occasional audio. Its emphasis is on breaking news.

Like his counterparts at larger papers, Bassett pushes reporters toward feeding the Web quickly.

Around noon the day I visit, a reporter files a short piece on a morning meeting. City Editor Carmean scans it, then calls the writer. "Just one quick question," he says, and then peppers him with seven questions. (Editors are like that.) A few minutes later, Carmean calls up the Web template, types in a headline and subhead and posts the story.

Sahler, 39, sees the Web as a vehicle for once again competing with broadcast to cover wrecks, fires and early meetings.

"If there is a murder, before I could be content to wait for the cops to gather information because I was only thinking of publishing for tomorrow," says reporter Ben Penserga, 27. "Now I have to grab what I can for the Web."

"The managing people part is similar, and the emphasis on storytelling, on getting it right, and, just as it was in my newspaper days, the idea that this is a public trust."

Carmean concedes that Web duties lengthen his day by about two hours, but he claims not to mind. "Sure it's long hours, and there are a lot of time-consuming elements," he says. "But I want to do it. I want this stuff on the Web. I want to reach a younger audience. There is no second place in journalism."

Back at the Houston Chronicle, Sylvia Wood has, before noon, posted a yearbook photo of the ninth grader and a staff-written story on the shooting. Now she is racing after other stories.

It is easy to imagine the time, coming soon, when the 24-hour Web cycle dominates the newsroom tempo, work flow and culture. It will bring new excitement, but giant demands for resources in a time of cutbacks and thin reserves. It may also bring serious quality-control issues. Print journalism's credibility has long been connected to its layers of editing.

As for tomorrow's journalists, they will more likely be identified by their function than by their medium. As newsrooms turn into diversified information retailers, the biggest distinction may be between those who develop the content and those who distribute it, via print, broadcast, the Internet or other channels.

Eventually, many editors foresee consolidated newsrooms with a single chain of command and few distinctions between print and online. For now, most aren't leaping quite that far.

First comes the physical merger. That will bring both groups into side-by-side cooperation but maintain, at least at first, their separate identities. After that, who knows?

"The endgame," says Chronicle Editor Jeff Cohen, "is to have all our excellent journalists producing content, and air traffic controllers putting it on the various platforms."

Or, as Sylvia Wood says: "Whether it is the Web or print or handhelds, the future is giving people news when they want it and how they want it."

Senior Editor **CARL SESSIONS STEPP** (cstepp@jmail.umd.edu) teaches at the Philip Merrill College of Journalism at the University of Maryland. He wrote about newspapers' increased interest in short-form narratives in AJR's August/September 2005 issue.

The Coming Robot Army

Introducing America's future fighting machines

STEVE FEATHERSTONE

A small gray helicopter was perched on the runway, its rotors beating slowly against the shroud of fog and rain blowing in from the Chesapeake Bay. Visibility was poor, but visibility did not matter. The helicopter had no windows, no doors, and, for that matter, no pilot. Its elliptical fuselage looked as if it had been carved out of wood and sanded smooth of detail. It hovered above the runway for a moment, swung its blind face toward the bay, and then dissolved into the mist.

The helicopter was the first among a dozen unmanned aerial vehicles (UAVs) scheduled to fly during the annual Association for Unmanned Vehicle Systems International conference in Baltimore. The live demonstration area at Webster Field, a naval air facility located seventy miles south of Washington, D.C., was laid out along the lines of a carnival midway. Big defense contractors and small engineering firms exhibited the latest military robots under white tents staked out alongside an auxiliary runway. Armed soldiers kept watch from towers and strolled through the throng of military officers and industry reps. I took a seat among rows of metal chairs arrayed in front of a giant video screen, which displayed a live feed from the helicopter's surveillance camera. There was little to see except clouds, so the announcer attempted to liven things up.

"Yesterday we saw some boats out there," he said, with an aggressive enthusiasm better suited to a monster-truck rally. "They didn't know they were being targeted by one of the newest UAVs!" Next, two technicians from AeroVironment, Inc., jogged onto the airfield and knelt in the wet grass to assemble what appeared to be a remote-controlled airplane. One of them raised it over his shoulder, leaned back, and threw it into the air like a javelin. The airplane—called the Raven—climbed straight up, stalled, dipped alarmingly toward the ground, and then leveled off at two hundred feet, its tiny electric motor buzzing like a mosquito. The screen switched to show the Raven's video feed: a bird's-eye view of the airstrip, at one end of which a large American flag flapped limply on a rope strung between two portable cranes next to an inflatable Scud missile launcher.

"A lot of the principles we use here are taken from the model industry," an AeroVironment spokesman told the announcer

as the Raven looped around the field. The U.S. military has purchased more than 3,000 Ravens, many of which have been deployed in Iraq and Afghanistan, but apparently none of the military officers present had ever seen one land. At the end of the Raven's second flight, the crowd went silent as the tiny plane plummeted from the sky and careered into the ground, tearing off its wings. The technicians scrambled to the crash site, stuck the wings back on, and held the Raven triumphantly above their heads.

"It's designed that way," the spokesman explained.

"Hey, if you can't fix it with duct tape," the announcer said, "it's not worth fixing, am I right?"

Other teams took the field to demonstrate their company's UAVs. The sheer variety of aircraft and their launching methods—planes were slung from catapults and bungee cords, shot from pneumatic guns and the backs of pickup trucks, or simply tossed by hand into the air—testified to the prodigious growth in demand for military robots since the terrorist attacks of September 11, 2001, and the subsequent "global war on terrorism." In his opening conference remarks, Rear Admiral Timothy Heely compared the embryonic UAV market with aviation in the first decades of the twentieth century, when the Wright brothers built planes in their workshop and dirigibles carried passengers. "It's all out there," he said. "You don't want to throw anything away."

Weaponized robots are the ultimate "force multiplier"—they can do the most damage with less people

It started to drizzle again. The military officers sought refuge under a catered VIP tent decorated with red, white, and blue bunting while the rest of us scattered in all directions. I headed to the unmanned ground vehicle (UGV) tent located at the far end of the runway. The tent's interior was dim; the air, sticky and hot. Tables stocked with brochures and laptops lined the vinyl walls. Robots rested unevenly on the grass. This was the first year UGVs were allowed demonstration time at the conference, and company reps were eager to show what their robots could do. A rep from iRobot, maker of the popular Roomba robotic vacuum cleaner, flipped open a shiny metal briefcase that contained an LCD monitor and a control panel studded with switches and buttons for operating the PackBots, a "man-packable" tracked robot not much bigger than a telephone book. Hundreds of PackBots have already been deployed in Iraq.

"If you can operate a Game Boy, you're good," the rep said.

A Raytheon engineer fired up an orange robot that looked like a track loader used in excavation. The only difference was a solid black box containing a radio receiver on top of the cage where the human driver normally sat. It rumbled out of the tent onto the airfield, followed by a camera crew.

"It's a Bobcat," the announcer shouted. "It's a *biiig* Bobcat!"

The Bobcat rolled up to a steel garbage bin containing a "simulated Improvised Explosive Device," hoisted it into the air with a set of pincers, and crumpled it like a soda can. A Raytheon spokesman listed all the things the tricked-out Bobcat could do, such as breach walls.

"You could also crush things like a car if you wanted to," he added.

"I never thought of crushing something," the announcer said. "But yeah, this would do very nicely."

After the Bobcat had dispatched the mangled garbage bin and returned to the tent, I asked a Raytheon engineer if the company had thought about arming it with machine guns. "Forget the machine guns," he said dismissively. "We're going lasers."

Military robots are nothing new. During World War II, Germans sent small, remote-controlled bombs on tank treads across front lines; and the United States experimented with unmanned aircraft, packing tons of high explosives into conventional bombers piloted from the air by radio (one bomber exploded soon after takeoff, killing Joseph Kennedy's eldest son, and the experiment was eventually shelved). But in a war decided by the maneuver of vast armies across whole continents, robots were a peculiar sideshow.

The practice of warfare has changed dramatically in the past sixty years. Since Vietnam, the American military machine has been governed by two parallel and complementary trends: an aversion to casualties and a heavy reliance on technology. The Gulf War reinforced the belief that technology can replace human soldiers on the battlefield, and the "Black Hawk down" incident in Somalia made this belief an article of faith. Today, any new weapon worth its procurement contract is customarily referred to as a "force multiplier," which can be translated as doing more damage with less people. Weaponized robots are the ultimate force multiplier, and every branch of the military has increased spending on new unmanned systems.

At $145 billion, the Army's Future Combat Systems (FCS) is the costliest weapons program in history, and in some ways the most visionary as well. The individual soldier is still central to the FCS concept, but he has been reconfigured as a sort of plug-and-play warrior, a node in what is envisioned as a sprawling network of robots, manned vehicles, ground sensors, satellites, and command centers. In theory, each node wilt exchange real-time information with the network, allowing the entire system to accommodate sudden changes in the "battle space." The fog of war would become a relic of the past, like the musket, swept away by crystalline streams of encrypted data. The enemy would not be killed so much as deleted.

FCS calls for seven new unmanned systems. It's not clear how much autonomy each system will be allowed. According to *Unmanned Effects (UFX): Taking the Human Out of the Loop*, a 2003 study commissioned by the U.S. Joint Forces Command, advances in artificial intelligence and automatic target recognition will give robots the ability to hunt down and kill the enemy with limited human supervision by 2015. As the study's title suggests, humans are the weakest link in the robot's "kill chain"—the sequence of events that occurs from the moment an enemy target is detected to its destruction.

At Webster Field, the latest link in the military's increasingly automated kill chain was on display: the Special Weapons Observation Reconnaissance Detection System, or SWORDS. I squatted down to take a closer look at it. Despite its theatrical name, SWORDS was remarkably plain, consisting of two thick rubber treads, stubby antennae, and a platform mounted with a camera and an M240 machine gun—all painted black. The robot is manufactured by a company named Foster-Miller, whose chief representative at the show was Bob Quinn, a slope-shouldered, balding man with bright blue eyes. Bob helped his engineer to get SWORDS ready for a quick demo. Secretary of the Army Francis Harvey, the VIP of VIPs, was coming through the UGV tent for a tour.

"The real demonstration is when you're actually firing these things," Bob lamented. Unfortunately, live fire was forbidden at Webster Field, and Bob had arrived too late to schedule a formal demonstration. At another conference two months before, he had been free to drive SWORDS around all day long. "I was going into the different booths and displays, pointing my gun, moving it up and down like the sign of the cross. People were going like this"—he jumped back and held up his hands in surrender—"then they would follow the robot back to me because they had no idea where I was. And that's the exact purpose of an urban combat capability like this."

Sunlight flooded into the tent as Secretary Harvey parted the canopy, flanked by two lanky Rangers in fatigues and berets. Bob ran his hand over his scalp and smoothed his shirt. It was sweltering inside the tent now. Beneath the brim of his tan baseball cap, Secretary Harvey's face was bright red and beaded with sweat. He nodded politely, leaning into the verbal barrage of specifications and payloads and mission packages the reps threw at him. When he got to SWORDS, he clasped his hands behind his back and stared down at the robot as if it were a small child. Someone from his entourage excitedly explained the various weapons it could carry.

Bob had orchestrated enough dog-and-pony shows to know that technology doesn't always impress men of Secretary Harvey's age and position. "We don't have it in the field yet," Bob interrupted, going on to say that SWORDS wasn't part of any official procurement plan. It was a direct result of a "bootstrap effort" by real soldiers at Picatinny Arsenal in New Jersey who were trying to solve real problems for their comrades in the field. "And soldiers love it," he added.

On the long bus ride back to Baltimore, I sat behind Master Sergeant Mike Gomez, a Marine UAV pilot. "All we are are battery-powered forward observers," he joked. Mike was biased against autonomous robots that could fire weapons or drop bombs with minimal, if any, human intervention. There were too many things that could go wrong, and innocent people could be killed as a result. At the same time, he wasn't opposed to machines that were "going to save Marines, save time, save manpower, save lives."

It wasn't the first time that day I'd heard this odd contradiction, and over the next three days I'd hear it again and again. It was as if everyone had rehearsed the same set of talking points. Robots will take soldiers out of harm's way. Robots will save lives. Allow robots to pull the trigger? No way, it'll never happen. But wasn't the logical outcome of all this fancy technology an autonomous robot force, no humans required save for those few sitting in darkened control rooms half a world away? Wasn't the best way to save lives—American lives, at least—to take humans off the battlefield altogether? Mike stared out the bus window at the passing traffic.

"I don't think that you can ever take him out," he said, his breath fogging the tinted glass. "What happens to every major civilization? At some point they civilize themselves right out of warriors. You've got sheep and you've got wolves. You've got to have enough wolves around to protect your sheep, or else somebody else's wolves are going to take them out."

Coming from a career soldier, Mike's views of war and humanity were understandably romantic. To him, bad wolves weren't the real threat. It was the idea that civilization might be able to get along without wolves, good or bad, or that wolves could be made of titanium and silicon. What would happen to the warrior spirit then?

Scores of scale-model UAVs dangled on wires from the ceiling of the exhibit hall at the Baltimore Convention Center, rotating lazily in currents of air-conditioning. Models jutted into the aisles, their wings canted in attitudes of flight. Company reps blew packing dust off cluster bombs and electronic equipment. They put out bowls of candy and trinkets. Everywhere I looked I saw ghostly black-and-white images of myself, captured by dozens of infrared surveillance cameras mounted inside domed gimbals, staring back at me from closed-circuit televisions.

In addition to cameras, almost every booth featured a large plasma monitor showing a continuous video loop of robots blowing up vehicles on target ranges, or robots pepper-spraying intruders, robots climbing stairs, scurrying down sewer pipes, circling above battlefields and mountain ranges. These videos were often accompanied by a narrator's bland voice-over, muttered from a sound system that rivaled the most expensive home theater.

I sat down in the concession area to study the floor map. An engineer next to me picked at a plate of underripe melon and shook his head in awe at the long lines of people waiting for coffee. "Four or five years ago it was just booths with concept posters pinned up," he said. "Now the actual stuff is here. It's amazing."

At the fringes of the exhibit hall, I wandered through the warrens of small companies and remote military arsenals squeezed side-by-side into 10×10 booths. I followed the screeching chords of thrash metal until I stood in front of a television playing a promotional video featuring a robot called Chaos. Chaos was built by Autonomous Solutions, a private company that had been spun out of Utah State University's robotics lab. In the video, it clambered over various types of terrain, its four flipper-like tracks chewing up dirt and rocks and tree bark. The real thing was somewhat less kinetic. A Chaos prototype lay motionless on the floor in front of the television. I nudged it with my foot and asked the company's young operations manager what it was designed to do.

"Kick the pants off the PackBot," he said, glancing around nervously. "No, I'm kidding."

A few booths down I encountered a group of men gathered around a robot the size of a paperback book. Apparently, it could climb walls by virtue of a powerful centrifuge in its belly. A picture showed it stuck to a building outside a second-story window, peering over the sill. But the rep holding the remote-control box kept ramming the robot into a doth-draped wall at the back of his booth. The robot lost traction on the loose fabric and flipped over on its back, wheels spinning. A rep from the neighboring booth volunteered use of his filing cabinet. The little robot zipped across the floor, bumped the cabinet, and, with a soft whir, climbed straight up the side. When it got to the top it extended a metal stalk bearing a tiny camera and scanned the applauding crowd.

I continued along the perimeter, trying to avoid eye contact with the reps. Since it was the first day of the show, they were fresh and alert, rocking on their heels at the edges of their booths, their eyes darting from name badge to name badge in search of potential customers. I picked up an M4 carbine resting on a table in the Chatten Associates booth. The gun's grip had been modified to simulate a computer mouse. It had two rubber keys and a thumb stick for operating a miniature radio-controlled tank sporting an assault rifle in its turret.

"You'll need this," said Kent Massey, Chatten's chief operating officer. He removed a helmet from a mannequin's head and placed it on mine. Then he adjusted the heads-up display, a postage stamp-sized LCD screen that floated in front of my right eye. The idea behind the setup was that a soldier could simultaneously keep one eye on the battlefield while piloting the robot via a video feed beamed back to his heads-up display. He never had to take his finger off the trigger.

I blinked and saw a robot's-eye view of traffic cones arranged on a fluorescent green square of artificial turf. I turned my head first to the left, then to the right. The gimbal-mounted camera in the tank mimicked the motion, swiveling left, then right. I pushed the thumb stick on the carbine's pistol grip. The tank lurched forward, knocking down a cone.

"Try not to look at the robot," Kent advised.

I turned my back to him and faced the aisle. It was difficult for me to imagine how the soldier of the future would manage both the stress of combat and the information overload that plagues the average office worker. Simply driving the tank made me dizzy, despite Kent's claims that Chatten's head-aiming system increased "situational awareness" and "operational efficiency" by 400 percent. Then again, I wasn't Army material. I was too old, too analog. As a Boeing rep would later explain to me, they were "building systems for kids that are in the seventh and eighth grades right now. They get the PDAs, the digital things, cell phones, IM."

As I crashed the tank around the obstacle course, conventioneers stopped in the aisle to determine why I was pointing a machine gun at them. I aimed the muzzle at the floor.

"The one mission that you simply cannot do without us is armed reconnaissance," Kent said over my shoulder. "Poke around a corner, clear a house . . . We lost thirty-eight guys in Fallujah in exactly those kinds of circumstances, plus a couple hundred wounded. If [the robot] gets killed, there's no letter to write home."

Robots have always been associated with dehumanization and, more explicitly, humanity's extinction. The word "robot" is derived from the Czech word for forced labor, "*robota*," and first appeared in Karel Capek's 1920 play, R.U.R (*Rossum's Universal Robots*), which ends with the destruction of mankind.

This view of robots, popularized in such movies as the *Terminator* series, troubles Cliff Hudson, who at the time coordinated robotics efforts for the Department of Defense. I ran into Cliff on the second day of the show, outside Carnegie Mellton's National Robotics Engineering Center's booth. Like the scientists in R.U.R., Cliff saw robots as a benign class of mechanized serfs. Military robots will handle most of "the three Ds: dull, dangerous, dirty-type tasks," he said, such as transporting supplies, guarding checkpoints, and sniffing for bombs. The more delicate task of killing would remain in human hands.

"I liken it to the military dog," Cliff said, and brought up a briefing given the previous day by an explosive-ordnance disposal (EOD) officer who had just returned from Iraq. The highlight of the briefing was an MTV-style video montage of robots disarming IEDs. It ended with a soldier walking away from the camera, silhouetted against golden evening sunlight, his loyal robot bumping along the road at his heels. Cliff pressed his hands together. "It's that partnership, it's that team approach," he said. "It's not going to replace the soldier. It's going to be an added capability and enhancer."

Adjacent to where we stood talking in the aisle was a prototype of the Gladiator, a six-wheeled armored car about the size of a golf cart, built by Carnegie Mellon engineers for the Marines. It was one mean enhancer. The prototype was equipped with a machine gun, but missiles could be attached to it as well.

"If you see concertina wire, you send this down range," Cliff said, maintaining his theme of man/robot cooperation. "And then the Marines can come up behind it. It's a great weapon." Despite its capabilities, the Gladiator hadn't won the complete trust of the Marines. "It's a little unstable," Cliff admitted. "Most people are uncomfortable around it when the safety is removed."

Reps proffering business cards began circling around Cliff and his entourage, sweeping me aside. Jörgen Pedersen, a young engineer with thin blond hair and a goatee, watched the scene with bemused detachment, his elbows propped on the Gladiator's turret. Jörgen had written the Gladiator's fire-control software.

"How safe is this thing?" I asked him.

"We wanted it to err on the side of safety first," Jörgen said. "You can always make something more *un*safe." In the early stages of the Gladiator's development, Jörgen had discovered that its communications link wasn't reliable enough to allow machine-gun bursts longer than six seconds. After six seconds, the robot would stop firing. So he reprogrammed the fire-control system with a fail-safe.

"You may have great communications here," Jörgen said, touching the Gladiator with his fingertips. "But you take one step back and you're just on the hairy edge of where this thing can communicate well."

The integrity of data links between unmanned systems and their operators is a major concern. Satellite bandwidth, already in short supply, will be stretched even further as more robots and other sophisticated electronics, such as remote sensors, are committed to the battlefield. There's also the possibility that radio signals could be jammed or hijacked by the enemy. But these problems are inherent to the current generation of teleoperated machines: robots that are controlled by humans from afar. As robots become more autonomous, fulfilling missions according to pre-programmed instructions, maintaining constant contact with human operators will be unnecessary. I asked Jörgen if robots would someday replace soldiers on the battlefield. He reiterated the need for a man in the loop.

"Maybe that's because I'm short-sighted based on my current experiences," he said. "Maybe the only way that it could happen is if there's no other people our on that field doing battle. It's just robots battling robots. At that point, it doesn't matter. We all just turn on the TV to see who's winning."

It is almost certain that robot deployment will save lives, both military and civilian. And yet the prospect of robot-on-human warfare does present serious moral and ethical, if not strictly legal, issues. Robots invite no special consideration under the laws of armed conflict, which place the burden of responsibility on humans, not weapons systems. When a laser-guided bomb kills civilians, responsibility falls on everyone involved in the kill chain, from the pilot who dropped the bomb to the commander who ordered the strike. Robots will be treated no differently. It will become vastly more difficult, however, to assign responsibility for noncombatant deaths caused by mechanical or programming failures as robots are granted greater degrees of autonomy. In this sense, robots may prove similar to low-tech cluster bombs or land mines, munitions that "do something that they're not supposed to out of the control of those who deploy them, and in doing so cause unintended death and suffering," according to Michael Byers, professor of global politics and international law at the University of British Columbia.

As robots become more autonomous, constant contact with human operators will be unnecessary

The moral issues are perhaps similar to those arising from the use of precision-guided munitions (PGMs). There's no doubt that PGMs greatly limit civilian casualties and collateral damage to civilian infrastructure such as hospitals, electrical grids, and water systems. But because PGM strikes are more precise compared with dropping sticks of iron bombs from B-52s, the civilian casualties that often result from PGM strikes are considered necessary, if horribly unfortunate, mistakes. One need look no further than the PGM barrage that accompanied the ground invasion of Iraq in 2003. "Decapitation strikes" aimed at senior Iraqi leaders pounded neighborhoods from Baghdad to Basra. Due to poor intelligence, none of the fifty known strikes succeeded in finding their targets. In four of the strikes forty-two civilians were killed, including six members of a family who had the misfortune of living next door to Saddam Hussein's half brother.

It's not difficult to imagine a similar scenario involving robots instead of PGMs. A robot armed only with a machine gun enters a house known to harbor an insurgent leader. The robot opens fire and kills a woman and her two children instead. It's later discovered that the insurgent leader moved to a different location at the last minute. Put aside any mitigating factors that might prevent a situation like this from occurring and assume that the robot did exactly what it was programmed to do. Assume the commander behind the operation acted on the latest intelligence, and that he followed the laws of armed conflict to the letter. Although the deaths of the woman and children might not violate the laws of armed conflict, they fall into a moral black hole where no one, no human anyway, is directly responsible. Had the innocents of My Lai and Haditha been slain not by errant men but by errant machines, would we know the names of these places today?

More troubling than the compromised moral calculus with which we program our killing machines is how robots reduce even further the costs, both fiscal and human, of the choice to wage war. Robots do not have to be recruited, trained, fed, or paid extra for combat duty. When they are destroyed, there are no death benefits to disburse. Shipping them off to hostile lands doesn't require the expenditure of political capital either. There will be no grieving robot mothers pitching camp outside the president's ranch gates. Robots are, quite literally, an off-the-shelf war-fighting capability—war in a can.

This bloodless vision of future combat was best captured by a billboard I saw at the exhibition, in the General Dynamics booth. The billboard was titled "Robots as Co-Combatants," and two scenes illustrated the concept in the garish style of toy-model-box art. One featured UGVs positioned on a slope near a grove of glossy palm trees. In the distance, a group of mud-brick buildings resembling a walled compound was set against a barren mountain range. Bright red parabolas traced the trajectories

of mortar shells fired into the compound from UGVs, but there were no explosions, no smoke.

The other scene was composed in the gritty vernacular of television news footage from Iraq. A squad of soldiers trotted down the cracked sidewalk of a city street, past stained concrete facades and terraces awash in glaring sunlight. A small, wingless micro-UAV hovered above the soldiers amid a tangled nest of drooping telephone lines, projecting a cone of white light that suggested an invisible sensor beam. And smack in the foreground, a UGV had maneuvered into the street, guns blazing. In both scenes, the soldiers are incidental to the action. Some don't even carry rifles. They sit in front of computer screens, fingers tapping on keyboards.

On the last day of the show, I sat in the concession area, chewing a stale pastry and scanning the list of the day's technical sessions. Most were dry, tedious affairs with such titles as "The Emerging Challenge of Loitering Attack Missiles." One session hosted by Foster-Miller, the company that manufactures the SWORDS robot, got my attention: "Weaponization of Small Unmanned Ground Vehicles." I filled my coffee cup and hustled upstairs.

I took a seat near the front of the conference room just as the lights dimmed. Hunched behind a podium, a Foster-Miller engineer began reading verbatim from a PowerPoint presentation about the history of SWORDS, ending with a dreary bullet-point list cataloguing the past achievements of the TALON robot, SWORDS's immediate predecessor.

"TALON has been used in most major, major . . ." The engineer faltered.

"Conflicts," someone in the audience stage-whispered. I turned to see that it was Bob Quinn. He winked at me in acknowledgment.

"Conflicts," the engineer said. He ended his portion of the talk with the same video montage that had inspired Cliff Hudson to compare robots to dogs. TALON robots were shown pulling apart tangles of wire connected to IEDs, plucking at garbage bags that had been tossed on the sides of darkened roads, extracting mortar shells hidden inside Styrofoam cups. Bob Quinn took the podium just as the final shot in the montage, that of the soldier walking down the road with his faithful TALON robot at his heels, faded on the screen behind him. The lights came up.

"The 800-pound gorilla, or the bully in the playpen, for weaponized robotics—for all ground-based robots—is Hollywood," Bob said. The audience stirred. Bob strolled off the dais and stood in the aisle, hands in his pockets. "It's interesting that UAVs like the Predator can fire Hellfire missiles at will without a huge interest worldwide. But when you get into weaponization of ground vehicles, our soldiers, our safety community, our nation, our world, are not ready for autonomy. In fact, it's quite the opposite."

Bob remained in the aisle, narrating a series of PowerPoint slides and video clips that showed SWORDS firing rockets and machine guns, SWORDS riding atop a Stryker vehicle,

SWORDS creeping up on a target and lobbing grenades at it. His point was simple: SWORDS was no killer robot, no Terminator. It was a capable weapons platform firmly in the control of the soldiers who operated it, nothing more. When the last video clip didn't load, Bob stalled for time.

"We've found that using Hollywood on Hollywood is a good strategy to overcome some of the concerns that aren't apparent with UAVs but are very apparent with UGVs," he said. Last February a crew from the History Channel had filmed SWORDS for an episode of *Mail Call*, a half-hour program hosted by the inimitable R. Lee Ermey, best known for his role as the profane drill sergeant in the movie *Full Metal Jacket*. Ermey's scowling face suddenly appeared onscreen, accompanied by jarring rock music.

"It's a lot smarter to send this robo-soldier down a blind alley than one of our flesh-and blood warriors," Ermey shouted. "It was developed by our troops in the field, not some suit in an office back home!"

Ermey's antic mugging was interspersed with quick cut-aways of SWORDS on a firing range and interviews with EOD soldiers.

"The next time you start thinking about telling the kids to put away that video game, think again!" Ermey screamed. He jabbed his finger into the camera. "Some day they could be using those same kinds of skills to run a robot that will save their bacon!"

"That's a good way to get off the stage," Bob said. He was smiling now, soaking in the applause. "I think armed robots will save soldiers' lives. It creates an unfair fight, and that's what we want. But they will be teleoperated. The more as a community we focus on that, given the Hollywood perceptions, the better off our soldiers will be."

Downstairs in the exhibit hall, I saw that Boeing had also learned the value of Hollywood-style marketing. I had stopped by the company's booth out of a sense of obligation more than curiosity: Boeing is the lead contractor for FCS. While I was talking to Stephen Bishop, the FCS business-development manager, I noticed a familiar face appear on the laptop screen behind him.

"Is that—MacGyver?"

Stephen nodded and stepped aside so that I could get a better view of the laptop. The face did indeed belong to Richard Dean Anderson, former star of the television series *MacGyver* and now the star of a five-minute promotional film produced by Boeing. Judging by the digital special effects, the film probably cost more to make than what most companies had spent on their entire exhibits. Not coincidentally, the film is set in 2014, when the first generation of FCS vehicles are scheduled for full deployment. An American convoy approaches a bridge near a snowy mountain pass somewhere in Asia, perhaps North Korea. The enemy mobilizes to cut the Americans off, but they are detected and annihilated by armed ground vehicles and UAVs.

At the center of this networked firestorm is Richard Dean Anderson, who sits inside a command vehicle, furrowing his brow and tapping a computer touchscreen. As the American forces cross the bridge, a lone enemy soldier hiding behind a boulder fires a rocket at the lead vehicle and disables it. The attack falters.

"I do not have an ID on the shooter!" a technician yells. Anderson squints grimly at his computer screen. It's the moment of truth. Does he pull back and allow the enemy time to regroup, or does he advance across the bridge, exposing his forces to enemy fire? The rousing martial soundtrack goes quiet.

"Put a 'bot on the bridge," Anderson says.

A dune-buggy-like robot darts from the column of vehicles and stops in the middle of the bridge in a heroic act of self-sacrifice. The lone enemy soldier takes the bait and fires another missile, destroying the robot and unwittingly revealing his position to a micro-UAV loitering nearby. Billions of dollars and decades of scientific research come to bear on this moment, on one man hiding behind a snow-covered boulder. He is obliterated.

"Good job," Anderson sneers. "Now let's finish this."

The film ends as American tanks pour across the bridge into enemy territory. The digitally enhanced point of view pulls back to reveal the FCS network, layer by layer, vehicle by vehicle, eighteen systems in all, until it reaches space, the network's outer shell, where a spy satellite glides by.

"Saving soldiers' lives," Stephen said, glancing at his press manager to make sure he was on message. I commended the film's production values. Stephen seemed pleased that I'd noticed. "Three-stars and four-stars gave it a standing ovation at the Pentagon last November," he told me.

"You can't argue with MacGyver," I said.

"Because it's all about saving soldiers' lives," Stephen said. "Works for congressmen, works for senators, works for the grandmother in Nebraska."

L ater that summer I visited Picatinny Arsenal, "Home of American Firepower," in New Jersey, to see a live-fire demonstration of the SWORDS robot. SWORDS was conceived at Picatinny by a small group of EOD soldiers who wanted to find a less dangerous way to "put heat on a target" inside caves in Afghanistan. Three years later, SWORDS was undergoing some final tweaks at Picatinny before being sent to Aberdeen Proving Ground for its last round of safety tests. After that, it would be ready for deployment.

"As long as you don't break my rules you'll be fine," said Sergeant Jason Mero, motioning for us to gather around him. Sgt. Mero had participated in the initial invasion of Iraq, including the assault on Saddam international Airport. He had buzzed sandy brown hair, a compact build, and the brusque authority common to non-commissioned officers. He told us exactly where we could stand, where we could set up our cameras, and assured us that he was there to help us get what we needed. Other than the "very, very loud" report of the M240 machine gun, there was little to worry about.

"The robot's not going to suddenly pivot and start shooting everybody," he said, without a hint of irony.

A crew from the Discovery Networks' Military Channel dragged their gear onto the range. They were filming a special on "Warbots," and the producer was disappointed to learn that the SWORDS robot mounted with a formidable-looking M202 grenade launcher wasn't operable. He would have to make do with the less telegenic machine-gun variant. The producer, Jonathan Gruber, wore a canvas fishing hat with the brim pulled down to the black frames of his stylish eyeglasses. Jonathan gave stage directions to Sgt. Mero, who knelt in the gravel next to SWORDS and began describing how the loading process works.

"Sergeant, if you could just look to me," Jonathan prompted. "Good. So, is a misfeed common?"

"No, not with this weapon system," Sgt. Mero said. "It's very uncommon." "My questions are cut out," Jonathan said. "So if you could repeat my question in the answer? So, you know, 'Misfeeds are not common . . .'"

"Mis—" Sgt. Mero cleared his throat. His face turned red. "However, misfeeds are not common with the M240 bravo."

"Okay, great, I'm all set for now, thanks."

The firing range was scraped out of the bottom of a shallow gorge, surrounded on all sides by trees and exposed limestone. Turkey vultures circled above the ridge. The weedy ground was littered with spent shell casings and scraps of scorched metal. Fifty yards from where I sat, two human silhouettes were visible through shoulder-high weeds in front of a concrete trap filled with sand. Sgt. Mero hooked a cable to SWORDS's camera, then flipped a red switch on the control box. I felt the M240's muzzle blast on my face as SWORDS lurched backward on its tracks, spilling smoking shells on the ground.

A cloud of dust billowed behind the silhouettes. Sgt. Mero fired again, then again. With each burst, recoil pushed SWORDS backward, and Sgt. Mero, staring at the video image on the control box's LCD screen, readjusted his aim. I could hear servos whining. When Sgt. Mero finished the ammunition belt, he switched off SWORDS and led us downrange to the targets.

"So, um, Sergeant?" Jonathan said. "As soon as you see our camera you can just start talking."

"As you see, the M240—"

"And Sergeant?" Jonathan interrupted. "I don't think you have to scream. You can just speak in a normal voice. We're all close to you."

"The problem with a heavy machine gun is, obviously, there's going to be a lot of spray," Sgt. Mero said, bending down to pick up one of the silhouettes that had fallen in the weeds. "Our second guy over here that we actually knocked down—he didn't get very many bullets, but he actually got hit pretty hard."

Through the weeds I spotted the SWORDS robot squatting in the dust. My heart skipped a beat. The machine gun was pointed straight at me. I'd watched Sgt. Mero deactivate SWORDS. I saw him disconnect the cables. And the machine gun's feed tray was empty. There wasn't the slightest chance of a misfire. My fear was irrational, but I still made a wide circle around the robot when it was time to leave.

Within our lifetime, robots will give us the ability to wage war without committing ourselves to the human cost of actually fighting a war. War will become a routine, a program. The great nineteenth-century military theorist Carl von Clausewitz understood that although war may have rational goals, the conduct of war is fundamentally irrational and unpredictable. Absent fear, war cannot be called war. A better name for it would be target practice.

Back on the firing line, Sgt. Mero booted up SWORDS and began running it around the range for the benefit of the cameras. It made a tinny, rattling noise as it rumbled over the rocks. A Discovery crewman waddled close behind it, holding his camera low to the ground. He stumbled over a clump of weeds, and for a second I thought he was going to fall on his face. But he regained his balance, took a breath, and ran to catch up with the robot.

"I think I'm good," Jonathan said after the driving demonstration. "Anything else you want to add about this?"

"Yeah," Sgt. Mero said, smiling wryly. "It kicks *ass*. It's *awesome*." In repentance for this brief moment of sarcasm, Sgt. Mero squared his shoulders, looked straight into the camera, and began speaking as if he were reading from cue cards. "These things are amazing," he said breathlessly. "They don't complain, like our regular soldiers do. They don't cry. They're not scared. This robot here has no fear, which is a good supplement to the United States Army."

"That's great," Jonathan said.

STEVE FEATHERSTONE is a writer and photographer in Syracuse, New York. His last article for *Harper's Magazine*, "The Line Is Hot," appeared in the December 2005 issue.

UNIT 6

Risk and Avoiding Risk

Unit Selections

Key Points to Consider

• The Overview to this unit mentions Michael Crichton's latest novel, *Prey.* The physicist Freeman Dyson reviews this novel in the February 13, 2002 issue of *The New York Review of Books.* Do you agree with what he has to say about the threats that technology holds for us?

• Who is Kevin Mitnick? Where does he work now? What does this say about the way we view white-collar crime in the United States?

• Use the Internet to find out more about Robert Tappan Morris, mentioned in the overview to this unit. His family history is interesting. Why?

• Do you feel safe giving your credit card number to merchants over the Internet? Find out how (or if) your number is protected from criminals who might intercept traffic between you and the merchants.

• The problems confronting government archivists in "The Fading Memory of the State," are also faced by librarians across the country. Interview librarians in your school. How are they contending with disintegrating media and changing file formats?

• Using peer-reviewed journals, find out what you can about the risk's posed to children who access social networking and dating sites.

• In January 2007, four families sued MySpace after their underage daughters were sexually abused by adults they met through the site. What is the status of that suit? Do you agree with the judgment?

Student Web Site
www.mhcls.com/online

Internet References
Further information regarding these Web sites may be found in this book's preface or online.

AntiOnline: Hacking and Hackers
    http://www.antionline.com/index.php
Copyright & Trademark Information for the IEEE Computer Society
    http://computer.org/copyright.htm
Electronic Privacy Information Center (EPIC)
    http://epic.org
Internet Privacy Coalition
    http://www.epic.org/crypto/
Center for Democracy and Technology
    http://www.cdt.org/crypto/
Survive Spyware
    http://www.cnet.com/internet/0-3761-8-3217791-1.html
An Electronic Pearl Harbor? Not Likely
    http://www.nap.edu/issues/15.1/smith.htm

If literature and film are guides, we in the United States and Western Europe have tangled feelings about technology. On the one hand, we embrace each technical marvel that enters the market place. On the other, a world in which machines have gained the upper hand is a cultural staple. Not long ago, Michael Crichton's novel, *Prey*, frightened us with killer robots that evolved by natural selection to inhabit bodies, snatch souls and take over the world. Teenagers around the country are still watching the handsome couple from *The Matrix*, Neo and Trinity, take on technology run amuck. This time our creations farm humankind and harvest their capacity to produce energy. More recently, *Children of Men* creates a world, torn by war, in which there has not been a human birth in twenty years.

As it happens, we have good reason to worry about technology, especially computer technology, but the risks are more prosaic. They include privacy intrusions, software that cannot be made error free, and deliberate sabotage. We even have grounds to fear that much of our cultural heritage, now digitized, will be inaccessible when the software used to encode it becomes obsolete. These are issues that concern practicing computer scientists and engineers. *The Communications of the ACM*, the leading journal in the field, has run a column in recent years called Inside Risks, dedicated to exploring the unintended consequences of computing. Another ACM journal, *Software Engineering Notes*, devotes a large part of each issue to chronicling software failures.

Spyware—software downloaded unknowingly—is receiving increasing attention. Harm caused by spyware ranges from gobbling up computer speed on your PC to enlisting your machine in attacks that can disrupt major businesses or the government (see "Why Spyware Poses Multiple Threats to Security").

Yet another unintended consequence of networked computers is the use of the Net by terrorist organizations. David Talbot's ("Terror's Server") tells us that "most experts agree that the Internet is not just a tool of terrorist organizations, but is central to their operations."

Ever since a Cornell graduate student, Robert Tappan Morris, released a worm onto the fledgling Internet in 1988, computer experts and users alike have been aware of computer network vulnerability. An increasingly common type in the world of hacking is the insider working for the good guys. The Web site www .happyhacker.org (retrieved 6/8/07), for example, offers this advice from someone who calls himself "Agent Steal," writing, he says, from an unnamed federal prison: ". . . let me tell you what this all means. You're going to get busted, lose everything you own, not get out on bail, snitch on your enemies, get even more time than you expected and have to put up with a bunch of idiots in prison. Sounds fun? Keep hacking." Good advice, of course.

RubberBall Productions

For a more personal view of Agent Steal and his friends, we offer a long piece from *The New York Times Magazine*, "The Virus Underground." The second para graph begins with these words: "When Mario is bored—and out here in the countryside, surrounded by soaring snowcapped mountains and little else, he's bored a lot—he likes to sit at his laptop and create computer viruses and worms."

With all of this potential mayhem in the news, it's nice to learn that the good guys have some tricks of their own in the form of fraud detection software. According to "Secrets of Digital Detectives," software intended to reduce credit card fraud has $250 million in annual sales and a growth-rate of 25 percent. Buying a diamond ring after filling your car with gas is puts you in a high risk category. Buy two pairs of running shoes in New York and you might get noticed.

The elderly are perhaps even more vulnerable than children who, in theory anyway, have adults to protect them. Of all the stories of identity theft that have circulated in the past few years, none are as poignant the tale of thieves, operating from lists of World War II veterans, who bilked 92-year old Richard Guthrie. Mr. Guthrie says he's lonelier since the con artists have stopped calling (see "Data on the Elderly, Marketed to Thieves").

Yet another risk associated with computer technology is implicit in the title of a piece from *Technology Review*: "The Fading Memory of the State." Government documents, from the 38 million e-mails generated by the Clinton administration to electronic records of the 1989 invasion of Panama, are on disintegrating electronic media, stored using now obsolete formats. In the worst scenario, they have been simply discarded. The reasons are legion, but one is sheer volume. One expert quoted in the article "says that in the next three years, humanity will generate more data—from Web sites to digital photos and video—than it generated in the previous 1,000 years."

Anyone who has spent time looking at Internet news sources knows that they can sometimes be unreliable. Paul Hitlin's "False Reporting on the Internet and the Spread of Rumors," examines Internet coverage of the Vince Foster suicide along with other stories to understand just why this is so.

What is a reasonable person to make of all of this? Terrorists, in setting up Web sites, are using software invented thirty years ago to help the U.S. sustain a nuclear attack. People around the world are actively trying to disrupt Internet traffic. Thieves get hold of computer-generated lists of names; lists presumably compiled so that government agencies could better serve their clients. Our digital records are disintegrating even as we digitize more and more of them. We debate whether young people sexually propositioned on social networking sites are propositioned by predators or peers. One strives for the equanimity of Neil Postman: "Technology giveth and technology taketh away."

Why Spyware Poses Multiple Threats to Security

ROGER THOMPSON

S pyware is becoming a relentless onslaught from those seeking to capture and use private information for their own ends. Spyware is annoying and negatively impacts the computing experience. Even worse, there are real and significant threats to corporate and even national security from those who use and abuse spyware.

There is much debate in Congress, state legislatures, and industry about what constitutes spyware. While that debate is an important one in terms of possible remedies, we can count the cost that unfettered spyware is having on individual users as well as on corporate networks. Regardless of whether we agree to divide the term spyware into various subsets such as adware or malware, the truth is any software application, if downloaded unknowingly or unwittingly, and without full explanation, is unacceptable and unwelcome.

With that understanding as a backdrop, the following is a working definition of spyware: Any software intended to aid an unauthorized person or entity in causing a computer, without the knowledge of the computer's user or owner, to divulge private information. This definition applies to legitimate business as much as to malicious code writers and hackers who are taking advantage of spyware to break into users' PCs.

Theft through spyware could be the most important and least understood espionage tactic in use today.

Many PC users have unwittingly loaded, or unknowingly had spyware downloaded onto their computers. This happens when a user clicks "yes" in response to a lengthy and often extremely technical or legalistic end user licensing agreement. Or it happens when a user simply surfs the Web, where self-activating code is simply dropped onto their machines in what is known as a "drive-by download."

Spyware Dangers Real and Pervasive

The dangers of spyware are not always known and are almost never obvious. Usually, you know when you have a virus or worm—they are quite obvious. Spyware silently installs itself on a PC, where it might start to take any number of different and unwanted actions, including:

- "Phone home" information about an individual, their computer, and their surfing habits to a third party to use to spam a computer user or push pop-up ads to their screen;
- Open a computer to a remote attacker using a Remote Access Trojan (RAT) to remotely control a computer;
- Capture every keystroke a user types—private or confidential email, passwords, bank account information—and report it back to a thief or blackmailer;
- Allow a computer to be hijacked and used to attack a third party's computers in a denial-of-service attack that can cost enterprises millions and expose them to legal liability; and
- Probe a system for vulnerabilities that can enable a hacker to steal files or otherwise exploit a computer system.

Spyware Harms Computer Performance

The misuse of technology and hijacking of spyware is a real and present danger to security and privacy. The ill effects of spyware do not stop there. Spyware seriously degrades computer performance and productivity.

Testing at our company's research laboratory earlier this year revealed that the addition of just one adware pest slowed a computer's boot time by 3.5 minutes. Instead of just under two minutes to perform this operation, it took the infected PC close to seven minutes. Multiply that by a large number of PCs and you have a huge productivity sinkhole. Add another pest and the slowdown doubles again.

We also tested Web page access, and again it took much longer once a pest was added to a clean machine. Almost five times longer in fact for a Web page to load on an infected PC. The pest also caused three Web sites to be accessed, rather than the one requested, and caused the PC to transmit and receive much greater amounts of unknown data—889 bytes transmitted compared to 281 transmitted from the clean machine, and 3,086 bytes received compared to 1,419 bytes received by the clean machine. This translates into significant increases in bandwidth utilization. Managing bandwidth costs money.

Increased costs due to unnecessary consumption of bandwidth on individual PCs, and the necessary labor costs in rebuilding systems to ensure they are no longer corrupt are virtually unquantifiable. System degradation is time consuming for the individual PC user and even more so for network administrators managing corporate networks. Even new PCs straight from the factory come loaded with thousands of pieces of spyware, all busy "phoning home" information about the user and slowing down computing speeds.

National Security Threats

As noted here, keystroke loggers and other programs embedded with spyware can be used to steal critical data. Literally thousands of spyware applications are downloaded every day in large organizations whose employees use the Internet. The probability is high that at least some of those applications are designed to steal passwords and other critical data. Theft through spyware could be the most important and least understood espionage tactic in use today.

Another disturbing threat posed by spyware goes directly to the ability of terrorists or others to disable computer networks in times of crisis. In the past year, spyware has been used to essentially hijack large numbers of personal computers and organize them into "Bot Armies." Some of the organizers of these armies use them to send millions of spam email messages without user knowledge. Advertisements offering this service have even appeared in Europe and Asia.

The potential exists to move beyond annoyance to something much worse—targeted distributed denial-of-service (DDoS) attacks aimed at disrupting major business or government activity. A DDoS attack coordinated through thousands of individual PCs, owned by innocent and even unwitting users, could be a very difficult threat to address quickly, effectively, and fairly.

Individual PC users are never aware their machine is being used to disrupt Internet traffic. There is currently little or no recourse to a legal solution even if the occurrence can be monitored.

Possible Solutions

Only a combination of education and protection, disclosure through legislation, active prosecution, and planning will provide the answer needed to address the spyware threat. None of these solutions by themselves is enough.

The first line of defense is education and protection. Any individual, business, or government agency currently connected to the Internet must realize they are part of a complex network that is inextricably intertwined. Creators of spyware take advantage of that fact, plus the knowledge that most PC users are not sophisticated technologists. The technology industry has begun to make computer users aware of the spyware threat by the creation of and active outreach by several groups and organizations, including the Consortium of Anti-Spyware Technology (COAST).

Consumer education about spyware and promotion of comprehensive anti-spyware software aimed at detecting and removing unwanted pests is fundamental to this outreach, which is modeled after the decade-long effort by anti-virus software companies to raise awareness about virus threats. However, individual computer users, precisely because of the insidious nature of spyware, can only do so much to protect themselves, and are not personally responsible for controlling the spread of spyware.

Which brings us to the second line of defense—disclosure legislation. All applications, including those bundled and downloaded along with free software and with legitimate commercial applications, should be readily identifiable by users prior to installation and made easy to remove or uninstall. It is this transparent disclosure, and the ability of individual users to decide what does and does not reside on their systems, that must be legislated. Individuals should have the ability to make fully informed decisions about what they choose to download onto their machines, while understanding the implications of doing so.

The third line of defense is aggressive prosecution. The deceptive practices employed by many spyware developers are already illegal under existing laws against consumer fraud and identity theft. Law enforcement agencies at the federal and state level should be encouraged to aggressively pursue and prosecute those who clandestinely use spyware to disrupt service, steal data, or engage in other illegal activity. Appropriate agencies should work closely with their counterparts in other countries to address this issue.

The final line of defense is planning. A spyware Bot Army DDoS targeted at key federal, state, or local agencies is well within the realm of possibility. Such an attack could be very damaging, especially if it was designed to conceal a more conventional attack, or disrupt a response to such an attack. Overcoming this type of DDoS attack could itself be highly disruptive to both individuals and businesses. It is critical that responsible bodies plan for both spyware-related DDoS attacks and responses to those attacks. If necessary, those plans should be coordinated with businesses and others. Again, this coordination should include working with responsible bodies in other countries.

Spyware is a significant threat to the effective functioning and continued growth of the Internet. It also poses threats to national security. Given the dangers it represents, it is important that business and government work together to address the issue and safeguard the productivity and security of the Internet computing environment.

ROGER THOMPSON is director of malicious content research at Computer Associates.

Terror's Server

**Fraud, gruesome propaganda, terror planning:
The Net enables it all. The online industry can help fix it.**

DAVID TALBOT

Two hundred two people died in the Bali, Indonesia, disco bombing of October 12, 2002, when a suicide bomber blew himself up on a tourist-bar dance floor, and then, moments later, a second bomber detonated an explosives-filled Mitsubishi van parked outside. Now, the mastermind of the attacks—Imam Samudra, a 35-year-old Islamist militant with links to al-Qaeda—has written a jailhouse memoir that offers a primer on the more sophisticated crime of online credit card fraud, which it promotes as a way for Muslim radicals to fund their activities.

Law enforcement authorities say evidence collected from Samudra's laptop computer shows he tried to finance the Bali bombing by committing acts of fraud over the Internet. And his new writings suggest that online fraud—which in 2003 cost credit card companies and banks $1.2 billion in the United States alone—might become a key weapon in terrorist arsenals, if it's not already. "We know that terrorist groups throughout the world have financed themselves through crime," says Richard Clarke, the former U.S. counterterrorism czar for President Bush and President Clinton. "There is beginning to be a reason to conclude that one of the ways they are financing themselves is through cyber-crime."

Online fraud would thereby join the other major ways in which terrorist groups exploit the Internet. The September 11 plotters are known to have used the Internet for international communications and information gathering. Hundreds of jihadist websites are used for propaganda and fund-raising purposes and are as easily accessible as the mainstream websites of major news organizations. And in 2004, the Web was awash with raw video of hostage beheadings perpetrated by followers of Abu Musab al-Zarqawi, the Jordanian-born terror leader operating in Iraq. This was no fringe phenomenon. Tens of millions of people downloaded the video files, a kind of vast medieval spectacle enabled by numberless Web hosting companies and Internet service providers, or ISPs. "I don't know where the line is. But certainly, we have passed it in the abuse of the Internet," says Gabriel Weimann, a professor of communications at the University of Haifa, who tracks use of the Internet by terrorist groups.

Meeting these myriad challenges will require new technology and, some say, stronger self-regulation by the online industry, if only to ward off the more onerous changes or restrictions that might someday be mandated by legal authorities or by the security demands of business interests. According to Vinton Cerf, a founding father of the Internet who codesigned its protocols, extreme violent content on the Net is "a terribly difficult conundrum to try and resolve in a way that is constructive." But, he adds, "it does not mean we shouldn't do anything. The industry has a fair amount of potential input, if it is to try to figure out how on earth to discipline itself. The question is, which parts of the industry can do it?" The roadblocks are myriad, he notes: information can literally come from anywhere, and even if major industry players agree to restrictions, Internet users themselves could obviously go on sharing content. "As always, the difficult question will be, Who decides what is acceptable content and on what basis?"

Some work is already going on in the broader battle against terrorist use of the Internet. Research labs are developing new algorithms aimed at making it easier for investigators to comb through e-mails and chat-room dialogue to uncover criminal plots. Meanwhile, the industry's anti-spam efforts are providing new tools for authenticating e-mail senders using cryptography and other methods, which will also help to thwart fraud; clearly, terrorist exploitation of the Internet adds a national-security dimension to these efforts. The question going forward is whether the terrorist use of the medium, and the emerging responses, will help usher in an era in which the distribution of online content is more tightly controlled and tracked, for better or worse.

The Rise of Internet Terror

Today, most experts agree that the Internet is not just a tool of terrorist organizations, but is central to their operations*. Some say that al-Qaeda's online presence has become more potent and pertinent than its actual physical presence since the September 11 attacks. "When we say al-Qaeda is a global ideology, this is where it existson the Internet," says Michael Doran, a Near

East scholar and terrorism expert at Princeton University. "That, in itself, I find absolutely amazing. Just a few years ago, an organization like this would have been more cultlike in nature. It wouldn't be able to spread around the world the way it does with the Internet."

The universe of terror-related websites extends far beyond al-Qaeda, of course. According to Weimann, the number of such websites has leapt from only 12 in 1997 to around 4,300 today. (This includes sites operated by groups like Hamas and Hezbollah, and others in South America and other parts of the world.) "In seven years it has exploded, and I am quite sure the number will grow next week and the week after," says Weimann, who described the trend in his report "How Modern Terrorism Uses the Internet," published by the United States Institute of Peace, and who is now at work on a book, *Terrorism and the Internet,* due out later this year.

These sites serve as a means to recruit members, solicit funds, and promote and spread ideology. "While the [common] perception is that [terrorists] are not well educated or very sophisticated about telecommunications or the Internet, we know that that isn't true," says Ronald Dick, a former FBI deputy assistant director who headed the FBI's National Infrastructure Protection Center. "The individuals that the FBI and other law enforcement agencies have arrested have engineering and telecommunications backgrounds; they have been trained in academic institutes as to what these capabilities are." (Militant Islam, despite its roots in puritanical Wahhabism, taps the well of Western liberal education: Khalid Sheikh Mohammed, the principal September 11 mastermind, was educated in the U.S. in mechanical engineering; Osama bin Laden's deputy Ayman al-Zawahiri was trained in Egypt as a surgeon.)

The Web gives jihad a public face. But on a less visible level, the Internet provides the means for extremist groups to surreptitiously organize attacks and gather information. The September 11 hijackers used conventional tools like chat rooms and e-mail to communicate and used the Web to gather basic information on targets, says Philip Zelikow, a historian at the University of Virginia and the former executive director of the 9/11 Commission. "The conspirators used the Internet, usually with coded messages, as an important medium for international communication," he says. (Some aspects of the terrorists' Internet use remain classified; for example, when asked whether the Internet played a role in recruitment of the hijackers, Zelikow said he could not comment.)

Finally, terrorists are learning that they can distribute images of atrocities with the help of the Web. In 2002, the Web facilitated wide dissemination of videos showing the beheading of *Wall Street Journal* reporter Daniel Pearl, despite FBI requests that websites not post them. Then, in 2004, Zarqawi made the gruesome tactic a cornerstone of his terror strategy, starting with the murder of the American civilian contractor Nicholas Berg—which law enforcement agents believe was carried out by Zarqawi himself. From Zarqawi's perspective, the campaign was a rousing success. Images of orange-clad hostages became a headline-news staple around the world—and the full, raw videos of their murders spread rapidly around the Web. "The Internet allows a small group to publicize such horrific and gruesome acts in seconds, for very little or no cost, worldwide, to huge audiences, in the most powerful way," says Weimann.

And there's a large market for such material. According to Dan Klinker, webmaster of a leading online gore site, Ogrish.com, consumption of such material is brisk. Klinker, who says he operates from offices in Western and Eastern Europe and New York City, says his aim is to "open people's eyes and make them aware of reality." It's clear that many eyes have taken in these images thanks to sites like his. Each beheading video has been downloaded from Klinker's site several million times, he says, and the Berg video tops the list at 15 million. "During certain events (beheadings, etc.) the servers can barely handle the insane bandwidths—sometimes 50,000 to 60,000 visitors an hour," Klinker says.

Avoiding the Slippery Slope

To be sure, Internet users who want to block objectionable content can purchase a variety of filtering-software products that attempt to block sexual or violent content. But they are far from perfect. And though a hodgepodge of Web page rating schemes are in various stages of implementation, no universal rating system is in effect—and none is mandated—that would make filters chosen by consumers more effective.

But passing laws aimed at allowing tighter filtering—to say nothing of actually mandating filtering—is problematical. Laws aimed at blocking minors access to pornography, like the Communications Decency Act and Childrens Online Protection Act, have been struck down in the courts on First Amendment grounds, and the same fate has befallen some state laws, often for good reason: the filtering tools sometimes throw out the good with the bad. "For better or worse, the courts are more concerned about protecting the First Amendment rights of adults than protecting children from harmful material," says Ian Ballon, an expert on cyberspace law and a partner at Manatt, Phelps, and Phillips in Palo Alto, CA. Pornography access, he says, "is something the courts have been more comfortable regulating in the physical world than on the Internet." The same challenges pertain to images of extreme violence, he adds.

The Federal Communications Commission enforces "decency" on the nation's airwaves as part of its decades-old mission of licensing and regulating television and radio stations. Internet content, by contrast, is essentially unregulated. And so, in 2004, as millions of people watched video of beheadings on their computers, the FCC fined CBS $550,000 for broadcasting the exposure of singer Janet Jacksons breast during the Super Bowl halftime show on television.

"While not flatly impossible, [Internet content] regulation is hampered by the variety of places around the world at which it can be hosted," says Jonathan Zittrain, codirector of the Berkman Center for Internet and Society at Harvard Law School—and that's to say nothing of First Amendment concerns. As Zittrain sees it, "its a gift that the sites are up there, because it gives us an opportunity for counterintelligence."

Industry adoption of tighter editorial controls would be a matter of good taste and of supporting the war on terror, says Richard Clarke.

As a deterrent, criminal prosecution has also had limited success. Even when those suspected of providing Internet-based assistance to terror cells are in the United States, obtaining convictions can be difficult. Early last year, under provisions of the Patriot Act, the U.S. Department of Justice charged Sami Omar al-Hussayen, a student at the University of Idaho, with using the Internet to aid terrorists. The government alleged that al-Hussayen maintained websites that promoted jihadist-related activities, including funding terrorists. But his defense argued that he was simply using his skills to promote Islam and wasn't responsible for the sites radical content. The judge reminded the jury that, in any case, the Constitution protects most speech. The jury cleared al-Hussayen on the terrorism charges but deadlocked on visa-related charges; al-Hussayen agreed to return home to his native Saudi Arabia rather than face a retrial on the visa counts.

Technology and ISPs

But the government and private-sector strategy for combatting terrorist use of the Internet has several facets. Certainly, agencies like the FBI and the National Security Agency—and a variety of watchdog groups, such as the Site Institute, a nonprofit organization based in an East Coast location that it asked not be publicized—closely monitor jihadist and other terrorist sites to keep abreast of their public statements and internal communications, to the extent possible.

It's a massive, needle-in-a-haystack job, but it can yield a steady stream of intelligence tidbits and warnings. For example, the Site Institute recently discovered, on a forum called the Jihadi Message Board, an Arabic translation of a U.S. Air Force Web page that mentioned an American airman of Lebanese descent. According to Rita Katz, executive director of the Site Institute, the jihadist page added, in Arabic, "This hypocrite will be going to Iraq in September of this year [2004]—I pray to Allah that his cunning leads to his slaughter. I hope that he will be slaughtered the Zarqawi's way, and then [go from there] to the lowest point in Hell." The Site Institute alerted the military. Today, on one if its office walls hangs a plaque offering the thanks of the Air Force Office of Special Investigations.

New technology may also give intelligence agencies the tools to sift through online communications and discover terrorist plots. For example, research suggests that people with nefarious intent tend to exhibit distinct patterns in their use of e-mails or online forums like chat rooms. Whereas most people establish a wide variety of contacts over time, those engaged in plotting a crime tend to keep in touch only with a very tight circle of people, says William Wallace, an operations researcher at Rensselaer Polytechnic Institute.

This phenomenon is quite predictable. "Very few groups of people communicate repeatedly only among themselves,"

A Window on Online Fraud

In 2003, 124,509 complaints of Internet fraud and crime were made to the U.S. Internet Crime Complaint Center, an offshoot of the FBI that takes complaints largely from the United States. The perpetrators' reported home countries broke down as follows:

Rank	Country	Reports
1	United States	76.4%
2	Canada	3.3%
3	Nigeria	2.9%
4	Italy	2.5%
5	Spain	2.4%
6	Romania	1.5%
7	Germany	1.3%
8	United Kingdom	1.3%
9	South Africa	1.1%
10	Netherlands	0.9%

Technology Review, February 2005

says Wallace. "It's very rare; they don't trust people outside the group to communicate. When 80 percent of communications is within a regular group, this is where we think we will find the groups who are planning activities that are malicious." Of course, not all such groups will prove to be malicious; the odd high-school reunion will crop up. But Wallaces group is developing an algorithm that will narrow down the field of so-called social networks to those that warrant the scrutiny of intelligence officials. The algorithm is scheduled for completion and delivery to intelligence agencies this summer.

And of course, the wider fight against spam and online fraud continues apace. One of the greatest challenges facing anti-fraud forces is the ease with which con artists can doctor their e-mails so that they appear to come from known and trusted sources, such as colleagues or banks. In a scam known as "phishing," this tactic can trick recipients into revealing bank account numbers and passwords. Preventing such scams, according to Clarke, "is relevant to counterterrorism because it would prevent a lot of cyber-crime, which may be how [terrorists] are funding themselves. It may also make it difficult to assume identities for one-time-use communications."

New e-mail authentication methods may offer a line of defense. Last fall, AOL endorsed a Microsoft-designed system called Sender ID that closes certain security loopholes and matches the IP (Internet Protocol) address of the server sending an inbound e-mail against a list of servers authorized to send mail from the message's purported source. Yahoo, the world's largest e-mail provider with some 40 million accounts, is now rolling out its own system, called Domain Keys, which tags each outgoing e-mail message with an encrypted signature that can be used by the recipient to verify that the message came from the purported domain. Google is using the technology with its Gmail accounts, and other big ISPs, including Earthlink, are following suit.

Finally, the bigger ISPs are stepping in with their own reactive efforts. Their "terms of service" are usually broad enough to allow them the latitude to pull down objectionable sites when asked to do so. "When you are talking about an online community, the power comes from the individual," says Mary Osako, Yahoo's director of communications. "We encourage our users to send [any concerns about questionable] content to us—and we take action on every report."

Too Little, or Too Much

But most legal, policy, and security experts agree that these efforts, taken together, still don't amount to a real solution. The new anti-spam initiatives represent only the latest phase of an ongoing battle. "The first step is, the industry has to realize there is a problem that is bigger than they want to admit," says Peter Neumann, a computer scientist at SRI International, a nonprofit research institute in Menlo Park, CA. "There's a huge culture change that's needed here to create trustworthy systems. At the moment we don't have anything I would call a trustworthy system." Even efforts to use cryptography to confirm the authenticity of e-mail senders, he says, are a mere palliative. There are still lots of problems with online security, says Neumann. "Look at it as a very large iceberg. This shaves off one-fourth of a percent, maybe 2 percent—but its a little bit off the top."

But if it's true that existing responses are insufficient to address the problem, it may also be true that we're at risk of an overreaction. If concrete links between online fraud and terrorist attacks begin emerging, governments could decide that the Internet needs more oversight and create new regulatory structures. "The ISPs could solve most of the spam and phishing problems if made to do so by the FCC," notes Clarke. Even if the Bali bombers writings don't create such a reaction, something else might. If no discovery of a strong connection between online fraud and terrorism is made, another trigger could be an actual act of "cyberterrorism"—the long-feared use of the Internet to wage digital attacks against targets like city power grids and air traffic control or communications systems. It could be some online display of homicide so appalling that it spawns a new drive for online decency, one countenanced by a newly conservative Supreme Court. Terrorism aside, the trigger could be a pure business decision, one aimed at making the Internet more transparent and more secure.

Zittrain concurs with Neumann but also predicts an impending overreaction. Terrorism or no terrorism, he sees a convergence of security, legal, and business trends that will force the Internet to change, and not necessarily for the better. "Collectively speaking, there are going to be technological changes to how the Internet functions—driven either by the law or by collective action. If you look at what they are doing about spam, it has this shape to it," Zittrain says. And while technological change might improve online security, he says, "it will make the Internet less flexible. If its no longer possible for two guys in a garage to write and distribute killer-app code without clearing it first with entrenched interests, we stand to lose the very processes that gave us the Web browser, instant messaging, Linux, and e-mail."

The first needed step: a culture change in the industry, to acknowledge a problem bigger than they want to admit, says Peter Neumann.

A concerted push toward tighter controls is not yet evident. But if extremely violent content or terrorist use of the Internet might someday spur such a push, a chance for preemptive action may lie with ISPs and Web hosting companies. Their efforts need not be limited to fighting spam and fraud. With respect to the content they publish, Web hosting companies could act more like their older cousins, the television broadcasters and newspaper and magazine editors, and exercise a little editorial judgment, simply by enforcing existing terms of service.

Is Web content already subject to any such editorial judgment? Generally not, but sometimes, the hopeful eye can discern what appear to be its consequences. Consider the mysterious inconsistency among the results returned when you enter the word "beheading" into the major search engines. On Google and MSN, the top returns are a mixed bag of links to responsible news accounts, historical information, and ghoulish sites that offer raw video with teasers like "World of Death, Iraq beheading videos, death photos, suicides and crime scenes." Clearly, such results are the product of algorithms geared to finding the most popular, relevant, and well-linked sites.

But enter the same search term at Yahoo, and the top returns are profiles of the U.S. and British victims of beheading in Iraq. The first 10 results include links to biographies of Eugene Armstrong, Jack Hensley, Kenneth Bigley, Nicholas Berg, Paul Johnson, and Daniel Pearl, as well as to memorial websites. You have to load the second page of search results to find a link to Ogrish.com. Is this oddly tactful ordering the aberrant result of an algorithm as pitiless as the ones that churn up gore links elsewhere? Or is Yahoo, perhaps in a nod to the victims' memories and their families' feelings, making an exception of the words "behead" and "beheading," treating them differently than it does thematically comparable words like "killing" and "stabbing?"

Yahoo's Osako did not reply to questions about this search-return oddity; certainly, a technological explanation cannot be excluded. But it's clear that such questions are very sensitive for an industry that has, to date, enjoyed little intervention or regulation. In its response to complaints, says Richard Clarke, "the industry is very willing to cooperate and be good citizens in order to stave off regulation." Whether it goes further and adopts a stricter editorial posture, he adds, "is a decision for the ISP [and Web hosting company] to make as a matter of good taste and as a matter of supporting the U.S. in the global war on terror." If such decisions evolve into the industry-wide assumption of a more journalistic role, they could, in the end, be the surest route to a more responsible medium—one that is less easy to exploit and not so vulnerable to a clampdown.

DAVID TALBOT is *Technology Review*'s chief correspondent.

The Virus Underground

Philet0ast3r, Second Part to Hell, Vorgon and guys like them around the world spend their Saturday nights writing fiendishly contagious computer viruses and worms. Are they artists, pranksters or techno-saboteurs?

CLIVE THOMPSON

This is how easy it has become.

Mario stubs out his cigarette and sits down at the desk in his bedroom. He pops into his laptop the CD of Iron Maiden's "Number of the Beast," his latest favorite album. "I really like it," he says. "My girlfriend bought it for me." He gestures to the 15-year-old girl with straight dark hair lounging on his neatly made bed, and she throws back a shy smile. Mario, 16, is a secondary-school student in a small town in the foothills of southern Austria. (He didn't want me to use his last name.) His shiny shoulder-length hair covers half his face and his sleepy green eyes, making him look like a very young, languid Mick Jagger. On his wall he has an enormous poster of Anna Kournikova—which, he admits sheepishly, his girlfriend is not thrilled about. Downstairs, his mother is cleaning up after dinner. She isn't thrilled these days, either. But what bothers her isn't Mario's poster. It's his hobby.

When Mario is bored—and out here in the countryside, surrounded by soaring snowcapped mountains and little else, he's bored a lot—he likes to sit at his laptop and create computer viruses and worms. Online, he goes by the name Second Part to Hell, and he has written more than 150 examples of what computer experts call "malware": tiny programs that exist solely to self-replicate, infecting computers hooked up to the Internet. Sometimes these programs cause damage, and sometimes they don't. Mario says he prefers to create viruses that don't intentionally wreck data, because simple destruction is too easy. "Anyone can rewrite a hard drive with one or two lines of code," he says. "It makes no sense. It's really lame." Besides which, it's mean, he says, and he likes to be friendly.

But still—just to see if he could do it—a year ago he created a rather dangerous tool: a program that autogenerates viruses. It's called a Batch Trojan Generator, and anyone can download it freely from Mario's Web site. With a few simple mouse clicks, you can use the tool to create your own malicious "Trojan horse." Like its ancient namesake, a Trojan virus arrives in someone's e-mail looking like a gift, a JPEG picture or a video, for example, but actually bearing dangerous cargo.

Mario starts up the tool to show me how it works. A little box appears on his laptop screen, politely asking me to name my Trojan. I call it the "Clive" virus. Then it asks me what I'd

like the virus to do. *Shall the Trojan Horse format drive C:?* Yes, I click. *Shall the Trojan Horse overwrite every file?* Yes. It asks me if I'd like to have the virus activate the next time the computer is restarted, and I say yes again.

Then it's done. The generator spits out the virus onto Mario's hard drive, a tiny 3k file. Mario's generator also displays a stern notice warning that spreading your creation is illegal. The generator, he says, is just for educational purposes, a way to help curious programmers learn how Trojans work.

But of course I could ignore that advice. I could give this virus an enticing name, like "britney_spears_wedding_clip.mpeg," to fool people into thinking it's a video. If I were to e-mail it to a victim, and if he clicked on it—and didn't have up-to-date anti-virus software, which many people don't—then disaster would strike his computer. The virus would activate. It would quietly reach into the victim's Microsoft Windows operating system and insert new commands telling the computer to erase its own hard drive. The next time the victim started up his computer, the machine would find those new commands, assume they were part of the normal Windows operating system and guilelessly follow them. Poof: everything on his hard drive would vanish— e-mail, pictures, documents, games.

I've never contemplated writing a virus before. Even if I had, I wouldn't have known how to do it. But thanks to a teenager in Austria, it took me less than a minute to master the art.

Mario drags the virus over to the trash bin on his computer's desktop and discards it. "I don't think we should touch that," he says hastily.

Computer experts called 2003 "the Year of the Worm." For 12 months, digital infections swarmed across the Internet with the intensity of a biblical plague. It began in January, when the Slammer worm infected nearly 75,000 servers in 10 minutes, clogging Bank of America's A.T.M. network and causing sporadic flight delays. In the summer, the Blaster worm struck, spreading by exploiting a flaw in Windows; it carried taunting messages directed at Bill Gates, infected hundreds of thousands of computers and tried to use them to bombard a Microsoft Web site with data. Then in August, a worm called

Sobig.F exploded with even more force, spreading via e-mail that it generated by stealing addresses from victims' computers. It propagated so rapidly that at one point, one out of every 17 e-mail messages traveling through the Internet was a copy of Sobig.F. The computer-security firm mi2g estimated that the worldwide cost of these attacks in 2003, including clean-up and lost productivity, was at least $82 billion (though such estimates have been criticized for being inflated).

The pace of contagion seems to be escalating. When the Mydoom.A e-mail virus struck in late January, it spread even faster than Sobig.F; at its peak, experts estimated, one out of every five e-mail messages was a copy of Mydoom.A. It also carried a nasty payload: it reprogrammed victim computers to attack the Web site of SCO, a software firm vilified by geeks in the "open source" software community.

You might assume that the blame—and the legal repercussions—for the destruction would land directly at the feet of people like Mario. But as the police around the globe have cracked down on cybercrime in the past few years, virus writers have become more cautious, or at least more crafty. These days, many elite writers do not spread their works at all. Instead, they "publish" them, posting their code on Web sites, often with detailed descriptions of how the program works. Essentially, they leave their viruses lying around for anyone to use.

Invariably, someone does. The people who release the viruses are often anonymous mischief-makers, or "script kiddies." That's a derisive term for aspiring young hackers, usually teenagers or curious college students, who don't yet have the skill to program computers but like to pretend they do. They download the viruses, claim to have written them themselves and then set them free in an attempt to assume the role of a fearsome digital menace. Script kiddies often have only a dim idea of how the code works and little concern for how a digital plague can rage out of control.

The modern virus epidemic is born of a symbiotic relationship between the people smart enough to write a virus and the people dumb enough—or malicious enough—to spread it.

Our modern virus epidemic is thus born of a symbiotic relationship between the people smart enough to write a virus and the people dumb enough—or malicious enough—to spread it. Without these two groups of people, many viruses would never see the light of day. Script kiddies, for example, were responsible for some of the damage the Blaster worm caused. The original version of Blaster, which struck on Aug. 11, was clearly written by a skilled programmer (who is still unknown and at large). Three days later, a second version of Blaster circulated online, infecting an estimated 7,000 computers. This time the F.B.I. tracked the release to Jeffrey Lee Parson, an 18-year-old in Minnesota who had found, slightly altered and re-released the Blaster code, prosecutors claim. Parson may have been seeking notoriety, or he may have had no clue how

much damage the worm could cause: he did nothing to hide his identity and even included a reference to his personal Web site in the code. (He was arrested and charged with intentionally causing damage to computers; when his trial begins, probably this spring, he faces up to 10 years in jail.) A few weeks later, a similar scene unfolded: another variant of Blaster was found in the wild. This time it was traced to a college student in Romania who had also left obvious clues to his identity in the code.

This development worries security experts, because it means that virus-writing is no longer exclusively a high-skill profession. By so freely sharing their work, the elite virus writers have made it easy for almost anyone to wreak havoc online. When the damage occurs, as it inevitably does, the original authors just shrug. *We may have created the monster,* they'll say, *but we didn't set it loose.* This dodge infuriates security professionals and the police, who say it is legally precise but morally corrupt. "When they publish a virus online, they *know* someone's going to release it," says Eugene Spafford, a computer-science professor and security expert at Purdue University. Like a collection of young Dr. Frankensteins, the virus writers are increasingly creating forces they cannot control—and for which they explicitly refuse to take responsibility.

"Where's the beer?" Philet0ast3r wondered.

An hour earlier, he had dispatched three friends to pick up another case, but they were nowhere in sight. He looked out over the controlled chaos of his tiny one-bedroom apartment in small-town Bavaria. (Most of the virus writers I visited live in Europe; there have been very few active in the United States since 9/11, because of fears of prosecution.) Philet0ast3r's party was crammed with 20 friends who were blasting the punk band Deftones, playing cards, smoking furiously and arguing about politics. It was a Saturday night. Three girls sat on the floor, rolling another girl's hair into thick dreadlocks, the hairstyle of choice among the crowd. Philet0ast3r himself—a 21-year-old with a small silver hoop piercing his lower lip—wears his brown hair in thick dreads. (Philet0ast3r is an online handle; he didn't want me to use his name.)

Philet0ast3r's friends finally arrived with a fresh case of ale, and his blue eyes lit up. He flicked open a bottle using the edge of his cigarette lighter and toasted the others. A tall blond friend in a jacket festooned with anti-Nike logos put his arm around Philet0ast3r and beamed.

"This guy," he proclaimed, "is the *best* at Visual Basic."

In the virus underground, that's love. Visual Basic is a computer language popular among malware authors for its simplicity; Philet0ast3r has used it to create several of the two dozen viruses he's written. From this tiny tourist town, he works as an assistant in a home for the mentally disabled and in his spare time runs an international virus-writers' group called the "Ready Rangers Liberation Front." He founded the group three years ago with a few bored high-school friends in his even tinier hometown nearby. I met him, like everyone profiled in this article, online, first e-mailing him, then chatting in an Internet Relay Chat channel where virus writers meet and trade tips and war stories.

Philet0ast3r got interested in malware the same way most virus authors do: his own computer was hit by a virus. He wanted to know how it worked and began hunting down virus-writers' Web sites. He discovered years' worth of viruses online, all easily downloadable, as well as primers full of coding tricks. He spent long evenings hanging out in online chat rooms, asking questions, and soon began writing his own worms.

One might assume Philet0ast3r would favor destructive viruses, given the fact that his apartment is decorated top-to-bottom with anticorporate stickers. But Philet0ast3r's viruses, like those of many malware writers, are often surprisingly mild things carrying goofy payloads. One worm does nothing but display a picture of a raised middle finger on your computer screen, then sheepishly apologize for the gesture. ("Hey, this is not meant to you! I just wanted to show my payload.") Another one he is currently developing will install two artificial intelligence chat-agents on your computer; they appear in a pop-up window, talking to each other nervously about whether your antivirus software is going to catch and delete them. Philet0ast3r said he was also working on something sneakier: a "keylogger." It's a Trojan virus that monitors every keystroke its victim types—including passwords and confidential e-mail messages—then secretly mails out copies to whoever planted the virus. Anyone who spreads this Trojan would be able to quickly harvest huge amounts of sensitive personal information.

Technically, "viruses" and "worms" are slightly different things. When a virus arrives on your computer, it disguises itself. It might look like an OutKast song ("hey_ya.mp3"), but if you look more closely, you'll see it has an unusual suffix, like "hey_ya.mp3.exe." That's because it isn't an MP3 file at all. It's a tiny program, and when you click on it, it will reprogram parts of your computer to do something new, like display a message. A virus cannot kick-start itself; a human needs to be fooled into clicking on it. This turns virus writers into armchair psychologists, always hunting for new tricks to dupe someone into activating a virus. ("All virus-spreading," one virus writer said caustically, "is based on the idiotic behavior of the users.")

Worms, in contrast, usually do not require any human intervention to spread. That means they can travel at the breakneck pace of computers themselves. Unlike a virus, a worm generally does not alter or destroy data on a computer. Its danger lies in its speed: when a worm multiplies, it often generates enough traffic to brown out Internet servers, like air-conditioners bringing down the power grid on a hot summer day. The most popular worms today are "mass mailers," which attack a victim's computer, swipe the addresses out of Microsoft Outlook (the world's most common e-mail program) and send a copy of the worm to everyone in the victim's address book. These days, the distinction between worm and virus is breaking down. A worm will carry a virus with it, dropping it onto the victim's hard drive to do its work, then e-mailing itself off to a new target.

Computer code blurs the line between speech and act. Posting a virus on a Web site, one expert says, is "like taking a gun and sticking bullets in it and sitting it on the counter and saying, 'Hey, free gun!'"

The most ferocious threats today are "network worms," which exploit a particular flaw in a software product (often one by Microsoft). The author of Slammer, for example, noticed a flaw in Microsoft's SQL Server, an online database commonly used by businesses and governments. The Slammer worm would find an unprotected SQL server, then would fire bursts of information at it, flooding the server's data "buffer," like a cup filled to the brim with water. Once its buffer was full, the server could be tricked into sending out thousands of new copies of the worm to other servers. Normally, a server should not allow an outside agent to control it that way, but Microsoft had neglected to defend against such an attack. Using that flaw, Slammer flooded the Internet with 55 million blasts of data per second and in only 10 minutes colonized almost all vulnerable machines. The attacks slowed the 911 system in Bellevue, Wash., a Seattle suburb, to such a degree that operators had to resort to a manual method of tracking calls.

Philet0ast3r said he isn't interested in producing a network worm, but he said it wouldn't be hard if he wanted to do it. He would scour the Web sites where computer-security professionals report any new software vulnerabilities they discover. Often, these security white papers will explain the flaw in such detail that they practically provide a road map on how to write a worm that exploits it. "Then I would use it," he concluded. "It's that simple."

Computer-science experts have a phrase for that type of fast-spreading epidemic: "a Warhol worm," in honor of Andy Warhol's prediction that everyone would be famous for 15 minutes. "In computer terms, 15 minutes is a really long time," says Nicholas Weaver, a researcher at the International Computer Science Institute in Berkeley, who coined the Warhol term. "The worm moves faster than humans can respond." He suspects that even more damaging worms are on the way. All a worm writer needs to do is find a significant new flaw in a Microsoft product, then write some code that exploits it. Even Microsoft admits that there are flaws the company doesn't yet know about.

Virus writers are especially hostile toward Microsoft, the perennial whipping boy of the geek world. From their (somewhat self-serving) point of view, Microsoft is to blame for the worm epidemic, because the company frequently leaves flaws in its products that allow malware to spread. Microsoft markets its products to less expert computer users, cultivating precisely the sort of gullible victims who click on disguised virus attachments. But it is Microsoft's success that really makes it such an attractive target: since more than 90 percent of desktop computers run Windows, worm writers target Microsoft in order to hit the largest possible number of victims. (By relying so exclusively on Microsoft products, virus authors say, we have created a digital monoculture, a dangerous thinning of the Internet's gene pool.)

Microsoft officials disagree that their programs are poor quality, of course. And it is also possible that their products are targeted because it has become cool to do so. "There's sort of a natural tendency to go after the biggest dog," says Phil Reitinger, senior security strategist for Microsoft. Reitinger says that the company is working to make its products more secure. But Microsoft is now so angry that it has launched a counterattack. Last fall, Microsoft set up a $5 million fund to pay for information leading to the capture of writers who target Windows machines. So far, the company has announced $250,000 bounties for the creators of Blaster, Sobig.F and Mydoom.B.

The motivations of the top virus writers can often seem paradoxical. They spend hours dreaming up new strategies to infect computers, then hours more bringing them to reality. Yet when they're done, most of them say they have little interest in turning their creations free. (In fact, 99 percent of all malware never successfully spreads in the wild, either because it expressly wasn't designed to do so or because the author was inept and misprogrammed his virus.) Though Philet0ast3r is proud of his keylogger, he said he does not intend to release it into the wild. His reason is partly one of self-protection; he wouldn't want the police to trace it back to him. But he also said he does not ethically believe in damaging someone else's computer.

So why write a worm, if you're not going to spread it?

For the sheer intellectual challenge, Philet0ast3r replied, the fun of producing something "really cool." For the top worm writers, the goal is to make something that's brand-new, never seen before. Replicating an existing virus is "lame," the worst of all possible insults. A truly innovative worm, Philet0ast3r said, "is like art." To allow his malware to travel swiftly online, the virus writer must keep its code short and efficient, like a poet elegantly packing as much creativity as possible into the tight format of a sonnet. "One condition of art," he noted, "is doing good things with less."

When he gets stuck on a particularly thorny problem, Philet0ast3r will sometimes call for help from other members of the Ready Rangers Liberation Front (which includes Mario). Another friend in another country, whom Philet0ast3r has never actually met, is helping him complete his keylogger by writing a few crucial bits of code that will hide the tool from its victim's view. When they're done, they'll publish their invention in their group's zine, a semiannual anthology of the members' best work.

The virus scene is oddly gentlemanly, almost like the amateur scientist societies of Victorian Britain, where colleagues presented papers in an attempt to win that most elusive of social currencies: street cred. In fact, I didn't meet anyone who gloated about his own talent until I met Benny. He is a member of 29A, a super-elite cadre within the virus underground, a handful of coders around the world whose malware is so innovative that even antivirus experts grudgingly admit they're impressed. Based in the Czech Republic, Benny, clean-cut and wide-eyed, has been writing viruses for five years, making him a veteran in the field at age 21. "The main thing that I'm most proud of, and that no one else can say, is that I always come up with a new idea," he said, ushering me into a bedroom so neat that it looked as if he'd stacked his magazines using a ruler and level. "Each worm shows something different, something new that hadn't been done before by anyone."

Benny—that's his handle, not his real name—is most famous for having written a virus that infected Windows 2000 two weeks before Windows 2000 was released. He'd met a Microsoft employee months earlier who boasted that the new operating system would be "more secure than ever"; Benny wrote (but says he didn't release) the virus specifically to humiliate the company. "Microsoft," he said with a laugh, "wasn't enthusiastic." He also wrote Leviathan, the first virus to use "multithreading," a technique that makes the computer execute several commands at once, like a juggler handling multiple balls. It greatly speeds up the pace at which viruses can spread. Benny published that invention in his group's zine, and now many of the most virulent bugs have adopted the technique, including last summer's infamous Sobig.F.

For a virus author, a successful worm brings the sort of fame that a particularly daring piece of graffiti used to produce: the author's name, automatically replicating itself in cyberspace. When antivirus companies post on their Web sites a new "alert" warning of a fresh menace, the thrill for the author is like getting a great book review: something to crow about and e-mail around to your friends. Writing malware, as one author e-mailed me, is like creating artificial life. A virus, he wrote, is "a humble little creature with only the intention to avoid extinction and survive."

Quite apart from the intellectual fun of programming, though, the virus scene is attractive partly because it's very social. When Philet0ast3r drops by a virus-writers chat channel late at night after work, the conversation is as likely to be about music, politics or girls as the latest in worm technology. "They're not talking about viruses—they're talking about relationships or ordering pizza," says Sarah Gordon, a senior research fellow at Symantec, an antivirus company, who is one of the only researchers in the world who has interviewed hundreds of virus writers about their motivations. Very occasionally, malware authors even meet up face to face for a party; Philet0ast3r once took a road trip for a beer-addled weekend of coding, and when I visited Mario, we met up with another Austrian virus writer and discussed code for hours at a bar.

The virus community attracts a lot of smart but alienated young men, libertarian types who are often flummoxed by the social nuances of life. While the virus scene isn't dominated by those characters, it certainly has its share—and they are often the ones with a genuine chip on their shoulder.

"I am a social reject," admitted Vorgon (as he called himself), a virus writer in Toronto with whom I exchanged messages one night in an online chat channel. He studied computer science in college but couldn't find a computer job after sending out 400 résumés. With "no friends, not much family" and no girlfriend for years, he became depressed. He attempted suicide, he said, by walking out one frigid winter night into a nearby forest for five hours with no jacket on. But then he got into the virus-writing scene and found a community. "I met a lot of cool people who were interested in what I did," he wrote. "They made me feel good again." He called his first virus FirstBorn to celebrate his new identity. Later, he saw that one of his worms had been written up as an alert on an antivirus site, and it thrilled him. "Kinda like when I got my first girlfriend," he wrote. "I was god for a couple days." He began work on another worm, trying to recapture the feeling. "I spent three months working on it just so I could have those couple of days of godliness."

Vorgon is still angry about life. His next worm, he wrote, will try to specifically target the people who wouldn't hire him. It will have a "spidering" engine that crawls Web-page links, trying to find likely e-mail addresses for human-resource managers, "like careers@microsoft.com, for example." Then it will send them a fake résumé infected with the worm. (He hasn't yet decided on a payload, and he hasn't ruled out a destructive one.) "This is a revenge worm," he explained—for "not hiring me, and hiring some loser that is not even half the programmer I am."

Many people might wonder why virus writers aren't simply rounded up and arrested for producing their creations. But in most countries, writing viruses is not illegal. Indeed, in the United States some legal scholars argue that it is protected as free speech. Software is a type of language, and writing a program is akin to writing a recipe for beef stew. It is merely a bunch of instructions for the computer to follow, in the same way that a recipe is a set of instructions for a cook to follow. A virus or worm becomes illegal only when it is activated—when someone sends it to a victim and starts it spreading in the wild, and it does measurable damage to computer systems. The top malware authors are acutely aware of this distinction. Most every virus-writer Web site includes a disclaimer stating that it exists purely for educational purposes, and that if a visitor downloads a virus to spread, the responsibility is entirely the visitor's. Benny's main virus-writing computer at home has no Internet connection at all; he has walled it off like an airlocked biological-weapons lab, so that nothing can escape, even by accident.

Vorgon is angry about life. His next worm, he says, will try to specifically target the people who wouldn't hire him. 'This is a revenge worm,' he explained.

Virus writers argue that they shouldn't be held accountable for other people's actions. They are merely pursuing an interest in writing self-replicating computer code. "I'm not responsible for people who do silly things and distribute them among their friends," Benny said defiantly. "I'm not responsible for those. What I like to do is programming, and I like to show it to people—who may then do something with it." A young woman who goes by the handle Gigabyte told me in an online chat room that if the authorities wanted to arrest her and other virus writers, then "they should arrest the creators of guns as well."

One of the youngest virus writers I visited was Stephen Mathieson, a 16-year-old in Detroit whose screen name is Kefi. He also belongs to Philet0ast3r's Ready Rangers Liberation Front. A year ago, Mathieson became annoyed when he found members of another virus-writers group called Catfish_VX plagiarizing his code. So he wrote Evion, a worm specifically designed to taunt the Catfish guys. He put it up on his Web site for everyone to see. Like most of Mathieson's work, the worm had no destructive intent. It merely popped up a few cocky messages, including: *Catfish_VX are lamers. This virus was constructed for them to steal.*

Someone did in fact steal it, because pretty soon Mathieson heard reports of it being spotted in the wild. To this day, he does not know who circulated Evion. But he suspects it was probably a random troublemaker, a script kiddie who swiped it from his site. "The kids," he said, shaking his head, "just cut and paste."

Quite aside from the strangeness of listening to a 16-year-old complain about "the kids," Mathieson's rhetoric glosses over a charged ethical and legal debate. It is tempting to wonder if the leading malware authors are lying—whether they do in fact circulate their worms on the sly, obsessed with a desire to see whether they will really work. While security officials say that may occasionally happen, they also say the top virus writers are quite likely telling the truth. "If you're writing important virus code, you're probably well trained," says David Perry, global director of education for Trend Micro, an antivirus company. "You know a number of tricks to write good code, but you don't want to go to prison. You have an income and stuff. It takes someone unaware of the consequences to release a virus."

But worm authors are hardly absolved of blame. By putting their code freely on the Web, virus writers essentially dangle temptation in front of every disgruntled teenager who goes online looking for a way to rebel. A cynic might say that malware authors rely on clueless script kiddies the same way that a drug dealer uses 13-year-olds to carry illegal goods—passing the liability off to a hapless mule.

"You've got several levels here," says Marc Rogers, a former police officer who now researches computer forensics at Purdue University. "You've got the guys who write it, and they know they shouldn't release it because it's illegal. So they put it out there knowing that some script kiddie who wants to feel like a big shot in the virus underground will put it out. They know these neophytes will jump on it. So they're grinning ear to ear, because their baby, their creation, is out there. But they didn't officially release it, so they don't get in trouble." He says he thinks that the original authors are just as blameworthy as the spreaders.

Sarah Gordon of Symantec also says the authors are ethically naïve. "If you're going to say it's an artistic statement, there are more responsible ways to be artistic than to create code that costs people millions," she says. Critics like Reitinger, the Microsoft security chief, are even harsher. "To me, it's online arson," he says. "Launching a virus is no different from burning down a building. There are people who would never toss a Molotov cocktail into a warehouse, but they wouldn't think for a second about launching a virus."

What makes this issue particularly fuzzy is the nature of computer code. It skews the traditional intellectual question about studying dangerous topics. Academics who research nuclear-fission techniques, for example, worry that their research could help a terrorist make a weapon. Many publish their findings anyway, believing that the mere knowledge of how fission works won't help Al Qaeda get access to uranium or rocket parts.

But computer code is a different type of knowledge. The code for a virus is itself the weapon. You could read it in the same way you read a book, to help educate yourself about malware. Or you could set it running, turning it instantly into an active agent. Computer code blurs the line between speech and act. "It's like taking a gun and sticking bullets in it and sitting it on the counter and saying, 'Hey, free gun!'" Rogers says.

Some academics have pondered whether virus authors could be charged under conspiracy laws. Creating a virus, they theorize, might be considered a form of abetting a crime by providing materials. Ken Dunham, the head of "malicious code intelligence" for iDefense, a computer security company, notes that there are certainly many examples of virus authors assisting newcomers. He has been in chat rooms, he says, "where I can see people saying, 'How can I find vulnerable hosts?' And another guy says, 'Oh, go here, you can use this tool.' They're helping each other out."

There are virus writers who appreciate these complexities. But they are certain that the viruses they write count as protected speech. They insist they have a right to explore their interests. Indeed, a number of them say they are making the world a better place, because they openly expose the weaknesses of computer systems. When Philet0ast3r or Mario or Mathieson finishes a new virus, they say, they will immediately e-mail a copy of it to antivirus companies. That way, they explained, the companies can program their software to recognize and delete the virus should some script kiddie ever release it into the wild. This is further proof that they mean no harm with their hobby, as Mathieson pointed out. On the contrary, he said, their virus-writing strengthens the "immune system" of the Internet.

These moral nuances fall apart in the case of virus authors who are themselves willing to release worms into the wild. They're more rare, for obvious reasons. Usually they are overseas, in countries where the police are less concerned with software crimes. One such author is Melhacker, a young man who reportedly lives in Malaysia and has expressed sympathy for Osama bin Laden. Antivirus companies have linked him to the development of several worms, including one that claims to come from the "Qaeda network." Before the Iraq war, he told a computer magazine that he would release a virulent worm if the United States attacked Iraq—a threat that proved hollow. When I e-mailed him, he described his favorite type of worm payload: "Stolen information from other people." He won't say which of his viruses he has himself spread and refuses to comment on his connection to the Qaeda worm. But in December on Indovirus.net, a discussion board for virus writers, Melhacker urged other writers to "try to make it in the wild" and to release their viruses in cybercafes, presumably to avoid detection. He also told them to stop sending in their work to antivirus companies.

Mathieson wrote a critical post in response, arguing that a good virus writer shouldn't need to spread his work. Virus authors are, in fact, sometimes quite chagrined when someone puts a dangerous worm into circulation, because it can cause a public backlash that hurts the entire virus community. When the Melissa virus raged out of control in 1999, many Internet service providers immediately shut down the Web sites of malware creators. Virus writers stormed online to pillory the Melissa author for turning his creation loose. "We don't need any more grief," one wrote.

If you ask cyberpolice and security experts about their greatest fears, they are not the traditional virus writers, like Mario or Philet0ast3r or Benny. For better or worse, those authors are a known quantity. What keeps antivirus people awake at night these days is an entirely new threat: worms created for explicit criminal purposes. These began to emerge last year. Sobig in particular alarmed virus researchers. It was released six separate times throughout 2003, and each time the worm was programmed to shut itself off permanently after a few days or weeks. Every time the worm appeared anew, it had been altered in a way that suggested a single author had been tinkering with it, observing its behavior in the wild, then killing off his creation to prepare a new and more insidious version. "It was a set of very well-controlled experiments," says Mikko Hypponen, the director of antivirus research at F-Secure, a computer security company. "The code is high quality. It's been tested well. It really works in the real world." By the time the latest variant, Sobig.F, appeared in August, the worm was programmed to install a back door that would allow the author to assume control of the victim's computer. To what purpose? Experts say its author has used the captured machines to send spam and might also be stealing financial information from the victims' computers.

No one has any clue who wrote Sobig. The writers of this new class of worm leave none of the traces of their identities that malware authors traditionally include in their code, like their screen names or "greetz," shout-out hellos to their cyberfriends. Because criminal authors actively spread their creations, they are cautious about tipping their hand. "The F.B.I. is out for the Sobig guy with both claws, and they want to make an example of him," David Perry notes. "He's not going to mouth off." Dunham of iDefense says his online research has turned up "anecdotal evidence" that the Sobig author comes from Russia or elsewhere in Europe. Others suspect China or other parts of Asia. It seems unlikely that Sobig came from the United States, because American police forces have been the most proactive of any worldwide in hunting those who spread malware. Many experts believe the Sobig author will release a new variant sometime this year.

Sobig was not alone. A variant of the Mimail worm, which appeared last spring, would install a fake pop-up screen on a computer pretending to be from PayPal, an online e-commerce firm. It would claim that PayPal had lost the victim's credit-card or banking details and ask him to type it in again. When he did, the worm would forward the information to the worm's still-unknown author. Another worm, called Bugbear.B, was programmed to employ sophisticated password-guessing strategies at banks and brokerages to steal personal information. "It was specifically designed to target financial institutions," said Vincent Weafer, senior director of Symantec.

The era of the stealth worm is upon us. None of these pieces of malware were destructive or designed to cripple the Internet with too much traffic. On the contrary, they were designed to be unobtrusive, to slip into the background, the better to secretly harvest data. Five years ago, the biggest danger was the "Chernobyl" virus, which deleted your hard drive. But the prevalence of hard-drive-destroying viruses has steadily declined to almost zero. Malware authors have learned a lesson that biologists have long known: the best way for a virus to spread is to ensure its host remains alive.

"It's like comparing Ebola to AIDS," says Joe Wells, an anti-virus researcher and founder of WildList, a long-established virus-tracking group. "They both do the same thing. Except one does it in three days, and the other lingers and lingers and lingers. But which is worse? The ones that linger are the ones that spread the most." In essence, the long years of experimentation have served as a sort of Darwinian evolutionary contest, in which virus writers have gradually figured out the best strategies for survival.

Given the pace of virus development, we are probably going to see even nastier criminal attacks in the future. Some academics have predicted the rise of "cryptoviruses"—malware that invades your computer and encrypts all your files, making them unreadable. "The only way to get the data back will be to pay a ransom," says Stuart Schechter, a doctoral candidate in computer security at Harvard. (One night on a discussion board I stumbled across a few virus writers casually discussing this very concept.) Antivirus companies are writing research papers that worry about the rising threat of "metamorphic" worms—ones that can shift their shapes so radically that antivirus companies cannot recognize they're a piece of malware. Some experimental metamorphic code has been published by Z0mbie, a reclusive Russian member of the 29A virus-writing group. And mobile-phone viruses are probably also only a few years away. A phone virus could secretly place 3 A.M. calls to a toll number, sticking you with thousand-dollar charges that the virus's author would collect. Or it could drown 911 in phantom calls. As Marty Lindner, a cybersecurity expert at CERT/CC, a federally financed computer research center, puts it, "The sky's the limit."

The profusion of viruses has even become a national-security issue. Government officials worry that terrorists could easily launch viruses that cripple American telecommunications, sowing confusion in advance of a physical 9/11-style attack. Paula Scalingi, the former director of the Department of Energy's Office of Critical Infrastructure Protection, now works as a consultant running disaster-preparedness exercises. Last year she helped organize "Purple Crescent" in New Orleans, an exercise that modeled a terrorist strike against the city's annual Jazz and Heritage Festival. The simulation includes a physical attack but also uses a worm unleashed by the terrorists designed to cripple communications and sow confusion nationwide. The physical attack winds up flooding New Orleans; the cyberattack makes hospital care chaotic. "They have trouble communicating, they can't get staff in, it's hard for them to order supplies," she says. "The impact of worms and viruses can be prodigious."

This new age of criminal viruses puts traditional malware authors in a politically precarious spot. Police forces are under more pressure than ever to take any worm seriously, regardless of the motivations of the author.

A young Spaniard named Antonio discovered that last fall. He is a quiet 23-year-old computer professional who lives near Madrid. Last August, he read about the Blaster worm and how it exploited a Microsoft flaw. He became intrigued, and after poking around on a few virus sites, found some sample code that worked the same way. He downloaded it and began tinkering to see how it worked.

Then on Nov. 14, as he left to go to work, Spanish police met him at his door. They told him the anti-virus company Panda Software had discovered his worm had spread to 120,000 computers. When Panda analyzed the worm code, it quickly discovered that the program pointed to a site Antonio had developed. Panda forwarded the information to the police, who hunted Antonio down via his Internet service provider. The police stripped his house of every computer—including his roommate's—and threw Antonio in jail. After two days, they let him out, upon which Antonio's employer immediately fired him. "I have very little money," he said when I met him in December. "If I don't have a job in a little time, in a few months I can't pay the rent. I will have to go to my parents."

The Spanish court is currently considering what charges to press. Antonio's lawyer, Javier Maestre, argued that the worm had no dangerous payload and did no damage to any of the computers it infected. He suspects Antonio is being targeted by the police, who want to pretend they've made an important cyberbust, and by an antivirus company seeking publicity.

Artificial life can spin out of control—and when it does, it can take real life with it. Antonio says he did not actually intend to release his worm at all. The worm spreads by scanning computers for the Blaster vulnerability, then sending a copy of itself to any open target. Antonio maintains he thought he was playing it safe, because his computer was not directly connected to the Internet. His roommate's computer had the Internet connection, and a local network—a set of cables connecting their computers together—allowed Antonio to share the signal. But what Antonio didn't realize, he says, was that his worm would regard his friend's computer as a foreign target. It spawned a copy of itself in his friend's machine. From there it leapfrogged onto the Internet—and out into the wild. His creation had come to life and, like Frankenstein's monster, decided upon a path of its own.

CLIVE THOMPSON writes frequently about science and technology. His last article for the magazine was about mobile-phone culture.

Secrets of the Digital Detectives

The pleasure of reading a classic detective story comes from the way that the sleuth puts together several clues to arrive at a surprising conclusion. What is enjoyable is not so much finding out who the villain is, but hearing the detectives explain their reasoning. Today, not all detectives are human. At insurance companies, banks and telecoms firms, fraud-detection software is used to comb through millions of transactions, looking for patterns and spotting fraudulent activity far more quickly and accurately than any human could. But like human detectives, these software sleuths follow logical rules and combine disparate pieces of data—and there is something curiously fascinating about the way they work.

Consider car insurance. Every Monday morning, telephone operators at insurance firms listen to stories of the weekend's motoring mishaps, typing the answers to several dozen standard questions into their computers. Once, each claim form then passed to a loss adjuster for approval; now software is increasingly used instead. The Monday-morning insurance claims, it turns out, are slightly more likely to be fraudulent than Tuesday claims, since weekends make it easier for policyholders who stage accidents to assemble friends as false witnesses. A single rule like that is straightforward enough for a human loss adjuster to take into account. But fraud-detection software can consider dozens of other variables, too.

If a claimant was nearly injured (because of an impact near the driver's seat, for example), the accident is less likely to have been staged and the claim less likely to be fraudulent, even if it is being filed on a Monday. Drivers of cars with low resale values are proportionately more likely to file fraudulent claims. But that factor is less important if the claimant also owns a luxury car, which suggests affluence. And if the insurance on the luxury car has expired, the likelihood of foul play drops further, since this increases the likelihood a person will drive a cheaper but properly insured car. And so on.

The staggering number of combinations, each an indication of fraud or legitimacy, underscores the limitations of human analysis. Fraud-detection software, however, can evaluate a vast number of permutations and deliver a fraud-probability score. And such programs are getting better as new claims provide extra statistics that can help tune the computational recipes, or algorithms, used to detect fraud.

German insurers, for example, recently noticed that claimants who call back shortly after filing, angrily demanding speedy settlement, are disproportionately more likely to be cheaters, says Jörg Schiller, an insurance expert at the Otto Beisheim School of Management in Vallendar, Germany. Evidently fraudsters consider themselves good actors. But when pugnacious policyholders call after the 20th of the month, the probability that they are acting decreases slightly, since funds from the previous month's paycheque may be dwindling. Mr Schiller says most car insurers in rich countries now use fraud-detection software, and those in developing countries are adopting it rapidly.

Play Your Cards Right

With an estimated $250m in annual sales, and yearly growth topping 25%, the largest and fastest-growing category of fraud-detection software is that used to spot fraudulent credit-card transactions. According to the Association for Payment Clearing Services, based in London, such software is largely responsible for reducing losses from credit-card fraud in Britain alone from £505m ($925m) in 2004 to £439m ($799m) in 2005. Merchants implementing anti-fraud software for the first time commonly see losses from fraud reduced by half. Such software evaluates many parameters associated with each credit-card transaction, including specific details of the items being purchased (derived from their bar codes), to evaluate the likelihood of foul play in the form of a numerical risk score. Any transactions that score above a certain pre-defined threshold are then denied or challenged.

Buying petrol seems innocent enough. If no attendant is present, however, the risk score goes up, because fraudsters prefer to avoid face-to-face purchases. Buying a diamond ring soon after buying petrol results in an even higher risk score: thieves often test a card's validity with a small purchase before buying something much bigger. A $100 purchase at a shop that sells hard liquor is more likely to be fraudulent than a more expensive shopping spree at a wine shop, because whisky is easier to fence. A purchase of sports shoes is risky because trainers appeal to a demographic with less money than, say, buyers of golf clubs. Buying two pairs of trainers increases the risk, as this may indicate plans to resell them. Shoes in teenage sizes bump up the score further, since pre-teens are less likely to buy stolen goods. Sales in London, New York or Miami, all cities with vibrant black markets for shoes, push scores higher, as do purchases made during school holidays. The fraud history of individual shops can also be taken into account.

Seasoned criminals can, of course, figure out such rules and change their behaviour in an attempt to avoid detection. Some types of purchases are less likely to be fraudulent. A shopping spree in a linen shop, however, does not have much appeal to most criminals. However, says Mike Davis, a fraud expert at Butler Group, a consultancy, the "vast majority" of fraudsters are low-level opportunists fairly easily foiled by today's fraud-detection software. The situation, he says, is "spectacularly better" than it was just a few years ago.

But the technology trips up cleverer fraudsters too, using a variety of tricks. The software can, for example, assign a customised scoring algorithm to each credit card, depending on its normal usage patterns. That algorithm can then be fine-tuned after each transaction. If a card belonging to a Berliner has never been used to purchase a plane ticket or buy goods outside Germany, the system may block an attempt to book a Moscow-Tokyo flight leaving in three hours. An attempt to charge a moped to an elderly woman's card may fail. Cards are often blocked when the volume of transactions for which they are used abruptly spikes.

E-businesses using anti-fraud software now block about 8% of all transactions. Some aborted orders, of course, are not fraudulent. Each "false positive" reduces profits and angers an honest shopper. To limit such damage, risk managers (employed by the software developers or the merchants themselves) study sales data compiled before the anti-fraud software was implemented. This analysis helps retailers find the optimal score threshold to determine which orders they accept.

Online fraudsters have tricks of their own, of course. Carl Clump, the boss of Retail Decisions, a fraud-detection firm based near London with clients including Wal-Mart, Sears and Bloomingdale's, offers an example. Not long ago, American scammers began buying CDs of classical music with their purchases of expensive items, apparently in an effort to deceive anti-fraud systems (since such music is generally assumed not to appeal to young, tech-savvy criminals). Retail Decisions' software, called PRISM, detected the trend. Now, purchases that combine classical or opera CDs with expensive goods receive a higher score than purchases of high-cost items alone.

By reading a computer's internet-protocol address, anti-fraud systems can "geolocate" online buyers, and raise or lower scores depending on where they are. Most systems penalise customers in places such as Eastern Europe, China, Thailand and Vietnam. More dramatically, many merchants block all transactions from certain countries. As this practice becomes more widespread, many countries, mostly in West Africa, are being completely shut out of international e-commerce. SN Brussels Airlines, for example, uses software developed by Ogone, a Belgian firm that protects more than 6,400 European merchants, to shut out all computers in Liberia and Congo. Without it, says Bruno Brusselmans, director of online sales, "I don't even want to think about what would happen."

Telecoms firms have always suffered heavily from fraud, which is thought to reduce industry revenues by around 5%. But new software that identifies fraudulent callers on mobile networks is helping some operators slash their losses. Telecom Italia's 140 anti-fraud engineers trimmed losses this year to less than 1% by freezing about 30,000 phones a month, says anti-fraud director Fabio Scarpelli.

Such spectacular drops in fraud are more commonplace in the developing world, where mobile operators now investing in the technology. David Ronen, of ECtel, a firm based in Rosh Ha'ayin, Israel, with more than 100 telecoms clients and galloping growth in poor countries, says his firm's software establishes the normal calling patterns of individuals in order to detect tell-tale "weird situations." For example, if a mobile account opened in Shanghai, and sparingly used for local calls, begins making numerous calls from Beijing to a few numbers in a distant western province, then it is likely that a phone thief is calling friends back home.

Fair Isaac, a large fraud-detection firm based in Minneapolis, operates a system so fast that it can block dialled calls before they are even connected. The software, called Falcon, is widely used, since laws prevent many telecoms firms from terminating non-prepaid calls once they are connected. Wily criminals are increasingly operating black-market phoning businesses based in parks and on street corners. "You may see 30 people with cell phones on one corner and one guy is dialling all the numbers for them," says Ted Crooks of Fair Isaac. The calls, often to expensive destinations in poor countries, sometimes last days, Mr Crooks says, because cheats use forwarding systems to serve many customers with a single call. Technology that can pinpoint handsets' locations, however, allows calls in "hot" areas renowned for such illicit operations to be blocked.

It is all a far cry from piecing together clues in a country house, or the drudgery of real-life detective work. But the result is the same. Life gets harder for the bad guys, and the honest citizens, who ultimately pick up the bill for fraud, are protected. The digital detectives, like those in mystery novels, arrive at their conclusions by combining apparently trivial morsels of information. But as Sherlock Holmes put it, "I am glad of all details, whether they seem to you to be relevant or not."

Data on the Elderly, Marketed to Thieves

CHARLES DUHIGG

The thieves operated from small offices in Toronto and hangar-size rooms in India. Every night, working from lists of names and phone numbers, they called World War II veterans, retired schoolteachers and thousands of other elderly Americans and posed as government and insurance workers updating their files.

Then, the criminals emptied their victims' bank accounts.

Richard Guthrie, a 92-year-old Army veteran, was one of those victims. He ended up on scam artists' lists because his name, like millions of others, was sold by large companies to telemarketing criminals, who then turned to major banks to steal his life's savings.

Mr. Guthrie, who lives in Iowa, had entered a few sweepstakes that caused his name to appear in a database advertised by InfoUSA, one of the largest compilers of consumer information. InfoUSA sold his name, and data on scores of other elderly Americans, to known lawbreakers, regulators say.

InfoUSA advertised lists of "Elderly Opportunity Seekers," 3.3 million older people "looking for ways to make money," and "Suffering Seniors," 4.7 million people with cancer or Alzheimer's disease. "Oldies but Goodies" contained 500,000 gamblers over 55 years old, for 8.5 cents apiece. One list said: "These people are gullible. They want to believe that their luck can change."

As Mr. Guthrie sat home alone—surrounded by his Purple Heart medal, photos of eight children and mementos of a wife who was buried nine years earlier—the telephone rang day and night. After criminals tricked him into revealing his banking information, they went to Wachovia, the nation's fourth-largest bank, and raided his account, according to banking records.

"I loved getting those calls," Mr. Guthrie said in an interview. "Since my wife passed away, I don't have many people to talk with. I didn't even know they were stealing from me until everything was gone."

Telemarketing fraud, once limited to small-time thieves, has become a global criminal enterprise preying upon millions of elderly and other Americans every year, authorities say. Vast databases of names and personal information, sold to thieves by large publicly traded companies, have put almost anyone within reach of fraudulent telemarketers. And major banks have made it possible for criminals to dip into victims' accounts without their authorization, according to court records.

The banks and companies that sell such services often confront evidence that they are used for fraud, according to thousands of banking documents, court filings and e-mail messages reviewed by *The New York Times*.

Although some companies, including Wachovia, have made refunds to victims who have complained, neither that bank nor infoUSA stopped working with criminals even after executives were warned that they were aiding continuing crimes, according to government investigators. Instead, those companies collected millions of dollars in fees from scam artists. (Neither company has been formally accused of wrongdoing by the authorities.)

"Only one kind of customer wants to buy lists of seniors interested in lotteries and sweepstakes: criminals," said Sgt. Yves Leblanc of the Royal Canadian Mounted Police. "If someone advertises a list by saying it contains gullible or elderly people, it's like putting out a sign saying 'Thieves welcome here.'"

In recent years, despite the creation of a national "do not call" registry, the legitimate telemarketing industry has grown, according to the Direct Marketing Association. Callers pitching insurance plans, subscriptions and precooked meals collected more than $177 billion in 2006, an increase of $4.5 billion since the federal do-not-call restrictions were put in place three years ago.

That growth can be partly attributed to the industry's renewed focus on the elderly. Older Americans are perfect telemarketing customers, analysts say, because they are often at home, rely on delivery services, and are lonely for the companionship that telephone callers provide. Some researchers estimate that the elderly account for 30 percent of telemarketing sales—another example of how companies and investors are profiting from the growing numbers of Americans in their final years.

While many telemarketing pitches are for legitimate products, the number of scams aimed at older Americans is on the rise, the authorities say. In 2003, the Federal Trade Commission estimated that 11 percent of Americans over age 55 had been victims of consumer fraud. The following year, the Federal Bureau of Investigation shut down one telemarketing ring that stole more than $1 billion, spanned seven countries and resulted in 565 arrests. Since the start of last year, federal agencies have filed lawsuits or injunctions against at least 68 telemarketing companies and individuals accused of stealing more than $622 million.

"Most people have no idea how widespread and sophisticated telemarketing fraud has become," said James Davis, a Federal Trade Commission lawyer. "It shocks even us."

Many of the victims are people like Guthrie, whose name was among the millions that infoUSA sold to companies under investigation for fraud, according to regulators. Scam artists stole more than $100,000 from Guthrie, his family says. How they took much of it is unclear, because Guthrie's memory is faulty and many financial records are incomplete.

What is certain is that a large sum was withdrawn from his account by thieves relying on Wachovia and other banks, according to banking and court records. Though 20 percent of the total amount stolen was recovered, investigators say the rest has gone to schemes too complicated to untangle.

Senior executives at infoUSA were contacted by telephone and e-mail messages at least 30 times. They did not respond.

Wachovia, in a statement, said that it had honored all requests for refunds and that it was cooperating with authorities.

Mr. Guthrie, however, says that thieves should have been prevented from getting access to his funds in the first place.

"I can't understand why they were allowed inside my account," said Guthrie. "I just chatted with this woman for a few minutes, and the next thing I knew, they took everything I had."

Sweepstakes a Common Tactic

Investigators suspect that Mr. Guthrie's name first appeared on a list used by scam artists around 2002, after he filled out a few contest entries that asked about his buying habits and other personal information.

He had lived alone since his wife died. Five of his eight children had moved away from the farm. Guthrie survived on roughly $800 that he received from Social Security each month. Because painful arthritis kept him home, he spent many mornings organizing the mail, filling out sweepstakes entries and listening to big-band albums as he chatted with telemarketers.

"I really enjoyed those calls," said. Mr. Guthrie "One gal in particular loved to hear stories about when I was younger."

Some of those entries and calls, however, were intended solely to create databases of information on millions of elderly Americans. Many sweepstakes were fakes, investigators say, and existed only to ask entrants about shopping habits, religion or other personal details. Databases of such responses can be profitably sold, often via electronic download, through list brokers like Walter Karl Inc., a division of infoUSA.

The list brokering industry has existed for decades, primarily serving legitimate customers like magazine and catalog companies. InfoUSA, one of the nation's largest list brokers and a publicly held company, matches buyers and sellers of data. The company maintains records on 210 million Americans, according to its Web site. In 2006, it collected more than $430 million from clients like Reader's Digest, Publishers Clearinghouse and Condé Nast.

But infoUSA has also helped sell lists to companies that were under investigation or had been prosecuted for fraud, according to records collected by the Iowa attorney general. Those records stemmed from a now completed investigation of a suspected telemarketing criminal.

By 2004, Mr. Guthrie's name was part of a list titled "Astroluck," which included 19,000 other sweepstakes players, Iowa's records show. InfoUSA sold the Astroluck list dozens of times, to companies including HMS Direct, which Canadian authorities had sued the previous year for deceptive mailings; Westport Enterprises, the subject of consumer complaints in Kansas, Connecticut and Missouri; and Arlimbow, a European company that Swiss authorities were prosecuting at the time for a lottery scam.

(In 2005, HMS's director was found not guilty on a technicality. Arlimbow was shut down in 2004. Those companies did not return phone calls. Westport Enterprises said it has resolved all complaints, complies with all laws and engages only in direct-mail solicitations.)

Records also indicate that infoUSA sold thousands of other elderly Americans' names to Windfall Investments after the F.B.I. had accused the company in 2002 of stealing $600,000 from a California woman.

Between 2001 and 2004, infoUSA also sold lists to World Marketing Service, a company that a judge shut down in 2003 for running a lottery scam; to Atlas Marketing, which a court closed in 2006 for selling $86 million of bogus business opportunities; and to Emerald Marketing Enterprises, a Canadian firm that was investigated multiple times but never charged with wrongdoing.

The investigation of Windfall Investments was closed after its owners could not be located. Representatives of Windfall Investments, World Marketing Services, Atlas Marketing and Emerald Marketing Enterprises could not be located or did not return calls.

The Federal Trade Commission's rules prohibit list brokers from selling to companies engaged in obvious frauds. In 2004, the agency fined three brokers accused of knowingly, or purposely ignoring, that clients were breaking the law. The Direct Marketing Association, which infoUSA belongs to, requires brokers to screen buyers for suspicious activity.

Yet internal infoUSA e-mail messages indicate that employees did not abide by those standards. In 2003, two infoUSA employees traded e-mail messages discussing the fact that Nevada authorities were seeking Richard Panas, a frequent infoUSA client, in connection with a lottery scam.

"This kind of behavior does not surprise me, but it adds to my concerns about doing business with these people," an infoUSA executive wrote to colleagues. Yet, over the next 10 months, infoUSA sold Panas an additional 155,000 names, even after he pleaded guilty to criminal charges in Nevada and was barred from operating in Iowa.

Panas did not return calls.

"Red flags should have been waving," said Steve St. Clair, an Iowa assistant attorney general who oversaw the infoUSA investigation. "But the attitude of these list brokers is that it's not their responsibility if someone else breaks the law."

Millions of Americans Are Called

Within months of the sale of the Astroluck list, groups of scam artists in Canada, the Caribbean and elsewhere had the names of Mr. Guthrie and millions of other Americans, authorities say. Such countries are popular among con artists because they are outside the United States jurisdiction.

The thieves began calling and posing as government workers or pharmacy employees. They would contend that the Social Security Administration's computers had crashed, or prescription records were incomplete. Payments and pills would be delayed, they warned, unless the older Americans provided their banking information.

Many people hung up, but Mr. Guthrie and hundreds of others gave the callers whatever they asked.

"I was afraid if I didn't give her my bank information, I wouldn't have money for my heart medicine," said Guthrie.

Criminals can use such banking data to create unsigned checks that withdraw funds from victims' accounts. Such checks, once widely used by gyms and other businesses that collect monthly fees, are allowed under a provision of the banking code. The difficult part is finding a bank willing to accept them.

In the case of Mr. Guthrie, criminals turned to Wachovia.

Between 2003 and 2005, scam artists submitted at least seven unsigned checks to Wachovia that withdrew funds from Guthrie's account, according to banking records. Wachovia accepted those checks and forwarded them to Mr. Guthrie's bank in Iowa, which in turn sent back $1,603 for distribution to the checks' creators.

Within days, however, Guthrie's bank, a branch of Wells Fargo, became concerned and told Wachovia that the checks had not been authorized. At Wells Fargo's request, Wachovia returned the funds, but it failed to investigate whether Wachovia's accounts were being used by criminals, according to prosecutors who studied the transactions.

In all, Wachovia accepted $142 million of unsigned checks from companies that made unauthorized withdrawals from thousands of accounts, federal prosecutors say. Wachovia collected millions of dollars in fees from those companies, even as it failed to act on warnings, according to records.

In 2006, after account holders at Citizens Bank were victimized by the same thieves that targeted Guthrie, an executive wrote to Wachovia that "the purpose of this message is to put your bank on notice of this situation and to ask for your assistance in trying to shut down this scam."

But Wachovia, which declined to comment on that communication, did not shut down the accounts.

Banking rules required Wachovia to periodically screen companies submitting unsigned checks. Yet there is little evidence Wachovia screened most of the firms that profited from the withdrawals.

In a lawsuit filed last year, the United States attorney in Philadelphia said Wachovia received thousands of warnings that it was processing fraudulent checks, but ignored them. That suit, against the company that printed those unsigned checks, Payment Processing Center, or P.P.C., did not name Wachovia as a defendant, though at least one victim has filed a pending lawsuit against the bank.

During 2005, according to the United States attorney's lawsuit, 59 percent of the unsigned checks that Wachovia accepted from P.P.C. and forwarded to other banks were ultimately refused by other financial institutions. Wachovia was informed each time a check was returned.

"When between 50 and 60 percent of transactions are returned, that tells you at gut level that something's not right," said the United States attorney in Philadelphia, Patrick L. Meehan.

Other banks, when confronted with similar evidence, have closed questionable accounts, but Wachovia continued accepting unsigned checks printed by P.P.C. until the government filed suit in 2006.

Wachovia declined to respond to the accusations in the lawsuit, citing the continuing civil litigation.

Although Wachovia is the largest bank that processed transactions that stole from Mr. Guthrie, at least five other banks accepted 31 unsigned checks that withdrew $9,228 from his account. Nearly every time, Mr. Guthrie's bank told those financial institutions the checks were fraudulent, and his money was refunded. But few investigated further.

The suit against P.P.C. ended in February. A court-appointed receiver will liquidate the firm and make refunds to consumers. P.P.C.'s owners admitted no wrongdoing.

Wachovia was asked in detail about its relationship with P.P.C., the withdrawals from Mr. Guthrie's account and the accusations in the United States attorney's lawsuit. The company declined to comment, except to say: "Wachovia works diligently to detect and end fraudulent use of its accounts. During the time P.P.C. was a customer, Wachovia honored all requests for returns related to the P.P.C. accounts, which in turn protected consumers from loss."

Prosecutors argue that many elderly accountholders never realized Wachovia had processed checks that withdrew from their accounts, and so never requested refunds. Wachovia declined to respond.

The bank's statement continued: "Wachovia is cooperating fully with authorities on this matter."

Some Afraid to Seek Help

By 2005, Mr. Guthrie was in dire straits. When tellers at his bank noticed suspicious transactions, they helped him request refunds. But dozens of unauthorized withdrawals slipped through. Sometimes, he went to the grocery store and discovered that he could not buy food because his account was empty. He didn't know why. And he was afraid to seek help.

"I didn't want to say anything that would cause my kids to take over my accounts," he said. Such concerns play into thieves' plans, investigators say.

"Criminals focus on the elderly because they know authorities will blame the victims or seniors will worry about their kids throwing them into nursing homes," said C. Steven Baker, a lawyer with the Federal Trade Commission. "Frequently, the victims are too distracted from dementia or Alzheimer's to figure out something's wrong."

Within a few months, Mr. Guthrie's children noticed that he was skipping meals and was behind on bills. By then, all of his savings—including the proceeds of selling his farm and money set aside to send great-grandchildren to college—was gone.

State regulators have tried to protect victims like Guthrie. In 2005, attorneys general of 35 states urged the Federal Reserve to end the unsigned check system.

"Such drafts should be eliminated in favor of electronic funds transfers that can serve the same payment function" but are less susceptible to manipulation, they wrote.

The Federal Reserve disagreed. It changed its rules to place greater responsibility on banks that first accept unsigned checks, but has permitted their continued use.

Today, just as he worried, Mr. Guthrie's financial freedom is gone. He gets a weekly $50 allowance to buy food and gasoline. His children now own his home, and his grandson controls his bank account. He must ask permission for large or unusual purchases.

And because he can't buy anything, many telemarketers have stopped calling.

"It's lonelier now," he said at his kitchen table, which is crowded with mail. "I really enjoy when those salespeople call. But when I tell them I can't buy anything now, they hang up. I miss the good chats we used to have."

From *The New York Times,* May 20, 2007, pp. 1, 18. Copyright © 2007 by The New York Times Company. Reprinted by permission.

The Fading Memory of the State

The National Archives struggles to ensure that endangered electronic records will be around for as long as the original Declaration of Independence.

DAVID TALBOT

The official repository of retired U.S. government records is a boxy white building tucked into the woods of suburban College Park, MD. The National Archives and Records Administration (NARA) is a subdued place, with researchers quietly thumbing through boxes of old census, diplomatic, or military records, and occasionally requesting a copy of one of the computer tapes that fill racks on the climate-controlled upper floors. Researchers generally don't come here to look for contemporary records, though. Those are increasingly digital, and still repose largely at the agencies that created them, or in temporary holding centers. It will take years, or decades, for them to reach NARA, which is charged with saving the retired records of the federal government (NARA preserves all White House records and around 2 percent of all other federal records; it also manages the libraries of 12 recent presidents). Unfortunately, NARA doesn't have decades to come up with ways to preserve this data. Electronic records rot much faster than paper ones, and NARA must either figure out how to save them permanently, or allow the nation to lose its grip on history.

One clear morning earlier this year, I walked into a fourth-floor office overlooking the woods. I was there to ask Allen Weinstein—sworn in as the new Archivist of the United States in February—how NARA will deal with what some have called the pending "tsunami" of digital records. Weinstein is a former professor of history at Smith College and Georgetown University and the author of *Perjury: The Hiss-Chambers Case* (1978) and coauthor of *The Story of America* (2002). He is 67, and freely admits to limited technical knowledge. But a personal experience he related illustrates quite well the challenges he faces. In 1972, Weinstein was a young historian suing for the release of old FBI files. FBI director J. Edgar Hoover—who oversaw a vast machine of domestic espionage—saw a *Washington Post* story about his efforts, wrote a memo to an aide, attached the *Post* article and penned into the newspaper's margin: "What do we know about Weinstein?" It was a telling note about the mind-set of the FBI director and of the federal bureaucracy of that era. And it was saved—Weinstein later found the clipping in his own FBI file.

But it's doubtful such a record would be preserved today, because it would likely be "born digital" and follow a convoluted electronic path. A modern-day J. Edgar Hoover might first use a Web browser to read an online version of the *Washington Post*. He'd follow a link to the Weinstein story. Then he'd send an e-mail containing the link to a subordinate, with a text note: "What do we know about Weinstein?" The subordinate might do a Google search and other electronic searches of Weinstein's life, then write and revise a memo in Microsoft Word 2003, and even create a multimedia PowerPoint presentation about his findings before sending both as attachments back to his boss.

What steps in this process can be easily documented and reliably preserved over decades with today's technology? The short answer: none. "They're all hard problems," says Robert Chadduck, a research director and computer engineer at NARA. And they are symbolic of the challenge facing any organization that needs to retain electronic records for historical or business purposes.

Imagine losing all your tax records, your high school and college yearbooks, and your child's baby pictures and videos. Now multiply such a loss across every federal agency storing terabytes of information, much of which must be preserved by law. That's the disaster NARA is racing to prevent. It is confronting thousands of incompatible data formats cooked up by the computer industry over the past several decades, not to mention the limited lifespan of electronic storage media themselves. The most famous documents in NARA's possession—the Declaration of Independence, the Constitution, and the Bill of Rights—were written on durable calfskin parchment and can safely recline for decades behind glass in a bath of argon gas. It will take a technological miracle to make digital data last that long.

But NARA has hired two contractors—Harris Corporation and Lockheed Martin—to attempt that miracle. The companies are scheduled to submit competing preliminary designs next month for a permanent Electronic Records Archives (ERA). According to NARA's specifications, the system must ultimately be able to absorb any of the 16,000 other software formats believed to be in use throughout the federal bureaucracy—and, at the same time, cope with any future changes in file-reading software and storage

Megabyte
1,024 kilobytes.
The length of a short novel or the storage available on an average floppy disk.

Gigabyte
1,024 megabytes.
Roughly 100 minutes of CD-quality stereo sound.

Terabyte
1,024 gigabytes.
Half of the content in an academic research library.

Petabyte
1,024 terabytes.
Half of the content in all U.S. academic research libraries.

Exabyte
1,024 petabytes.
Half of all the information generated in 1999.

Source: University of California, Berkeley

hardware. It must ensure that stored records are authentic, available online, and impervious to hacker or terrorist attack. While Congress has authorized $100 million and President Bush's 2006 budget proposes another $36 million, the total price tag is unknown. NARA hopes to roll out the system in stages between 2007 and 2011. If all goes well, Weinstein says, the agency "will have achieved the start of a technological breakthrough equivalent in our field to major 'crash programs' of an earlier era—our Manhattan Project, if you will, or our moon shot."

Data Indigestion

NARA's crash data-preservation project is coming none too soon; today's history is born digital and dies young. Many observers have noted this, but perhaps none more eloquently than a U.S. Air Force historian named Eduard Mark. In a 2003 posting to a Michigan State University discussion group frequented by fellow historians, he wrote: "It will be impossible to write the history of recent diplomatic and military history as we have written about World War II and the early Cold War. Too many records are gone. Think of Villon's haunting refrain, 'Ou sont les neiges d'antan?' and weep. . . . History as we have known it is dying, and with it the public accountability of government and rational public administration." Take the 1989 U.S. invasion of Panama, in which U.S. forces removed Manuel Noriega and 23 troops lost their lives, along with at least 200 Panamanian fighters and 300 civilians. Mark wrote (and recently stood by his comments) that he could not secure many basic records of the invasion, because a number were electronic and had not been kept. "The federal system for maintaining records has in many agencies—indeed in every agency with which I am familiar—collapsed utterly," Mark wrote.

Of course, managing growing data collections is already a crisis for many institutions, from hospitals to banks to universities. Tom Hawk, general manager for enterprise storage at IBM, says that in the next three years, humanity will generate more data—from websites to digital photos and video—than it generated in the previous 1,000 years. "It's a whole new set of challenges to IT organizations that have not been dealing with that level of data and complexity," Hawk says. In 1996, companies spent 11 percent of their IT budgets on storage, but that figure will likely double to 22 percent in 2007, according to International Technology Group of Los Altos, CA.

Still, NARA's problem stands out because of the sheer volume of the records the U.S. government produces and receives, and the diversity of digital technologies they represent. "We operate on the premise that somewhere in the government they are using every software program that has ever been sold, and some that were never sold because they were developed for the government," says Ken Thibodeau, director of the Archives' electronic records program. The scope of the problem, he adds, is "unlimited, and it's open ended, because the formats keep changing."

The Archives faces more than a Babel of formats; the electronic records it will eventually inherit are piling up at an ever accelerating pace. A taste: the Pentagon generates tens of millions of images from personnel files each year; the Clinton White House generated 38 million e-mail messages (and the current Bush White House is expected to generate triple that number); and the 2000 census returns were converted into more than 600 million TIFF-format image files, some 40 terabytes of data. A single patent application can contain a million pages, plus complex files like 3-D models of proteins or CAD drawings of aircraft parts. All told, NARA expects to receive 347 petabytes (*see definitions on this previous page*) of electronic records by 2022.

Currently, the Archives holds only a trivial number of electronic records. Stored on steel racks in NARA's 11-year-old facility in College Park, the digital collection adds up to just five terabytes. Most of it consists of magnetic tapes of varying ages, many of them holding a mere 200 megabytes apiece—about the size of 10 high-resolution digital photographs. (The electronic holdings include such historical gems as records of military psychological-operations squads in Vietnam from 1970 to 1973, and interviews, diaries, and testimony collected by the U.S. Department of Justice's Watergate Special Prosecution Force from 1973 to 1977.) From this modest collection, only a tiny number of visitors ever seek to copy data; little is available over the Internet.

Because the Archives has no good system for taking in more data, a tremendous backlog has built up. Census records, service records, Pentagon records of Iraq War decision-making, diplomatic messages—all sit in limbo at federal departments or in temporary record-holding centers around the country. A new avalanche of records from the Bush administration—the most electronic presidency yet—will descend in three and a half years, when the president leaves office. Leaving records sitting around at federal agencies for years, or decades, worked fine when everything was on paper, but data bits are nowhere near as reliable—and storing them means paying not just for the storage media, but for a sophisticated management system and extensive IT staff.

Data Under the Desk

The good news is that at least some of the rocket science behind the Archives' "moon shot" is already being developed by industry, other U.S. government agencies, and foreign governments. For example, Hewlett-Packard, IBM, EMC, PolyServe, and other companies have developed "virtual storage" technologies that automatically spread terabytes of related data across many storage devices, often of different types. Virtualization frees up IT staff, balances loads when demand for the data spikes, and allows hardware upgrades to be carried out without downtime. Although the Archives will need technologies far beyond virtual storage, the commercial efforts form a practical foundation. The Archives may also benefit from the examples of digital archives set up in other nations, such as Australia, where archivists are using open-source software called XENA (for XML Electronic Normalizing of Archives) to convert records into a standardized format that will, theoretically, be readable by future technologies. NARA will also follow the lead of the U.S. Library of Congress, which in recent years has begun digitizing collections ranging from early American sheet music to immigration photographs and putting them online, as part of a $100 million digital preservation program.

But to extend the technology beyond such commercial and government efforts, NARA and the National Science Foundation are funding research at places like the San Diego Supercomputer Center. There, researchers are, among other things, learning how to extract data from old formats rapidly and make them useful in modern ones. For example, San Diego researchers took a collection of data on airdrops during the Vietnam War—everything from the defoliant Agent Orange to pamphlets—and reformatted it so it could be displayed using nonproprietary versions of digital-mapping programs known as geographic information systems, or GIS (*see "Do Maps Have Morals?" June 2005*). Similarly, they took lists of Vietnam War casualties and put them in a database that can show how they changed over the years, as names were added or removed. These are the kinds of problems NARA will face as it "ingests" digital collections, researchers say. "NARA's problem is they will be receiving massive amounts of digital information in the future, and they need technologies that will help them import that data into their ERA—hundreds of millions of items, hundreds of terabytes of data," says Reagan Moore, director of data-knowledge computing at the San Diego center.

Another hive of research activity on massive data repositories: MIT. Just as the government is losing its grip on administrative, military, and diplomatic history, institutions like MIT are losing their hold on research data—including the early studies and communications that led to the creation of the Internet itself. "MIT is a microcosm of the problems [NARA] has every day," says MacKenzie Smith, the associate director for

technology at MIT Libraries. "The faculty members are keeping their research under their desks, on lots and lots of disks, and praying that nothing happens to it. We have a long way to go."

Now MIT is giving faculty another place to put that data. Researchers can log onto the Internet and upload information—whether text, audio, video, images, or experimental data sets—into DSpace, a storage system created in collaboration with Hewlett-Packard and launched in 2002 (*see "MIT's DSpace Explained," p. 50*). DSpace makes two identical copies of all data, catalogues relevant information about the data (what archivists call "metadata," such as the author and creation date), and gives each file a URL or Web address. This address won't change even if, say, the archivist later wants to put a given file into a newer format—exporting the contents of an old Word document into a PDF file, for instance. Indeed, an optional feature in DSpace will tell researchers which files are ready for such "migration."

Because the software behind DSpace is open source, it is available for other institutions to adapt to their own digital-archiving needs; scores have already done so. Researchers at MIT and elsewhere are working on improvements such as an auditing feature that would verify that a file hasn't been corrupted or tampered with, and a system that checks accuracy when a file migrates into a new format. Ann Wolpert, the director of MIT Libraries (and chair of *Technology Review's* board of directors), says DSpace is just a small step toward tackling MIT's problems, never mind NARA's. "These changes have come to MIT and other institutions so rapidly that we didn't have the technology to deal with it," Wolpert says. "The technology solutions are still emerging." Robert Tansley, a Hewlett-Packard research scientist who worked on DSpace, says the system is a good start but cautions that "it is still quite new. It hasn't been tested or deployed at a massive scale, so there would need to be some work before it could support what the National Archives is looking at."

Digital Marginalia

But for all this promise, NARA faces many problems that researchers haven't even begun to think about. Consider Weinstein's discovery of the Hoover marginalia. How could such a tidbit be preserved today? And how can any organization that needs to track information—where it goes, who uses it, and how it's modified along the way—capture those bit streams and keep them as safe as older paper records? Saving the text of e-mail messages is technically easy; the challenge lies in managing a vast volume and saving only what's relevant. It's important, for example, to save the e-mails of major figures like cabinet members and White House personnel without also bequeathing to history trivial messages in which mid-level bureaucrats make lunch arrangements. The filtering problem gets harder as the e-mails pile up. "If you have 300 or 400 million of anything, the first thing you need is a rigorous technology that can deal with that volume and scale," says Chadduck. More and more e-mails come with attachments, so NARA will ultimately need a system that can handle any type of attached file.

Version tracking is another headache. In an earlier era, scribbled cross-outs and margin notes on draft speeches were a boon to understanding the thinking of presidents and other public officials. To see all the features of a given Microsoft Word document, such as tracked changes, it's best to open the document using the same version of Word that the document's creator used. This means that future researchers will need not only a new piece of metadata—what software version was used—but perhaps even the software itself, in order to re-create fonts and other formatting details faithfully. But saving the functionality of software—from desktop programs like Word to the software NASA used to test a virtual reality model of the Mars Global Surveyor, for example—is a key research problem. And not all software keeps track of how it was actually used. Why might this matter? Consider the 1999 U.S. bombing of the Chinese embassy in Belgrade. U.S. officials blamed the error on outdated maps used in targeting. But how would a future historian probe a comparable matter—to check the official story, for example—when decision-making occurred in a digital context? Today's planners would open a map generated by GIS software, zoom in on a particular region, pan across to another site, run a calculation about the topography or other features, and make a targeting decision.

If a historian wanted to review these steps, he or she would need information on how the GIS map was used. But "currently there are no computer science tools that would allow you to reconstruct how computers were used in high-confidence decision-making scenarios," says Peter Bajcsy, a computer scientist at the University of Illinois at Urbana-Champaign. "You might or might not have the same hardware, okay, or the same version of the software in 10 or 20 years. But you would still like to know what data sets were viewed and processed, the methods used for processing, and what the decision was based on." That way, to stay with the Chinese embassy example, a future historian might be able to independently assess whether the database about the embassy was obsolete, or whether the fighter pilot who dropped the bomb had the right information before he took off. Producing such data is just a research proposal of Bajcsy's. NARA says that if such data is collected in the future, the agency will add it to the list of things needing preservation.

Data Curators

Even without tackling problems like this, NARA has its hands full. For three years, at NARA's request, a National Academy of Sciences panel has been advising the agency on its electronic records program. The panel's chairman, computer scientist Robert F. Sproull of Sun Microsystems Laboratories in Burlington, MA, says he has urged NARA officials to scale back their ambitions for the ERA, at least at the start. "They are going to the all-singing, all-dancing solution rather than an incremental approach," Sproull says. "There are a few dozen formats that would cover most of what [NARA] has to do. They should get on with it. Make choices, encourage people

submitting records to choose formats, and get on with it. If you become obsessed with getting *the* technical solution, you will never build an archive." Sproull counsels pragmatism above all. He points to Google as an example of how to deploy a workable solution that satisfies most information-gathering needs for most of the millions of people who use it. "What Google says is, 'We'll take all comers, and use best efforts. It means we won't find everything, but it does mean we can cope with all the data," Sproull says. Google is not an archive, he notes, but in the Google spirit, NARA should attack the problem in a practical manner. That would mean starting with the few dozen formats that are most common, using whatever off-the-shelf archiving technologies will likely emerge over the next few years. But this kind of preservation-by-triage may not be an option, says NARA's Thibodeau. "NARA does not have discretion to refuse to preserve a format," he says. "It is inconceivable to me that a court would approve of a decision not to preserve e-mail attachments, which often contain the main substance of the communication, because it's not in a format NARA chose to preserve."

Meanwhile, the data keep rolling in. After the 9/11 Commission issued its report on the attacks on the World Trade Center and the Pentagon, for example, it shut down and consigned all its records to NARA. A good deal of paper, along with 1.2 terabytes of digital information on computer hard disks and servers, was wheeled into NARA's College Park facility, where it sits behind a door monitored by a video camera and secured with a black combination lock. Most of the data, which consist largely of word-processing files and e-mails and their attachments, are sealed by law until January 2, 2009. They will probably survive that long without heroic preservation efforts. But "there's every reason to say that in 25 years, you won't be able to read this stuff," warns Thibodeau. "Our present will never become anybody's past."

It doesn't have to be that way. Projects like DSpace are already dealing with the problem. Industry will provide a growing range of partial solutions, and researchers will continue to fill in the blanks. But clearly, in the decades to come, archives such as NARA will need to be staffed by a new kind of professional, an expert with the historian's eye of an Allen Weinstein but a computer scientist's understanding of storage technologies and a librarian's fluency with metadata. "We will have to create a new profession of 'data curator'—a combination of scientist (or other data specialist), statistician, and information expert," says MacKenzie Smith of the MIT Libraries.

The nation's founding documents are preserved for the ages in their bath of argon gas. But in another 230 years or so, what of today's electronic records will survive? With any luck, the warnings from air force historian Mark and NARA's Thibodeau will be heeded. And historians and citizens alike will be able to go online and find that NARA made it to the moon, after all.

DAVID TALBOT is *Technology Review's* chief correspondent.

False Reporting on the Internet and the Spread of Rumors

Three Case Studies

PAUL HITLIN

Following the tragic events of September 11, 2001, a significant number of unsubstantiated rumors circulated around the Internet. One email pointed to the existence of prophecies by Nostradamus written hundreds of years earlier that predicted the attacks. Another accused Israel of masterminding the strikes and that thousands of Jews were told in advance to stay home from work that morning. The Internet allowed for a vast audience to spread these rumors along with the technology to facilitate their transmission, even though there was little evidence to support them and the rumors were later proven incorrect. Considering this spread of rumors, Stephen O'Leary (2002) writes:

> What may be hard for mainstream journalists to understand is that, in crisis situations, the social functions of rumor are virtually indistinguishable from the social functions of 'real news.' People spread rumors via the Net for the same reason that they read their papers or tune into CNN: they are trying to make sense of their world. (pg. 3)

O'Leary claims that these rumors fill a need for consumers of news that is very similar to the void that 'real news' fills. However, are the consequences the same? These Internet rumors help people to make sense of their world following a tragedy, although the lasting consequences are potentially much more harmful.

The Internet is certainly not responsible for errors in journalism. Every medium of news has a history of misreported stories. However, the nature of the Internet has created a new method for consumers to get their news and allowed for far greater numbers of people to become involved with the production and dissemination of news. As a consequence, cyberjournalism and the Internet have had real effects on both the process of reporting and subsequent public discourse.

How are errors in Internet journalism corrected online? What are the overarching consequences of errors that appear on Internet web sites? Jim Hall (2001) believes that one problem with instant news appearing on the Internet is that the way errors

are handled does not adequately address the fact that an error was made. He writes, "The problem with instant news is that when it is wrong it tends to be buried, sedimenting into and reinforcing its context, rather than corrected" (p. 133). Errors of Internet reporting do not often get identified and corrected as they do in newspapers. Instead, even if the editors of the Web site where the error first appeared change their site to remove the error, often the same false information will have already spread throughout other Web sites and emails. These rumors can become part of a public folklore even if there are no facts to support the original reports.

This paper will first consider Hall's assertion that errors are buried rather than corrected, and will examine the reasons Internet reporting leads to false reports. Then, three case studies of significant false reports on the Internet will be compared to the theories behind cyberjournalism in order to understand why the errors occurred and the impacts of these stories. Investigating these three examples will help us to begin to understand how we can decrease the influence of false reports in the future.

The first case study is the plane crash of TWA flight 800 in 1996. Even before full investigations were conducted, the Internet was full of reports of missiles or other causes behind the crash, the impacts of which would reach as far as the White House. The second case study will examine Matt Drudge's report that former White House special assistant Sidney Blumenthal physically abused his wife. The third case study will take a look at the pervasive rumors that the death of former Bill Clinton aide Vince Foster was a murder, not a suicide, even though numerous investigations have concluded that these accusations are unsupported. This incident is a clear example of how partisan politics can play a role in the spread of false reports on the Internet.

There has been much discussion about what distinguishes a 'journalist' working for a mainstream news source from a self-titled 'reporter' who never leaves his/ her computer and instead just links to reports on other sites. While these distinctions are important and worth discussing, it will not be within the realm of this study to draw out these distinctions. Instead, this paper will consider news reports that appear on the Internet regardless of whether or not the site displaying the report considers itself a news source. As we will see, public opinion can often be influenced as much from rumors on sites with little credibility as it can from more mainstream sources.

Reasons for Cyberjournalism Errors

Before considering the specific cases of false reporting, it is important to understand why the nature of the Internet may encourage reporting errors. Philip Seib (2001) points out that the Internet is not alone in containing factual errors. He writes, "the Web really is little different from other media in terms of its potential to abuse and be abused and its capability for self-governance" (pp. 129–130). The Internet itself, the actual technology, can not be held responsible for false reports since those reports have existed in all forms of media. However, there are qualities of the Internet and the manner in which news is reported on the Web that create differences in how frequently errors appear and what results as a consequence.

The causes of most cyberjournalism errors can be separated into four main categories. Let us now turn to each cause and examine it in turn.

1. The Need for Speed

The first and probably most significant reason for false reporting on the Internet is the 24-hour a day news cycle that the Internet promotes. With the development of newspapers, the news cycle was a daylong process that ended with having a story included in the next day's edition of the paper. This cycle changed with the expansion of cable television channels devoted entirely to news such as CNN and later MSNBC and Fox News. The cycle was expanded even further by the development of the Internet which is available to consumers 24-hours a day. Because of the constant need to keep both cable television and the Internet supplied with new information, expectations of news deadlines have shifted. As Seib notes, in the current information age, the deadline for reporters is always 'now' (p. 142).

Competitive pressures have also contributed to an emphasis being placed more on timeliness than accuracy. A number of Internet sites, such as Matt Drudge's *Drudge Report,* are one-person operations that issue reports on gossip and rumor without being constrained by traditional standards of reporting. These sites apply pressure to other news organizations to be the first to report a story or risk being scooped. Drudge himself believes that "absolute truth matters less than absolute speed" (Seib, 2001, p. 143). He also suggests that since we live in an information economy, complete accuracy is not possible or even necessary. Drudge focuses instead on immediacy and believes that the Web encourages this type of reporting (Hall, 2002, p. 148).

The pressure on reporters to be the first with a story has detracted from more traditional methods of journalism. Because the goal used to be to get a report into the next day's newspaper or that evening's nightly news television broadcast, reporters had more time for fact-checking. The 24-hour-a-day news cycle has decreased the time reporters have to assure accuracy and as a result, many errors found on the Internet can be attributed to the competitive pressure for journalists to be the first to break a specific news story.

2. The Desire to Attract 'Hits'

Competition among Web sites is also a cause for some false reports. Web sites have financial incentives to attract visitors to their sites, whether it is through advertising or a desire to widen the site's influence. Hall argues that journalism on the Web has promoted the idea that news is 'infotainment' and more at the mercy of the demands of the marketplace than to its audiences (Hall, 2001, p. 155). Web sites must fill the desires of consumers, or risk losing those consumers to other sites that either get the information first or are even more sensational in their reporting.

Furthermore, with the ability of Internet users to visit almost any news source in the world, as opposed to being confined to their local newspapers or television stations, the competition on the Web exacerbates the desire of sites to get the story first. Most news sites are updated several times a day, and competition forces those sites to get the story first or risk being thought of as irrelevant or out-of-date.

3. Political Gains

The specific source of many Internet rumors is often difficult to ascertain. However, certain rumors on the Internet are clearly promoted for partisan political gain and to advance a particular ideology.

Even after four investigations came to the same conclusions about Vince Foster's death, certain political groups were still spreading false reports in order to promote their own cause. For example, a fund-raising letter sent out by anti-Clinton groups asked for $1,000 donations in order to support the "Clinton Investigation Commission" which would investigate the claim that Foster was murdered (Piacente, 1997). Opponents of the Clinton administration perpetuated this false report to the exclusion of evidence in the case. These anti-Clinton groups were less concerned with accuracy than with forwarding a partisan agenda and the persistence of this specific rumor can be attributed to their political motives.

4. Attraction to Scandal

News, and specifically news on the Web, is often led by scandal and the concept of the spectacular rather than issues of depth (Hall, 2001, p. 137). For example, reports that TWA flight 800 was brought down by a missile were much more exciting than a report that a technical problem in the plane caused the crash. While some sites did wait for investigations into the cause of the crash to make conclusions about what actually brought the plane down, other sites used more dramatic rumors of missile fire to headline their reports. The competition between sites on the Web and the ability for consumers to move rapidly between those sites furthers the need for reporters to lead with scandal in order to catch consumers' attention. This desire for the spectacular, along with an emphasis on scandal, often leads to other false reports on the Internet.

Correction Policy, Social Cascades, and Online Credibility

Now that we have seen the four main reasons errors are found on the Internet, another key issue to understand is how those mistakes are corrected. There is still no singular method that Web sites use to correct errors, but as Seib (2001) writes:

The easiest way to fix a mistake is simply to erase it and replace it with the correct information. That is a temptation unique to electronic publication, since there is no "original" version in the print or video archives . . . This is fine for readers who come to the site after the correction has been made. But failure to post a formal notice of correction implies that there was never an error, and that is less than honest. (pp. 154–155)

The question of how to correct a mistake once it is discovered that causes Hall to suggest that the nature of Internet journalism reinforces the error's context rather than corrects the false information. While some retractions are clearly posted, as was the case with Matt Drudge following the accusations against Sidney Blumenthal, often the error has already spread to other sources. As a result, whether or not the original source is corrected no longer matters because the information will have already moved onto other places on the Web.

The result of this spread of Internet rumors is a phenomenon described by Cass Sunstein as one of 'social cascades.' Sunstein suggests that groups of people often move together in a direction of one set of beliefs or actions. He refers to this as a cascade effect (Sunstein, 2002, p. 80). Information can travel and become entrenched even if that information is incorrect. Sunstein argues that the Internet, with its wide reach and seemingly unending amount of Web sites and emails, greatly increases the likelihood of social cascades. Rumors can be passed to many users and spread quickly. The result is that the information appears believable solely due to the fact that the information has been repeated so many times. Richard Davis (1999) sums up the potential danger of this phenomenon:

Anyone can put anything on the Internet and seemingly does. Often, one cannot be sure of the reliability of the information provided. Reliability diminishes exponentially as the information is passed from user to user and e-mail list to e-mail list until it acquires a degree of legitimacy by virtue of its widespread dissemination and constant repetition. (p. 44)

A number of other factors also contribute to the believability of information passed on the Internet. Richard Davis and Diana Owen (1998) discuss many of the reasons why 'new media,' consisting of the Internet, talk radio, and interactive television, often engage users in different ways than previous forms of news. They claim that much of new media relies on active participation by users rather than a more passive relationship between users and newspapers or earlier television programs. Davis and Owen describe the influence of this connection:

The degree of involvement or interactivity with media is linked to the level of an audience member's media consumption and the strength of the effects of the communication. People who have a highly active relationship with a particular medium, such as callers to talk radio programs, may be more likely to establish a regular habit of attending to the medium and are more likely to be influenced by content than those whose acquaintance with the communication source is more casual. (p. 160)

Internet users who participate in online activities are not only more likely to be influenced by content they see online, but new media has a capacity to create strong psychological bonds between users and the media source. Davis and Owen add, "Individuals form personal relationships with their television sets and their computers. They treat computers as if they are people, talking to them, ascribing personalities to them and reacting to them emotionally when computers hand out praise or criticism during an interactive sessions" (p. 160). Users have greater influence over the content of media on the Web than in previous forms of media, whether it results from emailing articles of interest or responding to online polls and questionnaires. These interactions contribute to the perceived credibility that Internet users ascribe to information they receive over the Web. Stories that might be disregarded as false had they been disseminated through other forms of media often facilitate a social cascade effect if that information is spread online.

Having considered both why errors appear on the Internet and the difficulty in effectively correcting false information, let us now consider three cases of prominent false reports on the Internet and how those instances were handled.

Case Study One: The Crash of TWA Flight 800 in 1996

A clear example of how constant repetition of an erroneous report can result in widespread belief can be seen in the wake of the crash of TWA Flight 800. On July 17, 1996, the passenger flight left JFK International Airport in New York en route to Paris, but tragically crashed into the Long Island Sound. All 230 passengers and crew on board died.

Almost immediately, the National Transportation Safety Board (NTSB) began investigating the causes of the crash and rumors started to spread throughout the Internet as to what lead to the tragedy. Three main theories quickly surfaced as to what caused the crash: the crash was an act of terrorism conducted from onboard the flight; a mechanical malfunction was responsible for bringing down the plane; or the plane was shot down by a surface-to-air missile (Cobb & Primo, 2003, p. 104).

Some evidence initially indicated the crash could be a result of terrorism, either an onboard bomb or a projectile fired at the plane from the ground. The accident took place several days before the beginning of the 1996 Summer Olympics in Atlanta, which later become a target of a bombing attack. Some observers felt the timing of the plane crash indicated that it was somehow connected to international terrorism. In addition, numerous eyewitnesses reported having seen a streak of light approaching the plane before the explosion (Charles, 2001, p. 218). As the NTSB and the FBI began to investigate, numerous signals from the federal government indicated that all three potential theories were in play. As much as six months into a very public investigation, the NTSB was still declaring that all three theories remained as possibilities (Negroni, 2001). This did not change until March of 1997, when federal investigators began to dismiss theories of a missile bringing TWA Flight 800 down, claiming there was "no physical evidence" of such an attack (CNN.com, 1997).

As the investigation into the crash progressed and began to rule out terrorism, rumors persisted throughout the Internet that a government cover-up was concealing the real causes. At the forefront of those rumors was Pierre Salinger, a former press secretary to John F. Kennedy and correspondent for ABC News. Salinger insisted that he had a letter from French intelligence proving that a U.S. Navy missile ship shot down TWA Flight 800, and the FBI was covering up the act. Salinger's claims were reported in numerous news outlets. In addition, Salinger and several other journalists published a report in *Paris Match* stating that radar images existed that proved that a missile hit the plane (Harper, 1998, p. 85).

Salinger's credentials and his unwillingness to give up on his theory lent great credibility to the missile story. Many people on the Internet who believed the government was trying to hide something picked up on his writings. Interestingly enough, the letter that Salinger claimed had come from French intelligence was instead a memo that had been circulating on the Internet for several months written by a former United Air Lines pilot named Richard Russell.[1] As Mark Hunter writes in his Salon.com article, Salinger's insistence on promoting his conspiracy theory of both the missile and the FBI cover-up, even with scare evidence, actually harmed the real investigation by causing a significant distraction for investigators. It also caused further psychological stress on the family members of the victims of the crash who were forced to revisit the circumstances as a result of these repeated allegations.

By the time the NTSB issued its final report on the crash in August of 2000, much of the talk of conspiracy theories relating to the crash had disappeared. In 2001, the Federal Aviation Agency (FAA) acted in response to what was believed to be the actual cause of the crash and issued safety rules to minimize flammable vapors and decrease the risk of a tank igniting (Cobb & Primo, 2003, p. 117). However, the consequences of the crash rumors can be seen both in continuing public discourse and actions taken by upper levels of the federal government.

The immediate rumors following the crash about a possible bomb or missile attack led to direct government action. In the days that followed the accident, before much hard evidence was discovered, President Clinton issued a tightening of security at airports throughout the country in order to try to prevent any acts of terrorism (Cobb & Primo, 2003, p. 106). Clinton later created the White House Commission on Aviation Safety, led by Vice President Al Gore, which issued recommendations for improving airline safety (Cobb & Primo, 2003, pp. 110–111). Just the possibility of a terrorist or missile attack was enough for the federal government to react strongly and tighten security.

What role did the Internet play in promoting and maintaining the false rumors about the crash of TWA Flight 800? Internet sites were not alone in reporting the rumors about the crash. Many newspapers, including the *Washington Post* and *New York Times,* also reported the possibilities of a bomb or terror attack (Cobb & Primo, 2003, pp. 107–108). However, the Internet did allow for certain aspects of the story to persist even when the evidence against the rumors was mounting. For one thing, a letter written by Richard Russell that circulated by email throughout the Internet played a key role in Salinger's claims about a government cover-up. Whether or not Salinger knew the true source of the letter, the circulation of the note alone added some perceived credibility to the rumor. This Internet 'error' was not corrected and removed. Instead, as Hall suggested, the nature of the Internet embedded the rumor. The circulation continued even after the NTSB determined it was false: a clear example of a social cascade facilitated by the Internet, moving many to believe the government was hiding information and not telling the full story about the crash.

To further this notion about the impact of these rumors, one only has to look to the Internet today, more than seven years after the crash, to see how public discourse has been influenced. While the Internet is full of conspiracy theories and anti-government rhetoric, a simple search can still find many Web sites that maintain that the TWA crash was a government cover-up. A clear example is the Web site whatreallyhappened.com. One can still go to this site at any time and read about how the government is hiding secrets and promoting beliefs that the "witnesses who saw a missile hit the jumbo jet are all drunks" (whatreallyhappened.com, 2002). To any person deciding to conduct research into the causes of this plane crash today, the Internet is a rich resource consisting of both facts about the accident and significant rumor and innuendo.

Case Study Two: Sidney Blumenthal vs. Matt Drudge and Internet Libel

While some Internet rumors persist on numerous Web sites, others can be linked more closely with one specific site, as is the case with a report that appeared on Matt Drudge's Web site, drudgereport.com, in 1997. Matt Drudge's one-man newsroom is most well known for breaking the story about President Bill Clinton's Oval Office affair with a White House intern. Along with breaking that story, Drudge has had 'exclusives' with a number of other stories, some of which turned out not to be true at all. Included among these was the report that Bill Clinton had fathered an illegitimate black son, a report that was later proven to be false (Hall, 2001, p. 129).

On August 8, 1997, Drudge chose to report on his Web site allegations about White House special assistant Sidney Blumenthal. Writing about a Republican operative who was facing allegations of spousal abuse, Drudge issued the 'exclusive' on his Web site that included the following:

The *Drudge Report* has learned that top GOP operatives who feel there is a double-standard of only reporting [sic] shame believe they are holding an ace card: New White House recruit Sidney Blumenthal has a spousal abuse past that has been effectively covered up.

The accusations are explosive.

"There are court records of Blumenthal's violence against his wife," one influential Republican [sic], who demanded anonymity, tells the *Drudge Report.* (Blumenthal, 2003, pp. 239–240)

Drudge goes on to write that one White House source claimed the allegations were entirely false and that Drudge had been unsuccessful in his attempts to contact Blumenthal regarding these charges.

Three problems existed for Drudge in relation to this story. First, no court records existed that claimed Blumenthal abused his wife. Second, Drudge had not in fact made any attempts to contact Blumenthal. And third, Sidney Blumenthal decided to sue Matt Drudge and the Internet carrier of his column, American Online (AOL), for libel after other conservative news sources such as the *New York Post* and talk radio programs picked up the story (Blumenthal, 2003, p. 241).

This false Internet report was unique in that the origin of the rumor on the Web was clear along with who was responsible for spreading the rumor. Because of this, Blumenthal did have an opportunity to confront his accuser, which he did the day after the report first appeared. Blumenthal and his lawyer sent a letter to Drudge demanding to know the sources of the report. If Drudge did not comply, Blumenthal threatened to take "appropriate action" (Blumenthal, 2003, p. 244). In direct response to the threat, Drudge printed a retraction on his Web site that read, "I am issuing a retraction of my information regarding Sidney Blumenthal that appeared in the Drudge Report on August 11, 1997" (Blumenthal, 2003, p. 247). Drudge never officially apologized for the specific claim, although he was quoted as saying, "I apologize if any harm has been done. The story was issued in good faith. It was based on two sources who clearly were operating from a political motivation" (Kurtz, 1997).

While the lawsuit proceeded against Drudge with the blessing of President Clinton and the White House, the final result was not nearly as dramatic as the initial report. In May of 2001, Drudge and Blumenthal settled the suit out of court, and Blumenthal agreed to pay $2,500 to Drudge to reimburse travel expenses (Kurtz, 2001). Blumenthal claimed that he settled the suit because Drudge had endless financial backing from conservative groups and the suit was doing little more than providing additional exposure for Drudge (Blumenthal, 2003, p. 784). One interesting side note to this case is that early in the process,

a U.S. District judge had ruled that the Internet service provider, AOL, could not be a defendant in the libel case even though they had paid Drudge for his work. This decision was a significant victory for Internet service providers in protecting them from lawsuits concerning the content that appears on their own Web sites (Swartz, 1998).

Unlike the rumors about the TWA crash, this case study is much clearer in terms of who was responsible for placing the rumor online. Defamation of character is common in the Internet world, but Blumenthal viewed his lawsuit as an opportunity to make a larger point, "bringing the Internet under the same law that applied to the rest of the press" (Blumenthal, 2003, p. 471). Judging exactly how successful he was in doing so and whether future Internet sites will be as willing to publish unsubstantiated rumors is difficult. Drudge, for one, continues to publish numerous stories with seemingly little fear about being incorrect. However, this example does illustrate one occurrence where a retraction was issued on the same Internet site as the original error. Did the retraction correct the harm that resulted from a false story? Clearly Sidney Blumenthal did not feel so and continued his libel lawsuit even after the retraction was issued.

In addition, this news report was more a result of a partisan political agenda than it was an issue of Drudge trying to beat his competition by issuing an exclusive story not available on any other site. Drudge has been accused by many of having strong ties to conservative political groups who may have planted the Blumenthal story, but there seem to be no indications that other news sites were in competition with Drudge to be the first to issue this report. He would not thus have been facing a shortened time to check sources and facts. Drudge himself acknowledged that his sources for this story were acting on their own political agenda.

Case Study Three: The Suicide of White House Aide Vince Foster

Unlike the previous case study, the origins of the rumors involving the suicide of White House Aide Vince Foster are less clear. On July 20, 1993, the body of Vince Foster was discovered in a park in Washington, D.C. Foster had apparently committed suicide, and much of the initial evidence pointed to a self-inflicted gunshot wound as the cause of death. He had been showing tremendous signs of stress as he found himself the subject of political battles in Washington and a number of accusations against the Clinton administration. Foster had reportedly been very upset about the attention he was receiving in the "Travelgate" scandal and his role in questions about billing records involving Hillary Clinton and Whitewater investments (Tisdall, 1994). However, immediately after his body was found, rumors began circulating the Internet suggesting that Foster's death had not been a suicide. These reports claimed that the death was a murder that was covered-up by members of the Clinton administration who felt Foster knew too much about the Whitewater investigation being conducted by Independent Counsel Kenneth Starr.

Rumors of unresolved questions within the investigation of Foster's death began to spread throughout the Internet by members of conservative activist groups who made no secret of their hatred of President Clinton. Why was there no suicide note? Why were the keys on Foster's body not found at the scene, but only later, once the body was moved? What did the torn note say that was found near the body? Why were records missing from Vince Foster's office after the body was found? Those looking for sensational stories and rumors involving this story did not have to look hard on the Internet to find them.

The cascade effect of this story reached remarkable levels. Numerous Web sites published the rumor that Foster's death was a murder, including Matt Drudge's site (Scheer, 1999). Presidential candidate Pat Buchanan received criticism in 1996 by Jewish groups after an article published on his official campaign Web site claimed that Foster's death was ordered by Israel and that Hillary Clinton was secretly working as a Mossad agent (O'Dwyer, 1996). Rush Limbaugh, a conservative radio talk-show host, mentioned the accusations on his radio program and Representative John Linder, Republican of Georgia, even inserted the accusation into the record at Congressional hearings involving the Whitewater scandal (*Atlanta Journal and Constitution,* 1994). In fact, the rumors of murder were so persistent on the Internet and other mediums that a Time/CNN poll taken in 1995 during the Senate hearings of the aftermath of Foster's death showed that only 35 percent of respondents believed Foster's death was a suicide. Twenty percent believed he had been murdered (Weiner, 1995).

Rumors of a Clinton-led cover-up have continued to exist even after four separate investigations, conducted by the U.S. Park Police, the FBI, Special Counsel Robert Fiske, and Independent Counsel Ken Starr, all came to the same conclusion: Foster's death was a suicide. The persistent refusal to accept the conclusions of these investigations is demonstrated in a 1998 editorial in *The Augusta Chronicle* written five years after Foster's death. "Imagine [Ken Starr] ruling the Vince Foster killing a suicide when not one item of evidence would indicate suicide, but numerous items indicate obvious murder!" (*The Augusta Chronicle,* 1998).

Much of the persistent nature of these specific rumors can be traced to partisan political groups. Richard Scaife, a wealthy financier of many anti-Clinton groups, has been quoted as saying, "The death of Vincent Foster: I think that's the Rosetta Stone to the whole Clinton Administration" (Weiner, 1995). Scaife has supported groups, such as the Western Journalism Center, that have included work by Christopher Ruddy, a reporter who was dismissed by the *New York Post* for pursuing cover-up theories relating to the death. Ruddy, who refers to himself as part of the 'vast right-wing conspiracy' described by Hillary Clinton, has written and published numerous articles attacking both the Clinton administration and the Foster investigations. Even today, reports written by Ruddy questioning the investigations' findings can be found online (www.newsmax.com/ruddy/). In addition, fund-raising letters for conservative groups, including a 1997 letter from a group called "Clinton Investigation Committee," have been used to raise money to continue various investigations against Clinton, including the Foster case (Piacente, 1997). These organizations, Web sites, newspaper articles, and fund-raising letters, have all helped to perpetuate the rumors that Vince Foster's death was a murder, and somehow the Clinton administration was involved.

Because these rumors have persisted for years, their existence cannot be attributed to the timing pressure of the Internet news cycle. Instead, the theories involving Foster's death are a result of the desire for the sensational and partisan political efforts, in this instance from groups who opposed Bill Clinton. The possibility of a printed retraction seems impractical and would likely have no effect, since, unlike the Blumenthal case, there was no one specific site that started the rumors on the Internet, and because the rumors have extended far beyond the Internet into newspapers and even among members of Congress. The cascade effect of all of these rumors is that a certain contingent, in this case opponents of Bill Clinton, continues to believe that the Clintons were responsible for Vince Foster's death. The political consequences for such accusations, even after they have been disproved, can be far reaching because false information has to potential to unreasonably decrease the public's faith in public officials and the competency of their government.

Conclusion

The expansion of the Internet has great potential for promoting political discourse and allowing for far more citizens to be involved with the production and dissemination of news. Davis and Owen (1998) describe this positive potential:

> Increasingly, computer networks have become tools for political communication as well. Users gather political information, express their opinions, and mobilize other citizens and political leaders. The information superhighway is fast becoming an electronic town hall where anyone with a personal computer and a modem can learn about the latest bill introduced in Congress, join an interest group, donate money to a political candidate, or discuss politics with people they have never seen who may live half a world away. (pg. 110)

However, as these three case studies have shown, the potential for the Internet to be a conduit of false information or the spreading of rumors is also significant. The dilemma for those who are concerned about the role the Internet will play in the future of democracy will be to discover how to balance the positive democratizing aspects with the potentially harmful aspects that include the spread of false reports and misleading information.

The main goal of this investigation was to examine how errors of Internet reporting are handled online. These three case studies demonstrate that there is no single method as to how Internet errors are corrected. When one source for a rumor exists, as was the case with the Blumenthal story, a retraction is possible on that initial source which can somewhat lessen the impact of the false story. However, even that example was picked up by other mainstream newspaper and radio sources.

This study then supports Hall's assertion that the nature of the Internet reinforces the context of errors rather than corrects them. As seen with the Vince Foster case, significant numbers of people believed that his death was a murder even after several investigations had concluded otherwise. Public discourse was not shifted entirely even after the early reports were disproved or corrected. In fact, in all three of the cases presented here, the Internet rumors and false reports were picked up by other sources and continued to spread even after evidence pointed to contrary facts.

Another substantial conclusion that can be ascertained from this investigation is that Sunstein's assessment of social cascades is valid in regards to errors on the Internet. For those people who are interested in finding evidence to support their views, even if the evidence itself is questionable, the Internet can be a tremendous facilitator. And the reach of the influence of these reports is not just to conspiracy theorists. Their impact can be seen even in actions taken by government officials, such as President Clinton after the crash of TWA flight 800. These social cascades can have important political consequences, whether on airline safety regulations or in the perceptions of political figures. A connection appears to exist between the capabilities of the Internet and the vastness of the social cascading that can occur as a result of rumor and innuendo.

How, then, should the potential for social cascading as a result of misleading information be balanced with the positive potential of the Internet? Not all scholars agree that the implications of an 'anything goes' attitude of Internet reporting is entirely negative. Davis and Owen (1998) make an argument relating to old media that an increase of tabloid journalism may not be entirely destructive because it "can foster a sense of intimacy with the public," and also attract viewers to news sources (pg. 209). This same line of reasoning can be applied to the Internet sites such as Matt Drudge's that spread rumor while using standards for verification that are less than those that are utilized by traditional media. Consequently, it is possible that the lowering of journalistic norms that is apparent online will not have entirely negative consequences if the result encourages more people to search for news and connect with other Internet users.

Even if it is true that the Internet's impact on journalism and the increase of false reports is not entirely negative, this investigation has demonstrated that harmful effects can result from the cascade effects of misinformation. The question that arises from this investigation is regarding how to control or combat the prevalence of errors on the Internet. Sidney Blumenthal acknowledged that one of the goals of his lawsuit against Drudge was to bring the Internet under the same type of libel laws that newspaper and television journalists must follow. However, Blumenthal's attempt at forcing the Internet "reporter" to face negative consequences as a result of his false report was unsuccessful, and further attempts by the government to regulate the content of the Internet seem likely to be impractical, costly, and ineffective overall. There is simply too much online content for the government to be able to enforce the same types of journalistic laws that other news mediums must follow, not to mention the potential for excessive government censorship.

At the same time, it is incredibly unlikely that the four reasons mentioned earlier in this discussion that cause errors in reporting, that is, the need for speed, the desire to attract hits, the goal of advancing a partisan agenda, and the attraction to scandal, will lessen and lower the competitive pressures on Internet journalists in the next few years. If anything, those pressures are likely to increase as more and more people turn to the Internet for their news. The only probable method for improving the accuracy of online reporting would be for news producers themselves to make better attempts at following voluntary guidelines that are closer to the standards used by old media sources. Offering guidelines for reporters to follow is not new. Sabato, Stencel, and Lichter (2000) describe a number of guidelines reporters should follow in reporting political scandals in their book entitled *Peepshow* and journalism schools have been teaching professional norms for decades. Other sets of standards that are usually applied to traditional news outlets could be applied to Internet sources as well. These standards, such as the need for multiple sources for issuing a report, do not guarantee complete accuracy in reporting, as can be seen with the recent scandals of newspaper reporters Jayson Blair of the *New York Times* and Jack Kelley of *USA Today*. However, attempts to follow these more traditional guidelines would lessen the frequency and impact of Internet reporting errors.

Seib agrees with the need for online reporters to voluntarily follow traditional ethics of reporting. In his predictions for the future of Internet journalism, he notes that it will be increasingly important for reporters to aim at fairness and accuracy. He writes, "The 'Drudge effect—shoot-from-the-hip sensationalism—will give online journalism a bad name if the public perceives it to be a dominant characteristic of this medium" (p. 162). The best way for journalists to deal with this perceived 'Drudge effect' and the potentially harmful impact of Internet rumors is to deliver a consistently fair and accurate news product. The marketplace will in time come to rely on the high-quality product more than the hastily put together news site that does not have a good track record of accuracy. Seib's faith in the public's desire for quality reporting is the most hopeful and promising view as to how to lessen the impact of social cascades based on misleading or false information.

Along with offering positive aspects of the Internet, Davis and Owen (1998) also write, "new technologies have enhanced opportunities for the mass dissemination of misinformation" (p. 200). As this study has shown, this rapidly expanding technology can have potentially harmful effects if false reports are spread without supporting evidence. In order for us to reap the positive effects of the Internet, which include added convenience and the possibility of increased political discourse, the dangers of false information must also be confronted. The most effective method to lessen the amount and impact of false Internet errors will be for news producers on the Web to follow traditional journalistic standards of fact-checking and sourcing. False reporting will not disappear, but, we must make ourselves aware of the various types of reporting that can be found on the Web and hope that market forces will encourage high-quality reporting as opposed to unsubstantiated rumors passing as news. Awareness of the potential for both types of reporting is a central condition for encouraging effective and accurate online reporting.

References

The Atlanta Journal and Constitution (1994, July 29). "Hatemongers Who Cry Wolf . . . " Editorial, p. A14.

The Augusta Chronicle (Georgia) (1998, December 11). "Calls for Investigation, Not Cover-Up." Editorial, p. A4.

Blumenthal, Sidney (2003). *The Clinton Wars.* New York: Farrar, Straus and Giroux.

Charles, Michael T. (2001). "The Fall of TWA Flight 800." In Uriel Rosenthal, R. Arjen Boin, & Louise K. Comfort (Eds.), *Managing Crises: Threats, Dilemmas, Opportunities* (pp. 216–234). Springfield, IL.: Charles C. Thomas Publisher, Ltd.

CNN.com (1997, March 11). *NTSB: "No Physical Evidence" Missile Brought Down TWA 800.* Atlanta, GA: CNN.com. Retrieved October 18, 2003, from the CNN Interactive Web site: http://www.cnn.com/US/9703/11/twa.missile/

Cobb, Roger W., & Primo, David M. (2003*). The Plane Truth: Airline Crashes, the Media, and Transportation Policy.* Washington, D.C.: Brookings Institution Press.

Davis, Richard (1999). *The Web of Politics: The Internet's Impact on the American Political System.* New York: Oxford University Press.

Davis, Richard & Owen, Diana (1998). *New Media and American Politics.* New York: Oxford University Press.

Hall, Jim (2001). *Online Journalism: A Critical Primer.* London: Pluto Press.

Harper, Christopher (1998*). And That's the Way It Will Be: News and Information in a Digital World.* New York: New York University Press.

Hunter, Mark (1997). *The Buffoon Brigade: Pierre Salinger and His Conspiracy-Minded Colleagues are Stopping Investigators from Finding Out What Really Happened to TWA Flight 800.* San Francisco: Salon.com. Retrieved October 18, 2003, from the Salon.com Web site: http://www.salon.com/march97/ news/ news970326.html

Kurtz, Howard (1997, August 12). "Blumenthals Get Apology, Plan Lawsuit: Web Site Retracts Story of Clinton Aide." *The Washington Post,* p. A11.

Kurtz, Howard (2001, May 2). "Clinton Aide Settles Libel Suit Against Matt Drudge—At a Cost." *The Washington Post,* p. C1

Negroni, Christine (1997, January 17). *Six Months Later, Still No Answer to TWA Flight 800 Mystery.* Atlanta, GA: CNN.com. Retrieved October 18, 2003, from the CNN Interactive Web site: http://www.cnn.com/US/9701/17/twa/index.html

O'Dwyer, Thomas (1996, February 18). "Buchanan Web Site Blames Mossad for Clinton Aide's Death; Calls Hillary an Agent." *The Jerusalem Post,* p. 1.

O'Leary, Stephen (2002). *Rumors of Grace and Terror.* Los Angeles, CA: The Online Journalism Review. Retrieved September 29, 2003, from the Online Journalism Review Web site: http://www. ojr.org/ojr/ethics/1017782038.php

Piacente, Steve (1997, April 16). "Letter Claims Foster was Killed." *The Post and Courier*(Charleston, SC*)*, p. A9.

Ruddy, Christopher (1999). "A Memo: The Unanswered Questions in the Foster Case." West Palm Beach, FL: The Christopher Ruddy Web site. Retrieved November 27, 2003, from Newsmax.com: http://www.newsmax.com/articles/?a=1999/2/8/155138

Sabato, Larry J., Stencel, Mark, & Lichter, S. Robert (2000). *Peepshow: Media and Politics in an Age of Scandal.* Lanham, MD: Rowman & Littlefield Publishers, Inc.

Scheer, Robert (1999, January 14). "More Sludge From Drudge: The Story that Clinton Fathered An Illegitimate Son Turns Out to be a Hoax." *Pittsburgh Post-Gazette,* p. A15.

Seib, Philip (2001). *Going Live: Getting the News Right in a Real-Time, Online World.* Lanham, MD: Rowman & Littlefield Publishers, Inc.

Sunstein, Cass (2002). *Republic.com.* Princeton: Princeton University Press.

Swartz, Jon (1998, June 23). "Free-Speech Victory For Internet; AOL Off the Hook in Landmark Libel Case." *The San Francisco Chronicle,* p. A1.

Tisdall, Simon (1994, February 7). "The Body in the Park." *The Guardian*(London), p. 2.

Weiner, Tim (1995, August 13). "One Source, Many Ideas in Foster Case." *The New York Times,* pp. 1–19.

whatreallyhappened.com (2002, June 10). *Was TWA Flight 800 Shot Down by a Military Missile?* Retrieved October 18, 2003, from the whatreallyhappened.com Web site: http://www. whatreallyhappened.com/RANCHO/ CRASH/TWA/twa.html

Note

1. For complete text of the Internet letter written by Russell, see (Harper, 1998, pp. 85–86)

From *gnovis*, April 26, 2004. Copyright ©; 2004 by Communication, Culture and Technology Program (CCT), Georgetown University. Reprinted by permission. http://gnovis. georgetown.edu/

UNIT 7

International Perspectives and Issues

Unit Selections

Key Points to Consider

- Why is the year 1999 significant in the context of American information technology employment?

- A committed globalist might respond, "So what," to the litany of worries about Asia in "Is the Crouching Tiger a Threat." Economists call the theory underlying this response comparative advantage. Read about comparative advantage. Are you persuaded that the United States will suffer no ill effects if it cedes dominance in the information technology sector to Asia?

- "In Search of a PC for the People" mentions Nicholas Negroponte, an MIT professor and founder of the nonprofit group One Laptop Per Child. Use the Internet to find out more about this group. What do they have to say about the recent decision of a New York school district to drop its laptop for students program?

- Find out more about proxy servers. What is to prevent an authoritarian government from monitoring traffic to a proxy server within its borders? Suppose an authoritarian government sets up a Web site claiming to be anonymouse.org. How could it be distinguished from the real thing? What if a volunteer within a proxy server group sells a list of names and searched Web sites to authoritarian regimes. Do the proxy server Web sites you have visited address these issues?

Student Web Site
www.mhcls.com/online

Internet References
Further information regarding this Web site may be found in this book's preface or online.

Information Revolution and World Politics Project
http://www.ceip.org/files/projects/irwp/irwp_descrip.ASP

For the past several years we have been hearing a great deal about a global economy, with the exchange of goods, services, and labor across national boundaries. Yet human beings have been trading across long distances for centuries. The discovery of Viking artifacts in Baghdad and sea shells in the Mississippi Valley are two of many, many examples. The beginnings of capitalism in the 15th century accelerated an existing process. When most commentators speak of globalization, though, they refer increasingly to interdependent trade we have witnessed since the collapse of the former Soviet Union and the global availability of the Internet and satellite communications. Without the new information technologies, the global marketplace would not be possible. We can withdraw money from our bank accounts using ATM machines in Central Turkey, make cell phones calls from nearly anywhere on the planet, and check our e-mail from a terminal located in an Internet café in Florence or Katmandu. Businesses can transfer funds around the world and, if you happen to be a software developer, you can employ talented—and inexpensive—software engineers in growing tech centers like Bangalore, India.

Or China. Those of use old enough to remember the Chinese Red Guard waving copies of Chairman Mao's Little Red Book might be surprised to find that "Bill Gates has become the new idol of youths across China" (see "China's Tech Generation Finds a New Chairman to Venerate"). Though most commentators and politicians in the United States seem to celebrate the benefits of global trade, China's growing tech sector is worrisome to some of our homegrown computer scientists. Robert Glass' article from the *Communications of the ACM* ("Is the Crouching Tiger a Threat?) is a veritable catalog of worry: a dramatic drop in the number of American students majoring in computer science, increased number of Asian students in computer science at our top universities, growing computer science departments in China (and Korea), projections that the number of software developers in Asia and India will soon exceed those in the United States.

As a corrective, read David Patterson's short piece, "Restoring the Popularity of Computer Science." Though students seem to be voting with their feet after having read reports of smart, hardworking, and underpaid Indian software engineers, there is still plenty of work to go around in the United States. By May, 2004 the U.S. Bureau of Labor Statistics reported that employment in the American information technology sector was seventeen percent higher than in 1999.

Whether your believe Glass or Patterson, there is one aspect of the tech sector that does not inspire envy. What becomes of those many millions of computers that are retired each year? China appears to play a role here, too, as the excellent article from *The Progressive* shows (see "China's Computer Wasteland").

Not all international consequences of computer technology are economic. One of the most exciting developments in theoretical computer science in recent years has been strong cryptography, the art of enciphering messages. For practical purposes, freely available cryptographic software can produce unbreakable codes. Governments, including our own, have worried about this for a decade. Whatever you might think about making wiretap-proof software available to criminals in the United States, it is being put to good use in countries with repressive governments. Authoritarian governments find themselves in a fix, at lease with respect to encrypted e-mail.

Web sites are another story. Countries from Cuba to China find it easy enough to block sites they they disapprove of. The response from activists in the computer science community has been swift and disarmingly simple. A German computer science student created the first proxy Web site in less than a week. Now called Anonymouse.org, it is accessed daily by three million people. The idea is that you go to Anonymous.org and from there you can search the Web anonymously. Of course, the censors can block access to proxies once they find them. This leads to the cat and mouse game described in "Cat and Mouse, on the Web."

We in the United States, especially students on well-endowed university campuses, have grown accustomed to a cornucopia of computing devices that were not available anywhere a generation ago. They are still unavailable in the developing world. The computer industry is beginning to see that designing computers appropriate to the needs and resources of this emerging market is more than a good deed, it might well be good business. See "In Search of a PC for the People" and learn why "selling computers in the developing world is more complex than simply adding Mandarin, Hindi, or Arabic software to existing PCs."

The global interconnectedness that Marshall McLuhan observed forty years ago has only increased in complexity with developments in computer technology. Now instead of merely receiving one-way satellite feeds as in McLuhan's day, we can talk back through e-mail, Web sites, and blogs. It is not surprising that all of this communication is having unanticipated effects across the planet. Who, for instance, during the Tiananmen Square uprising of 1989 could have predicted that a newly market-centered China would also become a destination for America's computer trash, or, for that matter, the source of significant competition? Or, who could ever have predicted that Bill Gates would replace Chairman Mao in the hearts of the young Chinese? No one, in fact, which is why the study of computer use internationally is so fascinating.

References

De Palma, Paul, "http://www.when_is_enough_enough?.com, *The American Scholar* 68, 1 (Winter, 1999).

Merrett, Christopher D. "The Future of Rural Communities in a Global Economy." Retrieved 5/10/2004 from: http://www.uiowa.edu/ifdebook/features/perspectives/merrett.shtml

China's Tech Generation Finds a New Chairman to Venerate

KEVIN HOLDEN

Since the passing of Chairman Mao Zedong, a new chairman has come to represent the aims and aspirations of millions of Chinese youth—the chairman of Microsoft, Bill Gates.

"Chairman Mao was the great symbol of revolutionary China, but Bill Gates has become the new idol of youths across China," said a researcher with China's ministry of propaganda. "Gates has become more popular in China than any government leader."

Books by or about Microsoft's chairman are massive best sellers across China, even in the IT-impoverished countryside, and Gates has been cited as the ultimate role model by everyone, from the founders of internet startups to Chinese cyberdissidents.

"I read about Bill Gates before I had ever even seen a computer," said Dong Ruidong, who abandoned his rural village for the bright lights and cybercafes of the Chinese capital. "Even in the remotest villages of China, Gates is one of the most popular figures alive."

The Chinese edition of Gates' *The Road Ahead* "was one of the most successful books in our history," said Wang Mingzhou, who edited the Chinese edition. It is "among the most important works published since the founding of the People's Republic of China."

Wang, who rode the success of Gates' book to be named president of the Peking University Press, said *The Road Ahead* "helped launch the internet revolution across China, and gave it power and speed."

"Bill Gates is without doubt now one of the most influential foreigners in China," Wang said.

Chairman Gates is everything Chairman Mao was not. Mao crushed capitalists, closed newspapers and universities, and isolated China from the world. But Chairman Gates celebrates free enterprise and is busy forging partnerships with Chinese entrepreneurs, creating cybercolleges and integrating China's best and brightest into the web-linked world.

Gates has disbursed grants from his $30-billion philanthropic Gates Foundation to bring computers to rural China and health care to the poor, and in the process has acquired the aura of an internet-age angel.

Chinese youths stand to gain from the virtual universities Gates is helping create, and from student software packages Microsoft has begun offering for $3 (1/50th the retail price) each to governments buying computers for K–12 kids.

Microsoft Vice President Will Poole, who is helping spearhead the race to double the globe's cybercitizenry to 2 billion people by 2015, said Microsoft's software packages could be provided in tandem with the ultra-cheap XO machines being produced in China by the One Laptop Per Child group.

China's Ministry of Education, which paints Gates with an almost superhuman glow in books like *Junior English for China*, might use this software in its quest to churn out more internet-generation graduates.

China's internet population jumped by 23 percent to reach 130 million people in 2006, but nine-tenths of China's 1.3 billion citizens are still on the dark side of the digital divide.

At a recent Asian leadership forum in Beijing with Chinese technocrats and U.N. leaders, Gates outlined his latest goal—to extend internet access beyond the globe's 1 billion online elite to its 5 billion digitally dispossessed—many of whom are in China.

"Microsoft is now over 30 years old, and the original dream was about computers for everyone," he said. "As we go after this next 5 billion, it is really going back to the original roots, the original commitment of what Microsoft is all about."

Of course, meeting that goal would also position Microsoft to multiply, by a factor of 10, its current base of 600 million Windows users worldwide, and further expand Gates' global influence.

Microsoft's chairman is extending lots of incentives to new Windows users here, and has become a symbol of global fame and fortune, and of American-style freedoms. While hosting Chinese President Hu Jintao at an aristocratic feast at the Gates' private residence in Seattle last spring, Gates echoed Microsoft's testimony during U.S. congressional hearings on "The Internet in China: A Tool for Freedom or Suppression."

In remarks repeated across Chinese chat rooms, Gates told Hu: "Industry and government around the world should work even more closely to protect the privacy and security of internet users, and promote the exchange of ideas."

During his recent tour of China, Gates predicted the next global leader might be born here: "There was a survey done in the U.S. that asked where the next Bill Gates will come from," he said. "Sixty percent of the U.S. said the next stunning success would come from Asia."

Yet few Chinese believe that a clone of Gates, if born in China, could become *the* Bill Gates.

"Piracy is so widespread here that Microsoft would never generate such massive profits," said author Huang Wen.

Despite the massive, institutionalized piracy that has led the United States to file a complaint against China with the World Trade Organization, Gates has been amazingly tolerant of China's counterfeiters. This has created a paradoxical image of an internet-age Robin Hood and gained him universal admiration.

"Bill Gates deserves to win the Nobel Peace Prize," said the Chinese propaganda officer. "He gives people across the globe not only material help, but also inspiration that if they work very, very hard, they might one day become more important than a president."

Is the Crouching Tiger a Threat?

Considering the changing representation of the computing community.

Robert L. Glass

I'd like to share a concern with you. I've read a lot of things recently about the emergence of Asia as a computing/IT power, in an assortment of places. I'll tell you about those things later. But first, let me tell you where I'm going with this column. All of this is going to lead to a question. That question is, "Is the Asian Tiger preparing to take over the IT world?" Given the international distribution of the *Communications* readership, I'm quite interested to learn your answer.

Certainly one could answer "yes," based on adding up all of those things I'm about to tell you. Or all those things may really add up to just another example of the all-too-common hype that so often inundates our profession. The dilemma I'd like you to help me with is this: Does 2+2 really equal 6, as the press and others seem to be telling us these days? Or is it more likely 3?

OK, here are those things I promised to tell you about. Let me present them as a set of individual facts, each with an explanation of where that fact came from. Then your job, should you choose to accept it, is to take those facts, evaluate each one individually (after all, what passes as "fact" may in reality not be), and then form a conclusion out of the gestalt those facts create. And, if you wish, share that conclusion with me.

Fact 1: U.S. computer science academic programs are dominated by students from developing countries, especially. Asian ones. This fact came from a couple of sources: my own discussions with CS academics over the last decade, and the contribution of Don Reifer to a round-table discussion on offshore outsourcing that I included in the May 2005 issue of *The Software Practitioner*. Quoting Reifer is probably the best way to get this fact across: "When I did a straw poll of five of the top 10 schools offering degrees in computer science and software engineering about two years ago, I found that as many as 80% of the students came from abroad." The context of the quote makes it clear that a very large percentage of those "students from abroad" were from Asia.

Fact 2: There has been a 60% decline in the number of U.S. incoming college freshmen considering CS as a major during the period from 2000 to 2004. This fact comes from a survey performed by the Higher Educational Research Institute at UCLA. (Another fact from that survey, that there has been an 80% decline in the number of CS female undergraduates over approximately the same period, is fascinating, but not germane to what I'm discussing here).

Fact 3: The number of professional software developers in such Asian countries as China and India is increasing rapidly, such that (according to International Data Corp., the source of this particular fact), "the total software population of the Asia/Pacific region will over-take North America's in 2006." The study goes on to say that the growth rate of the programming population is 25.6% a year in China and 24.5% in India.

Fact 4: Asian Universities are beginning to dominate the Top Institutions portion of the Top Scholars and Institutions survey conducted and published by the *Journal of Systems and Software* each year in October. In the latest survey findings, published in October 2005, among the leading institutions of the world based on counting the number of software engineering research publications emerging from them, three of the top five institutions are Asian. Korea Advanced Institute of Science and Technology is number one, National Chiao Tung University of China is number two, and Seoul National University of Korea is number 4. The non-Asian institutions in the top five are Carnegie Mellon University (including its Software Engineering Institute), at number three; and Fraunhofer Institute for Experimental Software Engineering, at number five. What is striking about this particular fact is that as recently as three years ago, in earlier such survey findings, Asian schools were only marginally represented in the top 10, and the top institutions were clearly North American.

Fact 5: The Asian countries are beginning to work together to make IT a priority. According to [1], India and China are working on a "two pagoda" strategy in which India excels in software, and China in hardware. They envision that an "Asian century" in the IT industry will emerge.

Fact 6: Asian students are beginning to dominate the ACM-sponsored International Collegiate Programming contest. According to the July 2005 *Communications* "President's Letter" column, the most recent competition was won by a Chinese University (Shanghai Jiao Tong), and the sole U.S. entry (the University of Illinois) finished seventh [2].

Well, there you have it. These facts seem to add up to this:

- Student populations: The number of Asian students enrolling in computing courses is increasing; U.S. student enrollment is decreasing. The difference is dramatic.
- Student competition: Asian students are winning international programming contests.
- Practitioners: Asian practitioners are increasing at a rate sufficient to pass U.S. practitioner populations in 2006.
- Researchers: Asian institutional software engineering researchers are rapidly accelerating their publication productivity, to the point where they are leading the world in that category.
- Business collaboration: Asian nations are beginning to work together to make sure their advancements continue.

Now let me share a deeply personal thought with you here. I believe in something I call "the test of common sense" for help in making life's decisions. By that I mean this: when it comes time to make a decision about something, I step back a few paces and ask myself "does the conclusion I'm about to reach make sense?"

Let me apply that test here. Common sense tells me that the U.S. has dominated the computing profession for more than five decades now. It's hard for my common sense to accept the possibility that we're about to reach the point where that U.S. dominance is going to be overthrown.

So here's my dilemma. All of the facts stated in this column combine to suggest that something dramatic is happening in the computing world. But my common sense tells me that suggestion isn't valid. That's why I invited your consideration at the beginning of this column, as I would like to learn your opinion on this matter.

References

1. McDougall, P. Tech powerhouse. *Information Week* (Apr. 18, 2005).
2. Patterson, D. Reflections on a programming olympiad. *Commun. ACM 48, 7* (July 2005), 15.

ROBERT L. GLASS (rlglass@acm.org) is the publisher/editor of *The Software Practitioner* newsletter, and editor emeritus of Elsevier's *Journal of Systems and Software*. He is currently a visiting professor in the ARC Center for Complex Systems at Griffith University, Brisbane, Australia.

Restoring the Popularity of Computer Science

Inaccurate impressions of the opportunities of 21st century CS are shrinking the next generation of IT professionals. You can help by dispelling incorrect beliefs about employment and by helping improve pre-college education.

DAVID A. PATTERSON

Although universities were recently struggling to cope with an avalanche of computer science majors—some going so far as to erecting academic barriers to deflect the masses—they may soon need to reverse course and remove obstacles to the major, and even to recruiting to broaden participation in CS. Figure 1 tracks the change in popularity of the CS major among incoming freshmen over time in the U.S., which has been be a good predictor of graduates four to five years later [1].

Clearly, the CS major is now in a downward cycle in the U.S., especially for women. While the percentage of men intending to major in CS is no worse than the mid-1990s, the number of female CS majors is at a historic low. This drop is occurring while their academic numbers are increasing, as the majority of college students today are female. Colleagues outside North America suggest a similar decline in Europe. As an extreme example, a few CS departments were even closed in the U.K.

Everyone has an opinion as to why the CS numbers are down in this age group, so let me share mine: The expected negative impact of offshoring IT jobs in North America and Europe, and the current negative view of the CS profession by pre-college students, especially females. What can we do about these issues?

ACM's Job Migration Task Force has examined the impact of outsourcing extensively and is working to publish its findings, which we hope to complete this fall. I believe the truth will surely be better for our field than the worst fears of pre-college students and their parents. For example, Figure 2 shows the annual U.S. IT employment though May 2004. (The U.S. Bureau of Labor Statistics is about 15 months behind.)[1] Moreover, most of us believe things have gotten much better in the year since the survey was completed. Does anyone besides me know that U.S. IT employment was 17% higher than in 1999—5% higher than the bubble in 2000 and showing an 8% growth

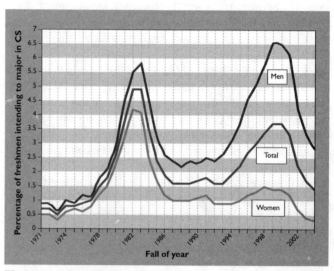

Figure 1 Computer science listed as probable major among incoming freshman.
Source: HERI at UCLA

in the most recent year—and that the compound annual growth rate of IT wages has been about 4% since 1999 while inflation has been just 2% per year? Such growth rates swamp predictions of the outsourcing job loss in the U.S., which most studies estimate to be 2% to 3% per year for the next decade.[2]

Regarding the negative CS impressions held by students not yet in college, we hope ACM's new Computer Science Teachers Association (CSTA) will help in this regard. CSTA is a membership organization that supports and promotes the teaching of CS and other computing disciplines. CSTA provides opportunities for pre-college teachers and students to better understand the computing disciplines and to more successfully prepare themselves to teach and learn. Remarkably, before ACM

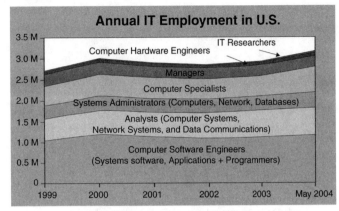

Figure 2   Annual IT employment in the U.S.

formed CSTA nine months ago, computer science was the only academic discipline within the U.S. high school curriculum without national professional representation.

To give you an idea what CSTA is trying to do to further the CS cause, here is the list of its existing committees: Curriculum, Equity, Finance, Funding Development, Governance, Membership, Policy and Advocacy, Professional Development, Publications and Communications, Research, and Standards and Certification (see csta.acm.org for details on all these groups and much more). I am particularly interested in the Equity committee, for I've long suspected that the drop in women CS majors was related to the initial unattractive impression of our field when high schools started teaching CS in the 1980s.

Although it only began in January, CSTA already has more than 2,000 members, and these members come from all over the world. CSTA members represent more than 60 countries and all 50 states in the U.S.

At the recent National Educational Computing Conference, panel speakers from Canada, Israel, Scotland, and South Africa described their current CS curriculum for students ages 12 to 18 and the issues that surround its implementation. They all emphasized the importance of supporting CS education as a means for ensuring the economic futures of their countries.

While all of the countries noted their efforts to implement a new national curriculum were initially hampered by issues such as lack of funding or insufficient time for teacher training, no point about the need for well-trained teachers was made more poignantly than by Michael Chiles from South Africa. He told the audience that the HIV/AIDS pandemic is taking the lives of so many teachers that it is becoming almost impossible to replace them. Not only are the teachers themselves dying, so many people in business are dying that industries looking for

technically skilled workers are luring the healthy CS teachers away from the classroom.

This panel discussion led to a CSTA project to create a white paper that will provide an international perspective on successful models for CS curriculum development and implementation. Judith Gal-Ezer, the panel speaker representing Israel, serves as an international director to the CSTA Board.

What can you do to help? First, please try to counteract the widespread impression that the CS field is not a good one for the future. For example, you can help publicize real employment data and the results of ACM's upcoming outsourcing study.

Second, if you know pre-college teachers, please suggest they consider joining CSTA. Studies of teachers belonging to such organizations suggest they gain important knowledge and psychological support as well as establish networking relationships that provide opportunities to share curricula. The resulting reform is also more widespread and long lasting.

CSTA could also use specific help on some of their committees. The Research committee is looking for volunteers to assist on statistical analysis of surveys. The Standards and Certification committee needs volunteers to create a database of teacher certification requirements in different regions. It could also use more practicing teachers on its Curriculum committee. Finally, if you really care about the issue of pre-college education, join CSTA.

It's difficult to imagine a more important topic for our future than trying to change public opinion about career opportunities in CS and to improve pre-college education, so thanks in advance for your help.

Notes

1. Private communication, John Sargent, Office of Technology, Policy Technology Administration, U.S. Department of Commerce, July 2005. For clarity, Figure 2 combines the 12 official U.S. Department of Labor titles into seven related categories.
2. Private communication, William Asprey, Indiana University, July 2005.

Reference

1. Vegso, J. Interest in CS as a major drops among incoming freshmen. *Computing Research News 17,* 3 (May 2005); www.cra.org/CRN/articles/may05/vegso.

DAVID A. PATTERSON (pattsn@eecs.berkeley.edu) is president of the ACM and the Pardee Professor of Computer Science at the University of California at Berkeley.

Article 38

China's Computer Wasteland

BENJAMIN JOFFE-WALT

"Shhh. Shhhhhhhhh!" the driver in Guangdong province whispers to us. He stares at the photographer out of the corner of his eye. When we stop, he won't even get out of the car. The photographer's every movement makes him jump a bit, and he receives the snap of her camera like the crack of a machine gun. "Careful!" he says. "They really will kill you."

We drive clandestinely, heads ducked, bodies curled up, eyes downward. "There, there it is!" the driver points. "They burn along the river." In front of us sprawl colossal piles of smoldering green computer circuit boards.

At first, Guiyu seems like any other rural Chinese town—flooded rice fields, streets swamped with produce vendors, migrant workers carrying bamboo on mopeds. But then you open the window. There is no smell more violent. The air is fierce, infected, as if the atmosphere itself had been viscously conquered by toxic paint, scorched bread, and burning plastic. An immediate noxious thickness enters your mouth, a toxic attack on all skin.

"I'm just trying to get some money," says Luo Yuan Chang, a newly arrived migrant from Hunan province who is burning old computers along the river. "Farming computers is more profitable than growing rice."

Computer waste from the West has made this poor mainland farming region an ecological disaster area. A large town along the Lianjiang River in southeastern China, Guiyu is the secret epicenter of illegal e-waste (electronic waste) processing in China. Workers there don't refurbish and sell the computers. They don't use them. Instead, they take hammers, chisels, and cutting torches to computers, keyboards, speakers, and other sorts of e-waste and smash them to bits for scrap metal, toner, gold, and reusable chips.

Chang stands shirtless atop scorched medical equipment, printing toner, and audio speakers. "I used to drive trucks, but I couldn't find a job so I had to come here and burn the rubbish," the forty-year-old says. "My family is here, and if I have no work we couldn't live, so I don't care how dangerous it is." When asked, though, he doesn't know much about the dangers involved.

It's plenty dangerous.

According to the Worldwatch Institute, workers breathe in all types of toxins: cadmium in chip resistors and semiconductors; beryllium on motherboards and connectors; brominated flame retardants in circuit boards and plastic casings; and lead, phosphor, barium, and hexavalent chromium in computer monitors.

The average CRT computer monitor contains four to eight pounds of lead, and the average LCD monitor contains four milligrams of mercury. Less than one-fourth of a teaspoon of mercury can contaminate more than 400 acres of a lake, making the fish unsafe to eat.

"There are many cases of lung problems, and the burning releases pollutants that cause diseases like silicosis, heart attacks, and pulmonary edema," says Dr. Chen at a local health clinic.

International watchdog groups estimate that the United States alone exported more than $1 billion worth of electronic waste to China last year while receiving virtually none from China. Though particularly pronounced in China, the e-waste of the Western world is being dumped all over Asia. *The Times of India* reports that "electronic waste is giving the country a big headache" and that India has become a "favorite dumping ground for countries like the U.S., Malaysia, Sweden, Canada, and Singapore."

Toxics Link, an Indian environmental group, claims that recycling a computer in India costs $2 on average, compared to $20 in the United States. Policymakers in the United States also understand the dynamics of dumping in Asia. After a pilot project to recycle computer monitors, the U.S. Environmental Protection Agency estimated that it is ten times cheaper to ship them to Asia than to recycle them in the United States.

China is not only a computer dumping ground. It also produces many of the 150 million computers that head out yearly on a peculiar round trip. For instance, IBM, Apple, Hewlett-Packard, Dell, and Sony all manufacture electronic goods in China. They then sell these products to Western countries. Finally, China gets them back as rubbish.

"Most of it is coming from recycling programs in countries that are trying to prevent pollution of their own territory," says Lai Yun, a Chinese environmentalist.

Today, more than 50 percent of U.S. households own a computer and have, on average, two to three old computers stored away in the basement or garage. Studies estimate that 315 million to 600 million computers in the United States will be obsolete by 2006.

"That's the same as a twenty-two-story pile of e-waste covering the entire 472 square miles of the City of Los Angeles," says the Computer TakeBack Campaign, an effort by a consortium of thirteen environmental organizations.

"Farming computers is more profitable than growing rice."

Two member groups, the Basel Action Network and the Silicon Valley Toxics Coalition, say in a report that 80 percent of e-waste collected in the United States is exported to Asia.

The United States is using "hidden escape valves to export the crisis to developing countries of Asia," the report states. "The poor of the world," it adds, are forced to "bear a disproportionate share of the e-waste environmental burden. This current reality is the dirty little secret of the electronics industry."

"The real crime," says Jim Puckett of the Basel Action Network, "is the unwillingness of countries like the United States and Japan to take responsibility for preventing the global dumping of their own toxic waste."

Guiyu is a cyber desert. Desolate mountains of electronic trash are everywhere, as hundreds of trucks drive over burnt circuit boards, the intricate crunch audible from almost a mile away. Dogs with diseased eyes are chained to e-waste "farmhouses" of moldy concrete walls. Circuit boards are used to hole up corrugated iron shacks housing migrants right next to heaps of junk along the river. The streams running through the migrants' riverside tenements are a blinding, shiny silver due to mercury and other toxins. Private traders import millions of gallons of water to the town and sell it at a premium to residents.

"Even if the work would kill me, I'd continue," says He Ti Guang, a wire cutter in an e-waste factory downtown. "I have no choice. My family is poor, so I came here to earn money." A thirty-five-year-old migrant from Sichuan province, Guang has warts, burns, and rashes up and down his arms.

"This waste is too hot, and it burns. My skin itches all the time," he says. "I think the wires are toxic, but I don't know."

His wife works in a plastics e-waste factory, melting old wires, computer monitors, TVs, and cellphones to be used for plastic chairs and thermoses.

"I've had many health problems," Li Sheng Cui says. "My body is weak and my stomach hurts when I laugh." She cringes and blinks erratically. "Your tongue tastes like sugar, and your skin is itchy," she says, holding her finger in her mouth. "It's impossible to wear a white shirt. You wash it and it turns yellow."

China's e-waste crisis is a byproduct of its unequal development. "China's opening to international markets and capital has greatly exacerbated the divide between urban middle class wealth and the rural poor," says Yun Xien,

a local environmental activist. "E-waste is just one profitable coping mechanism for rural China."

E-waste sweatshops often sit in secluded areas off the street. Inside are migrant workers, usually women, stripping wires, banging circuits, and disassembling broken motors. Workers say the average salary for sweatshop work is $3 to $4 per day for men, and about half that for women.

"The law has no effect here," says He Hai, who smuggled circuit boards to Guiyu as the e-waste boom took off. "Everyone here gets money from this kind of thing, so no one can afford to let it stop."

Hai says bribery is prevalent, as is intimidation. "Everything seems peaceful, but this place is very dangerous," he says. "The migrant workers fear the local people will beat them if they talk about it to anyone."

This is the underbelly of China's economic boom.

"The more developed areas won't do it," says Zhao Jun, who migrated to Guiyu twelve years ago as a teenager to work in e-waste. "This area was so poor, and it was hard to grow rice, so about a decade ago people began picking up rubbish to look for valuables. Gradually, they realized computer rubbish is better than other rubbish and started getting into e-waste. When I came, it was a one-story village with all dirt roads; now it's a city with big buildings and rich people."

Local residents got rich scouring the trash and brought in migrants to start scouring it for them. "The most dangerous and hardest jobs they give to the migrant workers," says Jun. "The locals who used to do the e-waste work are now wealthy e-waste bosses."

James Songqing is one such boss. His office is in a large building that makes up part of the new Juiyu skyline. He sits on his posh furniture next to a buddy holding a slingshot. Young women enter to pour them tea as Chinese soap operas play in the background.

Since my guide warned me that e-waste bosses want to keep all journalists out and would even kill me if they knew what I was doing, I pretend I'm interested in buying ten tons of bronze a month for a South African company.

"It is outside," Songqing says. On his front patio lie about two tons of untreated bronze in large white sacks. It sells for $1.50 a kilo, he says. "It takes me two weeks to produce twenty tons of the stuff."

By my calculations, his street-side sweatshop is making upwards of $30,000 per month in profit.

Hai does not approve of this trade. "It's in the interests of our country to stop e-waste," he says. "We should stop e-waste altogether because it is foreign countries' rubbish."

Sound computer recycling programs are available. But, given the volume of e-waste produced each year, domestic reuse and recycling is wishful thinking for the time being.

Computers are not built to be recycled, environmentalists say, and their dismantling is extremely dangerous, labor-intensive, and costly.

The Computer TakeBack Campaign seeks to pressure "consumer electronics manufacturers and brand owners to take full responsibility for the lifecycle of their products." The groups in the campaign call on consumers to use their buying power to promote greater corporate responsibility, computer recycling, and a reduction in hazardous e-waste.

Outside the United States, there have been some successes. In May of 2001, the European Union adopted a directive that requires producers of electronics to take financial responsibility for the recovery and recycling of e-waste and to phase out the use of hazardous materials.

But reforms are lagging in the United States. "Brand owners and manufacturers in the U.S. have dodged their responsibility for management of products at the end of their useful life, while public policy has failed to promote producer take back, clean design, and clean production," says the Computer TakeBack Campaign.

We head back to the river to thank Chang. He is meandering on top of crumbled, smoking circuit boards, in a burning pile of e-waste. Chang must work late. He competes with eight other migrants, and he has a month-old baby.

We try to ask him more about his life, but his tune has changed. He is tight-lipped, redder in the face, unyielding. He gets frustrated immediately and says he has to go.

"I don't care for these questions of health and responsibility," he says. "Life is better here because I can get more money."

He turns away from us, coughs a bit, and bikes home along the banks of the Lianjiang River.

BENJAMIN JOFFE-WALT is a freelance writer based in South Africa. Research for this article was supported by a grant from the Fund for Investigative Journalism, Inc.

Cat and Mouse, on the Web

Techniques to evade censorship of internet traffic are improving, to the chagrin of authoritarian regimes

For a website lashed together in a week by a college student, Anonymouse.org is not to be sniffed at. Alexander Pircher, a computer-science student in Darmstadt, Germany, created the site in 1997. Users simply type a web address into a box on the Anonymouse home page and click a button, and the Anonymouse server (rather than the user's own computer) fetches the page and displays it. To many people this might seem pointless: rerouting data through another server makes for slower surfing, fonts and graphics are sometimes slightly skewed and video may not work properly.

But for many others the manoeuvre is anything but pointless, for this redirection allows them to surf the web anonymously. It enables people living under repressive regimes to visit censored websites because, technically speaking, they are only visiting Anonymouse.org. More than 3 million people access the web through Anonymouse.org every day and Mr Pircher, who now upgrades his software with help from friends, says he receives plenty of thank-you messages from censorship-dodgers in countries like Cuba, Iran, North Korea and Saudi Arabia. "We're bringing people the Universal Declaration of Human Rights," he says, referring to Article 19 of the United Nations document, which says freedom of information is a fundamental right.

Anonymouse.org is not alone. It is part of a large and growing constellation of similar computer servers, known as proxies, put online for the most part by activists living in free countries. These proxy servers play a central role in the global struggle to outsmart censors working to protect undemocratic regimes from political and social dissent. Mokhtar Yahyaoui, a lawyer in Tunisia, says that in his country proxies "are pretty much the only way to get information that's not official government information."

But censors have an effective countermeasure. Once they identify a proxy, they can block access to it, just as they block access to other sites. The difficult part is finding the proxies, but the software used by censors, called censorware, is getting better at it. China's censors are leading the way. The estimated 30,000 government censors behind the world's most elaborate censorship programme—known as the Great Firewall of China by detractors, and as the Golden Shield by the Communist Party—work hard to hunt down proxies and prevent them from relaying data into the country.

The anti-censorship community is developing new ways to evade censors in response. For example, when China blocks a proxy (Anonymouse.org's fate in that country), internet users can find a replacement by consulting a growing number of websites that compile and post lists of working proxies. E-mailed newsletters that provide links to proxy servers are also available. Some anti-censorship organisations spread the word via instant-messaging services: people looking for a proxy simply send an instant message to one of these groups and immediately receive an automated reply with a recently updated list of proxies.

These methods work because it usually takes censors a little while to identify and block new proxies. China's censors are probably the fastest to react, but even then some proxies survive for a week or more, in part because the firewall is maintained by a complex network of private and state-controlled telecommunications operators, and national, provincial and municipal government agencies that don't always act in concert. Lesser-known proxies handling small amounts of traffic generally go undetected the longest, sometimes for months. "It's a game called cat and rat," says Mao Xianghui, a partner in an investment firm in Shanghai. His blog provided advice on using proxies to sidestep censorship, until authorities shut it down last year.

An American non-profit group called Tor operates one of the most robust anti-censorship systems. Using money provided by America's Naval Research Laboratory and the Electronic Frontier Foundation, a free-speech advocacy group, Tor developed free software that can be downloaded from many websites. The software works in conjunction with a web browser (the developers recommend Firefox) to encrypt traffic and route it through three proxy servers chosen at random from a network of around 1,000 proxies run by Tor volunteers worldwide. This makes it difficult for censors to determine what information is being sent, where it came from, and who received it. A Tor spokeswoman says many human-rights groups advise their activists in authoritarian countries to use the software to avoid government snooping.

This is not the only tool available to activists. In June of last year Huang Qi, an outspoken human-rights activist from Chengdu, China, was released after serving five years in prison on charges of subversion. He promptly downloaded a free "circumvention" programme that had been developed during his detention. Now, when Mr Huang opens his browser, the software, called Wujie, automatically searches the internet until it locates a functioning proxy server through which to connect. "It opens the doors to the world," he says.

Censorship firewalls rely heavily on keyword-blocking software, which can catch and block e-mails and instant messages containing words and phrases deemed dangerous. Bill Xia, a Chinese dissident living in North Carolina, employs a number of tricks to sneak words past censors. He is the founder of Dynamic Internet Technology, a company paid by the American government's International Broadcasting Bureau to e-mail more than 2 million pro-democracy Voice of America and Radio Free Asia newsletters into China and Vietnam every day.

To foil keyword filters, Mr Xia replaces sensitive words such as "freedom" and "elections" with uncommon or approximate synonyms, or descriptive phrases. He inserts random characters, such as asterisks, between Vietnamese letters or the ideograms that make up Chinese words. Other techniques include writing words in a mixture of several fonts, replacing parts of words with syllables that sound similar, and replacing words with pictures of those words.

Employing such ruses makes for tedious writing and choppy reading. And having to bother with proxy servers to surf the web can be a hassle. But for those who are victims of censorship, the increasingly elaborate efforts required to outmanoeuvre censors are liberating, empowering and well worth the effort.

The Digital Divide

In Search of a PC for the People

The race is on to serve "the next billion" in emerging markets. Whose low-cost model will win?

BRUCE EINHORN

In Silicon Valley, "the next billion" is shorthand for the vast potential market in the developing world, where few people have access to PCs. For Mark J. Beckford, it's almost an obsession. The 39-year-old Intel Corp. general manager has spent most of the past decade trying to create computers for that next billion. From his office in Shanghai, he oversees a team of about two dozen engineers in China, Brazil, Egypt, and India, all designing PCs suited to the needs and wallets of customers in emerging markets. "The next billion isn't going to come by pushing the same things," he says. "It requires new levels of affordability, access methods, ease of use, connectivity, and power."

These days lots of companies are trying to serve that same billion. Intel's biggest rival, Advanced Micro Devices Inc., is working on various possibilities, including a PC in India that sells for about $200. Taiwan's VIA Technologies Inc., the world's No. 3 designer of microprocessors, has launched a business group focusing on low-cost computers for emerging markets. Microsoft Corp. in late May introduced a low-cost solution. And Nicholas Negroponte, a professor at Massachusetts Institute of Technology, is leading a group called One Laptop Per Child, which aims to produce a machine for $140 or so by yearend, and as little as $50 by 2010. "I think of digital access for kids as a human right," Negroponte said in an e-mail interview.

But as they target emerging markets, the world's info-tech powers are grappling with a host of difficult issues. How do you design a PC that's affordable to almost anyone? What traditional features do you ditch to do that? Will users in developing countries be satisfied with these computers, or will they resent the idea of getting dumbed-down machines? Do they want global brands, or are they happy to accept no-name alternatives?

Leaner and Greener

Just about everybody agrees selling computers in the developing world is more complex than simply adding Mandarin, Hindi, or Arabic software to existing PCs. In many places, PCs must withstand desert heat and sand—and cope with frequent electricity outages. That requires more rugged designs that are also energy-efficient. "In emerging markets we see a huge appetite for PCs," says Richard Brown, a VIA vice-president who heads the new PC-1 business unit, set up early this year to sell computers in developing countries. "But they need to be smaller, cooler, quieter, and greener."

Microsoft, meanwhile, has come up not with computers, but with an innovative way to finance them. On May 22, the software giant announced FlexGo, software that keeps machines from working until users type in a number from a pre-paid card. The idea is that consumers in developing countries, who might not be able to shell out $500 or more in one go, can afford perhaps half the cost of a PC up front, then pay for the actual hours they use the machine via the cards. After a certain number of hours—and payments—the computer becomes the property of the consumer. In the developing world, computers are "simply out of reach for people who would like a PC in the home," says Will Poole, senior vice-president of Microsoft's Market Expansion Group. "What do we do to change the equation?"

Most companies are seeking to solve that equation through innovative design. For instance, Intel in March launched its "Community PC," targeted at Indian villages where those who can't afford computers of their own share a common machine. The Community PC, which costs about $550, has a filter to keep out dust, can run on a car battery when blackouts occur, and is equipped with a one-button "recover" feature in case of crashes. Also in March, Intel introduced a $250 to $350 miniaturized desktop computer (with the clunky name of Low Cost Full Featured PC); Mexican officials have ordered 400,000 for delivery by November. And the company in May revealed a prototype of a new notebook called the ClassMate PC that carries a price tag below $400.

Designing machines for developing countries can be taxing for engineers accustomed to building PCs from off-the-shelf, commodity parts. "Before, it was just cut and paste, follow the guidelines," says Kent Geeng, president of iDot Computers Inc.,

Laptops for All

More low-cost computers are being developed for emerging markets

INTEL

Has hardy "Community PCs" for India, systems for Net cafes in China, and the ClassMate, a $400 notebook for students.

MICROSOFT

On May 22, the software giant announced a pay-as-you-go computer for low- and middle-income countries.

AMD

Offers a PC in India with local partner HCL for around $200. Also sells the low-cost Personal Internet Communicator.

VIA

This Taiwanese chipmaker is building PCs powered by car batteries or solar cells, with sand-resistant cases for use in Africa.

One Laptop Per Child

Founded by Nicholas Negroponte of MIT's Media Lab, this nonprofit aims to build a laptop for $100 or less.

which designs VIA's low-cost PCs. To reach the target price of $230, his engineers had to start from scratch. "A cost-effective machine is much more difficult than doing the high end," says Geeng. "It's like building a Nissan to drive at the same speed as a Porsche."

That's just what bothers some critics, who don't believe people in poor countries need to compute at Autobahn speeds. Stephen Dukker, who founded low-cost computing pioneer eMachines Inc. in 1998, now runs Seoul-based Ncomputing Ltd. His goal is to sell not PCs but "thin clients," diskless machines that work only if connected to a server. Since a single PC can run 10 of these devices, schools and libraries in impoverished areas could get computers in front of many more people far more cheaply than by buying actual PCs for everyone. Dukker's device—little more than a chip surrounded by plastic—costs just $70 or so. "Why are we trying to force people to use a computing technology that's not appropriate for them?" says Dukker.

Do Third World users need to compute at Autobahn speeds?

PC alternatives, though, don't have a great track record. Oracle Corp. and Sun Microsystems Inc. tried to push thin clients in the late 1990s, without much success. Negroponte has attracted a lot of attention, but skeptics say that children—and their parents—may not really want a machine that cheap. "You have a low-cost device, but it's very limited," says Beckford's colleague, Intel Vice-President Bill M. Siu.

The real demand, says Microsoft's Poole, is for "a solid, midrange PC." With so many companies targeting emerging markets, there's a lot riding on the right answer.

With Jay Greene, in Seattle and Peter Burrows, in San Mateo, Calif.

UNIT 8
The Frontier of Computing

Unit Selections

Key Points to Consider

- 2003 marked the 30th anniversary of the publication of an essay entitled "Animals, Men and Morals" by Peter Singer in the *New York Review of Books.* This essay is often credited with beginning the animal rights movement. Singer argues that because animals have feelings, they can suffer. Because they can suffer, they have interests. Because they have interests, it is unethical to conduct experiments on them. Suppose scientists succeed in developing machines that feel pain and fear. What obligations will we have towards them? If this is difficult to imagine, watch the movie *Blade Runner* with Harrison Ford. What do you think now?

- The overview to this unit says that the dollar value of the output of the meat and poultry industries exceeds the dollar value of the output of the computer industry. The overview mentions one reason why we hear so much more about software than chickens. Can you think of others?

- Suppose you were provided with a robot whose task is to filter spam from your e-mail. Now suppose you are provided with a real secretary to do the same task. Both of these assistants will make judgment calls. That is, based on what you have told them, each will make best guesses as to whether e-mail is spam or not. How do you feel about your robot making the occasional error? How do you feel about your secretary making a mistake?

- Professor Turkle's disturbing question is quoted in the To The Reader section of this book: "Are you really you if you have a baboon's heart inside, had your face resculpted by Brazil's finest plastic surgeons, and are taking Zoloft to give you a competitive edge." Are you?

- What is a digital certificate? Who issues them and what are they used for? See if you can find out what digital certificates are on your computer and where they came from.

Student Web Site
www.mhcls.com/online

Internet References
Further information regarding these Web sites may be found in this book's preface or online.

Introduction to Artificial Intelligence (AI)
http://www-formal.stanford.edu/jmc/aiintro/aiintro.html
Kasparov vs. Deep Blue: The Rematch
http://www.chess.ibm.com/home/html/b.html
PHP-Nuke Powered Site: International Society for Artificial Life
http://alife.org/

According to U.S. Census Bureau statistics not long ago, the output of the meat and poultry industry was worth more than the output of the computer and software industries. Though this is not exactly a fair comparison—computers are used to build still other products—it does get at something significant about computers: they figure more importantly in our imaginations than they do in the economy. Why is this? Part of the answer has to do with who forms opinions in developed nations. The computer is an indispensable tool for people who staff the magazine, newspaper, publishing and education sectors. If meat packers were the opinion makers, we might get a different sense of what is important. Recall "Five Things We Need to Know about Technological Change." Postman says that "Embedded in every technology there is a powerful idea . . . . To a person with a computer, everything looks like data."

We can concede Postman's point but still insist that there is something special about computing. Before computers became a household appliance, it was common for programmers and users alike to attribute humanlike properties to them. Joseph Weizenbaum, developer of Eliza in the 1970's, a program that simulated a Rogerian psychotherapist, became a severe critic of certain kinds of computing research, in part, because he noticed that staff in his lab had begun to arrive early to ask advice from the program. In 1956 a group of mathematicians interested in computing gathered at Dartmouth College and coined the term "Artificial Intelligence." AI, whose goal is to build into machines something that we can recognize as intelligent behavior, has become perhaps the best-known and most criticized area of computer science. Since intelligent behavior, like the ability to read and form arguments, is often thought to be the defining characteristic of humankind (we call ourselves "homo sapiens," after all), machines that might exhibit intelligent behavior have occupied the dreams and nightmares of western culture for hundreds of years.

All of our ambiguous feelings about technology are congealed in robots. The term itself is surprisingly venerable, having been invented by the Czech playwright Karel Copek in 1921. They can be loveable like R2D2 from *Star Wars* or Robbie from *The Forbidden Planet* of a generation earlier. They can be forbidding but loyal, like Gort from *The Day the Earth Stood Still.* They can even be outfitted with logical safety mechanisms that render them harmless to humans. This last, an invention of Isaac Asimov in *I, Robot,* is a good thing, too, since so many of our robotic imaginings look like *The Terminator.* Sherry Turkle of MIT has been studying the relationship between humans and their machines for twenty years. In "A Nascent Robotics Culture," she asks the jarring question, "What is a robot kind of love?"

Though robots don't figure beyond the clever title in "March of the Robolawyers," the article itself describes a novel application of game theory to family law, specifically to how divorcing cou-

Photodisc Collection/Getty Images

ples divide their property. The software encourages couples to rank items they most want in a settlement. Developers have found that by using the software, each party ends up with 70–80% of what he or she originally wanted, rather than the strict 50% split of all items. For those interested in a more aggressive approach, the developer has another program that models what happens in bitterly contested divorces. Plaintiffs "generally diminish their prospects of getting what they want."

As mentioned in the overview to Unit 7, the development of public-key cryptography in the late seventies was a significant achievement in computer science. Since classical times, cryptographers have grappled with a serious weak point in any cryptographic system. Suppose Alice encrypts a message and sends it to Bob. She also needs to send Bob instructions, known as the key, telling him how to decrypt the message. Since the key can be intercepted, this is a problem. In the late seventies, a Stanford engineer and an itinerant mathematician developed a mechanism that avoids it. Called public-key cryptography, it is used to encrypt the secret key Alice must send to Bob, and this can be done without risk of *that* encrypting key being intercepted. If all this seems a little obscure, look at your browser the next time you purchase something on-line. The web address should begin with *https,* indicating that it is making use of public-key techniques to encrypt your credit card number.

Thirty years is a long time in computing, and public-key systems are beginning to show their age. The much-awaited quantum computers could have the capacity to break public-key encryption systems. But if quantum computers arrive, quantum cryptography will have arrived too. Read the fascinating "Best-Kept Secrets" from *Scientific American* to learn how researchers are using principles of quantum mechanics to develop the next generation of cryptographic systems.

As I write this introduction, researchers from around the world are preparing for GECCO 2007, the Genetic Algorithm and Computation Conference to be held in London. In the mid-seventies, John Holland, at the University of Michigan, proposed a mechanism for problem solving based loosely on the idea of Darwinian natural selection. Since that time researchers have use genetic algorithms, as Holland called them, to solve problems too difficult to be solved using conventional computing techniques. The genetic algorithm is one of several computing techniques based on a "paradigm that draws on the principles of self-organization of complex systems." The article, "Toward Nature-Inspired Computing," is an excellent introduction.

For a more nuts and bolts view of what is to come, read "The Intelligent Internet." Here, among many other sources, you will learn that the Internet will be the "main method used in 30 percent of courses" by 2014. The final article, "Mind Control," describes how advanced software enables quadriplegics to play video games. The next step is to develop robot soldiers controlled by the thoughts of real soldiers far from the battle front. Though one should take these predictions and inventions with a grain of salt—futurists in the 60's thought we would all be commuting in levitated automobiles by now—they give a sense of the excitement that surrounds computing.

Robots, quantum cryptography, processors embedded in the brain, the articles in this unit have ranged widely but with this common theme: none of the technologies described are fully formed and, more to the point, their impact on society has not been large. Computing history is filled with bad predictions. Perhaps the most spectacularly wrong prediction is widely attributed to Thomas Watson, head of IBM, who in 1943 is reputed to have said, "I think there is a world market for maybe five computers." But there have been many, many other predictions or questions. Will robots get no further than furbies? Will the distance limitations of quantum cryptography not be overcome? Will captured electroencephalograms get stuck at the pong-playing stage? It is hard to know. But no one wants to be the next Thomas Watson.

A Nascent Robotics Culture
New Complicities for Companionship

Encounters with humanoid robots are new to the everyday experience of children and adults. Yet, increasingly, they are finding their place. This has occurred largely through the introduction of a class of interactive toys (including Furbies, AIBOs, and My Real Babies) that I call "relational artifacts." Here, I report on several years of fieldwork with commercial relational artifacts (as well as with the MIT AI Laboratory's Kismet and Cog). It suggests that even these relatively primitive robots have been accepted as companionate objects and are changing the terms by which people judge the "appropriateness" of machine relationships. In these relationships, robots serve as powerful objects of psychological projection and philosophical evocation in ways that are forging a nascent robotics culture.

SHERRY TURKLE

Introduction

The designers of computational objects have traditionally focused on how these objects might extend and/or perfect human cognitive powers. But computational objects do not simply do things *for* us, they do things *to* us as people, to our ways of being the world, to our ways of seeing ourselves and others (Turkle 2005[1984], 1995). Increasingly, technology also puts itself into a position to do things *with* us, particularly with the introduction of "relational artifacts," here defined as technologies that have "states of mind" and where encounters with them are enriched through understanding these inner states (Turkle 2004a, 2004b). Otherwise described as "sociable machines (Breazeal 2000, 2002, Breazeal and Scasselati 1999, 2000, Kidd 2004), the term relational artifact evokes the psychoanalytic tradition with its emphasis on the meaning of the person/machine encounter.

In the late 1970s and early 1980s, children's style of programming reflected their personality and cognitive style. And computational objects such as Merlin, Simon, and Speak and Spell provoked questions about the quality of aliveness and about what is special about being a person. (Turkle 2005[1984]) Twenty years later, children and seniors confronting relational artifacts as simple as Furbies, AIBOs and My Real Babies (Turkle 2004a) or as complex as the robots Kismet and Cog (Turkle et al. 2004) were similarly differentiated in their style of approach and

similarly provoked to ask fundamental questions about the objects' natures.

Children approach a Furby or a My Real Baby and explore what it means to think of these creatures as alive or "sort of alive"; elders in a nursing play with the robot Paro and grapple with how to characterize this creature that presents itself as a baby seal (Taggart, W. et al. 2005, Shibata 1999, 2005). They move from inquiries such as "Does it swim?" and "Does it eat?" to "Is it alive?" and "Can it love?"[1]

These similarities across the decades are not surprising. Encounters with novel computational objects present people with category-challenging experiences. The objects are liminal, betwixt—and between, provoking new thought. (Turner 1969; Bowker and Star 1999). However, there are significant differences between current responses to relational artifacts and earlier encounters with computation. Children first confronting computer toys in the late 1970s and early 1980s were compelled to classification. Faced with relational artifacts, children's questions about classification are enmeshed in a new desire to *nurture and be nurtured by* the artifacts rather than simply categorize them; in their dialogue with relational artifacts, children's focus shifts from cognition to affect, from game playing to fantasies of mutual connection. In the case of relational artifacts for children and the elderly, nurturance is the new "killer app." We attach to what we nurture (Turkle 2004, 2005b).

We Attach to What We Nurture

In *Computer Power and Human Reason,* Joseph Weizenbaum wrote about his experiences with his invention, ELIZA, a computer program that seemed to serve as self object as it engaged people in a dialogue similar to that of a Rogerian psychotherapist (1976). It mirrored one's thoughts; it was always supportive. To the comment: "My mother is making me angry," the program might respond, "Tell me more about your mother," or "Why do you feel so negatively about your mother." Weizenbaum was disturbed that his students, fully knowing that they were talking with a computer program, wanted to chat with it, indeed, wanted to be alone with it. Weizenbaum was my colleague at MIT at the time; we taught courses together on computers and society. And at the time that his book came out, I felt moved to reassure him. ELIZA seemed to me like a Rorschach through which people expressed themselves. They became involved with ELIZA, but the spirit was "as if." The gap between program and person was vast. People bridged it with attribution and desire. They thought: "I will talk to this program 'as if' it were a person; I will vent, I will rage, I will get things off my chest." At the time, ELIZA, seemed to me no more threatening than an interactive diary. Now, thirty years later, I ask myself if I had underestimated the quality of the connection.

A newer technology has created computational creatures that evoke a sense of mutual relating. The people who meet relational artifacts feel a desire to nurture them. And with nurturance comes the fantasy of reciprocation. They wanted the creatures to care about them in return. Very little about these relationships seemed to be experienced "as if." The experience of "as if" had morphed into one of treating robots "as though." The story of computers and their evocation of life had come to a new place.

Children have always anthropomorphized the dolls in their nurseries. It is important to note a difference in what can occur with relational artifacts. In the past, the power of objects to "play house" or "play cowboys" with a child has been tied to the ways in which they enabled the child to project meanings onto them. They were stable "transitional objects." (Winnicott 1971) The doll or the teddy bear presented an unchanging and passive presence. But today's relational artifacts take a decidedly more active stance. With them, children's expectations that their dolls want to be hugged, dressed, or lulled to sleep don't only come from the child's projection of fantasy or desire onto inert playthings, but from such things as the digital dolls' crying inconsolably or even saying: "Hug me!" or "It's time for me to get dressed for school!" *In the move from traditional transitional objects to contemporary rela-*

tional artifacts, the psychology of projection gives way to a relational psychology, a psychology of engagement. Yet, old habits of projection remain: robotic creatures become enhanced in their capacities to enact scenarios in which robots are Rorschachs, projective screens for individual concerns.

From the perspective of several decades of observing people relating to computational creatures, I see an evolution of sensibilities.

- Through the 1980s, people became deeply involved with computational objects—even the early computer toys became objects for profound projection and engagement. Yet, when faced with the issue of the objects' affective possibilities, a modal response might be summed up as "Simulated thinking may be thinking; simulated feeling is never feeling. Simulated love is never love.

- Through the 1990s, the development of a "culture of simulation" brought the notion of simulation (largely through participation in intensive game spaces) into the everyday. The range and possibilities of simulation became known to large numbers of people, particularly young people.

- By the late 1990s, the image of the robot was changing in the culture. A robotics presence was developing into a robotics culture increasingly shaped by the possibility if not the reality of robots in the form of relational artifacts. Alongside a tool model, people are learning about a notion of cyber-companionship. Acceptance of this notion requires a revisiting of old notions of simulation to make way for a kind of companionship that feels appropriate to a robot/person relationship.

The Evolution of Sensibilities: Two Moments

A first moment: I take my fourteen-year-old daughter to the Darwin exhibit at the American Museum of Natural History. The exhibit documents Darwin's life and thought, and with a somewhat defensive tone (in light of current challenges to evolution by proponents of intelligent design), presents the theory of evolution as the central truth that underpins contemporary biology. The Darwin exhibit wants to convince and it wants to please. At the entrance to the exhibit is a turtle from the Galapagos Islands, a seminal object in the development of evolutionary theory. The turtle rests in its cage, utterly still. "They could have used a robot," comments my daughter. She considers it a shame to bring the turtle all this way and put it in a cage for a performance that draws so little on the turtle's "aliveness." I am startled by her comments, both solicitous of the imprisoned turtle because it is alive and unconcerned about its authenticity. The museum has been advertising these turtles as wonders, curiosities, marvels—among the plastic models of life at the museum, here is the life that Darwin saw. I begin to talk with others at the exhibit, parents and children. It is Thanksgiving weekend. The line is long, the crowd frozen in place. My question, "Do you care that the turtle is alive?" is welcome diversion. A ten-year-old girl would prefer a robot turtle because aliveness comes with aesthetic inconvenience: "its water looks dirty. Gross." More usually, votes for the robots echo my daughter's sentiment that in this setting, aliveness doesn't seem worth the trouble. A twelve-year-old girl opines: "For what the turtles do, you didn't have to have the live ones." Her father looks at her, uncomprehending: "But the point is that they are real, that's the whole point."

The Darwin exhibit gives authenticity major play: on display are the actual magnifying glass that Darwin used, the actual notebooks in which he recorded his observations, indeed, the very notebook in which he wrote the famous sentences that first described his theory of evolution *But in the children's reactions to the inert but alive Galapagos turtle, the idea of the "original" is in crisis.* I recall my daughter's reaction when she was seven to a boat ride in the postcard blue Mediterranean. Already an expert in the world of simulated fish tanks, she saw a creature in the water, pointed to it excitedly and said: "Look mommy, a jellyfish! It looks so realistic!" When I told this story to a friend who was a research scientist at the Walt Disney Company, he was not surprised. When Animal Kingdom opened in Orlando, populated by "real," that is, biological animals, its first visitors complained that these animals were not as "realistic" as the animatronic creatures in Disney World, just across the road. The robotic crocodiles slapped their tails, rolled their eyes, in sum, displayed "essence of crocodile" behavior. The biological crocodiles, like the Galapagos turtle, pretty much kept to themselves. What is the gold standard here?

I have written that now, in our culture of simulation, the notion of authenticity is for us what sex was to the Victorians—"threat and obsession, taboo and fascination" (Turkle, 2005[1984]). I have lived with this idea for many years, yet at the museum, I find the children's position strangely unsettling. For them, in this context, aliveness seems to have no intrinsic value. Rather, it is useful only if needed for a specific purpose. "If you put in a robot instead of the live turtle, do you think people should be told that the turtle is not alive?" I ask. Not really, say several of the children. Data on "aliveness" can be shared on

a "need to know" basis, for a purpose. But what *are* the purposes of living things? When do we need to know if something is alive?

A second moment: an older woman, 72, in a nursing home outside of Boston is sad. Her son has broken off his relationship with her. Her nursing home is part of a study I am conducting on robotics for the elderly. I am recording her reactions as she sits with the robot Paro, a seal-like creature, advertised as the first "therapeutic robot" for its ostensibly positive effects on the ill, the elderly, and the emotionally troubled. Paro is able to make eye contact through sensing the direction of a human voice, is sensitive to touch, and has "states of mind" that are affected by how it is treated—for example, it can sense if it is being stroked gently or with some aggressivity. In this session with Paro, the woman, depressed because of her son's abandonment, comes to believe that the robot is depressed as well. She turns to Paro, strokes him and says: "Yes, you're sad, aren't you. It's tough out there. Yes, it's hard." And then she pets the robot once again, attempting to provide it with comfort. And in so doing, she tries to comfort herself.

Psychoanalytically trained, I believe that this kind of moment, if it happens between people, has profound therapeutic potential. What are we to make of this transaction as it unfolds between a depressed woman and a robot? When I talk to others about the old woman's encounter with Paro, their first associations are usually to their pets and the solace they provide. The comparison sharpens the questions about Paro and the quality of the relationships people have with it. I do not know if the projection of understanding onto pets is "authentic." That is, I do not know whether a pet could feel or smell or intuit some understanding of what it might mean to be with an old woman whose son has chosen not to see her anymore. What I do know is that Paro has understood nothing. Like other "relational artifacts" its ability to inspire relationship is not based on its intelligence or consciousness, but on the capacity to push certain "Darwinian" buttons in people (making eye contact, for example) that cause people to respond *as though* they were in relationship. For me, relational artifacts are the new uncanny in our computer culture, as Freud (1960) put it, "the long familiar taking a form that is strangely unfamiliar."

Confrontation with the uncanny provokes new reflection. Do plans to provide relational robots to children and the elderly make us less likely to look for other solutions for their care? If our experience with relational artifacts is based on a fundamentally deceitful interchange (artifacts' ability to persuade us that they know and care about our existence) can it be good for us? Or might it be good for us in the "feel good" sense, but bad for us in our lives as moral beings? The answers to such questions are not dependent on what computers can do today or what they are likely to be able to do in the future. These questions ask what *we* will be like, what kind of people are *we* becoming as we develop increasingly intimate relationships with machines.

Rorschach and Evocation

We can get some first answers by looking at the relationship of people—here I describe fieldwork with children and seniors—with these new intimate machines. In these relationship it is clear that the distinction between people using robots for projection of self (as Rorschach) and using robots as philosophically evocative objects, is only heuristic. They work together: children and seniors develop philosophical positions that are inseparable from their emotional needs. Affect and cognition work together in the subjective response to relational technologies. This is dramatized by a series of case studies, first of children, then of seniors, in which the "Rorschach effect" and the "evocative object effect" are entwined.[2]

Case Studies of Children

I begin with a child Orelia, ten, whose response to the robot AIBO serves as commentary on her relationship to her mother, a self-absorbed woman who during her several sessions with her daughter and the robot does not touch, speak, or make eye contact with her daughter. One might say that Orelia's mother acts robotically and the daughter's response is to emphasize the importance and irreducibility of the human heart. In a life characterized by maternal chill, Orelia stressed warmth and intuition as ultimate human values.

Orelia: Keeping a Robot In Its Place

I met Orelia at a private Boston-area middle school where we were holding group sessions of fifth graders with a range of robotic toys. Orelia received an AIBO to take home; she kept a robot "diary." We met several times with Orelia and her parents in their Charlestown home. (Turkle 2004a)

Orelia is bright and articulate and tells us that her favorite hobby is reading. She makes determined distinctions between robots and biological beings. "AIBO is not alive like a real pet; it does not breathe." There is no question in her mind that she would choose a real dog over an AIBO. She believes that AIBO can love but only because "it is programmed to." She continues: "If [robots] love, then it's artificial love. [And] if it's an artificial love, then there really isn't anything true . . . I'm sure it would be programmed to [show that it likes you], you know, the computer inside of it telling it to show artificial love, but it doesn't love you."

Orelia is sure that she could never love an AIBO. "They [robots] won't love you back if you love them. In order to love an AIBO, Orelia says it would need "a brain and a heart." Orelia feels that it is not worth investing in something that does not have the capacity to love back, a construction that is perhaps as much about the robot as about her relationship with her mother.

Orelia's brother Jake, nine, the baby of the family, is more favored in his mother's eyes. Unlike his sister, Jake assumes that AIBO has feelings. Orelia speaks to the researchers *about* AIBO; Jake addresses AIBO directly. He wants to stay on AIBO's good side, asking, "Will he get mad if you pick him up?" When Jake's style of addressing AIBO reveals that Jake finds the robot's affective states genuine, Orelia corrects her brother sharply: "It [AIBO] would just be mad at you because it's programmed to know 'if I don't get the ball, I'll be mad.'" The fact that AIBO is programmed to show emotions, make these artificial and not to be trusted.

Orelia expands on real versus programmed emotion:

A dog, it would actually feel sorry for you. It would have sympathy, but AIBO, it's artificial. I read a book called *The Wrinkle in Time,* where everyone was programmed by this thing called "It." And all the people were completely on routine. They just did the same thing over and over. I think it'd be the same thing with the [artificial] dog. The dog wouldn't be able to do anything else.

For Orelia, only living beings have real thoughts and emotions:

With a real dog if you become great friends with it, it really loves you, you know, it truly . . . has a brain, and you know somewhere in the dog's brain, it loves you, and this one [AIBO], it's just somewhere on a computer disk . . . If a real dog dies, you know, they have memories, a real dog would have memories of times, and stuff that you did with him or her, but this one [AIBO] doesn't have a brain, so it can't.

Orelia wants the kind of love that only a living creature can provide. She fears the ability of any creature to behave 'as if' it could love. She denies a chilly emotional reality by attributing qualities of intuition, transparency, and connectedness to all people and animals. A philosophical position about robots is linked to an experience of the machine-like equalities of which people are capable, a good example of the interdependence of philosophical position and psychological motivation.

Melanie: Yearning to Nurture a Robotic Companion

The quality of a child's relationship with a parent does not determine a *particular* relationship to robotic companions. Rather, feelings about robots can represent different strategies for dealing with one's parents, and perhaps for working through difficulties with them. This is illustrated by the contrast between Orelia and ten-year-old Melanie. Melanie, like Orelia, had sessions with AIBO and My Real Baby at school and was given both to play with at home. In Melanie's case, feelings that she did not have enough of her parent's attention led her to want to nurture a robotic creature. Melanie was able to feel more loved by loving another; the My Real Baby and AIBO were "creature enough" for this purpose.

Melanie is soft-spoken, intelligent, and well mannered. Both of her parents have busy professional lives; Melanie is largely taken care of by nannies and baby-sitters. With sadness, she says that what she misses most is spending time with her father. She speaks of him throughout her interviews and play sessions. Nurturing the robots enables her to work through feelings that her parents, and her father in particular, are not providing her with the attention she desires.

Melanie believes that AIBO and My Real Baby are sentient and have emotions. She thinks that when we brought the robotic dog and doll to her school "they were probably confused about who their mommies and daddies were because they were being handled by so many different people." She thinks that AIBO probably does not know that he is at her particular school because the school is strange to him, but "almost certainly does knows that he is outside of MIT and visiting another school." She sees her role with the robots as straightforward; it is maternal.

One of Melanie's third-grade classmates is aggressive with My Real Baby and treats the doll like an object to explore (poking the doll's eyes, pinching its skin to test its "rubberness," and putting her fingers roughly inside its mouth). Observing this behavior, Melanie comes over to rescue the doll. She takes it in her arms and proceeds to play with it as though it were a baby, holding it close, whispering to it, caressing its face. Speaking of the My Real Baby doll that she is about to take home, Melanie says, "I think that if I'm the first one to interact with her then maybe if she goes home with another person [another study participant] she'll cry a lot . . . because she doesn't know, doesn't think that this person is its Mama." For Melanie, My Real Baby's aliveness is dependent on its animation and relational properties. Its lack of biology is not in play. Melanie understands that My Real Baby is a machine. This is clear in her description of its possible "death."

Hum, if his batteries run out, maybe [it could die]. I think it's electric. So, if it falls and breaks, then it would die, but if people could repair it, then I'm not really sure. [I]f it falls and like totally shatters I don't think they could fix it, then it would die, but if it falls and one of its ear falls off, they would probably fix that.

Melanie combines a mechanical view of My Real Baby with confidence that it deserves to have her motherly love. At home, Melanie has AIBO and My Real Baby sleep near her bed and believes they will be happiest on a silk pillow. She names My Real Baby after her three-year old cousin Sophie. "I named her like my cousin . . . because she [My Real Baby] was sort of demanding and said most of the things that Sophie does." She analogies the AIBO to her dog, Nelly. When AIBO malfunctions, Melanie does not experience it as broken, but as behaving in ways that remind her of Nelly. In the following exchange that takes place at MIT, AIBO makes a loud, mechanical, wheezing sound and its walking becomes increasingly wobbly. Finally AIBO falls several times and then finally is still. Melanie gently picks up the limp AIBO and holds it close, petting it softly. At home, she and a friend treat it like a sick animal that needs to be rescued. They give it "veterinary care."

In thinking about relational artifacts such as Furbys, AIBOs, My Real Babies, and Paros, the question is posed: how these objects differ from "traditional" (non-computational) toys, teddy bears, and Raggedy-Ann dolls. Melanie, unbidden, speaks directly to this issue. With other dolls, she feels that she is "pretending." With My Real Baby, she feels that she is really the dolls's mother: "[I feel] like I'm her real mom. I bet if I really tried, she could learn another word. Maybe Da-da. Hopefully if I said it a lot, she would pick up. It's sort of like a real baby, where you wouldn't want to set a bad example."

For Melanie, not only does My Real Baby have feelings, Melanie sees it as capable of complex, mixed emotions. "It's got similar to human feelings, because she can really tell the differences between things, and she's happy a lot. She gets happy, and she gets sad, and mad, and excited. I think right now she's excited and happy at the same time."

Our relationship, it grows bigger. Maybe when I first started playing with her she didn't really know me so she wasn't making as much of these noises, but now that she's played with me a lot more she really knows me and is a lot more outgoing. Same with AIBO.

When her several weeks with AIBO and My Real Baby come to an end, Melanie is sad to return them. Before leaving them with us, she opens the box in which they are housed and gives them an emotional good bye. She hugs each one separately, tells them that she will miss them very much but that she knows we [the researchers] will take good care of them. Melanie is concerned that the toys will forget her, especially if they spend a lot of time with other families.

Melanie's relationship with the AIBO and My Real Baby illustrates their projective qualities: she nurtures them because getting enough nurturance is an issue for her. But in providing nurturance to the robots, Melanie provided it to herself as well (and in a way that felt more authentic than developing a relationship with a "traditional" doll). In another case, a seriously ill child was able to use relational robots to speak more easily in his own voice.

Jimmy: From Rorschach to Relationship

Jimmy, small, pale, and thin, is just completing first grade. He has a congenital illness that causes him to spend much time in hospitals. During our sessions with AIBO and My Real Baby he sometimes runs out of energy to continue talking. Jimmy comes to our study with a long history of playing computer games. His favorite is Roller Coaster Tycoon. Many children play the game to create the wildest roller coasters possible; Jimmy plays the game to maximize the maintenance and staffing of his coasters so that the game gives him awards for the safest park. Jimmy's favorite toys are Beanie Babies. Jimmy participates in our study with his twelve-year-old brother, Tristan.

Jimmy approaches AIBO and My Real Baby as objects with consciousness and feelings. When AIBO slams into the red siding that defines his game space, Jimmy interprets his actions as "scratching a door, wanting to go in . . . I think it's probably doing that because it wants to go through the door . . . Because he hasn't been in there yet." Jimmy thinks that AIBO has similar feelings toward him as his biological dog, Sam. He says that AIBO would miss him when he goes to school and would want to jump in to the car with him. In contrast, Jimmy does not believe that his Beanie Babies, the stuffed animal toys, have feelings or 'aliveness,' or miss him when he is at school. Jimmy tells us that other relational artifacts like Furbies 'really do' learn and are the same 'kind of alive' as AIBO.

During several sessions with AIBO, Jimmy talks about AIBO as a super dog that show up his own dog as a limited creature. Jimmy says: "AIBO is probably as smart as Sam and at least he isn't as scared as my dog [is]." When we ask Jimmy if there are things that his dog can do that AIBO can't do, Jimmy answers not in terms of his dog's strengths but in terms of his deficiencies: "There are some things that Sam can't do and AIBO can. Sam can't fetch a ball. AIBO can. And Sam definitely can't kick a ball." On several other occasions, when AIBO completed a trick, Jimmy commented "My dog couldn't do that!" AIBO is the "better" dog. AIBO is immortal, invincible. AIBO cannot get sick or die. In sum, AIBO represents what Jimmy wants to be.

During Jimmy's play sessions at MIT, he forms a strong bond with AIBO. Jimmy tells us that he would probably miss AIBO as much as Sam if either of them died. As we talk about the possibility of AIBO dying, Jimmy explains that he believes AIBO could die if he ran out of power. Jimmy wants to protect AIBO by taking him home.

> If you turn him off he dies, well, he falls asleep or something . . . He'll probably be in my room most of the time. And I'm probably going to keep him downstairs so he doesn't fall down the stairs. Because he probably, in a sense he would die if he fell down the stairs. Because he could break. And. Well, he could break and he also could . . . probably or if he broke he'd probably . . . he'd die like.

Jimmy's concerns about his vulnerable health are expressed with AIBO in several ways. Sometimes he thinks the dog is vulnerable, but Jimmy thinks he could protect him. Sometimes he thinks the dog is invulnerable, a super-hero dog in relation to his frail biological counterpart. He tests AIBO's strength in order to feel reassured.

Jimmy "knows" that AIBO does not have a real brain and a heart, but sees AIBO as a mechanical kind of alive, where it can function as if it had a heart and a brain. For Jimmy, AIBO is "alive in a way," because he can "move around" and "[H]e's also got feelings. He shows . . . he's got three eyes on him, mad, happy, and sad. And well, that's how he's alive." As evidence of AIBO's emotions, Jimmy points to the robot's lights: "When he's mad, then they're red. [And when they are green] he's happy."

Jimmy has moments of intense physical vulnerability, sometimes during our sessions. His description of how AIBO can strengthen himself is poignant. "Well, when he's charging that means, well he's kind of sleepy when he's charging but when he's awake he remembers things more. And probably he remembered my hand because I kept on poking in front of his face so he can see it. And he's probably looking for me."

AIBO recharging reassures Jimmy by providing him with a model of an object that can resist death. If AIBO can be alive through wires and a battery then this leaves hope that people can be "recharged" and "rewired" as well. His own emotional connection to life through technology motivates a philosophical position that robots are "sort of alive."

At home, Jimmy likes to play a game in which his Bio Bugs attack his AIBO. He relishes these contests in which he identifies with AIBO. AIBO lives through technology and Jimmy sees AIBO's survival as his own. AIBO symbolizes Jimmy's hopes to someday be a form of life that defies death. The Bio Bugs are the perfect embodiment of threat to the body, symbolizing the many threats that Jimmy has to fight off.

Jimmy seems concerned that his brother, Tristan, barely played with AIBO during the time they had the robot at home. Jimmy brings this up to us in a shaky voice. Jimmy explains that his brother didn't play with AIBO because "he didn't want to get addicted to him so he would be sad when we had to give him back." Jimmy emphasizes that he did not share this fear. Tristan is distant from Jimmy. Jimmy is concerned that his brother's holding back from him is because Tristan fears that he might die. Here, AIBO becomes the "stand in" for the self.

When he has to return his AIBO, Jimmy says that AIBO he will miss the robot "a little bit" but that it is AIBO that will probably miss him more.

Researcher: Do you think that you'll miss AIBO?

Jimmy: A little bit. He'll probably miss me.

Seniors: Robots as a Prism for the Past

In bringing My Real Babies into nursing homes, it was not unusual for seniors to use the doll to re-enact scenes from their children's youth or important moments in their relationships with spouses. Indeed, seniors were more comfortable playing out family scenes with robotic dolls than with traditional ones. Seniors felt social "permission" to be with the robots, presented as a highly valued and "grownup" activity. Additionally, the robots provided the elders something to talk about, a seed for a sense of community.

As in the case of children, projection and evocation were entwined in the many ways seniors related to the robots. Some seniors, such as Jonathan, wanted the objects to be transparent as a clockwork might be and became anxious when their efforts to investigate the robots' "innards" were frustrated. Others were content to interact with the robot as it presented itself, with no window onto how it 'worked' in any mechanical sense. They took the relational artifact 'at interface value' (Turkle 1995). In each case, emotional issues were closely entwined with emergent philosophies of technology.

Jonathan: Exploring a Relational Creature, Engineer-Style

Jonathan, 74, has movements that are slow and precise; he is well spoken, curious, and intelligent. He tells us that throughout his life he has been ridiculed for his obsessive ways. He tends to be reclusive and has few friends at the nursing home. Never married, with no children, he has always been a solitary man. For most of his life, Jonathan worked as an accountant, but was happiest when he worked as a computer programmer. Now, Jonathan approaches AIBO and My Real Baby with a desire to analyze them in an analytical, engineer's style.

From his first interaction with the My Real Baby at a group activity to his last interview after having kept the robot for four months in his room, Jonathan remained fascinated with how it functioned. He handles My Real Baby with detachment in his methodical explorations.

When Jonathan meets My Real Baby the robot is cooing and giggling. Jonathan looks it over carefully, bounces it up and down, pokes and squeezes it, and moves its limbs. With each move, he focuses on the doll's reactions. Jonathan tries to understand what the doll says and where its voice comes from. Like Orelia, Jonathan talks to the researchers about the robot, but does not speak to the robot itself. When he discovers that My Real Baby's voice comes from its stomach, he puts his ear next to the stomach and says: "I think that this doll is a very remarkable toy. I have never seen anything like this before. But I'd like to know, how in the entire universe is it possible to construct a doll that talks like this?"

Despite his technical orientation to the robot, Jonathan says that he would be more comfortable speaking to a computer or robot about his problems than to a person.

> Because if the thing is very highly private and very personal it might be embarrassing to talk about it to another person, and I might be afraid of being ridiculed for it . . . And it wouldn't criticize me . . . Or let's say that if I wanted to blow off steam, it would be better to do it to a computer than to do it to a living person who has nothing to do with the thing that's bothering me. [I could] express with the computer emotions that I feel I could not express with another person, to a person.

Nevertheless, Jonathan, cannot imagine that his bond with My Real Baby could be similar to those he experiences with live animals, for example the cats he took care of before coming to the nursing home:

> Some of the things I used to enjoy with the cat are things I could never have with a robot animal. Like the cat showing affection, jumping up on my lap,

letting me pet her and listening to her purr, a robot animal couldn't do that and I enjoyed it very much.

Jonathan makes a distinction between the affection that can be offered by something alive and an object that acts as if it were alive.

Andy: Animation in the Service of Working Through

Andy, 76, at the same nursing home as Jonathan, is recovering from a serious depression. At the end of each of our visits to the nursing home, he makes us promise to come back to see him as soon as we can. Andy feels abandoned by family and friends. He wants more people to talk with. He participates in a day-program outside the home, but nevertheless, often feels bored and lonely. Andy loves animals and has decorated his room with scores of cat pictures; he tells us that some of his happiest moments are being outside in the nursing home's garden speaking to birds, squirrels, and neighborhood cats. He believes they communicate with him and considers them his friends. Andy treats robotic dolls and pets as sentient; they become stand-ins for the people he would like to have in his life. Like Jonathan, we gave Andy a My Real Baby to keep in his room for four months. He never tired of its company.

The person Andy misses most is his ex-wife Rose. Andy reads us songs he has written for her and letters she has sent him. My Real Baby helps him work on unresolved issues in his relationship with Rose. Over time, the robot comes to represent her.

Andy: Rose, that was my ex-wife's name.

Researcher: Did you pretend that it was Rose when you talked to her?

Andy: Yeah. I didn't say anything bad to her, but some things that I would want to say to her, it helped me to think about her and the time that I didn't have my wife, how we broke up, think about that, how I miss seeing her . . . the doll, there's something about her, I can't really say what it is, but looking at her reminds me of a human being. She looks just like her, Rose, my ex-wife, and her daughter . . . something in her face is the same, looking at her makes me feel more calm, I can just think about her and everything else in my life.

Andy speaks at length about his difficulty getting over his divorce, his feelings of guilt that his relationship with Rose did not work out, and his hope that he and his ex-wife might someday be together again. Andy explains how having the doll enables him to try out different scenarios that might lead to a reconciliation with Rose. The doll's presence enables him to express his attachment and vent his feelings of regret and frustration.

Researcher: How does it make you feel to talk to the doll?

Andy: Good. It lets me take everything inside me out, you know, that's how I feel talking to her, getting it all out of me and feel not depressed . . . when I wake up in the morning I see her over there, it makes me feel so nice, like somebody is watching over you.

Andy: It will really help me [to keep the doll] because I am all alone, there's no one around, so I can play with her, we can talk. It will help me get ready to be on my own.

Researcher: How?

Andy: By talking to her, saying some of the things that I might say when I did go out, because right now, you know I don't talk to anybody right now, and I can talk much more right now with her than, I don't talk to anybody right now.

Andy holds the doll close to his chest, rubs its back in a circular motion, and says lovingly, "I love you. Do you love me?" He makes funny faces at the doll, as if to prevent her from falling asleep or just to amuse her. When the doll laughs with perfect timing as if responding to his grimaces, Andy laughs back, joining her. My Real Baby is nothing if not an "intimate machine."

Intimate Machines: A Robot Kind of Love

The projective material of the children and seniors is closely tied to their beliefs about the nature of the relational artifacts in their care. We already know that the "intimate machines" of the computer culture have shifted how children talk about what is and is not alive (Turkle 2005[1984]). For example, children use different categories to talk about the aliveness of "traditional" objects than they do when confronted with computational games and toys. A traditional wind-up toy was considered "not alive" when children realized that it did not move of its own accord. Here, the criterion for aliveness was in the domain of physics: autonomous motion. Faced with computational media, children's way of talking about aliveness became psychological. Children classified computational objects as alive (from the late 1970s and the days of the electronic toys Merlin, Simon, and Speak and Spell) if they could *think* on their own. Faced with a computer toy that could play tic-tac-toe, what counted to a child was not the object's physical but psychological autonomy.

Children of the early 1980s came to define what made people special in opposition to computers, which they saw as our "nearest neighbors." Computers, the children reasoned, are rational machines; people are special because they are emotional. Children's use of the category "emotional machines" to describe what makes people special was a fragile, unstable definition of human uniqueness. In 1984, when I completed my study of a first generation of children who grew up with electronic toys and games, I thought that other formulations would arise from generations of children who might, for example, take the intelligence of artifacts for granted, understand how it was created, and be less inclined to give it philosophical importance. But as if on cue, robotic creatures that presented themselves as having both feelings and needs entered mainstream American culture. By the mid-1990s, as emotional machines, people were not alone.

With relational artifacts, the focus of discussion about whether computational artifacts might be alive moved from the psychology of projection to the psychology of engagement, from Rorschach to relationship, from creature competency to creature connection. Children and seniors already talk about an "animal kind of alive" and a "Furby kind of alive." The question ahead is whether they will also come to talk about a "people kind of love" and a "robot kind of love."

What is a robot kind of love?

In the early 1980s, I met a thirteen-year-old, Deborah, who responded to the experience of computer programming by speaking about the pleasures of putting "a piece of your mind into the computer's mind and coming to see yourself differently." Twenty years later, eleven-year-old Fara reacts to a play session with Cog, a humanoid robot at MIT that can meet her eyes, follow her position, and imitate her movements, by saying that she could never get tired of the robot because "it's not like a toy because can't teach a toy; it's like something that's part of you, you know, something you love, kind of like another person, like a baby."

In the 1980s, debates in artificial intelligence centered on the question of whether machines could "really" be intelligent. These debates were about the objects themselves, what they could and could not do. Our new debates about relational and sociable machines—debates that will have an increasingly high profile in mainstream culture—are not about the machines' capabilities but about our vulnerabilities. In my view, decisions about the role of robots in the lives of children and seniors cannot turn simply on whether children and the elderly "like" the robots. What does this deployment of "nurturing technology" at the two most dependent moments of the life cycle say about us? What will it do to us? What kinds of relationships are appropriate to have with machines? And what is a relationship?

My work in robotics laboratories has offered some images of how future relationships with machines may look, appropriate or not. For example, Cynthia Breazeal was leader on the design team for Kismet, the robotic head that was designed to interact with humans "sociably," much as a two-year-old child would. Breazeal was its chief programmer, tutor, and companion. Kismet needed Breazeal to become as "intelligent" as it did and then Kismet became a creature Breazeal and others could interact with. Breazeal experienced what might be called a maternal connection to Kismet; she certainly describes a sense of connection with it as more than "mere" machine. When she graduated from MIT and left the AI Laboratory where she had done her doctoral research, the tradition of academic property rights demanded that Kismet be left behind in the laboratory that had paid for its development. What she left behind was the robot "head" and its attendant software. Breazeal described a sharp sense of loss. Building a new Kismet would not be the same.

In the summer of 2001, I studied children interacting with robots, including Kismet, at the MIT AI Laboratory (Turkle et. al. 2006). It was the last time that Breazeal would have access to Kismet. It is not surprising that separation from Kismet was not easy for Breazeal, but more striking, it was hard for the rest of us to imagine Kismet without her. One ten-year-old who overheard a conversation among graduate students about how Kismet would be staying in the A.I. lab objected: "But Cynthia is Kismet's mother."

It would be facile to analogize Breazeal's situation to that of Monica, the mother in Spielberg's *A.I.,* a film in which an adopted robot provokes feelings of love in his human caretaker, but Breazeal is, in fact, one of the first people to have one of the signal experiences in that story, separation from a robot to which one has formed an attachment based on nurturance. At issue here is not Kismet's achieved level of intelligence, but Breazeal's experience as a "caregiver." My fieldwork with relational artifacts suggests that being asked to nurture a machine that presents itself as an young creature of any kind, constructs us as dedicated cyber-caretakers. Nurturing a machine that presents itself as dependent creates significant attachments. We might assume that giving a sociable, "affective" machine to our children or to our aging parents will change the way we see the lifecycle and our roles and responsibilities in it.

Sorting out our relationships with robots bring us back to the kinds of challenges that Darwin posed to his generation: the question of human uniqueness. How will interacting with relational artifacts affect people's way of thinking about what, if anything, makes people special? The sight of children and the elderly exchanging tendernesses with robotic pets brings science fiction into everyday life and techno-philosophy down to earth. The question here is not whether children will love their robotic pets more than their real life pets or even their parents, but rather, what will loving come to mean?

One woman's comment on AIBO, Sony's household entertainment robot startles in what it might augur for the future of person-machine relationships: "[AIBO] is better than a real dog . . . It won't do dangerous things, and it won't betray you . . . Also, it won't die suddenly and make you feel very sad." Mortality has traditionally defined the human condition; a shared sense of mortality has been the basis for feeling a commonality with other human beings, a sense of going through the same life cycle, a sense of the preciousness of time and life, of its fragility. Loss (of parents, of friends, of family) is part of the way we understand how human beings grow and develop and bring the qualities of other people within themselves (Freud 1989).

Relationships with computational creatures may be deeply compelling, perhaps educational, but they do not put us in touch with the complexity, contradiction, and limitations of the human life cycle. They do not teach us what we need to know about empathy, ambivalence, and life lived in shades of gray. To say all of this about our love of our robots does not diminish their interest or importance. It only puts them in their place.

Notes

1. A note on method: the observations presented here are based on open-ended qualitative fieldwork. This is useful in the study of human/robot interaction for several reasons. Case studies and participant-observation in natural settings enable the collection of empirical data about how people think about and use technology outside the laboratory. Qualitative methods are well-positioned to bring cultural beliefs and novel questions to light. Open-ended qualitative work puts the novelty of the technology at the center of things and says, "When you are interested in something new: *observe, listen, ask.*" Additionally, qualitative approaches to human-robot interaction provide analytical tools that help us better understand both the technologies under study and the social and cultural contexts in which these technologies are deployed. Differences in individual responses to technology are a window onto personality, life history, and cognitive style. Seeing technology in social context helps us better understand social complexities.

2. My case studies of robots and seniors with AIBO and My Real Baby are drawn from work conducted through weekly visits to schools and nursing homes from 2001 to 2003, studies that encompassed several hundred participants. In my discussion of Paro, I am reporting on studies of the same two nursing homes during the spring of 2005, a study that took place during twelve site visits

and recruited 23 participants, ranging in age from 60–104, six males, and seventeen females. Researchers on these projects include Olivia Dasté, for the first phase of work, and for the second phase, Cory Kidd and Will Taggart.

References

Bowker, G.C., and Star, S.L. 1999. *Sorting Things Out: Classification and Its Consequences,* Cambridge, Mass.: MIT Press.

Breazeal, C. "Sociable Machines: Expressive Social Exchange Between Humans and Robots." 2000. PhD Thesis, Massachusetts Institute of Technology.

Breazeal, C. 2002. *Designing Sociable Robots,* Cambridge: MIT Press.

Breazeal, C., and Scassellati, B. 1999. "How to Build Robots that Make Friends and Influence People", in *Proceedings of the IEEE/RSJ International Conference on Intelligent Robots and Systems (IROS-99),* pp. 858–863.

Breazeal, C., and Scassellati, B., 2000. "Infant-like Social Interactions Between a Robot and a Human Caretaker", *Adaptive Behavior,* 8, pp. 49–74.

Freud, S. 1960. "The Uncanny," in *The Standard Edition of the Complete Psychological Works of Sigmund Freud,* vol. 17, J. Strachey, trans. and ed. London: The Hogarth Press, pp. 219–252.

Freud, S. 1989. "Mourning and Melancholia," in *The Freud Reader.* P. Gay, ed. New York: W.W. Norton & Company, p. 585.

Kahn, P., Friedman, B., Perez-Granados, D.R., and Freier, N.G. 2004. "Robotic Pets in the Lives of Preschool Children," in *CHI Extended Abstracts,* ACM Press, 2004, pp. 1449–1452.

Kidd, C.D. "Sociable Robots: The Role of Presence and Task in Human-Robot Interaction." 2004. Master's Thesis, Massachusetts Institute of Technology.

Shibata, T., Tashima, T., and Tanie, K. 1999. "Emergence of Emotional Behavior through Physical Interaction between Human and Robot", in *Proceedings of the IEEE International Conference on Robotics and Automation,* 1999, pp. 2868–2873.

Shibata, T. (accessed 01 April 2005). "Mental Commit Robot," Available online at: http://www.mel.go.jp/soshiki/robot/biorobo/shibata/

Taggard, W., Turkle, S., and Kidd, C.D. 2005. "An Interactive Robot in a Nursing Home: Preliminary Remarks, in *Proceedings of CogSci Workshop on Android Science,* Stresa, Italy, pp. 56–61.

Turkle, S. 2005 [1984]. The Second Self: Computers and the Human Spirit. Cambridge, Mass.: MIT Press.

Turkle, S, *Life on the Screen.* 1995. New York: Simon and Schuster.

Turkle, S. 2004. "Relational Artifacts," NSF Report, (NSF Grant SES-0115668).

Turkle, S. 2005a. "Relational Artifacts/Children/Elders: The Complexities of CyberCompanions," in *Proceedings of the CogSci Workshop on Android Science,* Stresa, Italy, 2005, pp. 62–73.

Turkle, S. 2005b. "Caring Machines: Relational Artifacts for the Elderly." Keynote AAAI Workshop, "Caring Machines." Washington, D.C.

Turkle, S., Breazeal, C., Dasté, O., and Scassellati, B. 2006. "First Encounters with Kismet and Cog: Children's Relationship with Humanoid Robots," in *Digital Media: Transfer in Human Communication,* P. Messaris and L. Humphreys, eds. New York: Peter Lang Publishing.

Turner, V. 1969. The Ritual Process. Chicago: Aldine.

Weizenbaum, J. 1976. *Computer Power and Human Reason: From Judgment to Calculation.* San Francisco, CA: W. H. Freeman.Winnicott. D. W. (1971). *Playing and Reality.* New York: Basic Books.

March of the Robolawyers

A new program uses game theory to produce fairer outcomes when dividing the property of divorcing couples

When it comes to the difficult problem of deciding who gets to keep the holiday home, the dog and the Barry Manilow albums, divorcing couples now have somewhere new to turn. Researchers in Australia have developed a computer program that relies on a branch of mathematics known as game theory to produce a fairer outcome when dividing property. Instead of the traditional approach of dividing a couple's property in half, the system, called Family Winner, guides the couple through a series of trade-offs and compensation strategies. According to John Zeleznikow, a computer scientist at Victoria University in Melbourne, who developed the software with his colleague Emilia Bellucci, the results are fairer because both parties end up with what they value most.

The software was tested last year on 50 divorcing couples, with the outcomes evaluated by Victoria Legal Aid. Each party is given a limited number of points, which they are asked to allocate to the items of property they wish to keep. Through a multi-step process of modification, the parties are encouraged to give priority to the items they most value. The researchers found that, using the software, each party ended up with 70–80% of what they originally wanted, rather than the usual 50–50 split.

Applying game theory in this way is a welcome development in an area of law where parties are normally encouraged to be combative when going through the courts, says Richard Susskind, a law professor who is technology adviser to England's Lord Chief Justice. In the eyes of the law, this approach to conflict resolution would appear to be superior, he says, because it produces a more equitable outcome than the courts. But, he notes, it can

be employed only if both parties consent to its use, which is unlikely in the most acrimonious cases. "The ones that perhaps need it the most may be the ones most resistant to using it," he warns.

Dr Zeleznikow admits that despite the system's merits, divorcing couples do not necessarily always want what is fair. But, he says, the system is intended for use by couples seeking out-of-court mediation as they separate, rather than those already involved in legal battles. The software will be aimed at mediation services when it goes on sale later this year.

This is not Dr Zeleznikow's first venture into the field of robolawyer software. Indeed, for those determined to take their former spouses for everything they've got, he has already developed a different program, called SplitUp, which can encourage them to reconsider mediation. It uses techniques from the field of artificial intelligence to draw inferences based on past rulings in the Family Court of Australia. This allows parties to play out risky or aggressive courtroom strategies to see just how successful they might actually be, but without any of the risks. "By going for the jugular, disputants generally diminish their prospects of getting what they want," says Dr Zeleznikow. SplitUp can help people realise this, and thus encourage them to give mediation another look.

Game theory can be applied to many other fields besides family law, notes Dr Zeleznikow. The availability of a purely rational approach to dividing property means that the same approach could be particularly suitable for resolving industrial disputes, he suggests. By forcing the parties to focus on what matters most to them, it could bypass the emotional and political elements of a dispute that so often inhibit progress.

Resolving disputes more efficiently through software is a laudable aim. But is there not a risk that it might trigger a legal arms race? After all, says Dr Susskind, if a system can be developed to inject fairness and rationality into divorce, then someone else could just as easily design a system that suggests more aggressive or Machiavellian strategies—to help clients take their exes to the cleaners.

Best-Kept Secrets

Quantum cryptography has marched from theory to laboratory to real products

GARY STIX

At the IBM Thomas J. Watson Research Laboratory, Charles Bennett is known as a brilliant theoretician—one of the fathers of the emerging field of quantum computing. Like many theorists, he has not logged much experience in the laboratory. His absentmindedness in relation to the physical world once transformed the color of a teapot from green to red when he left it on a double boiler too long. But in 1989 Bennett and colleagues John A. Smolin and Gilles Brassard cast caution aside and undertook a groundbreaking experiment that would demonstrate a new cryptography based on the principles of quantum mechanics.

The team put together an experiment in which photons moved down a 30-centimeter channel in a light-tight box called "Aunt Martha's coffin." The direction in which the photons oscillated, their polarization, represented the 0s or 1s of a series of quantum bits, or qubits. The qubits constituted a cryptographic "key" that could be used to encrypt or decipher a message. What kept the key from prying eavesdroppers was Heisenberg's uncertainty principle—a foundation of quantum physics that dictates that the measurement of one property in a quantum state will perturb another. In a quantum cryptographic system, any interloper tapping into the stream of photons will alter them in a way that is detectable to the sender and the receiver. In principle, the technique provides the makings of an unbreakable cryptographic key.

Today quantum cryptography has come a long way from the jury-rigged project assembled on a table in Bennett's office. The National Security Agency or one of the Federal Reserve banks can now buy a quantum-cryptographic system from two small companies—and more products are on the way. This new method of encryption represents the first major commercial implementation for what has become known as quantum information science, which blends quantum mechanics and information theory. The ultimate technology to emerge from the field may be a quantum computer so powerful that the only way to protect against its prodigious code-breaking capability may be to deploy quantum-cryptographic techniques.

The challenge modern cryptographers face is for sender and receiver to share a key while ensuring that no one has filched a copy. A method called public-key cryptography is often used to distribute the secret keys for encryption and decoding of a full-length message. The security of public key cryptography depends on factorization or other difficult mathematical problems. It is easy to compute the product of two large numbers but extremely hard to factor it back into the primes. The popular RSA cipher algorithm, widely deployed in public-key cryptography, relies on factorization. The secret key being transferred between sender and receiver is encrypted with a publicly available key, say, a large number such as 408,508,091 (in practice, the number would be much larger). It can be decrypted only with a private key owned by the recipient of the data, made up of two factors, in this case 18,313 and 22,307.

The difficulty of overcoming a public-key cipher may hold secret keys secure for a decade or more. But the advent of the quantum information era—and, in particular, the capability of quantum computers to rapidly perform monstrously challenging factorizations-may portend the eventual demise of RSA and other cryptographic schemes. "If quantum computers become a reality, the whole game changes," says John Rarity, a professor in the department of electrical and electronics engineering at the University of Bristol in England.

Unlike public-key cryptography, quantum cryptography should remain secure when quantum computers arrive on the scene. One way of sending a quantum-cryptographic key between sender and receiver requires that a laser transmit single photons that are polarized in one of two modes. In the first, photons are positioned vertically or horizontally (rectilinear mode); in the second, they are oriented 45 degrees to the left or right of vertical (diagonal mode). In either mode, the opposing positions of the photons represent either a digital 0 or a 1.

Who Sells "Unbreakable" Keys

id Quantique Geneva, Switzerland	An optical-fiber-based system sends quantum-cryptographic keys over tens of kilometers
MagiQ Technologies	An optical-fiber system sends quantum-cryptographic keys up to 100 kilometers; also includes hardware and software for integration into existing networks
NEC	Scheduled to release an optical-fiber product at the earliest next year after a 2004 demonstration that transferred keys over a record 150 kilometers
QinetiQ	Provides systems on a contract basis that transfer keys through the air at distances up to 10 kilometers; has supplied a system to BBN Technologies in Cambridge, Mass.

The sender, whom cryptographers by convention call Alice, sends a string of bits, choosing randomly to send photons in either the rectilinear or the diagonal modes. The receiver, known as Bob in crypto-speak, makes a similarly random decision about which mode to measure the incoming bits. The Heisenberg uncertainty principle dictates that he can measure the bits in only one mode, not both. Only the bits that Bob measured in the same mode as sent by Alice are guaranteed to be in the correct orientation, thus retaining the proper value [see table on next page].

After transmission, Bob then communicates with Alice, an exchange that need not remain secret, to tell her which of the two modes he used to receive each photon. He does not, however, reveal the 0- or 1-bit value represented by each photon. Alice then tells Bob which of the modes were measured correctly. They both ignore photons that were not observed in the right mode. The modes measured correctly constitute the key that serves as an input for an algorithm used to encrypt or decipher a message.

If someone tries to intercept this stream of photons—call her Eve—she cannot measure both modes, thanks to Heisenberg. If she makes the measurements in the wrong mode, even if she resends the bits to Bob in the same way she measured them, she will inevitably introduce errors. Alice and Bob can detect the presence of the eavesdropper by comparing selected bits and checking for errors.

Beginning in 2003, two companies—id Quantique in Geneva and MagiQ Technologies in New York City—introduced commercial products that send a quantum-cryptographic key beyond the 30 centimeters traversed in Bennett's experiment. And, after demonstrating a record transmission distance of 150 kilometers, NEC is to come to market with a product at the earliest next year. Others, such as IBM, Fujitsu and Toshiba, have active research efforts [see table above].

The products on the market can send keys over individual optical-fiber links for multiple tens of kilometers. A system from MagiQ costs $70,000 to $100,000. "A small number of customers are using and testing the system, but it's not widely deployed in any network," comments Robert Gelfond, a former Wall Street quantitative trader who in 1999 founded MagiQ Technologies.

Some government agencies and financial institutions are afraid that an encrypted message could be captured today and stored for a decade or more—at which time a quantum computer might decipher it. Richard J. Hughes, a researcher in quantum cryptography at Los Alamos National Laboratory, cites other examples of information that must remain confidential for a long time: raw census data, the formula for Coca-Cola or the commands for a commercial satellite. (Remember Captain Midnight, who took over HBO for more than four minutes in 1986.) Among the prospective customers for quantum cryptographic systems are telecommunications providers that foresee offering customers an ultrasecure service.

The first attempts to incorporate quantum cryptography into actual networks—rather than just point-to-point connections—have begun. The Defense Advanced Research Projects Agency has funded a project to connect six network nodes that stretch among Harvard University, Boston University and BBN Technologies in Cambridge, Mass., a company that played a critical role in establishing the Internet. The encryption keys are sent over dedicated links, and the messages ciphered with those keys are transmitted over the Internet. "This is the first continuously running operational quantum-cryptography network outside a laboratory," notes Chip Elliott of BBN, who heads the project. The network, designed to merely show that the technology works, transfers ordinary unclassified Internet traffic. "The only secrets I can possibly think of here are where the parking spaces are," Elliott says. Last fall, id Quantique and a partner, the Geneva-based Internet services provider Deckpoint, put on display a network that allowed a cluster of servers in Geneva to have its data backed up at a site 10 kilometers away, with new keys being distributed frequently through a quantum-encrypted link.

The current uses for quantum cryptography are in networks of limited geographic reach. The strength of the technique—that anyone who spies on a key transmittal will change it unalterably—also means that the signals that carry quantum keys cannot be amplified by network equipment that restores a weakening signal and allows it to be relayed along to the next repeater. An optical amplifier would corrupt qubits.

To extend the distance of these links, researchers are looking beyond optical fibers as the medium to distribute quantum keys. Scientists have trekked to mountaintops—where the altitude minimizes atmospheric turbulence—to prove the feasibility of sending quantum keys through the air. One experiment in 2002 at Los Alamos National Laboratory created a 10-kilometer link. Another, performed that same year by QinetiQ, based in Farnborough, England, and Ludwig Maximilian University in Munich, stretched 23 kilometers between two mountaintops in the southern Alps. By optimizing this technology—using bigger telescopes for detection, better filters and antireflective coatings—it might be possible to build a system that could transmit and receive signals over more than 1,000 kilometers, sufficient to reach satellites in low earth orbit. A network of satellites would allow for worldwide coverage. The European Space Agency is in the early stages of putting together a plan for an earth-to-satellite experiment. (The European Union also launched an effort in April to develop quantum encryption over communications networks, an effort spurred in part by a desire to prevent eavesdropping by Echelon, a system that intercepts electronic messages for the intelligence services of the U.S., Britain and other nations.)

Ultimately cryptographers want some form of quantum repeater—in essence, an elementary form of quantum computer that would overcome distance limitations. A repeater would work through what Albert Einstein famously called "'spukhafte Fernwirkungen," spooky action at a distance. Anton Zeilinger and his colleagues at the Institute of Experimental Physics in Vienna, Austria, took an early step toward a repeater when they reported in the August 19, 2004, issue of Nature that their group had strung an optical-fiber cable in a sewer tunnel under the Danube River and stationed an "entangled" photon at each end. The measurement of the state of polarization in one photon (horizontal, vertical, and so on) establishes immediately an identical polarization that can be measured in the other.

Entanglement spooked Einstein, but Zeilinger and his team took advantage of a link between two entangled photons to "teleport" the information carried by a third photon a distance of 600 meters across the Danube. Such a system might be extended in multiple relays, so that the qubits in a key could be transmitted across continents or oceans. To make this a reality will require development of esoteric components, such as a quantum memory capable of actually storing qubits without corrupting them before they are sent along to a subsequent link. "This is still very much in its infancy. It's still in the hands of physics laboratories," notes Nicolas Gisin, a professor at the University of Geneva, who helped to found id Quantique and who has also done experiments on long-distance entanglement.

A quantum memory might be best implemented with atoms, not photons. An experiment published in the October 22 issue of Science showed how this might work. Building on ideas of researchers from the University of Innsbruck in Austria, a group at the Georgia Institute of Technology detailed in the paper how two clouds of ultracold rubidium atoms could be entangled and, because of the quantum linkage, could be inscribed with a qubit, the clouds storing the qubit for much longer than a photon can. The experiment then transferred the quantum state of the atoms, their qubit, onto a photon, constituting information transfer from matter to light and showing how a quantum memory might output a bit. By entangling clouds, Alex Kuzmich and Dzmitry Matsukevich of Georgia Tech hope to create repeaters that can transfer qubits over long distances.

The supposed inviolability of quantum cryptography rests on a set of assumptions that do not necessarily carry over into the real world. One of those assumptions is that only a single photon represents each qubit. Quantum cryptography works by taking a pulsed laser and diminishing its intensity to such an extent that typically it becomes unlikely that any more than one in 10 pulses contains a photon—the rest are dark—one reason that the data transfer rate is so low. But this is only a statistical likelihood. The pulse may have more than one photon. An eavesdropper could, in theory, steal an extra photon and use it to help decode a message. A software algorithm, known as privacy amplification, helps to guard against this possibility by masking the values of the qubits.

But cryptographers would like to have better photon sources and detectors. The National Institute of Standards and Technology (NIST) is one of many groups laboring on these devices. "One very interesting area is the development of detectors that can tell the difference between one, two or more photons arriving at the same time," says Alan Migdall of NIST. Researchers there have also tried to address the problem of slow transmission speed by generating quantum keys at a rate of one megabit per second—100 times faster than any previous efforts and enough to distribute keys for video applications.

Quantum cryptography may still prove vulnerable to some unorthodox attacks. An eavesdropper might sabotage a receiver's detector, causing qubits received from a sender to leak back into a fiber and be intercepted. And an inside job will always prove unstoppable.

"Treachery is the primary way," observes Seth Lloyd, an expert in quantum computation at the Massachusetts Institute of Technology. "There's nothing quantum mechanics can do about that." Still, in the emerging quantum information age, these new ways of keeping secrets may be better than any others in the codebooks.

Quantum Mechanics Hides a Secret Code Key

Alice and Bob try to keep a quantum-cryptographic key secret by transmitting it in the form of polarized photons, a scheme invented by Charles Bennett of IBM and Gilles Brassard of the University of Montreal during the 1980s and now implemented in a number of commercial products.

1. To begin creating a key, photon Alice sends a through either the 0 or 1 slot of the rectilinear or diagonal polarizing filters, while making a record of the various orientations.

2. For each incoming bit, Bob chooses randomly which filter slot he uses for detection and writes down both the polarization and the bit value.

3. If Eve the eavesdropper tries to spy on the train of photons, quantum mechanics prohibits her from using both filters to detect the orientation of a photon. If she chooses the wrong filter, she may create errors by modifying their polarization.

4. After all the photons have reached Bob, he tells Alice over a public channel, perhaps by telephone or an e-mail, the sequence of filters he used for the incoming photons, but not the bit value of the photons.

5. Alice tells Bob during the same conversation which filters he chose correctly. Those instances constitute the bits that Alice and Bob will use to form the key that they will use to encrypt messages.

Toward Nature-Inspired Computing

NIC-based systems utilize autonomous entities that self-organize to achieve the goals of systems modeling and problem solving.

JIMING LIU AND K.C. TSUI

Nature-inspired computing (NIC) is an emerging computing paradigm that draws on the principles of self-organization and complex systems. Here, we examine NIC from two perspectives. First, as a way to help explain, model, and characterize the underlying mechanism(s) of complex real-world systems by formulating computing models and testing hypotheses through controlled experimentation. The end product is a potentially deep understanding or at least a better explanation of the working mechanism(s) of the modeled system. And second, as a way to reproduce autonomous (such as lifelike) behavior in solving computing problems. With detailed knowledge of the underlying mechanism(s), simplified abstracted autonomous lifelike behavior can be used as a model in practically any general-purpose problem-solving strategy or technique.

Neither objective is achievable without formulating a model of the factors underlying the system. The modeling process can begin with a theoretical analysis from either a macroscopic or microscopic view of the system. Alternatively, the application developer may adopt a blackbox or whitebox approach. Blackbox approaches (such as Markov models and artificial neural networks) normally do not reveal much about their working mechanism(s). On the other hand, whitebox approaches (such as agents with bounded rationality) are more useful for explaining behavior [7].

The essence of NIC formulation involves conceiving a computing system operated by population(s) of autonomous entities. The rest of the system is referred to as the environment. An autonomous entity consists of a detector (or set of detectors), an effector (or set of effectors), and a repository of local behavior rules (see Figure 1) [5,8].

A detector receives information related to its neighbors and to the environment. For example, in a simulation of a flock of birds, this information would include the speed and direction the birds are heading and the distance between the

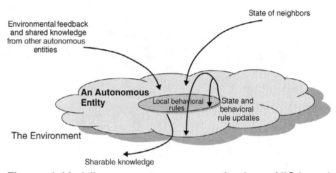

Figure 1 Modeling an autonomous entity in a NIC-based system.

birds in question. The details of the content and format of the information must be defined according to the system to be modeled or to the problem to be solved. The notion of neighbors may be defined in terms of position (such as the bird(s) ahead, to the left, and to the right), distance (such as a radial distance of two grids), or both (such as the birds up to two grids ahead of the nominal viewpoint bird).

Environmental information conveys the status of a certain feature of interest to an autonomous entity. The environment can also help carry sharable local knowledge. The effector of an autonomous entity refers collectively to the device for expressing actions. Actions can be changes to an internal state, an external display of certain behaviors, or changes to the environment the entity inhabits. An important role of the effector, as part of the local behavior model, is to facilitate implicit information sharing among autonomous entities.

Central to an autonomous entity are the rules of behavior governing how it must act or react to the information collected by the detector from the environment and its neighbors. These rules determine into what state the entity should change and also what local knowledge should be released via the effector to the environment. An example of sharable local knowledge is the role pheromones play in an ant colony. It is untargeted, and the communication via the environment is undirected; any ant can pick up the information and react according to its own behavior model.

In order to adapt itself to a problem without being explicitly told what to do in advance, an autonomous entity must modify the rules of its behavior over time. This ability, responding to local changing conditions, is known as the individual's learning capability. Worth noting is that randomness plays a part in the decision-making process of an autonomous entity despite the presence of a rule set. It allows an autonomous entity to explore uncharted territory despite evidence that it should exploit only a certain path. On the other hand, randomness helps the entity resolve conflict in the presence of equal support for suggestions to act in different ways in its own best interests and avoid being stuck by randomly choosing an action in local optima.

The environment acts as the domain in which autonomous entities are free to roam. This is a static view of the environment. The environment of a NIC system can also act as the "noticeboard" where the autonomous entities post and read local information. In this dynamic view, the environment is constantly changing For example, in the N-queen constraint satisfaction problem [7], the environment can tell a particular queen on a chessboard how many constraints are violated in her neighborhood after a move is made. In effect, this violations, or conflicts, report translates a global goal into a local goal for a particular entity. The environment also keeps the central clock that helps synchronize the actions of all autonomous entities, as needed.

Before exploring examples of NIC for characterizing complex behavior or for solving computing problems, we first highlight the central NIC ideas, along with common NIC characteristics, including autonomous, distributed, emergent, adaptive, and self-organized, or ADEAS [5]:

Autonomous. In NIC systems, entities are individuals with bounded rationality that act independently. There is no central controller for directing and coordinating individual entities. Formal computing models and techniques are often used to describe how the entities acquire and improve their reactive behavior, based on their local and/or shared utilities, and how the behavior and utilities of the entities become goal-directed.

Distributed. Autonomous entities with localized decision-making capabilities are distributed in a heterogeneous computing environment, locally interacting among themselves to exchange their state information or affect the states of others. In distributed problem solving (such as scheduling and optimization), they continuously measure, update, and share information with other entities following certain predefined protocols.

Emergent. Distributed autonomous entities collectively exhibit complex (purposeful) behavior not present or predefined in the behavior of the autonomous entities within the system. One interesting issue in studying the emergent behaviors that leads to some desired computing solutions (such as optimal resource allocation) is how to mathematically model and measure the interrelationships among the local goals of the entities and the desired global goal(s) of the NIC system in a particular application.

Adaptive. Entities often change their behavior in response to changes in the environment in which they are situated. In doing so, they utilize behavioral adaptation mechanisms to continuously evaluate and fine-tune their behavioral attributes with reference to their goals, as well as to ongoing feedback (such as intermediate rewards). Evolutionary approaches may be used to reproduce high-performing entities and eliminate poor-performing ones.

Self-organized. The basic elements of NIC-based systems are autonomous entities and their environment. Local interactions among them are the most powerful force in their evolution toward certain desired states. Self-organization is the essential process of a NIC system's working mechanism. Through local interactions, these systems self-aggregate and amplify the outcome of entity behavior.

Characterizing Complex Behavior

A complex system can be analyzed and understood in many different ways. The most obvious is to look at it from the outside, observing its behaviors and using models to try to identify and list them. Assumptions about unknown mechanisms must be made to start the process. Given observable behaviors of the desired system, NIC designers verify the model by comparing its behavior with the desired features. This process is repeated several times before a good, though not perfect, prototype can be found. Apart from obtaining a working model of the desired system, an important by-product is the discovery of the mechanisms that were unknown when the design process began.

The human immune system is an example of a highly sensitive, adaptive, self-regulated complex system involving numerous interactions among a vast number of cells of different types. Despite numerous clinical case studies and empirical findings [1], the working mechanism underlying the complex process of, say, HIV invasion and the erosion and eventual crash of the immune system (including how the local interactions in HIV, T-cells, and B-cells affect the process) are still not fully understood (characterized and predicted).

The usefulness of conventional modeling and simulation technologies is limited due to computational scale and costs.

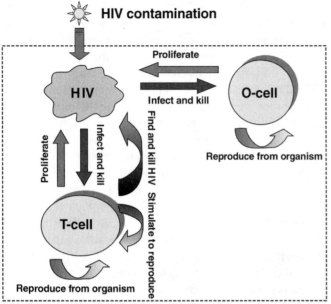

Figure 2 Modeling HIV, T-cells, and O(ther) cells in a NIC-based system.

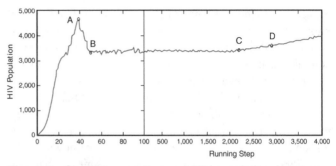

Figure 3 Simulation results on an HIV population during several phases of AIDS development.

Understanding and modeling complex systems (such as the human immune system) is a major challenge for the field of computing for two main reasons: the task of computing is seamlessly carried out in a variety of physical embodiments, and no single multipurpose or dedicated machine is able to accomplish the job. The key to success for simulating self-regulated complex systems lies in the large-scale deployment of computational entities or agents able to autonomously make local decisions and achieve collective goals.

Seeking to understand the dynamics of the immune system during an HIV attack, NIC researchers can use a 2D lattice to build a NIC model. The lattice is circular so the edges wrap around one another. Each site can be inhabited by HIV, as well as by immune cells. HIV and immune cells behave in four main ways:

Interaction. T-cells recognize HIV by its signature (protein structure); HIV infects and kills cells;

Proliferation. Reactions stimulate lymphoid tissue to produce more T-cells, which are reproduced naturally;

Death. Besides being killed by drugs and other deliberate medical intervention, HIV and T-cells die naturally; and

Diffusion. HIV diffuses from densely populated sites to neighboring sites (see Figure 2).

Figure 3 outlines the temporal emergence of three-stage dynamics in HIV infection generated from the NIC model [12]:

Before B. Primary response;

B ~ C. Clinical latency; and

After D. Onset of AIDS.

At A, the HIV population reaches a maximum point. Starting from C, the mechanism that decreases the natural ability of an organism to reproduce T-cells is triggered. These NIC-generated results are consistent with empirically observed phenomena [1]. Experiments in [12] have also found that AIDS cannot break out if HIV destroys only T-cells without weakening the T-cell reproduction mechanism. The emergence in "shape space" indicates it is because of HIV's fast mutation that the immune system cannot eradicate HIV as readily as it does other invaders. These discoveries are helping immunology researchers understand the dynamics of HIV-immune interaction.

The NIC approach to systems modeling starts from a microscopic view of the immune system. The elements of the model are the basic units—HIV and immune cells—of the immune system. The model aims to capture the essence of the immune system, though simplification is inevitable. Note that the autonomous entities in the model that belong to the same species types normally have a similar set of behavior rules. The only difference among them is the parameters of the rules, which may be adapted throughout the lifetime of the entities. Probabilistic selection of certain behavior is also common in the entities. It must be emphasized that the environment of the model can also be viewed as a unique entity in the model, with its own behavior rules.

Self-Organized Web Regularities

Researchers have identified several self-organized regularities related to the Web, ranging from its growth and evolution to usage patterns in Web surfing. Many such regularities are best represented by characteristic distributions following a Zipf law or a power law. Random-walk models [4] have been used to simulate some statistical regularities empirically observed on the Web. However, these models do not relate the emergent regularities to the dynamic interactions between users and the Web, nor do they reflect the interrelationships between user behavior and the contents or structure of the Web. User interest and motivation in navigating the

Web are among the most important factors determining user navigation behavior.

As part of the NIC approach to regularity characterization, [6] proposed a computational model of Web surfing that includes user characteristics (such as interest profiles, motivations, and navigation strategies). Users are viewed as information-foraging entities inhabiting the Web environment or as a collection of Web sites connected by hyperlinks. When an entity finds certain Web sites with content related to its topic(s) of interest, it will be motivated to search sites deeper into the Web. On the other hand, when an entity finds no interesting information after a certain amount of foraging or finds enough content to satisfy its interest, it stops foraging and goes offline, leaving the Web environment.

Experiments in [6] classified users into three groups: recurrent users familiar with the Web structure; rational users new to a particular Web site but who know what they are looking for; and random users with no strong intention to retrieve information but are just "wandering around." The results, which used both synthetic and empirical data from visitors to NASA Web site(s), showed that the foraging agent-entity-oriented model generates power-law distributions in surfing and link-click-frequency, similar to those found in the real world and hence offer a whitebox explanation of self-organized Web regularities.

Solving Computing Problems

The key factors contributing to the success of these NIC-based models are the distinctive characteristics of their elements. Marvin Minsky of MIT suggested in his 1986 book *Society of Mind* that "To explain the mind, we have to show how minds are built from mindless stuff, from parts that are much smaller and simpler than anything we'd consider smart." So, if we want to formulate a problem-solving strategy based on some observation from nature, how and where should we begin? To formulate a NIC problem-solving system, we must identify and gain a deep understanding of a working system in the natural or physical world from which models can be extracted. As with complex-systems modeling, the abstracted behavior of the working system becomes the property of the elements to be modeled.

Basing their approach on the general principles of survival of the fittest (whereby poor performers are eliminated) and the "law of the jungle" (whereby weak performers are eaten by stronger ones), several NIC systems have been devised [7, 9] to solve some well-known constraint-satisfaction problems. One is the N-queen problem, in which N queens are placed on an N × N chessboard, so no two queens ever appear in the same row, column, or diagonal. Based on the rules of the problem, a NIC model is formulated in the following way: Each queen is modeled as an autonomous entity in the system, and multiple queens are assigned to each row

of the chessboard (a grid environment). This process allows for competition among the queens in the same row, so the queen with the best strategy survives. The system calculates the number of violated constraints for each position on the grid. This represents the environmental information all queens can access when making decisions about where to move, with possible movements being restricted to positions in the same row.

Three movement strategies are possible: random-move (involving the random selection of a new position for a queen); least-move (involving selection of the position with the least number of violations, or conflicts); and coop-move (promoting cooperation among the queens by eliminating certain positions in which one queen's position may create conflicts with other queens). All three are selected probabilistically.

This NIC system gives an initial amount of energy to each queen. Like a character in a video game, a queen "dies" if its energy falls below a predefined threshold. A queen's energy level changes in one of two ways: losing it to the environment and absorbing it from another queen. When a queen moves to a new position that violates the set constraint with m queens, it loses m units of energy. This also causes the queens that attack this new position to lose one unit of energy. The intention is to encourage the queens to find a position with the fewest violations, or conflicts. The law of the jungle is implemented by having two or more queens occupy the same grid position and fight over it. The queen with the greatest amount of energy wins and eats the loser(s) by absorbing all its (their) energy. This model efficiently solves the N-queen problem with only a moderate amount of computation.

As with complex-systems modeling, the abstracted behavior of the working system becomes the property of the elements to be modeled.

In the commonly used version of a genetic algorithm [3], a member of the family of evolutionary algorithms, the process of sexual evolution is simplified to selection, recombination, and mutation, without the explicit identification of male and female (such as in the gene pool). John Holland of the University of Michigan, in his quest to develop a model to help explain evolution, has developed a genetic algorithm for optimization. The basic unit in this artificial evolution is a candidate solution to the optimization problem, commonly termed a chromosome. A genetic algorithm has a pool of them. Interactions among candidate solutions are achieved through artificial reproduction where operations mimicking natural evolution allow the candidate solutions to produce offspring that carry part of either parent (crossover) with occasional variation (mutation). While reproduction can be viewed as the cooperative side of all the chromosomes, competition among chromosomes for a position in the next generation directly reflects the principle of survival of the fittest.

On the other hand, evolutionary autonomous agents [10] and evolution strategies [11] are closer to asexual reproduction, with the addition of constraints on mutation and the introduction of mutation operator evolution, respectively. Despite this simplification and modification, evolutionary algorithms capture the essence of natural evolution and are proven global multi-objective optimization techniques. Another successful NIC algorithm that has been applied in similar domains is the Ant System [2], which mimics the food-foraging behavior of ants.

Autonomy-Oriented Computing

As a concrete manifestation of the NIC paradigm, autonomy-oriented computing (AOC) has emerged as a new field of computer science to systematically explore the metaphors and models of autonomy offered in nature (such as physical, biological, and social entities of varying complexity), as well as their role in addressing practical computing needs. It studies emergent autonomy as the core behavior of a computing system, drawing on such principles as multi-entity formulation, local interaction, nonlinear aggregation, adaptation, and self-organization [5, 8].

Three general approaches help researchers develop AOC systems: AOC-by-fabrication, AOC-by-prototyping, and AOC-by-self-discovery. Each has been found to be promising in several application areas [6, 7, 10, 12]. Work on AOC in our research laboratory over the past decade [5, 8] has opened up new ways to understand and develop NIC theories and methodologies. They have provided working examples that demonstrate the power and features of the NIC paradigm toward two main goals: characterizing emergent behavior in natural and artificial systems involving a large number of self-organizing, locally interacting entities; and solving problems in large-scale computation, distributed constraint satisfaction, and decentralized optimization [5].

Conclusion

The NIC paradigm differs from traditional imperative, logical, constraint, object-oriented, and component-based paradigms, not only in the characteristics of its fundamental concepts and constructs, but in the effectiveness and efficiency of the computing that can be achieved through its ADEAS characteristics. NIC approaches have been found most effective in dealing with computational problems characterized by the following dimensions:

High complexity. Problems of high complexity (such as when the system to be characterized involves a large number of autonomous entities or the computational computing problem to be solved involves large-scale, high-dimension, highly nonlinear interactions/relationships, and highly interrelated/constrained variables);

Locally interacting problems. They are not centralized or ready or efficient enough for batch processing;

Changing environment. The environment in which problems are situated is dynamically updated or changes in real time; and

Deep patterns. The goal of modeling and analysis is not to extract some superficial patterns/relationships, data transformation, or association from one form to another, but to discover and understand the deep patterns (such as the underlying mechanisms and processes that produce the data in the first place or help explain their cause and origin).

We will continue to see new NIC theories and methodologies developed and learn to appreciate their wide-ranging effect on computer science, as well as on other disciplines, including sociology, economics, and the natural sciences. Promising applications will help explain gene regulatory networks and drug-resistance mechanisms for anti-cancer drug design, predict the socioeconomic sustainability of self-organizing online markets or communities, and perform real-time autonomous data processing in massive mobile sensor networks for eco-geological observations.

References

1. Coffin, J. HIV population dynamics in vivo: Implications for genetic variation, pathogenesis, and therapy. *Science 267* (1995), 483–489.

2. Dorigo, M., Maniezzo, V., and Colorni, A. The Ant System: Optimization by a colony of cooperative agents. *IEEE Transactions on Systems, Man, and Cybernetics, Part B, 26,* 1 (1996), 1–13.

3. Holland, J. *Adaptation in Natural and Artificial Systems.* MIT Press, Cambridge, MA, 1992.

4. Huberman, B., Pirolli, P., Pitkow, J., and Lukose, R. Strong regularities in World Wide Web surfing. *Science 280* (Apr. 3, 1997), 96–97.

5. Liu, J., Jin, X., and Tsui, K. *Autonomy-Oriented Computing: From Problem Solving to Complex Systems Modeling.* Kluwer Academic Publishers/Springer, Boston, 2005.

6. Liu, J., Zhang, S., and Yang, J. Characterizing Web usage regularities with information foraging agents. *IEEE Transactions on Knowledge and Data Engineering 16,* 5 (2004), 566–584.

7. Liu, J., Han, J., and Tang, Y. Multi-agent-oriented constraint satisfaction. *Artificial Intelligence 136,* 1 (2002), 101–144.

8. Liu, J. *Autonomous Agents and Multi-Agent Systems: Explorations in Learning, Self-Organization and Adaptive Computation*, World Scientific Publishing, Singapore, 2001.

9. Liu, J. and Han, J. ALife: A multi-agent computing paradigm for constraint satisfaction problems. *International Journal of Pattern Recognition and Artificial Intelligence 15*, 3 (2001), 475–491.

10. Liu, J., Tang, Y., and Cao, Y. An evolutionary autonomous agents approach to image feature extraction. *IEEE Transactions on Evolutionary Computation 1*, 2 (1997), 141–158.

11. Schwefel, H.P. *Numerical Optimization of Computer Models.* John Wiley & Sons, Inc., New York, 1981.

12. Zhang, S. and Liu, J. A massively multi-agent system for discovering HIV-immune interaction dynamics. In *Proceedings of the First International Workshop on Massively Multi-Agent Systems* (Kyoto, Japan, Dec. 10–11). Springer, Berlin, 2004.

JIMING LIU (jiming@uwindsor.ca) is a professor in and director of the School of Computer Science at the University of Windsor, Windsor, Ontario, Canada. **K.C. TSUI** (tsuikc@comp.hkbu.edu.hk) is an IT manager in the Technical Services and Support Department of Hongkong and Shanghai Banking Corporation, Hong Kong, China.

From *Communications of the ACM*, 49(10), October 2006, pp. 59–64. Copyright © 2006 by Association for Computing Machinery, Inc. Reprinted by permission.

The Intelligent Internet

The Promise of Smart Computers and E-Commerce

Information and communication technologies are rapidly converging to create machines that understand us, do what we tell them to, and even anticipate our needs.

WILLIAM E. HALAL

W e tend to think of intelligent systems as a distant possibility, but two relentless super-trends are moving this scenario toward near-term reality. Scientific advances are making it possible for people to talk to smart computers, while more enterprises are exploiting the commercial potential of the Internet.

This synthesis of computer intelligence and the Internet is rapidly creating a powerful new global communication system that is convenient, productive, and transformative—the Intelligent Internet. Here are three simple examples of what should become common soon.

- The UCLA Cultural Virtual Reality Laboratory has developed a Web site that recreates ancient Rome. Visitors are able to virtually walk around 3-D images of reconstructed temples, monuments, and plazas as though they were living in Rome 2,000 years ago. The head of UCLA's lab calls it "a kind of time machine."
- Amtrak has installed speech recognition software to replace the button-pressing menus that drive many people mad. Now you can talk to a virtual salesperson named Julie to get train schedules, make reservations, pay for tickets, and discuss problems. Customers are happier, and Amtrak is saving money.
- The Waldorf-Astoria Hotel in New York City leases out a five-by-seven-foot videoconferencing system that allows guests to hold virtual meetings with other people at remote locations.

Business people find it so useful that the system is always busy.

It may seem foolhardy to claim that the Internet will soon thrive again when economies around the globe struggle out of recession. After all, it was the unrealistic type of endless growth we heard during the dot-com boom that caused today's economic pain. But forecasts conducted under the TechCast Project at George Washington University indicate use should reach 30% "takeoff" adoption levels during the second half of this decade to rejuvenate the economy. Meanwhile, the project's technology scanning finds that advances in speech recognition, artificial intelligence, powerful computers, virtual environments, and flat wall monitors are producing a "conversational" human-machine interface.

> **"We are poised at the cusp of another major technology transition, much as the 1980s brought the PC and the 1990s brought the Internet."**

These powerful trends will drive the next generation of information technology into the mainstream by about 2010. Rather than forcing us to hunch over a keyboard, this Intelligent Internet should allow people everywhere to converse naturally and comfortably with life-sized, virtual people while shopping, working, learning, and conducting most social relationships.

E-Commerce Technology Timeline

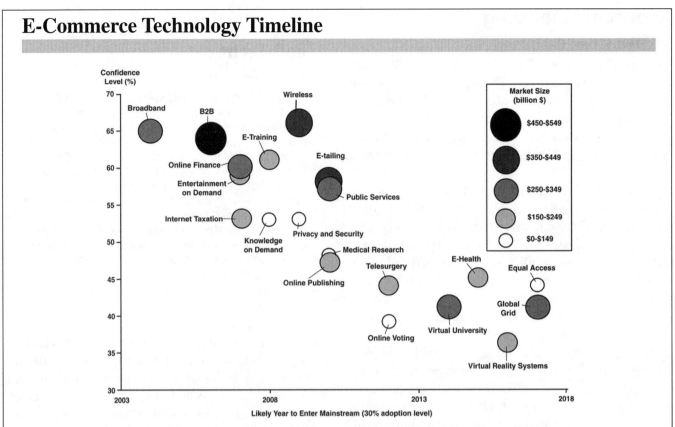

Notes: "Likely Year" is the most likely year that each e-commerce is expected to reach its stated adoption level in industrialized nations. Adoption levels are defined as a percent of the total that is possible. for instance, broadband is defined as the percent of households, while e-tailing is the percent of retail sales. "Confidence Level" is the confidence experts place in their forecast of "Likely Year." "Market Size" is a relative measure of the economic market resulting from each e-commerce service, on a scale from a low of less than $150 billion to a high of about $550 billion. See www.TechCast.org, "Emerging Technologies," The Futurist (November–December 1997): and "The Top Ten Emerging Technologies," The Futurist (July–August 2000).

Original graph construction by Paul Williams GWU graduate assistant.

Broadband High-speed channels (DSL, cable, Ethernet, and satellite) are used in 30% of homes: 2004.

B2B 30% of commercial transactions are conducted online: 2006.

E-Health Online systems are used 30% of the time to prescribe drugs, order lab tests, monitor patients, etc.: 2015.

Entertainment on Demand 30% of music, movies, games, and other entertainment is sold online: 2007.

Equal Access Most (90%) of underprivileged people have Internet access: 2017.

E-tailing 30% of goods and services are sold online: 2010.

E-Training Distance learning (Internet, video, e-mail) is the main method used in 30% of training programs: 2008.

Global Grid Half of the world population has access to PCs, Internet, etc.: 2017.

Internet Taxation Internet sales are taxed by major nations: 2007.

Knowledge on Demand Focused educational programs are used online to serve 30% of specific needs: 2008.

Medical Research 30% of clinical research is conducted us ing computerized systems: 2010.

Online Finance 30% of banking, investments, and other financial services are performed online: 2007.

Online Publishing 30% of newspapers, magazines, journals, and books are sold online: 2010.

Online Voting ATM-type machines or PCs on the Internet are used in 30% of elections: 2012.

Privacy and Security A majority of the public feels safe about the privacy and security of their information: 2009.

Public Services 30% of government services (auto registration, licenses, fees, etc.) are conducted online: 2010.

Telesurgery Surgical procedures are performed at remote locations: 2012.

Virtual Reality Systems are used by 30% of the public to experience exotic environments (Mars), entertainment (games, virtual sex), education, testing designs, etc.: 2016.

Virtual University Distance learning (Internet, video, e-mail) is the main method used in 30% of courses: 2014.

Wireless Web phones, handheld devices, etc., are used by 30% of the population for Internet, video, etc.: 2009.

Economic Maturing of the Internet

The TechCast system, formerly called The GW Forecast, is a database-driven Web site in which panels of experts provide online estimates to carefully researched questions. The estimates are pooled automatically to produce the best possible forecast of when each technology is likely to take off, the associated confidence level, and size of the potential market—in real time.

Results are presented in the E-Commerce Technology Timeline for 20 applications of e-commerce. The expert panel convened for this study comprises 38 authorities from a variety of backgrounds, including CEOs of high-tech firms, technology officers, scientists and engineers, consultants, academics, and futurists. Not all experts respond to every question, so the typical number of respondents averages 22. Delphi forecasts of this type are generally considered sound if they use a dozen or more experts, which makes these results fairly reliable.

These results portray a striking scenario in which the dominant forms of e-commerce—broadband, business-to-business (B2B), online finance, entertainment-on-demand, wireless, e-training, knowledge-on-demand, electronic public services, online publishing, e-tailing—grow from their present 5%–20% adoption levels to 30% between 2004 and 2010. TechCast considers the 30% penetration level significant because this roughly marks the "take-off point" when technologies move from their early-adopter phase into the mainstream, where they permeate economic and social life. Andrew Grove, former CEO of Intel, told *Business Week* (May 5, 2003), "Everything we ever said about the Internet is happening now."

Many think the Internet is mainstream now, but that's only true for nonpaying use, such as surfing for free information. As of 2003, commercial operations involving monetary exchange were limited to about 23% for broadband, 10% for e-tailing, 12% for B2B, 10% for distance learning, and 5% for music. And these are the most popular Internet applications. Others hardly register in adoption levels at all.

TechCast's other results suggest that more-complex applications—online voting, e-health, the virtual university, virtual reality, and the global grid—are likely to follow later. These forms of e-commerce lag because they involve more exotic and costly technology, difficult institutional changes, and new forms of consumer behavior. Making the virtual university a reality, for instance, requires professors to switch from tradi-

About the GW Forecast and TechCast

The George Washington University Forecast of Emerging Technologies (GW Forecast) is a research project initiated by William Halal, management professor, that has been in operation for a decade. In order to provide a source of funding to support this work, TechCast was formed two years ago as a limited liability corporation (LLC), with the goal of commercializing the results. TechCast is jointly owned by Halal and the other officers of the project, by George Washington University, and by partner George Mason University. TechCast intends to offer individuals and organizations access to the information on its new Web site, www.TechCast.org, on a subscription basis.

tional lectures to communication technologies that are poorly developed, college administrators to justify the economic feasibility of more expensive systems, and students to feel comfortable and trusting in a virtual setting. E-health demands a similar transformation among physicians, hospitals, and patients.

The remaining developments in our forecast—taxation, privacy and security, computerized research, telesurgery, and equal access—should appear at varying times throughout the next two decades. These applications differ because they do not serve major new social needs but involve modifications of existing systems.

Interwoven through these advances in e-commerce are other trends leading to a new generation of intelligent systems expected to emerge during the same time period. The TechCast project calls it TeleLiving—a conversational human-machine interface that allows a more comfortable and convenient way to shop, work, educate, entertain, and conduct most other social relationships [see *The Futurist*, January–February 2003]. The following are a few of the advances in speech recognition, artificial intelligence, powerful chips, virtual environments, and flat-screen wall monitors that are likely to produce this intelligent interface.

Reliable Speech Recognition Should Be Common by 2010

- IBM has a Super Human Speech Recognitionw Program to greatly improve accuracy, and in the next decade Microsoft's program is expected to reduce the error rate of speech recognition, matching human capabilities.

- MIT is planning to demonstrate their Project Oxygen, which features a voice-machine interface. Project director Rodney Brooks says, "I wanted to bring the machine into our world, a machine that will look you in the eye, let you ask questions in casual English, and answer them the same way."
- Amtrak, Wells Fargo, Land's End, and many other organizations are replacing keypad-menu call centers with speech-recognition systems because they improve customer service and recover investment in a year or two. Analysts think most companies will make the conversion soon.
- Internet search engines such as Google and Yahoo operate voice-recognition systems that help users find what they seek.
- General Motors OnStar driver assistance system relies primarily on voice commands, with live staff for backup; the number of subscribers has grown from 200,000 to 2 million and is expected to increase by 1 million per year. The Lexus DVD Navigation System responds to over 100 commands and guides the driver with voice and visual directions.
- Even more pervasive yet simpler, Sprint offers voice dialing on most cell phones and networks.

Smart Computers Will Be Learning and Adapting within a Decade

- The Defense Advanced Research Projects Agency is developing a hypersmart computer that can maintain itself, assess its performance, make adaptive changes, and respond to different situations.
- The Department of Energy is creating an intelligent computer that can infer intent, remember prior experiences, analyze problems, and make decisions.
- IBM's "autonomic computing" program will allow servers and networks to solve problems and reconfigure themselves to accomplish a goal, just as organisms rely on an autonomic nervous system to regulate heartbeat and body temperature.
- Norton provides PC software that can eliminate virus infections, optimize computer performance,

fix registry mistakes, and perform other tasks without user intervention.

- AI is being used to intelligently guide human action figures in computer games, such as *Sims, Metal Gear Solid, Unreal Tournament,* and *Halo.*
- Pattern matching and text parsing are used to improve searches by Google and AltaVista.
- BCC Corporation estimates total AI sales to grow from $12 billion in 2002 to $21 billion in 2007.

A New Generation of Computer Power Is Here

Intel and AMD are introducing 64-bit processors to replace the 32-bit chips that brought us the Windows operating system a decade ago. The 64-bit chips mark a new generation of computer power that features cinematic displays rivaling the most sophisticated science-fiction movies, accurate speech recognition, and artificial intelligence.

Virtual Robots/Environments Will Populate the Web by 2010

- Virtual robots, or avatars, are becoming common, such as Ananova, a female robot who presents weather reports. In Japan, Yuki Terai is a virtual rock star who has become a national idol.
- "There" is a multimedia Web site featuring 3-D computer-generated environments populated with avatars that interact with users and other avatars.
- According to the CEO of Native Minds, a virtual robot maker, "The Internet will be filled with robots by 2010."

Flat Wall Monitors Should Become Common in a Few Years

- Sales of liquid crystal display (LCD) monitors now surpass cathode ray tube (CRT) sales, introducing an era of flat monitors that use one-third the power of CRTs. "Ultimately, the flat panel is less expensive," according to a Dell manager.
- Leading TV makers are all bringing out 60-inch wall-mounted digital TV monitors.
- Albeit expensive now, as the switch from CRTs to LCDs gathers momentum, costs and prices should fall dramatically, making $1,000 wall monitors the size of a movie screen fairly common. A fully functional three-by-five-foot wall monitor should sell for less than $500.

These are formidable undertakings, to be sure, and some may not succeed as planned. But such remarkable developments promise to transform the human-computer interface. Powerful new scientific capabilities are being applied now for simple uses, and if current trends hold, a modest version of the talking computer made famous in *2001: A Space Odyssey* should be available about 2010. Rather than use a keyboard or mouse, the PC will disappear into a corner while we talk to life-sized virtual persons on large wall monitors.

A few years ago, Microsoft chairman Bill Gates claimed, "The future lies with computers that talk, see, listen, and learn." This view is now supported by computer industry leaders. Robert McClure of IDC stated recently, "What the graphical user interface was in the 1990s, the natural user interface will be in this decade." Sony President Kunitake Ando expects the PC of 2005 to be a more personalized, intelligent system, acting as a "teacher, agent, and guide." Ian Pearson at British Telecom sees a resumption of Internet growth in 2005 and 2006, driven by "better interface technology . . . and artificial intelligence." And computer scientist Ray Kurzweil forecasts, "It will be routine to meet in full-immersion virtual reality for business meetings and casual conversations in five to seven years."

The Next Information Technology [IT] Generation

The enormous gap between today's depressed IT industry and the vibrant trends noted above signifies that we are poised at the cusp of another major technology transition, much as the 1980s brought the PC and the 1990s brought the Internet.

The economic recession left in the wake of the dot-com bust may linger awhile, but all technological revolutions go through a similar boom-and-bust cycle. The introduction of railroads, telephones, and radios invited wild speculation similar to the dot-com bubble. But a few years after the inevitable crash, renewed economic growth and more prudent business practices caused these fledgling industries to boom again.

A similar resumption of growth is likely for dot-coms. Economically sound e-practices are common now and should continue to expand. As the economic recession runs its course, venture capital is also appearing to support new startups. And broadband is reaching the critical 30% take-off level, which will soon create huge markets for exciting new applications that need lots of bandwidth. The TechCast Project participants therefore see no serious obstacles to the first wave of relatively straightforward e-commerce services noted in the forecast, which is likely to reach the 30% adoption level during this take-off period running roughly from 2005 to 2010.

This time, however, the intelligent interface holds the key to putting today's underutilized IT to work. Many more examples like those noted above are being developed by Web entrepreneurs, and competition could mount as customers demand these attractive new benefits. The first "wired generation" of college students is entering work, expecting the unlimited bandwidth and sophisticated Internet features they grew accustomed to on campus. The nagging problem of selling entertainment online—the digital rights management conundrum—is also likely to be resolved soon, which could unleash a huge market for music, videos, movies, and other intellectual property.

These emerging markets are perfect for the lifelike, conversational multimedia of TeleLiving, encouraging a new generation of IT that should be extremely appealing and relieves today's exploding complexity. Ninety percent of Americans say today's computers are too complex and time-consuming. The huge advantages of this next-generation IT could fuel demand for the Intelligent Internet to blossom sometime around 2010, as the trends above suggest. *Business Week's* special issue, "The E-Biz Surprise" (May 5, 2003), noted, "The Web is the same age color TV was when it turned profitable."

Almost any social transaction—teleworking with colleagues, buying and selling online, education, consulting with your physician, entertainment, or just a casual talk with a distant friend—could soon be conducted in a conversational mode, speaking with life-sized images as comfortably as we now use the telephone and television. It should feel as though virtual people are right there in the same room with you.

This scenario is not without uncertainties. Cynicism persists over unrealized promises of AI, and the Intelligent Internet will present its own problems. If you think today's dumb computers are frustrating, wait until you find yourself shouting at a virtual robot that repeatedly fails to grasp what you badly want it to do. And this forecast for a glorious IT future may seem extravagant amidst the dismal mood of IT today.

The main obstacle is a lack of vision among industry leaders, customers, and the public as scars of the dot-com bust block creative thought. Yes, the dot-com boom was unrealistic to a large extent, but it was driven by a powerful image that inspired huge gains in many areas. Bold innovations always require equally bold imagination, and so unleashing pent-up demand for online social transactions will require an imaginative understanding of how IT can improve life in the difficult years ahead. The evidence suggest the future lies in developing an Intelligent Internet, and that the world could benefit enormously by focusing on this concept with clarity and determination.

WILLIAM E. HALAL, director of the TechCast Project (formerly The GW Forecast), is a professor of management in the Department of Management Science, Monroe Hall, George Washington University, Washington, D.C. 20052. Telephone 1-202-994-5975; Web site www.TechCast.org or www.gwforecast.gwu.edu; e-mail halal@gwu.edu.

Mind Control

Matt Nagle is paralyzed. He's also a pioneer in the new science of brain implants.

RICHARD MARTIN

Matthew Nagle is beating me at Pong. "OK, baby," he mutters. The creases in his forehead deepen as he moves the onscreen paddle to block the ball. "C'mon—here you go," he says, sending a wicked angle shot ricocheting down the screen and past my defense. "Yes!" he says in triumph, his voice hoarse from the ventilator that helps him breathe. "Let's go again, dude."

The remarkable thing about Nagle is not that he plays skillfully; it's that he can play at all. Nagle is a C4 quadriplegic, paralyzed from the neck down in a stabbing three years ago. He pilots a motorized wheelchair by blowing into a sip-and-puff tube, his pale hands strapped to the armrests. He's playing Pong with his thoughts alone.

A bundle of wires as thick as a coaxial cable runs from a connector in Nagle's scalp to a refrigerator-sized cart of electronic gear. Inside his brain, a tiny array of microelectrodes picks up the cacophony of his neural activity; processors recognize the patterns associated with arm motions and translate them into signals that control the Pong paddle, draw with a cursor, operate a TV, and open e-mail.

Nagle, 25, is the first patient in a controversial clinical trial that seeks to prove brain-computer interfaces can return function to people paralyzed by injury or disease. His BCI is the most sophisticated ever tested on a human being, the culmination of two decades of research in neural recording and decoding. A Foxborough, Massachusetts-based company called Cyberkinetics built the system, named BrainGate.

After we play Pong for a while, I ask Nagle to try something I'd seen him do in a video: draw a circle. This is more fundamental and difficult than playing Pong. Drawing a circle freehand is a classic test of motor function, a species marker. Legend has it that Leonardo da Vinci was among the few humans who could sketch a perfect one.

Today, Nagle barely gets to imperfect. The line keeps shooting off the screen or crossing itself. Maybe it's my presence or fatigue or some subtle shift in Nagle's brain chemistry due to who knows what. Abe Caplan, the Cyberkinetics techni-cian overseeing the computer gear that dominates a corner of Nagle's room at New England Sinai Hospital, urges him on softly.

The room fills with static—the sound of another human being's thoughts.

"I'm tryin', dude," Nagle says, cursing softly. "C'mon, you bitch."

Caplan taps on one of his keyboards to adjust a setting, averaging the system's motion prediction over a longer time to smooth out the line. Finally, Nagle manages to produce a collapsed half circle. He's exhilarated but clearly exhausted. As they finish the session, Caplan nods his head toward the computers and says, "Want to hear it?"

He flicks a switch, and a loud burst of static fills the room—the music of Nagle's cranial sphere. This is raw analog signal, Nagle's neurons chattering. We are listening to a human being's thoughts.

Roughly the size of a deflated volleyball, your brain weighs about 3 pounds. Its 100 billion neurons communicate via minute electrochemical impulses, shifting patterns sparking like fireflies on a summer evening, that produce movement, expression, words. From this ceaseless hubbub arose *Ode to Joy,* thermonuclear weapons, and *Dumb and Dumber.*

Nobody really knows how all that electricity and meat make a mind. Since Freud, scientists have wrangled over "the consciousness problem" to little effect. In fact, it's only in the past 20 years that researchers have learned how to listen in on—or alter—brain waves. Neuroscientists can record and roughly translate the neural patterns of monkeys, and thousands of humans with Parkinson's disease and epilepsy have cerebral pacemakers, which control tremors and seizures with electrical impulses.

John Donoghue, head of neuroscience at Brown University and the founder of Cyberkinetics, eventually wants to hook BrainGate up to stimulators that can activate muscle tissue, bypassing a damaged nervous system entirely. In theory, once you can control a computer cursor, you can do anything from drawing circles to piloting a battleship. With enough computational power, "everything else is just engineering," says Gerhard Friehs, the neurosurgeon from Brown who implanted Nagle's device.

For now, that engineering remains a challenge. Cyberkinetics is just one of a dozen labs working on brain-computer interfaces, many of them funded by more than $25 million in grants from the US Department of Defense, which frankly envisions a future of soldier-controlled killer robots. Before that can happen, BCIs must become safe enough to be implanted in a human, durable enough to function reliably for years, and sensitive enough to pick up distinctive neural patterns. Many physicians doubt useful information can ever be extracted from neural activity, and some who believe in the promise of BCIs worry that putting one into Nagle's head was premature, even reckless, considering less invasive technological options still on the table—electrode-studded skullcaps or devices that rest on the brain's surface. They worry that a failure could set the entire field back a decade.

"The technology required is very complex," Donoghue admits. "There are still many issues to be resolved. But it's here. It's going to happen. Just look at Matt."

On July 3, 2001, Matthew Nagle and several friends went to a fireworks display at Wessagussett Beach, 20 miles south of Boston. The 6' 2", 180-pound Nagle had been a football standout at Weymouth High and was a devoted Patriots and Red Sox fan. That summer he was driving a van delivering kitchenware and had just passed the postal service exam. As Nagle and his buddies were leaving the beach, one of them got into a scuffle. Nagle jumped out of the car to help his friend. "The last thing I remember is sitting in the car," Nagle says. "My friend told me I went over to this guy and he pulled a knife."

The 8-inch blade entered the left side of Nagle's neck just under his ear, severing his spinal cord. Nagle spent four months in rehabilitation before moving back to his parents' house. He can't breathe without a respirator, and though he has at times managed to wiggle a finger, doctors give him no chance of regaining the use of his limbs. Nagle's mother ran across the BrainGate experiments while researching spinal-cord injuries online, and she brought him an article about Cyberkinetics from *The Boston Globe*. Nagle, who had been trying unsuccessfully to wean himself from the ventilator, begged his doctors for the chance to be the first subject. "My mother was scared of what might happen, but what else can they do to me?" Nagle rasps, jutting his chin at his wheelchair. "I was in a corner, and I had to come out fighting."

Nagle's doctor contacted the people running the trial. "A week later I got a call," Nagle says. "I told them, 'You can treat me like a lab rat, do whatever. I want this done as soon as possible.'"

Nagle turned out to be an ideal subject—young, strong-willed, and convinced that he will walk again. The only problem: Because Nagle's brain had been cut off from his spinal cord, no one knew if he could still produce the coherent neural signals necessary for movement. It wouldn't matter how well the BrainGate could read patterns if Nagle's brain was broadcasting noise. Donoghue's experiments had used healthy, fully functioning monkeys.

"That was the great unknown," says Donoghue. "When he thinks 'move left,' were we going to get one neuron firing one time, 20 the next time? Or maybe not anything? Could he still imagine motion enough to make those cells modulate, to change those spikes?"

There was only one way to find out: implant the chip.

On the morning of June 22, 2004, Friehs—an expert in gamma knife surgery, which uses focused radiation to treat brain diseases like Parkinson's—opened Nagle's skull using a high-speed drill called a craniotome. With a number 15 scalpel, he carefully sliced through the protective membranes that surround the brain.

The living brain is a gory sponge, a mass of blood vessels shot through with a delicate mesh of fiber. Magnetic resonance imaging allowed Friehs to plot in advance the region on Nagle's motor cortex most likely to provide readable arm-movement signals to the BrainGate. One revelation of BCI research has been that brain functions are highly distributed: Any spot within a given region can provide neural signals to operate a prosthetic. Get the BrainGate to the right place, and it would pick up signals not just from the neurons it touches, but from important neural clusters nearby as well. Using a small pneumatic inserter, Friehs tapped in the tiny array—100 electrodes, each just 1 millimeter long and 90 microns across at its base. Friehs closed Nagle's skull with titanium screws, leaving a tiny hole. Through that he threaded gold wires from the array to an external pedestal connector attached to Nagle's skull. Matthew Nagle was now part biological, and part silicon, platinum, and titanium.

It took Nagle three weeks to sufficiently recover from surgery to start learning to use the BrainGate. The first session would answer Donoghue's foremost question: Could Nagle's brain still produce usable signals?

As Donoghue looked on, Caplan asked Nagle to think left, right, then relax. "When we watched the system monitor, we could plainly see that neurons were briskly modulating," Donoghue recalls. "My reaction was 'This is it!'"

Nagle had even more confidence. "I learned to use it in two or three days—it's supposed to take 11 months," he says. "I totally knew this was going to work."

Four months after the operation, I watched Caplan take Nagle through a typical training session. He tracked Nagle's mental activity on two large monitors, one of which displayed a graph of red and green spiking lines. Each spike represented the firing of clusters of neurons. As Nagle performed specific actions in his mind's eye—move arm left, move arm up—the electrodes picked up the patterns of nearby neuron groups. Then BrainGate amplified and recorded the corresponding electrical activity. Over dozens of trials the computer built a filter that associated specific neural patterns with certain movements. Later, when Nagle again mentally pictured the motions, the computer translated the signals to guide a cursor.

Then they moved on to some more complicated neural gymnastics, with Nagle willing a large green cursor onto a picture of a money bag that popped up in different spots onscreen. Sometimes the cursor moved shakily, or shot off course; sometimes it landed almost immediately where Nagle wanted to place it. It was like watching a 3-year-old learn to use a mouse. Slowly, the cursor grew more controlled. The machine was memorizing Nagle's characteristic neural firing patterns.

"Let's see what you can do with this thing, Matt," Caplan said.

Nagle turned the TV on and off and switched channels (trapped in his hospital room, he's become a daytime-TV addict). Then he opened and read the messages in his dummy email program. "Now I'm at the point where I can bring the cursor just about anywhere," he said. "I can make it hover off to the side, not doing anything. When I first realized I could control it I said, 'Holy shit! I like this.'"

What are you thinking about when you move the cursor? I asked.

"For a while I was thinking about moving the mouse with my hand," Nagle replied. "Now, I just imagine moving the cursor from place to place." In other words, Nagle's brain has assimilated the system. The cursor is as much a part of his self as his arms and legs were.

F resh out of Boston University undergrad, John Donoghue went to work at the Fernald School, a facility for mentally handicapped children in Waltham, Massachusetts. His boss, Harvard neuroanatomist Paul Yakovlev, had studied in Russia under Ivan Pavlov, who turned his conditioned-reflex work with dogs and bells into the first map of the human motor cortex—left foot controlled here, right foot over there, and so on. At Fernald, Yakovlev and assistants like Donoghue spent hours a day slicing human brains, mostly damaged or defective ones, into 1/1,000-inch sections for study.

Whenever he looked up from his microscope, Donoghue could see the results of those defects roaming the halls of Fernald. Looking for ways to help people recover from cerebral injury, he became interested in plasticity, the brain's ability to adapt and form neural pathways. "By understanding how the plasticity of the brain can be captured and controlled," Donoghue says, "I believed we could promote the recovery of function in severely impaired patients." He set out to learn the grammar and syntax of interneuron communication.

Ten years later, with a PhD in neuroscience from Brown, Donoghue was using microelectrodes to record neural activity in rats, one neuron at a time. It wasn't enough. "Listening to just one neuron is like hearing only the second violinist," says Donoghue. "With multiple neurons, it's like hearing the whole orchestra." The problem was, nobody knew how to record multiple neurons reliably.

In 1992, he went to the Society for Neuroscience meeting in search of a solution. "I went to every poster session that had innovative multielectrode recording methods," Donoghue says, "and finally I found Dick Normann."

Normann is the kind of person who shows up often in the history of scientific revolutions: more tinkerer than basic researcher, more inventor than visionary. In the early 1990s he created the Utah electrode array, a thin substrate of silicon that rests on the surface of the cortex, embedding platinum-tipped electrodes into the gray matter. Normann designed it to send signals into the brain, as part of a visual prosthetic. Donoghue realized it could also be an uplink.

A few weeks after the conference, he visited Normann's lab in Utah. "We placed the implant in a cat, went to lunch, and let the animal recover," Donoghue says. "When we came back we had good signals. It worked!"

Other researchers were chasing the same goal. In 2002, Miguel Nicolelis, a neurobiologist at Duke, provided the best evidence yet of the brain's plasticity. He and his team plugged 86 microwires into the brain of a monkey and taught the animal to use a joystick to move an onscreen cursor (the reward: a sip of juice). After the computer had learned to interpret the animal's brain activity, Nicolelis disconnected the joystick. For a while, the monkey kept working it. But he eventually figured it out. The monkey dropped the joystick and stopped moving his arm; the cursor still moved to the target. As the monkey calmly downed another swallow of juice, Nicolelis' lab fell silent in awe. The mammalian brain could assimilate a device—a machine.

Now the cursor is as much a part of him as his arms and legs ever were.

Still, the Utah array had a few advantages over other designs. It "floats" with the movement of respiration and blood pumping, remaining stable in relation to the surrounding neurons. Years of refinement stripped much of the metal away, making it more biocompatible and less likely to cause scarring. By 2003, Donoghue and Normann had tested the device, now called BrainGate, in 22 monkeys. That got them the FDA approval they'd been looking for: a small trial with five human subjects. Their first was Matthew Nagle.

A t a conference in 2002, Anthony Tether, the director of Darpa, envisioned the military outcome of BCI research. "Imagine 25 years from now where old guys like me put on a pair of glasses or a helmet and open our eyes," Tether said. "Somewhere there will be a robot that will open its eyes, and we will be able to see what the robot sees. We will be able to remotely look down on a cave and think to ourselves,

'Let's go down there and kick some butt.' And the robots will respond, controlled by our thoughts. Imagine a warrior with the intellect of a human and the immortality of a machine."

Some scientists have further suggested that implants designed to restore cognitive abilities to Alzheimer's and stroke victims could enhance the brainpower of healthy people. There's talk of using BCIs to stifle antisocial tendencies and "program" acceptable behavior.

Of course, as spooky as these scenarios may be, they first require that BCIs actually work. A few months into the trial, Donoghue's device looks safe enough, and it clearly reads useful (albeit rudimentary) signals from Nagle's brain. No one knows if it will still work a year from now, much less five or ten. If Nagle's brain rejects the implant, other researchers might shy away from implants altogether. "The key is what functions you want to restore," says Duke's Nicolelis. "If you only want to play a videogame or turn on your TV, you don't need to get into the brain. It's really a question of cost-benefit and risk. That's why I'm concerned about things moving too fast; we need to know more about the risks of leaving these things in people's heads for long periods. We don't know much yet."

That's why some BCI researchers are looking for less invasive methods. A team of Austrian researchers taught a quadriplegic patient to open and close a prosthetic hand using an electrode-studded skullcap that picked up electroencephalograms, waves of electricity generated by the entire brain. It was impressive, but the patient required five months of training to pull it off. And this past December, researchers at the Wadsworth Center in Albany, New York, reported that a patient was able to move a cursor around on a monitor using externally detected signals—no implant. Another group has tried an electrode array that rests on the surface of the brain without penetrating the cortex. "I don't think anybody really knows which method is going to be the safest and still give detailed pictures of brain activity," says Wadsworth's Gerwin Schalk.

Donoghue remains convinced that the only way to give people with immobile bodies full interaction with their environment is through embedded electrodes. "No other method gives you the power and clarity you need to transform this noisy signal into something that a patient can use," he says. "The people who question whether this will really work, I don't think they realize how much has already been done. We've got a 1,098-day monkey, who had a working BCI for almost three years. The question is, how long do you want to keep doing this in monkeys?"

Nagle has the fervor of the saved. He's convinced that BrainGate will restore him to movement. "It's just around the corner," he says. "I know I'm going to beat this." Already he can control a prosthetic hand—it's an eerie sight, rubberized, disembodied fingers grasping and relaxing on a tabletop a few feet from the motionless Nagle. "Thirty-nine months I've been paralyzed," he says. "I can stick with it another two years, till they get this thing perfected."

But controlling a robotic hand is a long way from walking. Near the end of our interview, I ask Donoghue if he thinks he's giving Nagle false hope for a cure.

"I don't know that it's false," he replies. "It's hope."

Test Your Knowledge Form

We encourage you to photocopy and use this page as a tool to assess how the articles in *Annual Editions* expand on the information in your textbook. By reflecting on the articles you will gain enhanced text information. You can also access this useful form on a product's book support Web site at *http://www.mhcls.com/online/*.

NAME: DATE:

_____

TITLE AND NUMBER OF ARTICLE:

_____

BRIEFLY STATE THE MAIN IDEA OF THIS ARTICLE:

_____

LIST THREE IMPORTANT FACTS THAT THE AUTHOR USES TO SUPPORT THE MAIN IDEA:

_____

WHAT INFORMATION OR IDEAS DISCUSSED IN THIS ARTICLE ARE ALSO DISCUSSED IN YOUR TEXTBOOK OR OTHER READINGS THAT YOU HAVE DONE? LIST THE TEXTBOOK CHAPTERS AND PAGE NUMBERS:

_____

LIST ANY EXAMPLES OF BIAS OR FAULTY REASONING THAT YOU FOUND IN THE ARTICLE:

_____

LIST ANY NEW TERMS/CONCEPTS THAT WERE DISCUSSED IN THE ARTICLE, AND WRITE A SHORT DEFINITION:

We Want Your Advice

ANNUAL EDITIONS revisions depend on two major opinion sources: one is our Advisory Board, listed in the front of this volume, which works with us in scanning the thousands of articles published in the public press each year; the other is you—the person actually using the book. Please help us and the users of the next edition by completing the prepaid article rating form on this page and returning it to us. Thank you for your help!

ANNUAL EDITIONS: Computers in Society 08/09

ARTICLE RATING FORM

Here is an opportunity for you to have direct input into the next revision of this volume.
We would like you to rate each of the articles listed below, using the following scale:

1. **Excellent: should definitely be retained**
2. **Above average: should probably be retained**
3. **Below average: should probably be deleted**
4. **Poor: should definitely be deleted**

Your ratings will play a vital part in the next revision.
Please mail this prepaid form to us as soon as possible.
Thanks for your help!

RATING		ARTICLE	RATING		ARTICLE
	1.	Five Things We Need to Know About Technological Change		25.	Can Blogs Revolutionize Progressive Politics?
	2.	Slouching Toward the Ordinary		26.	Center Stage
	3.	On the Nature of Computing		27.	The Coming Robot Army
	4.	The Subprime Loan Machine		28.	Why Spyware Poses Multiple Threats to Security
	5.	Click Fraud		29.	Terror's Server
	6.	The Big Band Era		30.	The Virus Underground
	7.	The Beauty of Simplicity		31.	Secrets of the Digital Detectives
	8.	The Software Wars		32.	Data on the Elderly, Marketed to Thieves
	9.	Scan This Book!		33.	The Fading Memory of the State
	10.	National ID		34.	False Reporting on the Internet and the Spread of Rumors
	11.	Brain Circulation		35.	China's Tech Generation Finds a New Chairman to Venerate
	12.	The New Face of the Silicon Age		36.	Is the Crouching Tiger a Threat?
	13.	Computer Software Engineers		37.	Restoring the Popularity of Computer Science
	14.	The Computer Evolution		38.	China's Computer Wasteland
	15.	Making Yourself Understood		39.	Cat and Mouse, on the Web
	16.	Privacy, Legislation, and Surveillance Software		40.	In Search of a PC for the People
	17.	Romance in the Information Age		41.	A Nascent Robotics Culture
	18.	How Do I Love Thee?		42.	March of the Robolawyers
	19.	The Perfect Mark		43.	Best-Kept Secrets
	20.	Back-to-School Blogging		44.	Toward Nature-Inspired Computing
	21.	E-Mail Is for Old People		45.	The Intelligent Internet
	22.	The Copyright Paradox		46.	Mind Control
	23.	Piracy, Computer Crime, and IS Misuse at the University			
	24.	Facing Down the E-Maelstrom			

‖‖‖

BUSINESS REPLY MAIL
FIRST CLASS MAIL PERMIT NO. 551 DUBUQUE IA

POSTAGE WILL BE PAID BY ADDRESSEE

McGraw-Hill Contemporary Learning Series
501 BELL STREET
DUBUQUE, IA 52001

ABOUT YOU

Name   Date

Are you a teacher? ❑ A student? ❑
Your school's name

Department

Address   City   State   Zip

School telephone #

YOUR COMMENTS ARE IMPORTANT TO US!

Please fill in the following information:
For which course did you use this book?

Did you use a text with this ANNUAL EDITION? ❑ yes ❑ no
What was the title of the text?

What are your general reactions to the Annual Editions concept?

Have you read any pertinent articles recently that you think should be included in the next edition? Explain.

Are there any articles that you feel should be replaced in the next edition? Why?

Are there any World Wide Web sites that you feel should be included in the next edition? Please annotate.

May we contact you for editorial input? ❑ yes ❑ no
May we quote your comments? ❑ yes ❑ no